Indirect Expropriation in International Law

LEUVEN GLOBAL GOVERNANCE

Series Editor: Jan Wouters, *Katholieke Universiteit Leuven, Belgium*

The *Leuven Global Governance* series comprises high-quality monographs and edited volumes dedicated to innovative research on global governance. The series focuses particularly on the following themes: European Union and global multilateral governance; trade and sustainable development; peace and security studies; human rights, democracy and the rule of law; space governance and comparative federalism. In full recognition of the complex issues involved, the series favours studies approaching global governance from a multidisciplinary, multi-level and multi-actor perspective.

Titles in the series include:

China, the European Union and Global Governance
Edited by Jan Wouters, Tanguy de Wilde, Pierre Defraigne and Jean-Christophe Defraigne

Private Standards and Global Governance
Legal and Economic Perspectives
Edited by Axel Marx, Miet Maertens, Johan F.M. Swinnen and Jan Wouters

The Governance of Climate Relations between Europe and Asia
Evidence from China and Vietnam as Key Emerging Economies
Edited by Hans Bruyninckx, Qi Ye, Nguyen Quang Thuan and David Belis

Indirect Expropriation in International Law
Sebastián López Escarcena

Indirect Expropriation in International Law

Sebastián López Escarcena

Lecturer in International Law, Pontificia Universidad Católica de Chile

LEUVEN GLOBAL GOVERNANCE

Edward Elgar

Cheltenham, UK • Northampton, MA, USA

Published by
Edward Elgar Publishing Limited
The Lypiatts
15 Lansdown Road
Cheltenham
Glos GL50 2JA
UK

Edward Elgar Publishing, Inc.
William Pratt House
9 Dewey Court
Northampton
Massachusetts 01060
USA

A catalogue record for this book
is available from the British Library

Library of Congress Control Number: 2013949821

This book is available electronically in the ElgarOnline.com Law Subject Collection, E-ISBN 978 1 78254 411 1

FSC
www.fsc.org
MIX
Paper from responsible sources
FSC® C013056

ISBN 978 1 78254 410 4

Typeset by Columns Design XML Ltd, Reading
Printed and bound in Great Britain by T.J. International Ltd, Padstow

To my family

pero aquí abajo abajo
cerca de las raíces
es donde la memoria
ningún recuerdo omite
y hay quienes se desmueren
y hay quienes se desviven
y así entre todos logran
lo que era un imposible
que todo el mundo sepa
que el sur también existe

Mario Benedetti

Contents

Preface

Prof. Dr. Jan Wouters, General Editor

As General Editor of the Leuven Global Governance Series I am delighted to write a short preface to this monograph written by my good friend and esteemed colleague Prof. Dr. Sebastián López Escarcena from the Pontificia Universidad Católica de Chile, Santiago.

As the reader will soon discover, this insightful and highly informative book on the problem of indirect takings provides a thorough examination of the international law of expropriation. Some may have thought that, with such a complex problématique, involving plenty of tricky and sensitive issues, with case-law spread over a large variety of international courts, from the Iran–US Claims Tribunal to the European Court of Human Rights, the book would be a rather dry and technical read. The contrary is the case: the book reads like a novel. Engaging in style and thought-provoking, it covers the shift in the international debate from the problem of compensation to that of indirect takings; the expropriation clause in friendship, commerce and navigation treaties, bilateral and plurilateral investment treaties, and the investment chapters of economic integration agreements; and the case-law of the main tribunals settling expropriation cases, including – apart from the ones indicated above – the Inter-American Court of Human Rights and arbitral panels in investment treaty arbitrations.

For sure, such a book could not have been written by a novice in international law. It deals with an awesome multitude of intersecting questions under the international law of expropriation, including the concept of property; the right to expropriate; the distinction between lawful and unlawful takings; the requirements of a lawful expropriation (public purpose, non-discrimination, payment of compensation, and now due process); the Hull formula; the distinction made by the European Court of Human Rights between deprivations, controls on the use of property and other interferences; the proportionality test; the margin of appreciation; the bilateral and plurilateral protection against expropriation; the failed attempts to regulate takings in a universal treaty; the soft-law instruments currently available on the issue; the effects and the police-powers doctrine; the concept of substantial and permanent deprivation; the police-powers exception within the effects rule; the principle of respect for prior and distinct legitimate expectations; the interplay between the protection against expropriation and the fair and equitable treatment clause; the global administrative law theory and its approach to international investment law; the constant presence of the US regulatory takings doctrine in the international law of expropriation; the mutual influence of the case-law of the Iran-United States Claims Tribunal, the European Court of Human Rights, and investment treaty arbitrations; the relation between the protection of property in regional conventions of human rights and investment treaties; and the natural orientation of these treaties towards reducing political risk and promoting good governance through the encouragement of the rule of law.

This incisive and stimulating book studies the problem of indirect takings from the standpoint of the minimum standard of treatment offered at present by regional human rights conventions and investment treaties. It is well argued, coherent and bold in its scholarly and compelling support of a not particularly 'trendy' position in international law nowadays: the effects doctrine.

I should not let the reader wait any longer. This is a lucid and comprehensively researched book, offering a detailed analysis of the customary and conventional law of expropriation, as construed by international case-law and doctrine. It is an excellent and timely contribution to the understanding of a complex legal topic, for which we should be very grateful to Sebastián.

Leuven, 14 July 2013

Acknowledgements

A renowned Spanish law professor used to assert something that is applicable to any research project: one does not finish a PhD dissertation, one leaves it. The manuscript that you have now in your hands began as mine, successfully defended at the School of Law of the University of Edinburgh. Updated and converted into a book, Edward Elgar publishes it years later with the original title. Much changed between one text and the other, but not the central tenets of my project – its thesis remains essentially the same. This book of the Leuven Global Governance Series therefore reflects my unfinished research in the international law of expropriation, as I left it in 2013.

My debt of gratitude is deep, and has many creditors. Firstly, my family who have always supported me: most of all my admirable parents, Luis and Patricia, to whom I owe my education and values, and my lovely daughter, Amelia, ever-cheerful and positive. Secondly, all the talented academics and good friends who helped me with this project: particularly, Lorand Bartels, Alan Boyle and Jan Wouters; Stephen Neff and Federico Ortino; Manuel Núñez P. and Sebastián Zárate R.; and of course Roberto Guerrero V. and Arturo Yrarrázaval C., who made it possible. Thirdly, those institutions that allowed me to focus on this research, in its different stages: the *Pontificia Universidad Católica de Chile*, my alma mater and current place of work; the University of Edinburgh, where I had the chance of teaching as a tutor and guest lecturer while being a probationer research student and PhD candidate; the *Katholieke Universiteit Leuven*, who generously received me as a post-doctoral visiting fellow with a Coimbra Group scholarship; the University of Florida and the University of Wisconsin–Madison, whose journals of international law published parts of the preliminary findings of Chapters 3 and 4;[1] Cornell University, where I recently stayed as a Rudolf B. Schlesinger post-doctoral fellow with a grant from the Chilean

[1] *See* S López Escarcena, 'Interferences with Property under European Human Rights Law', (2012) 24/3 *Florida Journal of International Law* 513; and S López Escarcena, 'Expropriations and Other Measures Affecting Property Rights in the Case Law of the Iran–United States Claims Tribunal', (2013) 31/2 *Wisconsin International Law Journal* 176.

state[2]; and certainly Edward Elgar, an independent, extremely professional and yet friendly publishing house. To all of them, thanks!

As a Jesuit alumnus, I humbly try to live up to Saint Ignatius of Loyola's motto: *ad maiorem Dei gloriam.* Consequently, years of hard work lie in the following pages. I started this text as a student, and I finished it as a lecturer. It is fair to say that in the process of writing this book, I became a researcher. Whether a good or a bad one, that is not for me to say.

Sebastián López E.
Santiago de Chile, June 2013.

[2] *Fondo Nacional para el Desarrollo de la Ciencia y la Tecnologia* (FONDECYT), project Nr. 11110045.

Abbreviations

African Commission HPR	African Commission on Human and Peoples' Rights
AJCL	American Journal of Comparative Law
AJIL	American Journal of International Law
AMDI	Anuario Mexicano de Derecho Internacional
ASEAN	Association of Southeast Asian Nations
ASIL Proc.	American Society of International Law Proceedings
BIT	Bilateral Investment Treaty
Brook. JIL	Brooklyn Journal of International Law
BYIL	British Year Book of International Law
BYU LR	Brigham Young University Law Review
CAFTA–DR	Central America–Dominican Republic–USA Free Trade Agreement
Cal. West. ILJ	California Western International Law Journal
CARICOM	Caribbean Community
Chic. JIL	Chicago Journal of International Law
Colum. JTL	Columbia Journal of Transnational Law
Colum. LR	Columbia Law Review
COMESA	Common Market for Eastern and Southern Africa
Corn. ILJ	Cornell International Law Journal
Corn. LQ	Cornell Law Quarterly (now Cornell Law Review)
ECJ	European Court of Justice
ECOSOC	Economic and Social Council of the United Nations
ECT	Energy Charter Treaty
EIA	Economic Integration Agreement
EJIL	European Journal of International Law
Emory ILR	Emory International Law Review
Eur. Commission HR	European Commission of Human Rights
Eur. Court HR	European Court of Human Rights
Eur. ELR	European Environmental Law Review

Eur. HRLR	European Human Rights Law Review
Eur. HR Rep.	European Human Rights Reports
EPIL	Max Planck Encyclopedia of Public International Law
FCN	Friendship, Commerce and Navigation Treaty
Fed. LR	Federal Law Review
FET	Fair and Equitable Treatment
Fordh. ILJ	Fordham International Law Journal
Fordh. LR	Fordham Law Review
FORUM	International Law FORUM du Droit International
FTA	Free Trade Agreement
GAL	Global Administrative Law
GATT	General Agreement on Tariffs and Trade
Geo. IELR	Georgetown International Environmental Law Review
GYIL	German Yearbook of International Law
Harv. HRJ	Harvard Human Rights Journal
Harv. ILJ	Harvard International Law Journal
Hast. ICLR	Hastings International and Comparative Law Review
I/A Commission HR	Inter-American Commission of Human Rights
I/A Court HR	Inter-American Court of Human Rights
ICC	International Chamber of Commerce
ICJ	International Court of Justice
ICJ Rep.	Reports of Judgments, Advisory Opinions and Orders (ICJ)
ICLQ	International & Comparative Law Quarterly
ICSID	International Centre for Settlement of Investment Disputes
ICSID Rev.	ICSID Review – Foreign Investment Law Journal
IILJ	NYU Institute for International Law and Justice
ILC	International Law Commission
ILJWP	International Law and Justice Working Papers
IL	International Lawyer
IL-RCDI	International Law – Revista Colombiana de Derecho Internacional
ILM	International Legal Materials
ILR	International Law Reports
Iran–US CT	Iran–United States Claims Tribunal
Iran–US CTR	Iran–United States Claims Tribunal Reports

JDI	Journal du Droit International
JIA	Journal of International Arbitration
JIEL	Journal of International Economic Law
JPL	Journal of Public Law (now Emory Law Journal)
JTLP	Journal of Transnational Law & Policy
JWIT	Journal of World Investment & Trade
LCIA	London Court of International Arbitration
LCP	Law and Contemporary Problems
LPICT	Law and Practice of International Courts and Tribunals
LQR	Law Quarterly Review
LSEWP	London School of Economics and Political Science (LSE) Law Society and Economy Working Papers
LSE Res. On.	London School of Economics and Political Science Research Online
MAI	Multilateral Agreement on Investment
Marq. LR	Marquette Law Review
MERCOSUR	Mercado Común del Sur (Common Market of the South)
MFN	Most-Favoured-Nation Treatment
Mich. JIL	Michigan Journal of International Law
MIGA	Multilateral Investment Guarantee Agency
NAFTA	North American Free Trade Agreement
NC JILCR	North Carolina Journal of International Law and Commercial Regulation
Neth. ILR	Netherlands International Law Review
Neth. YIL	Netherlands Yearbook of International Law
NGO	Non-Governmental Organisation
NIEO	New International Economic Order
Nord. JIL	Nordic Journal of International Law
Nw JILB	Northwestern Journal of International Law and Business
NYU ELJ	New York University Environmental Law Journal
NYU JILP	New York University Journal of International Law and Politics
NYU LR	New York University Law Review
OAS	Organization of American States
OECD	Organisation for Economic Cooperation and Development

OPEC	Organization of the Petroleum Exporting Countries
PCIJ	Permanent Court of International Justice
PCIJ Rep.	Collection of Judgments (PCIJ)
RCADI	Recueil des Cours (Académie de Droit International de La Haye)
RIAA	Reports of International Arbitration Awards
SCC	Stockholm Chamber of Commerce
SJICL	Singapore Journal of International & Comparative Law (now Singapore Year Book of International Law)
Suff. TLR	Suffolk Transnational Law Review
Sw JIL	Southwestern Journal of International Law
Tex. ILF	Texas International Law Forum (now Texas International Law Journal)
Tul. LR	Tulane Law Review
UC-Davis JILP	University of California–Davis Journal of International Law and Policy
U.Ill. LR	University of Illinois Law Review
UNCITRAL	United Nations Commission for International Trade Law
UNCTAD	United Nations Conference on Trade and Development
UK	United Kingdom
UN	United Nations
UNGA	United Nations General Assembly
U. Penn. JIEL	University of Pennsylvania Journal of International Economic Law (now University of Pennsylvania Journal of International Law)
US	United States of America
Vand. JTL	Vanderbilt Journal of Transnational Law
Virg. JIL	Virginia Journal of International Law
Virg. LR	Virginia Law Review
WTAM	World Trade and Arbitration Materials
Yale JIL	Yale Journal of International Law
Yale LERP	Yale Law and Economics Research Paper
Yale LJ	Yale Law Journal
Yale LSDWP	Yale Law School Draft Working Paper

Cases

PCIJ & ICJ

HUMAN RIGHTS COURTS AND COMMISSIONS

IRAN–US CLAIMS TRIBUNAL

AD HOC, ICSID, SCC & UNCITRAL ARBITRATIONS

OTHER INTERNATIONAL TRIBUNALS

DOMESTIC COURTS

Treaties and other instruments

TREATIES

UN GENERAL ASSEMBLY RESOLUTIONS

OTHER

1. Introduction

It is a truism that foreign investment creates a long-term relationship between aliens and host-states, which exposes the former to eventual shifts in the public policies of the latter. To encourage foreign investment within its borders, many states offer foreigners treaty-protections against potential interferences with their property. Because the main interference risked by the alien is the expropriation of his/hers/its property, it is not surprising that the protection against takings is at the centre of what is now called international investment law. Foreign investors require clarity in this regard, but not only them: treaty-protections may constrain the exercise of regulatory powers by the host-state. Foreign investors are highly sensitive concerning any interference against their property, just like host-states are concerning any restriction on their sovereignty. How to protect aliens without unduly limiting the exercise of state powers is today the prime challenge of international investment law.

Two cases illustrate the difficulties of achieving this result, and the consequences of failing in the attempt. On 3 August 2005, an international arbitral tribunal concluded that the USA had not expropriated a substantial portion of Methanex's investment, as claimed by the Canadian investor who started this arbitration under Chapter 11 of the North American Free Trade Agreement (NAFTA).[1] According to *Methanex*, a regulation which affects a foreign investor is not expropriatory, and therefore not compensable, if it had been adopted for a public purpose, in a non-discriminatory manner, in accordance with due process, and no specific commitments had been given to the investor by the host-state.[2] The claimant in this case argued for a different approach, then followed recently by *Metalclad*, another NAFTA Chapter 11 arbitration. On 30 August 2000, this award had stated that the term expropriation includes any interference with property which has the effect of depriving the owner of it, in whole or in significant part, even if not necessarily to the obvious benefit of the host-state.[3] From this viewpoint, the tribunal deemed the measure adopted by Mexico to be expropriatory against the US investor and, as a consequence, compensable.[4] Had the arbitral panel in *Methanex* followed the approach of *Metalclad*, the measure adopted by the USA might have also been considered an expropriation, and compensation would have been awarded to the Canadian investor.

Two opposite rulings, then, for cases involving the application of the same treaty provision to not so dissimilar situations. Can international law provide legal certainty to someone investing abroad, or to the state where that investment is being made, if an essential article guiding their future conduct may be construed in such contradictory ways? This is only an example of a problem that is not exclusive to NAFTA, but is common to all the expropriation provisions included in other investment chapters of economic integration agreements (EIA), or in bilateral investment treaties (BIT).

That aliens should be protected is an old principle of the law of nations. Known to the Romans since Cicero's time, it was only developed in the 19th century as a consequence of the evolution of world economy.[5] This protective principle offers a minimum standard of treatment to foreigners, which provides essentially for two things: security of the person from injury or restraint, and the preservation of property from political risk in the host-state.[6] That is to say, it provides for the protection of property from potential interferences based on ideological hostility towards foreign investment, nationalism, and changes in industry patterns and domestic state policy considerations. These interferences have generally adopted the form of the taking of foreign property, whether as an outright deprivation or a major infringement of it.[7] The articulation of an area of international law aimed at reducing political risk is a relatively recent development. Known as international investment law, it largely contains today an older and smaller area of the law of nations – the international law of expropriation. The latter is founded on three distinct but closely related concepts: property, taking and compensation.[8]

Rosalyn Higgins observes that the right to hold property reflects a social instinct. As a consequence, it has a very long history.[9] It is not uncommon to find a reference to property in the sources of international law; a definition, however, is hardly ever seen.[10] A certain consensus among lawyers and scholars has evolved over its content, comprising a positive and negative aspect.[11] On its positive side, property is a generally unlimited right of disposal. On its negative side, it is an exclusive right, conferring upon its holder the power to forbid any other to perform an act of disposal. This notion of property is not restricted to tangibles: rights have been accepted as an integral part of the concept of property in international law by tribunals and scholars.[12] Not only the right to hold property, but also its social function have been commonly recognised by conservative and liberal authors as well as Marxist ones. Such a notion, which can be traced back to medieval times, is found today in virtually all nations.[13] There is an inherent tension in the coexistence of private property and its social function, as the requirements of society sometimes come into conflict with individual property rights. This tension between personal and community interests is at the core of the notion of takings.

There is no unanimously agreed-upon definition of expropriation.[14] The term is generally equated to the taking of property by the state:[15] *i.e.*, to its actual or effective deprivation, either by ousting the owner and claiming the title, or by destroying the property or severely impairing its utility.[16] Exceptionally, taking and expropriation have been distinguished in international case-law. In the *ELSI* case, for instance, the International Court of Justice (ICJ) had to interpret the terms taking and *espropriati*, used in the English and Italian versions – respectively – of a friendship, commerce and navigation treaty (FCN) concluded between Italy and the USA. In that opportunity, the ICJ considered the former to be 'wider and looser' than the latter.[17] Some authors have also perceived taking and expropriation to be different. For example, Jan Paulsson and Zachary Douglas distinguish them on their effects. While a taking is non-compensable, they argue, an expropriation requires compensation.[18]

Expropriations have received other names too. In the 1970s, Burns Weston called them wealth deprivations, in a rather unsuccessful attempt to introduce a 'normatively neutral statement' that would replace wealth for 'the more popular "property"'.[19] The other notions of expropriation normally used in doctrine, and sometimes in treaties and judicial decisions, refer to specific forms of takings. Nationalisations are the expropriation of one or more major industries or resources within a general programme of social and economic reform.[20] Rudolf Dolzer and Margrete Stevens call the transfer of property, to nationals of the host-state, indigenisation.[21] Requisition refers to the power of an occupant state to use the resources and services in an occupied state for the maintenance of its military forces, in return for compensation.[22] Takings or expropriation, however, should not be confused with sequestration, defined in comparative law as the action ordered by national authorities under its domestic law, by which the state assumes temporary control over private property belonging to someone subject to its jurisdiction, without transfer of title and without the payment of compensation.[23] An example of this form of measure is the seizure of property as a result of a sanction imposed by the state in the exercise of its police-powers.[24] In all, there is an extensive literature on the terminology and classification of expropriations, a topic that remains not fully clear, consistent or established,[25] probably because it originates in domestic law and practice, and is not easily translated to the international level.[26]

International law traditionally recognises the state's right to expropriate foreign property, under certain conditions. The state measure resulting in a deprivation will be considered lawful under international norms if it is for a public purpose, of a non-discriminatory nature and followed by the payment of compensation. More recently, treaty and international case-law have added a fourth requirement: due process of law in the execution of the respective measure.[27] If the national authorities fail to comply with any of these requirements, the taking would constitute a confiscation.[28] The state would incur international responsibility and would be liable for breaching the minimum standard governing the treatment of aliens. These norms only come into play where the property of foreigners is involved: international law does not generally provide a remedy to domestic claimants for the expropriation of their property by their own authorities.[29] These apparently simple rules have lacked, however, clarity not only at the moment of establishing the time, form and amount of compensation that should be paid in case of a lawful or even an unlawful expropriation, but also at the moment of finding whether compensation is due at all.

According to the 2001 Articles on State Responsibility of the International Law Commission (ILC), a wrongful act entails two obligations for the responsible state under general international law: cessation and reparation.[30] The latter was expressly recognised in 1928 by the Permanent Court of International Justice (PCIJ), in an often-quoted passage from the *Chorzow Factory* case:

> The essential principle contained in the actual notion of an illegal act – a principle which seems to be established by international practice and in particular by the decisions of arbitral tribunals – is that reparation must, so far as possible, wipe out all the consequences of the illegal act and re-establish the situation which would, in all probability, have existed if that act had not been committed. Restitution in kind, or, if this is not possible, payment of a sum corresponding to the value which a restitution in kind would bear; the award if need be, of damages for loss sustained which would not be covered by restitution in kind or payment in place of it – such are the principles which should serve to determine the amount of compensation due for an act contrary to international law.[31]

In conformity with Article 34 of the ILC's Articles, full reparation for the injury caused by an internationally wrongful act shall take the form of restitution, compensation and satisfaction, either singly or in combination.[32] Restitution is the re-establishment of the situation which existed before the wrongful act was committed, when it is materially possible and the burden derived from it is proportional to the benefit to be obtained.[33] It might involve returning physical assets, or paying the replacement value for damaged assets or the costs for their repair, as long as the respective assets are replaceable and marketable in a used condition.[34] Restitution should normally prevail over compensation in international law.[35] This means that the obligation to compensate will come into play only when the injury is not made good by restitution, covering any financially assessable damage, including loss of profits.[36] In many cases it is simply not possible to restore the situation that existed before the commission of the wrongful act. For this reason, states and other subjects of international law commonly seek compensation, which will normally consist of a monetary payment.[37] Its determination is, therefore, an essential aspect of international law.

Compensation is also one of the requirements of a lawful taking. In doctrine, this term is distinguished from that of damages, which refers to the consequence of a breach of an international obligation. No such obligation is violated when a state lawfully expropriates foreign property.[38] The ILC made no distinction between compensation and damages in its Articles, largely because it relied on the case-law of the PCIJ and the ICJ, and neither of these tribunals has distinguished them carefully in their judicial decisions.[39] The issue is further confounded by the fact that international case-law generally recognises the same financial effect for both lawful and unlawful expropriations.[40] The practical difference between the two types of takings is usually found elsewhere – in the obligation of restitution, which would only originate from the commission of a wrongful act, like an unlawful expropriation.[41] However, as Irmgard Marboe points out:

> Claimants in their written and oral submissions sometimes rely on the standard of compensation for a lawful expropriation, even if they are of the opinion that the expropriation was unlawful. This can be explained by the fact that restitution is often not regarded as the best or the most desirable remedy. Claimants and tribunals thus frequently turn immediately to the secondary remedy, the 'compensation'. Furthermore, the choice of this standard perhaps is considered to be helpful for the acceptability of their claim by the court or tribunal and by the respondent State because it does not 'punish' the State for having acted illegally.[42]

The problem of compensation was highly debated by capital-importing and capital-exporting states, after the emergence of the notion of nationalisation in the first half of the 20th century, particularly in regard to the question of the amount of compensation required for an expropriation to be considered lawful.[43] This issue has been largely settled by treaty practice in the last decades.[44] Ironically, the same changes in international economy and politics that brought the clarification of the problem of compensation have highlighted a long-present and, until not so long ago, dormant issue in the international law of expropriation: that of indirect takings.[45]

Expropriations may occur as an outright taking or as measures having an equivalent effect. Normally referred to as direct expropriation, the former may come as a nationalisation or an expropriation, depending on whether the actual taking is of a general kind or is property or enterprise specific.[46] Direct expropriation has been defined in recent international case-law as 'the forcible appropriation by the State, of the tangible and intangible property of individuals by means of administrative or legislative action'.[47] Historically, these outright takings were the first and most common form of expropriation, but are nowadays rare.[48] Only occasionally, modern cases relate to direct takings.[49] It is generally easy to establish when a direct expropriation has occurred, for expropriations are normally adopted through legislative or administrative measures. If one does occur, compensation is due, no matter what the cause of the taking was.[50] Indirect expropriation refers to those measures that, falling short of a direct taking, amount in their effects to one, thus requiring compensation. This type of taking, the form prevalent today, has received different names and definitions in international law. The terms *de facto*, disguised, creeping, consequential, or constructive expropriation, as well as regulatory takings, stress certain aspects of indirect expropriations in their definitions. The development of these notions has been progressive, which explains why some of them relate to behaviour that would not have provided a sound legal basis for an expropriation claim under an FCN, but would do so under a bilateral investment treaty (BIT).[51]

Contrary to a *de jure* or formal taking, a *de facto* or informal one involves no express legislative or administrative measure announcing the expropriation. The benefit of the property is, however, effectively neutralised by the corresponding governmental act.[52] The name disguised expropriation indicates that it is not visibly recognisable as a taking.[53] The notion of creeping expropriation emphasises the slow and incremental encroachment of the property rights of the alien by a group of measures that only retrospectively will become evident as a taking.[54] Creeping expropriations are comprised of a number of elements, none of which can separately constitute the international wrong.[55] Modern investment treaty case-law has defined them as:

> a form of indirect expropriation with a distinctive temporal quality in the sense that it encapsulates the situation whereby a series of acts attributable to the State over a period of time culminate in the expropriatory taking of such property.[56]

Consequential expropriations are closely related to the concept of good governance, the main objective of international investment law.[57] According to Michael Reisman and Robert Sloane, they refer to the failure of the host-state to create, maintain and properly manage the legal and administrative regulatory framework established in an investment treaty.[58] A constructive expropriation points to the fact that effects similar to a taking are produced, though externally the situation remains unchanged.[59] Lately, regulatory takings have been added to the lexicon of international law to designate those measures that relate to the exercise of the host-state's powers to govern the social and economic activity within its boundaries. This concept derives from the doctrine on the Fifth Amendment of the US Constitution, and although it has not yet been formally used in treaties, it can be recognised in modern forms of expropriation described as tantamount or equivalent to the latter.[60] All these forms of indirect takings are subsumed in the following definition: state measures that are not openly expropriatory, but result in the deprivation of property.[61] Or as the tribunal in *Parkerings-Compagniet* said, 'the negative effect of government measures on the investor's property rights, which does not involve a transfer of property but a deprivation of the enjoyment of the property'.[62] This notion is already recognisable in the decisions of early arbitral tribunals and the PCIJ.[63] Illegality is the general rule for indirect expropriation, since normally aliens receive no compensation from the host-states adopting the challenged measures.[64]

The conceptual analysis of indirect takings only illustrates how they may appear in practice, but leaves its main question unanswered: when does a state measure become compensable, as an indirect expropriation, under international law? The problem is somehow shrouded by the fact that not all expropriations give rise to compensation. In this respect, the term police-powers is a source of significant confusion.[65] Because in international law the state has a right to regulate society, it can interfere with property to the point of deprivation without paying compensation, but only in exceptional circumstances,[66] for instance in those described under its criminal law, or in certain cases of imminent and grave danger to the public health. Notwithstanding exceptions of this kind, the answer to the main question lies in the degree of interference required to consider a regulatory measure as expropriatory.[67] Two factors are relevant here: the severity of the impact of the interference on the affected property, and the duration of the measure.[68] Besides degree, the respect of the foreign investor's legitimate expectations also plays an important role in indirect takings.[69] As Rudolf Dolzer and Christoph Schreuer remark on the issue:

> Not surprisingly, significant lacunae and open issues remain in the law governing indirect expropriation. Domestic courts have grappled with the same issues much longer. Despite the benefit of constitutional texts and the homogeneity of their national legal systems, they have been unable to resolve all problems.[70]

The only possible definitive approach to the problem of indirect takings is case-by-case. This has been widely accepted in doctrine, and expressly recognised in recent treaties.[71] It is obviously not a method that is specific to the issue of indirect expropriation, but one that will be used in most instances in which an adjudicator applies legal standards to a particular set of facts.[72] In the words of Paulsson and Douglas:

> [t]he only real guidance with respect to the threshold of interference for state measures affecting investments is the product of inductive generalizations from the findings of international tribunals and domestic courts as to the factual circumstances that give rise to a [...] taking.[73]

Decision-makers in international law normally refer to the statements of other tribunals. According to Article 38 of the Statute of the ICJ, judicial decisions are subsidiary means for the determination of the rules of law. Though not a proper source of international law, they will be generally treated as authoritative statements by other decision-makers. Judicial decisions will aid them to settle a dispute in two situations: when there is no applicable treaty or clear interpretation of an existing one, and when it is not easy to ascertain the existence or meaning of an international custom or general principle of law.[74]

The PCIJ and the ICJ have seldom referred to indirect expropriation in their judgments.[75] The case-law on this issue derives mainly from the ever-growing number of arbitral awards in investor-to-state disputes, mostly based on BITs or investment chapters of EIAs.[76] Outside international investment law, the protection of property from deprivation has been addressed by regional human-rights bodies, particularly in Europe.[77] Important judicial decisions for the international law of expropriation also emerge from *ad hoc* dispute-settlement institutions, most notably the Iran–United States Claims Tribunal (Iran–US CT).[78] The case-law of US domestic courts is highly instructive as well, and should not be overlooked in any study on the law of indirect expropriation.[79] In this regard, Andrew Newcombe and Lluís Paradell rightly point out that:

> The importance of the jurisprudence rests, however, not in short-hand definitions of what constitutes expropriation that can be applied as a template

> case-by-case. Rather, its importance lies in identifying a number of legally significant factors that must be assessed in deciding an expropriation claim.[80]

Two doctrines provide guidelines on the threshold problem, *i.e.* that of defining the boundaries between non-compensable state measures and compensable indirect takings.[81] The first one is the effects doctrine. According to this position, the central factor for establishing whether an indirect taking has occurred is the result of the governmental measures on the affected property. The purpose of these measures is not essential to this determination, nor is the fact that the actual title of the asset remains with the owner.[82] The effects approach goes back to the 1922 *Norwegian Shipowners* claim and the 1928 *Chorzow Factory* case.[83] This view has received the express or tacit support of many scholars.[84] Its constitutive elements are already found in the concept of indirect taking given by George Christie in the 1960s:

> [an] interference with an alien's property [that] amount[s] to expropriation even when no explicit attempt is made to affect the legal title to the property, and even though the respondent State may specifically disclaim any such intention.[85]

The second position is the so-called police-powers doctrine. Besides the effect on the alien's property, it takes into account the purpose and context of the respective measures when establishing whether the regulatory action of the state amounts to an indirect expropriation. This doctrine maintains that non-discriminatory measures adopted for a legitimate public purpose are necessarily lawful under international norms, and do not give rise to compensation.[86] The police-powers solution can be traced back to the 1934 *Oscar Chinn* case.[87] It has been recently endorsed by last-generation US BITs and free trade agreements (FTAs).

Both positions offer useful guidance to any decision-maker addressing the threshold problem. Nonetheless, choosing one doctrine or the other is not a matter of indifference for the chief actors of international investment law. Dolzer and Stevens rightly explain that:

> to the investor, the line of demarcation between measures for which no compensation is due and actions qualifying as indirect expropriations may well make the difference between the burden to operate (or abandon) a non-profitable enterprise and the right to receive full compensation (either from the host State or under an insurance contract). For the host State, the definition determines the scope of the State's power to enact legislation that regulates the rights and obligations of owners in instances where compensation may fall due.[88]

The effects doctrine clearly stresses the interests of the foreign investors; the police-powers position, those of the host-state.[89] Until recently, an effects approach had been the general rule for the solution of the threshold problem in international law. However, not only the regulatory powers of developed states might be challenged at present, but also those of developed countries. The police-powers doctrine, once exceptional, has thus strongly re-emerged, particularly in North America.

The protection of property in international law has been traditionally based on one core principle: the international minimum standard. Without it, there is no international law of expropriation. This principle has historically received the full support of capital-exporting countries – until not so long ago, an exclusive club composed only of developed states. Other countries, capital-importing and mostly developing, defended another principle: the national standard of treatment. Because the content of this standard was provided by the domestic laws of the undeveloped states receiving foreign investment, capital-exporting countries staunchly refused to accept it as the sole basis for the protection of aliens in international law. Nevertheless, the current flow of foreign investment is not unilateral, as it was before. Some developing states have become capital-exporting countries, while several developed states have become capital-importing ones. This situation has prompted the latter to endorse the once-rejected standard, but with an important caveat: the only national treatment accepted must be similar to that given by its domestic law.

The USA, followed by Canada, have tried to avoid unwanted applications of their BITs, and of the investment chapters of their EIAs, through interpretative declarations aimed at decision-makers in eventual investment disputes.[90] These pragmatic efforts have found a much-needed theoretical background in the doctrine of global administrative law (GAL), generally developed in the USA and Europe.[91] A somewhat related approach advocates the application of the proportionality principle developed in European human rights law, as a possible solution to the threshold problem of indirect takings.[92] The intent of the host-state and the fair balance test now threaten to replace the deprivation of the foreign investor's property as the chief factor shaping indirect expropriations. But, are these solutions in conformity with international investment law, as it currently stands? And, do they provide more legal certainty to investors and states than the effects rule?

The present work is aimed at offering guidelines to identify non-compensable state measures and compensable indirect expropriations, according to international law. For this purpose, the next chapters analyse the international law of expropriation, focusing on the solutions to the problem of indirect takings adopted in the different *fora* of contemporary international law, in which property and its deprivation have been addressed. Chapter 2 outlines the evolution of the law of expropriation in the 19th, 20th and 21st centuries. Interferences with property under international human rights law are studied in Chapter 3, which traces the difficulties in incorporating property as a human right in multilateral instruments, and its progressive recognition in the regional systems of Europe, the Americas and Africa. This third chapter is centred on the case-law of the European Court of Human Rights, the most developed, complex and influential jurisprudence on the issue of the protection of property in this area of international law. The work of the Iran–US CT is addressed in Chapter 4. It deals with the judicial interpretation and application of the concepts on which the competence of this tribunal was based: expropriations and other measures affecting property rights. Even though most of the case-law of the Iran–US CT pre-dates the emergence of international investment law, arbitral panels in investor-to-state disputes have generally followed its views in aspects such as the requirements of a legal expropriation and the threshold problem of indirect takings.

Foreign investment and its expropriation, as regulated in bilateral treaties and construed in international arbitration, are examined in Chapter 5. This part analyses FCNs and BITs, centring on the latter. The problems of degree and intent, and the issue of legitimate expectations, are addressed here. Chapter 6 studies multilateral treaties currently protecting property from expropriation, and their case-law. This section surveys the failed attempts to establish a multilateral framework for the protection of foreign investment, as well as relevant soft-law instruments on the topic. Chapter 7 assesses, from a legal perspective, the new interpretation given to the national treatment standard by certain entities and individuals in mostly developed countries, and the purported application of the proportionality principle of European human rights law to the threshold problem in international investment law. This last part explains the rationale behind the rules and principles of the international law of expropriation, and the role of good governance in the reduction of political risk, relating the protection of property against takings with the rule of law – *i.e.* with the stable, predictable, consistent, transparent and coherent legal and administrative framework at present required from states by investment treaties and regional human rights conventions.

NOTES

1. *Methanex Corporation v. United States of America*, NAFTA, UNCITRAL arbitration, Final Award, 3 August 2005, Part IV, Chapter D, paras. 6 & 15. The awards and decisions of international arbitral tribunals in investment treaty disputes are available at http://italaw.com (last visited 30 June 2013).
2. *Methanex*, Final Award, 3 August 2005, Part IV, Chapter D, para. 7.
3. *Metalclad Corporation v. United Mexican States*, NAFTA, ICSID case No. ARB(AF)/97/1, Award, 30 August 2000, para. 103.
4. *Ibid.*, paras. 105–7 & 112.
5. *See* F Dunn, 'International Law and Private Property Rights', (1928) 28/2 *Colum. LR* 166, at 171–3; and J Herz, 'Expropriation of Foreign Property', (1941) 35/2 *AJIL* 243, at 244.
6. Dunn (1928), at 176.
7. *See* P Comeaux and N Kinsella, *Protecting Foreign Direct Investment under International Law. Legal Aspects of Political Risk* (1996), xvii; S Schill, *The Multilateralization of International Investment Law* (2009), 3; S Robert-Cuendet, *Droits de l'investisseur étranger et protection de l'environnement: contribution à l'analyse de l'expropriation indirect* (2010), 101–2; J Salacuse, *The Law of International Investment Treaties* (2010), 285–6; and M Sornarajah, *The International Law on Foreign Investment* (2010), 69–79.
8. R Dolzer, 'Indirect Expropriation of Alien Property', (1986) 1/1 *ICSID Rev.* 41, at 41; and R Dolzer and C Schreuer, *Principles of International Investment Law* (2012), 99.
9. R Higgins, 'The Taking of Property by the State: Recent Developments in International Law', (1982) 176/3 *RCADI* 259, at 273.
10. *See ibid.*, 269.
11. *Ibid.*, 270. *See* K Katzarov, *The Theory of Nationalisation* (1964), 103. *See also* B Wortley, 'Protection of Property Situated Abroad', (1960) 35/4 *Tul. LR* 739, at 740.
12. On the broad notion of property in the international law of expropriation, *see e.g.* Hertz (1941), 244–5; B Wortley, *Expropriation in Public International Law* (1959), 8–12; Higgins (1982), 271; M Pellonpää and M Fitzmaurice, 'Taking of Property in the Practice of the Iran–United States Claims Tribunal', (1988) 19 *Neth. YIL* 53, at 58; Comeaux and Kinsella (1996), 1–2; G Sacerdoti, 'Bilateral Treaties and Multilateral Instruments on Investment Protection', (1997) 269 *RCADI* 251, at 381; H Sedigh, 'What Level of Host State Interference Amounts to a Taking under Contemporary International Law', (2001) 2/2 *JWIT* 631, at 647; T Waelde and A Kolo, 'Environmental Regulation, Investment Protection and "Regulatory Taking" in International Law', (2001) 50/4 *ICLQ* 811, at 835; Y Dinstein, 'Deprivation of Property of Foreigners under International Law', in N Ando et al (eds.), *Liber Amicorum Judge Shigeru Oda* (2002), 856; G Sampliner, 'Arbitration of Expropriation Cases under U.S. Investment Treaties – a Threat to Democracy or the Dog That Didn't Bark?', (2003) 18/1 *ICSID Rev.* 1, at 14; Y Fortier and S Drymer, 'Indirect Expropriation in the Law of International Investment: I Know It When I See It, or Caveat Investor', (2004) 19/2 *ICSID Rev.* 293, note 9 at 296; J Paulsson and Z Douglas, 'Indirect Expropriation in Investment Treaty Arbitrations', in N Horn (ed.), *Arbitrating Foreign Investment Disputes. Procedural and Substantive Legal Aspects* (2004), 152–3; A Reinisch, 'Expropriation', in P Muchlinski, F Ortino and C Schreuer (eds.), *The Oxford Handbook of International Investment Law* (2008), 410–20; A Newcombe and L Paradell, *Law and Practice of Investment Treaties: Standards of Treatment* (2009), note 7 at 322; Salacuse (2010), 19–20 & 290–1; K Yannaca-Small, 'Indirect Expropriation and the Right to Regulate: How to Draw the

Line?', in K Yannaca-Small (ed.), *Arbitration under International Investment Agreements: A Guide to the Key Issues* (2010), 449–50; and I Alvik, *Contracting with Sovereignty: State Contracts and International Arbitration* (2011), 162–3.
13. *See* Higgins (1982), 274–5. *See also* F Mann, 'Outlines of a History of Expropriation', (1959) 75/2 *LQR* 188, at 189; and B Wortley, 'Some Early but Basic Theories of Expropriation', (1977) 20 *GYIL* 236, at 236–7 & 240.
14. For a comparative account of expropriation, from an historical point of view, *see generally* S Reynolds, *Before Eminent Domain: Toward a History of Expropriation of Land for the Common Good* (2010).
15. *See e.g.* Pellonpää and Fitzmaurice (1988), at 55; A Mouri, *The International Law of Expropriation as Reflected in the Work of the Iran–U.S. Claims Tribunal* (1994), 66; A Avanessian, *Iran–United States Claims Tribunal in Action* (1993), 29; Comeaux and Kinsella (1996), 3; R Jennings and A Watts, *Oppenheim's International Law* (1996), note 9 at 916; C Brower and J Brueschke, *The Iran–United States Claims Tribunal* (1998), note 1718 at 369; F. Beveridge, *The Treatment and Taxation of Foreign Investment under International Law* (2000), at 13; J Dugard, *International Law. A South African Perspective* (2000), 225; and D Wallace, 'Case Study under NAFTA: Lessons for the Wise?', in N Horn (ed.), *Arbitrating Foreign Investment Disputes. Procedural and Substantive Legal Aspects* (2004), 255; A Hoffmann, 'Indirect Expropriation', in A Reinisch (ed.), *Standards of Investment Protection* (2008), 153; Salacuse (2010), 294; and Alvik (2011), 161.
16. *See* B Garner (ed.), *Black's Law Dictionary* (2009), 662 & 1591.
17. *Elettronica Sicula, S.p.A.* (ELSI) (USA v. Italy), International Court of Justice, Judgment, 20 July 1989, (1989) 28/5 *ILM* 1111, para. 113.
18. Paulsson and Douglas (2004), 148–50.
19. B Weston, '"Constructive Takings" under International Law: A Modest Foray into the Problem of "Creeping Expropriation"', (1975) 16/1 *Virginia LR* 103, at 112–3.
20. J Crawford, *Brownlie's Principles of Public International Law* (2012), 620–2 & 624. *See* Newcombe and Paradell (2009), 324; and Salacuse (2010), 288.
21. R Dolzer and M Stevens, *Bilateral Investment Treaties* (1995), 98.
22. R Dolzer, 'Requisitions', in R Bernhardt (ed.), *EPIL* (2000), Vol. 4, 205. *See* Newcombe and Paradell (2009), 324.
23. R Dolzer, 'Sequestration', in R Bernhardt (ed.), *EPIL* (2000), Vol. 4, 383.
24. In comparative law, the term confiscation is sometimes used as sequestration. *See e.g.* Wortley (1959), 38–45 & 105; Newcombe and Paradell (2009), 324–5; and S Nikièma, *L'expropriation indirecte en droit international des investissements* (2012), 99–100.
25. *See e.g.* the distinction between vertical and horizontal state-measures and its application to the law of expropriation, in Nikièma (2012).
26. UNCTAD, *International Investment Agreements: Key Issues* (2004), Vol. 1, 236.
27. *See* Chapter 5 below.
28. Crawford (2012), 621. Some authors refer to confiscation as spoliation. *See e.g.* Wortley (1977), 242; Newcombe and Paradell (2009), 325; and Nikièma (2012), 98–9.
29. Comeaux and Kinsella (1996), 5. *See* Chapters 3 & 5 below.
30. *See* Arts. 30 and 31 of the Articles on Responsibility of States for Internationally Wrongful Acts, adopted by the International Law Commission in 2001. Available at http://untreaty.un.org/ilc/texts/instruments/english/draft%20articles/9_6_2001.pdf (last visited 30 June 2013).
31. *Factory at Chorzow* (Germany v. Poland), PCIJ, Judgment, 13 September 1928, (1928) *PCIJ Rep.* Series A No 17, at 47. *See* J Crawford, *The International Law Commission's Articles on State Responsibility. Introduction, Text and Commentaries* (2005), 211.

32. *See* Art. 34 of the ILC Articles.
33. *See* Art. 35 of the ILC Articles.
34. I Marboe, 'Compensation and Damages in International Law. The Limits of the "Fair Market Value"', (2006) 7/5 *JWIT* 723, at 744–5.
35. The primacy of restitution can be traced back to the *Chorzow Factory* case. Arts. 35 and 36 of the ILC Articles refer to it too. *See* Crawford (2005), 213–14; and Marboe (2006), 744.
36. *See* Art. 36 of the ILC Articles.
37. *See* Crawford (2005), 218–19.
38. Marboe (2006), 725–6. *See* T Waelde and B Sabahi, 'Compensation, Damages, and Valuation', in P Muchlinski, F Ortino and C Schreuer (eds.), *The Oxford Handbook of International Investment Law* (2008), 1052–3.
39. Marboe (2006), note 3 at 724 & note 14 at 726. On compensation in international investment law, *see generally* S Ripinski and K Williams, *Damages in International Investment Law* (2008); Waelde and Sabahi (2008); I Marboe, *Calculation of Compensation and Damages in International Investment Law* (2009); M Kinnear, 'Damages in Investment Treaty Arbitration', in K Yannaca-Small (ed.), *Arbitration under International Investment Agreements: A Guide to the Key Issues* (2010); and B Sabahi, *Compensation and Restitution in Investor-State Arbitration: Principles and Practice* (2011).
40. This situation has been exceptionally and properly criticised by tribunals, judges and authors. *See* Marboe (2006), 726–8. *See also* D Bowett, 'State Contracts with Aliens: Contemporary Developments on Compensation for Termination or Breach', (1988) 59 *BYIL* 49, at 61; G Sacerdoti, 'The Admission and Treatment of Foreign Investment under Recent Bilateral and Regional Treaties', (2000) 1/1 *JWIT* 105, at 123; and Dolzer and Schreuer (2012), 100.
41. *See* Dolzer and Schreuer (2012), 100–1.
42. Marboe (2006), 728.
43. *See* U Kriebaum, 'Regulatory Takings: Balancing the Interests of the Investor and the State', (2007) 8/5 *JWIT* 717, at 717.
44. *See* Chapter 2 below.
45. The literature on the topic is illustrative of this. Even though there are numerous articles on indirect expropriation, monographs on the issue are scarce. *See e.g.* Robert-Cuendet (2010); and Nikièma (2012).
46. UNCTAD (2004), 235. Both involve the physical taking of property. *Ibid.*, 236. *See* Salacuse (2010), 288, 294 & 296.
47. *LG&E Energy Corp., LG&E Capital Corp., LG&E International Inc. v. Argentine Republic*, ICSID case No. ARB/02/1, Decision on Liability, 3 October 2006, para. 187. *See BC Group Plc. v. Republic of Argentina*, UNCITRAL arbitration, Final Award, 24 December 2007, para. 259.
48. *See* UNCTAD (2004), 236 & 240; Hoffmann (2008), 151; M Sornarajah, 'A Coming Crisis: Expansionary Trends in Investment Treaty Arbitration', in K Sauvant (ed.), *Appeals Mechanism in International Investment Disputes* (2008), 61; Newcombe and Paradell (2009), 341; Salacuse (2010), 286–7 & 296; and Dolzer and Schreuer (2012), 101.
49. *See e.g. Franz Sedelmayer v. The Russian Federation*, SCC arbitration, Award 7 July 1998; *Compañía del Desarrollo de Santa Elena S.A. v. Republic of Costa Rica*, ICSID case No. ARB/96/1, Award, 17 February 2000; *Swembalt AB, Sweden v. The Republic of Latvia*, UNCITRAL arbitration, Award 23 October 2000; *ADC Affiliate Limited and ADC & ADMC Management Limited v. The Republic of Hungary*, ICSID case No. ARB/03/16, Award, 2 October 2006; *Bernardus Henricus Funnekotter and others v. Republic of Zimbabwe*, ICSID case No. ARB/05/6, Award 22 April 2009; *Waguih Elie George Siag and Clorinda Vecchi v. Arab Republic of Egypt*, ICSID case

No. ARB/05/15, Award, 1 June 2009; and *Ioannis Kardassopoulos v. Republic of Georgia*, ECT, ICSID case No. ARB/05/18, Award, 3 March 2010.
50. Kriebaum (2007), at 717; and Newcombe and Paradell (2009), 340–1.
51. M Reisman and R Sloane, 'Indirect Expropriation and Its Valuation in the BIT Generation', (2003) 74 *BYIL* 115, at 119. *See* Chapter 5 below.
52. *See* Mouri (1994), 70. *See also* J Stanley, 'Keeping Big Brother Out of Our Backyard: Regulatory Takings as Defined in International Law and Compared to American Fifth Amendment Jurisprudence', (2001) 15/1 *Emory ILR* 349, at 360–5.
53. Sornarajah (2010), 368. *See Barcelona Traction* (Belgium v. Spain), ICJ, Judgment, 5 February 1970, Separate Opinion of Judge Fitzmaurice, (1970) 9/2 *ILM* 227, para. 71; and *CME Czech Republic B.V. v. The Czech Republic*, UNCITRAL arbitration, Partial Award, 13 September 2001, para. 604.
54. Reisman and Sloane (2003), 124; Newcombe and Paradell (2009), 343–4; Sornarajah (2010), 368; K Vandevelde, *Bilateral Investment Treaties: History, Policy, and Interpretation* (2010), 278–9; and Dolzer and Schreuer (2012), 125–6. *See* Reinisch, 'Expropriation' (2008), 426–31; and F González de Cossío, *Arbitraje de inversión* (2009), 236–40.
55. *See Waste Management, Inc. v. United Mexican States*, NAFTA, ICSID case No. ARB(AF)/98/2, Award, 2 June 2000 ('Waste Management 1'), Dissenting Opinion of Keith Highet, para. 17.
56. *Generation Ukraine, Inc. v. Ukraine*, ICSID case No. ARB/00/9, Award, 16 September 2003, para. 20.22. *See Tradex Hellas S.A. v. Republic of Albania*, ICSID case No. ARB/94/2, Award, 29 April 1999, para. 191; *Siemens A.G. v. The Argentine Republic*, ICSID case No. ARB/02/8, Award, 6 February 2007, para. 263; *Biwater Gauff (Tanzania) Ltd. v. United Republic of Tanzania*, ICSID case No. ARB/05/22, Award, 24 July 2008, para. 455–6; and *Impregilo S.p.A. v. Argentine Republic*, ICSID case No. ARB/07/17, Award, 21 June 2011, para. 270.
57. *See e.g.* Salacuse (2010), 6–9, 109–11 & 114; and Vandevelde (2010), 2–4; and Dolzer and Schreuer (2012), 24–5.
58. Reisman and Sloane (2003), 128–9. *Cf.* Newcombe and Paradell (2009), 339.
59. Sornarajah (2010), 368. *See* Reinisch, 'Expropriation' (2008), 426–7.
60. Waelde and Kolo (2001), note 46 at 821; and Z AlQurashi, 'Indirect Expropriation in the Field of Petroleum', (2004) 5/6 *JWIT* 897, at 901.
61. *See* A Newcombe, 'The Boundaries of Regulatory Expropriation in International Law', (2005) 20/1 *ICSID Rev.* 1, at 10. *See also* Newcombe and Paradell (2009), 323; Vandevelde (2010), 277–8; and Dolzer and Schreuer (2012), 101.
62. *Parkerings-Compagniet AS v. Republic of Lithuania*, ICSID case No. ARB/05/8, Award, 11 September 2007, para. 437. *See Biwater Gauff*, Award, 24 July 2008, para. 452. These measures need not benefit the host-state. Reinisch, 'Expropriation' (2008), 442–4.
63. Dolzer and Schreuer (2012), 101–2.
64. *See* Dolzer and Schreuer (2012), 100. *See also* Vandevelde (2010), 307.
65. *See* Newcombe (2005), 26.
66. *See e.g.* F. Beveridge, *The Treatment and Taxation of Foreign Investment under International Law* (2000), 5–6; and S Montt, *State Liability in Investment Treaty Arbitration: Global Constitutional and Administrative Law in the BIT Generation* (2009), 191–8 & 232–5.
67. *See e.g.* Waelde and Kolo (2001) 825; C Schreuer, 'The Concept of Expropriation under the ECT and Other Investment Protection Treaties', in C Ribeiro (ed.), *Investment Arbitration and the Energy Charter Treaty* (2006), 145; Hoffmann (2008), 156 & 158–9; and Newcombe and Paradell (2009), 341, 344–6, 350–1 & 358.
68. *See e.g.* Hoffmann (2008), 156–60; Salacuse (2010), 307–11; and Yannaca–Small (2010), 460–9.

69. *See e.g.* Salacuse (2010), 311–13; and Yannaca-Small (2010), 474–6.
70. Dolzer and Schreuer (2012), 112.
71. *See e.g.* G Christie, 'What Constitutes a Taking of Property under International Law?', (1962) *BYIL* 307, at 308; American Law Institute, *Restatement of the Law Third, the Foreign Relations Law of the United States* (1987), § 712, Reporter's Note 6, at 211; Dolzer and Stevens (1995), 100; Z AlQurashi, 'Indirect Expropriation in the Field of Petroleum', (2004) 5/6 *JWIT* 897, at 905; Paulsson and Douglas (2004), 146; B Kunoy, 'Developments in Indirect Expropriation Case Law in ICSID Transnational Arbitration', (2005) 6/3 *JWIT* 467, at 467 & 473; Newcombe (2005), 6; M Gutbrod and S Hindelang, 'Externalization of Effective Legal Protection against Indirect Expropriation. Can the Legal Order of Developing Countries Live up to the Standards Required by International Investment Agreements? A Disenchanting Comparative Analysis', (2006) 7/1 *JWIT* 59, at 63; Hoffmann (2008), 169; C McLachlan, L Shore and M Weiniger, *International Investment Arbitration: Substantive Principles* (2008), 298; Reinisch, 'Expropriation' (2008), 438; González de Cossío (2009), 222; Newcombe and Paradell (2009), 344 & 366–8; J Waincymer, 'Balancing Property Rights and Human Rights in Expropriation', in P Dupuy, F Francioni and E Petersmann (eds.), *Human Rights in International Investment Law and Arbitration* (2009), 291; and Yannaca-Small (2010), 446–7, 455 & 459. *See also e.g.* Annex B of the 2004 Treaty concerning the Encouragement and Reciprocal Protection of Investment between Uruguay and the USA; or Annex B.13 (1) of the 2006 Agreement for the Promotion and Protection of Investments between Canada and Perú. BITs are available at http://www.unctadxi.org/templates/docsearch____779.aspx (last visited 30 June 2013).
72. Fortier and Drymer (2004) 19/2 *ICSID Rev.* 293, at 314.
73. Paulsson and Douglas (2004), 146.
74. *See* A Boyle and C Chinkin, *The Making of International Law* (2006), 293–300. *See also* Pellonpää and Fitzmaurice (1988), 56; Brower and Brueschke (1998), 642–3; and Sornarajah (2010), note 6 at 333 & 368–9.
75. *See* Chapter 7 below.
76. *See* Chapters 5 & 6 below.
77. *See* Chapter 3 below.
78. *See* Chapter 4 below.
79. *See* Chapters 5, 6 & 7 below.
80. Newcombe and Paradell (2009), 367.
81. *See e.g.* M Brunetti, 'Indirect Expropriation in International Law', (2003) 5/3 *FORUM* 150, at 151; R Dolzer, 'Indirect Expropriations: New Developments?', (2003) 11/1 *NYU ELJ* 64, at 79–80; R Dolzer and F Bloch, 'Indirect Expropriation: Conceptual Realigments?', (2003) 5/3 *FORUM* 155, at 158; V Heiskanen, 'The Contribution of the Iran–United States Claims Tribunal to the Development of the Doctrine of Indirect Expropriation', (2003) 5/3 *FORUM* 176, at 176–8; A Weiner, 'Indirect Expropriations: The Need for a Taxonomy of "Legitimate" Regulatory Purposes', (2003) 5/3 *FORUM* 166, at 166; Fortier and Drymer (2004), at 300; Kunoy (2005), 471; Newcombe (2005), 5–6, 9–10, 22 & 25–9; Gutbrod and Hindelang (2006), 63–6; V Heiskanen, 'The Doctrine of Indirect Expropriation in Light of the Practice of the Iran–United States Claims Tribunal', (2007) 8/2 *JWIT* 215, at 217; and Kriebaum (2007), at 724–9.
82. This doctrine is better known as 'sole-effect', a name given by Rudolf Dolzer. Dolzer (2003), 79–90. *See* Hoffmann (2008), 156; and Nikièma (2012), 141. Such a name, however, is not used throughout the following pages because it can be misleading: the effect is a relevant factor in finding a compensable indirect expropriation, but not the only one. *See* Chapter 7 below.

83. *See Norwegian Shipowners* (Norway v. USA), Anderson, Vogt and Valloton, arbitrators, Award, 13 October 1922. (1922) 1 *RIAA* 307, and *Factory at Chorzow* (Germany v. Poland), PCIJ, Judgment, 13 September 1928. *See also* Christie (1962), 311, Higgins (1982), 323; Sedigh (2001), 647; and Reisman and Sloane (2003), 119–20. For an early exposition of the effects doctrine, *see* Herz (1928), 248 & 253.
84. *See e.g.* Higgins (1982), 331; Waelde and Kolo (2001), 824–5, 827 & 846; Dinstein (2002), 869; F Orrego Vicuña, 'Carlos Calvo, Honorary NAFTA Citizen', (2002) 11/1 *NYU ELJ* 19, at 27; B Appleton, 'Regulatory Takings: The International Law Perspective', (2003) 11/1 *NYU ELJ* 35, at 37; I Madalena, 'Foreign Direct Investment and the Protection of the Environment: The Border between National Environmental Regulation and Expropriation', (2003) 12/3 *Eur. ELR* 70, at 70; Reisman and Sloane (2003), 130 & 141; Paulsson and Douglas (2004), 158; Kunoy (2005), 468 & 474; Gutbrod and Hindelang (2006), 66; Reinisch, 'Expropriation' (2008), 444–7; González de Cossío (2009), 220–1, 230 & 241–2; N Blackaby et al, *Redfern & Hunter on International Arbitration* (2009), 497–8; Newcombe and Paradell (2009), 325–6 & 341–8; and Salacuse (2010), 298.
85. Christie (1962), 309.
86. Heiskanen (2003), 177.
87. *See Oscar Chinn* (UK v. Belgium), PCIJ, Judgment, 12 December 1934. (1934) *PCIJ Rep.* Series A/B No 63. *See also* Dolzer and Bloch (2003), 159. An embryonic version of this view can be found in Dunn (1928), 180.
88. Dolzer and Stevens (1995), 99–100.
89. *See* Waelde and Kolo (2001), 822–3.
90. *See e.g.* Annex B of the 2004 Uruguay–USA BIT; Annex B.13 (1) of the 2006 Canada–Perú BIT; Annex B of the 2008 Treaty between Rwanda and the USA concerning the Encouragement and Reciprocal Protection of Investments; Annex B of the 2009 Agreement between Canada and Latvia for the Promotion and Protection of Investments; and Annex A of the 2010 Agreement between Canada and the Slovak Republic for the Promotion and Protection of Investments. *See also e.g.* Annex 10-D of the 2003 Chile–USA FTA; Annex 10-C of the 2004 Central America–Dominican Republic–USA FTA; Annex 10-B of the 2006 Oman–USA FTA; Annex 11-B of the 2007 Korea–USA FTA; Annex 811 of the 2008 Canada-Colombia FTA; and Annex 9.11 of the 2010 Canada–Panamá FTA. US FTAs are available at http://www.ustr.gov/trade-agreements/free-trade-agreements (last visited 30 June 2013). Canadian FTAs are available at http://www.international.gc.ca/trade-agreements-accords-commerciaux/agr-acc/index.aspx?lang=en&view=dChromeHTML\Shell\Open\Command#free (last visited 30 June 2013). *See* Chapters 5, 6 & 7 below.
91. *See e.g.* the GAL Project at New York University School of Law, available at http://www.iilj.org/GAL/ (last visited 30 June 2013); or the project of the Max Planck Institute for Comparative Public Law and International Law, titled 'Transnational Private–Public Arbitration as Global Regulatory Governance: Charting and Codifying the Lex Mercatoria Publica', available at http://www.mpil.de/ww/en/pub/organization/lex_mp.cfm (last visited 30 June 2013). *See* Chapter 7 below.
92. *See e.g.* Kriebaum (2007) 8/5 *JWIT* 717, at 727–4; Hoffmann (2008), 167–70; J Kommendijk and J Morijn, 'Proportional by What Measure(s)? Balancing Investor Interests and Human Rights by Way of Applying the Proportionality Principle in Investor–State Arbitration', in P Dupuy et al (2009), 423, 432–46 & 448–51; U Kriebaum, 'Human Rights of the Population of the Host State in International Investment Arbitration', (2009) 10/5 *JWIT* 653, at 670; and Salacuse (2010), 313–5 & 317–8. *See* Chapters 3, 5, 6 & 7 below.

2. From compensation to indirect takings

The long debate on the payment of compensation for the expropriation of aliens was based on historical and ideological differences between capital-exporting and capital-importing states. According to developed countries, an international minimum standard stressing the need for a prompt, adequate and effective compensation was required in cases of expropriation of foreign property, guaranteeing the full value of the lost investment. Developing and communist states, as well as those countries that gained their independence from colonial rule in the aftermath of the Second World War, proposed national treatment as a minimum and maximum standard requiring appropriate compensation, to be determined by the expropriating state, in conformity with its municipal law. In practice, this meant the payment of a compensation that would range from the full value of the taken property to none, depending on each particular case. While these two views collided at the UN General Assembly, significant changes in international economy and politics gradually reshaped state policies, legislation and practice on the protection of aliens.

The collapse of communism and the progressive liberalisation of national and international economies led erstwhile statist-orientated countries to desire foreign investment. For this purpose, they enacted investment codes and concluded international agreements that promote and protect foreign investment in the traditional terms advanced by capital-exporting states. Both the national and international treatment standards were included in these treaties. The exclusive standard of national treatment, advocated diplomatically by second- and third-world countries, was thus conventionally defeated. Capital-importing states also discarded their position on compensation, part of which had achieved international consensus at the UN in 1962. This situation and the increased governmental regulation in areas formerly run by the state, like the industrial exploitation of natural resources, or of current public concern, like the protection of the environment, have modified the nature of the international legal debate. The problem of compensation has given way to that of indirect takings as the most controversial issue in the law of expropriation today.

The present chapter deals with the classical international norms on takings and the main challenges to them, which include the 19th-century Calvo doctrine and clause; the 1917 Russian revolution; the Mexican constitution of the same year; the nationalisations of the second half of the 20th century and their lump-sum agreements; and the diplomatic controversy on the permanent sovereignty over natural resources and the new international economic order (NIEO) that took place at the UN in the 1960s and 1970s. An introduction to the current doctrinal debate in the international law of expropriation completes this brief historical survey on the protection against takings.

2.1 CALVO DOCTRINE AND NATIONALISATIONS

Prior to the Second World War, imperial-powers provided the necessary degree of legal and administrative certainty to those investing in their colonial territories through their domestic laws and institutions.[1] For those investing in non-colonial territories, mainly independent Latin American countries, the imperial-powers developed an absolute international standard of treatment.[2] According to it, aliens should be granted a minimum degree of protection, regardless of how the nationals of the host-state country were treated by their own authorities. Against this principle, Latin American states advanced the relative standard of national treatment. In conformity with it, aliens should not be treated differently from the nationals of the country that hosted them.[3] The classical norms on the responsibility of states derive from this dispute, which explains why there was normally no distinction in the past between the rules of state responsibility and the substantive rules on the treatment of aliens, both in the writings of scholars and the practice of states. Today, it is generally acknowledged that these two types of norms refer to different, but related, areas of international law.[4]

By the first half of the 20th century, the so-called international minimum standard had prevailed.[5] Non-compliance with it by the host government makes it now liable under the international law of state responsibility. The authorities infringing an international obligation are responsible for that breach and have to repair it. The government of the injured foreigner is entitled to ask for reparation through diplomatic means.[6] It can resort to self-help, in the form of non-forcible action, so as to constrain the other state to correct the wrong, or even punish it for the violation of the international norm. Such action might take the form of economic sanctions, or the suspension or termination of a treaty, among other possibilities. Forcible measures involving armed reprisals and war were also an option in classical international law.[7]

Also known as international standard of justice, the principle advanced by the USA and Western European states was first described by the US–Mexican General Claims Commission in the 1926 *Roberts* case as a treatment 'in accordance with ordinary standards of civilization'.[8] In its early formulations, this minimum treatment included certain protections: that against denial of justice; indecent treatment if imprisoned; disorders, violence and deportation in abusive ways; and expropriation.[9] The latter did not mean that the host-state had no right to take the property of aliens. It meant that the host-state could only take their property if the respective measure was lawful, *i.e.* if it was adopted following three requirements: for public purposes, without discrimination, and accompanied by compensation.[10]

2.1.1 Against the International Standard

Although the institution of diplomatic protection can be traced back to the 18th century, it was mostly developed as a result of the relations between the newly independent Latin American states and European imperial powers, later joined by the USA.[11] In other parts of the world, like Africa and Asia, the system of extraterritorial jurisdiction had been employed to protect the rights of aliens. For instance, nationals of certain European countries in the Ottoman empire benefited from capitulations, by which the Sultan allowed them to be subject to the law of their nationality, and not to Ottoman law.[12] But it was not only diplomatic protection that developed from the relations between Latin American states and European imperial powers and the USA – so did its negation.[13] The initial assault on the 19th-century international protection of aliens came from Argentina, and took the name of Calvo doctrine.[14] It proposed the standard of national treatment, derived from the principles of non-intervention and sovereign equality of states. This doctrine was an application of the principle of non-discrimination, both as a minimum and maximum standard of treatment.[15] Calvo did not consider the content of the international standard to be unacceptable. He only claimed that both nationals and non-nationals of the host country should be protected by the domestic law of the latter. As a consequence, disputes arising from its application should be settled by the courts of this state, under its municipal norms.[16] The doctrine accepted only one set of exceptions, to the otherwise exclusive settlement of disputes by domestic courts under national law. In cases of denial of justice, aliens could resort to diplomatic protection.[17]

Even though Carlos Calvo did not create the doctrine that bears his name, he was the one to popularise it. The doctrine first appeared in Latin America in the writings of the Venezuelan Andrés Bello, who also strongly advocated for the principles of non-intervention and sovereign equality of states.[18] Bello himself relied on the writings of the Swiss Emer de Vattel.[19] Calvo's version of the doctrine originated in the negative perception held in Latin America towards US foreign investment. Muthucumaraswamy Sornarajah explains that in this region:

> foreign investment and the claims relating to the international law that protected it were perceived as instruments through which the United States was able to maintain its economic dominance in the region. [...] The idea that there were supranational norms which permitted the protection of the foreign investor was anathema to the Latin American jurists who argued that only protection that existed for foreign investment was to be found in the domestic legal systems of the host state.[20]

Not surprisingly, the USA itself had embraced this position when it was a recipient of investment from Europe. Its authorities only changed their mind when the USA became an exporter of capital into Latin America.[21] European countries investing in the region also adopted the international minimum standard, and its name abusively exercised their right of diplomatic protection in Latin America during the late 19th and early 20th centuries. The most famous example of abuse was the naval blockade of the Venezuelan coast by Germany, Italy and the United Kingdom in 1902, who all demanded reparation for Venezuela's sovereign-debt default and damages for their nationals.[22] Calvo's theory was a direct reaction to this type of situation.[23]

As a corollary to his doctrine, Latin American countries inserted a clause in those concession contracts concluded with foreigners, by which the alien waived the right of diplomatic protection.[24] Known as the Calvo clause, it meant that a foreign investor would be in the same position as a local one, both of them subject to the exclusive jurisdiction of the host-state's courts at the moment of determining their rights and obligations.[25] Unlike the doctrine of the same name, some Calvo clauses did not include an exception for cases of denial of justice.[26] Article 9 paragraph 2 of the 1934 Montevideo Convention on the Rights and Duties of States illustrates the Calvo doctrine. It stated that '[n]ationals and foreigners are under the same protection of the law and the national authorities and the foreigners may not claim rights other or more extensive than those of the nationals'.[27] Examples of the Calvo doctrine include Article 21 of the 1892 Treaty of Friendship, Commerce and Navigation between Colombia and Italy, and Article 7 of the 1948 American Treaty of Pacific Settlements (Pact of Bogotá). The Colombia–Italy FCN provided that:

> Both Contracting Parties wish to avoid disputes which could affect their friendly relationship and agree that in connection with disputes involving private parties arising out of criminal, civil or administrative matters, their diplomatic agents will abstain from intervention, save in case of denial of justice or extraordinary unlawful delay in the administration of justice.[28]

The Pact of Bogotá says:

> The High Contracting Parties bind themselves not to make diplomatic representations in order to protect their nationals, or to refer a controversy to a court of international jurisdiction for that purpose, when the said nationals have had available the means to place their case before competent domestic courts of the respective State.[29]

Although the debate over the Calvo clause developed almost exclusively in the Americas, it became one of the most controversial issues in international law.[30] Overall, this doctrine has not been generally well received in the international *fora*.[31] The PCIJ recognised diplomatic protection as a right of the state, derived from international law, in the *Mavrommatis* case.[32] Critics of the Calvo clause have referred to this judgment in concluding that diplomatic protection cannot be renounced by nationals. Several claims commissions and courts have dealt with the validity of the clause. The most famous of these cases is *North American Dredging Company of Texas*, settled by the US–Mexican General Claims Commission in 1926.[33] In this landmark case, the tribunal adopted the rule known as limited validity of the Calvo clause: with it, the claims commission avoided having to choose between upholding the clause altogether, or denying its efficacy completely. According to this rule, there is no generally accepted norm of international law forbidding an individual or legal entity to relinquish, to any extent and under any circumstances or conditions, the protection of his/her/its government. Although the individual or legal entity would be legally bound by the clause to which he/she/it contractually agreed, the state of his/hers/its nationality would not be bound by an agreement to which it was not a party. In other words, the respective government would not be deprived of the exercise of its right of diplomatic protection. The Calvo clause would therefore only insist on the requirement of the exhaustion of local remedies before such an exercise.[34] In practice, this solution downgraded the clause to an altogether superfluous provision, repeating a condition already included in the general rules of admissibility of diplomatic protection.[35] Other judicial decisions followed this view.

In 2006, the ILC expressly decided 'to leave open the question whether the State exercising diplomatic protection does so in its own right or that of its national – or both'.[36] The ILC's Articles on Diplomatic Protection acknowledged that the Calvo clause was viewed as a regional custom in Latin America and 'formed part of the national identity of many States'.[37] Nevertheless, they failed to observe that several Latin American countries have enacted national legislation to promote the flow of investment into their economies. Furthermore, the Articles did not acknowledge what Nico Schrijver pointed out almost ten years before their adoption:

> [t]he changing attitude of a number of Latin American countries towards foreign investment is also reflected in their increasing participation in multilateral investment instruments such as ICSID and MIGA as well as in the increasing number of bilateral investment treaties they have concluded in recent years.[38]

The ILC did, however, recognise that capital-exporting states have vigorously disputed the validity of this clause. Quoting *North American Dredging Co.*, the ILC finally endorsed the limited validity of the Calvo clause, as put forward in that case, expressly stating that this clause:

> is difficult to reconcile with international law if it is to be interpreted as a complete waiver of recourse to international protection in respect of an action by the host State constituting an internationally wrongful act (such as denial of justice) or where the injury to the alien was of direct concern to the State of nationality of the alien. The objection to the validity of the 'Calvo clause' in respect of general international law are certainly less convincing if one accepts that the right protected within the framework of diplomatic protection are those of the individual protected and not those of the protecting State.[39]

2.1.2 The Road to Lump-sum Agreements

Two events would further undermine the international protection of foreign investment. Until 1917, the right of private property was recognised by the municipal legislation of almost every state, and protected by the international minimum standard of treatment. This consensus among nations was broken by the Russian Revolution and its repudiation of the right of private property. The newly created Soviet Union introduced to the international lexicon the term nationalisation to designate expropriations of a general character.[40] Subsequent takings of the property of

Russian nationals and aliens followed, without compensation. The communist authorities justified the lack of payment to foreigners invoking the principle of national treatment. Western states slowly came to terms with the Soviet nationalisations, but never formally accepted these measures as legal.[41]

Another revolution, this time in Mexico, led to the establishment of the social function of property at a constitutional level. In the early 20th century, Mexican law was built on individualism and private property as an absolute, untouchable right.[42] One of the main purposes of the revolution that started in 1910 was the redefinition of this approach.[43] The 1917 constitution, still in force in Mexico, achieved the objective in its article 27:

> Ownership of the lands and waters included within the boundaries of the national territory belongs originally to the Nation, which has had and continues to have the right to transmit ownership thereof to private parties, thereby constituting private property.
>
> Expropriations may only be made for reasons of public utility and by means of compensation.
>
> The Nation shall have at all times the right to impose on private property the modalities required by public interest, as well as to regulate, for social benefit, the exploitation of natural resources capable of appropriation, in order to make an equitable distribution of public wealth, conserve them, achieve the balanced development of the country and improve the life conditions of the rural and urban population.[44]

This remodelled notion of property, subordinated to the common welfare of the society, was in no case a new concept in the history of law. The social function of property had already been advanced by St. Thomas Aquinas in the medieval period, and was included in the influential Napoleonic civil code of 19th-century France.[45] As Andreas Lowenfeld explains, the Mexican version did not mean taking without compensation, but instead meant:

> distinctions between state-taking of a private home where a school or highway was to be built, and state ownership (or acquisition of ownership) of a major industry, such as electric power generation, petroleum exploration, or railroads. For the former, compensation, generally prior and more or less in full value, was contemplated, if not always implemented. For the latter, as well as for redistribution of land pursuant to agrarian reform programmes, compensation was not excluded, but it need not be prior or prompt, and the state's ability to pay was an important factor in determining the appropriate level of compensation.[46]

The famous 1938 diplomatic exchange between the governments of the USA and Mexico, derived from the agrarian expropriations which began in 1917 in the latter, summarised the opposed positions of capital-exporting and capital-importing countries regarding the issue of compensation.[47] At the outset of this exchange, Cordell Hull declared:

> The issue is not whether Mexico should pursue social and economic policies designed to improve the standard of living of its people. The issue is whether in pursuing them the property of American nationals may be taken by the Mexican Government without making prompt payment of just compensation to the owner in accordance with the universally recognized rules of law and equity.[48]

Reaffirming the principle of international treatment, the US Secretary of State noted that 'no government is entitled to expropriate private property, for whatever purpose, without provision for prompt, adequate, and effective payment therefor'.[49] Hull called this position the doctrine or principle of just compensation, and claimed that it was recognised both in international and comparative law.[50] This principle meant that compensation should not only correspond to the value of the property taken, but should also be paid speedily to the owner in a transferable currency.[51] For the US government, the taking of property without compensation is confiscation, rather than expropriation.[52] Mexico distinguished nationalisations from expropriations, admitted that only adequate compensation was due, under the laws of the expropriating state, and insisted on the Calvo doctrine, declaring that international law merely required aliens to be treated no less favourably than nationals of the host-state.[53] As a consequence of the 1938 nationalisation of the oil industry in Mexico, another diplomatic exchange between the two countries ensued.[54] Eventually, the two governments agreed on the compensation to be paid, each insisting on their respective legal positions until the end.[55]

In the following years, nationalisations occurred in Eastern Europe, former Western colonies, and Latin America. All the countries under communist control nationalised private property, whether owned by their own citizens or by foreigners. So did Bulgaria, Czechoslovakia, Hungary and Poland, from 1945 to 1948; China, from 1949 to 1957; and Cuba, from 1959 onwards.[56] In the decolonised states of Africa and Asia, as in Latin American countries, nationalisations befell on major natural resources. The Anglo-Iranian Oil Company's properties in Iran, for example, were nationalised in 1951; the Suez Canal Company in Egypt in 1956; and Dutch properties in Indonesia in 1958/9. In the early 1970s, nearly all the Arab states abrogated the concessions of the major Western oil companies or directly nationalised them. Mines and other major enterprises were subject to general expropriations in Argentina, Bolivia, Brazil, Chile, Guatemala and Perú, among other Latin American states.[57]

Expropriations were followed by state-to-state or state/former-owner negotiations, sometimes with the participation of intermediaries, like the World Bank which offered its good offices in the negotiations between Egypt and the Suez Canal Company.[58] Negotiations normally led to lump-sum agreements. Through these treaties, the expropriating state allocated a single sum of money, determined on the basis of various criteria, which generally met halfway the conflicting interests of the two countries concerned.[59] Lump-sum agreements settled, in a definitive form, difficult disputes arising from nationalisations, and were concluded in large numbers: around 200 since the end of the Second World War.[60] They involved a compromise where the seized property was never returned, and the amounts given were lower than those originally claimed by the foreigner whose property had been disposed of. The negotiations which took place to conclude these treaties with the UK and USA, for instance, were described by Lowenfeld as follows:

> In the case of the nationalizations in Eastern Europe, […] the United States negotiated so-called 'lump-sum agreements' with each state, between 1948 (Yugoslavia) and 1982 (Czechoslovakia), under which the taking state kept the property but agreed to payment of stated sums over an extended period, and the United States agreed to adjudicate the claims of eligible former owners and make pro rata payments to them out of the funds recovered. In most cases the United States held some 'bargaining chips', such as frozen assets or promise of economic assistance. The United Kingdom also negotiated lump-sum agreements with the Eastern European states as well as Egypt but, with fewer bargaining chips (and less willingness to jeopardize its position as a financial centre by blocking bank accounts), settled sooner than the United States and generally for lesser amounts relative to the value of the properties in question.[61]

Lump-sum agreements were concluded almost exclusively under political and economic considerations. For the host-state, law played a role only at the moment of deciding whether to adopt the measure, negotiate settlements and pay compensation.[62] Sole-arbitrator René-Jean Dupuy, in the *TOPCO/CALASIATIC* case, considered lump-sum agreements to have no evidentiary value in international law because they were 'inspired basically by considerations of expediency and not of legality'.[63] The Iran–US CT reached a similar conclusion in a number of its decisions.[64] This circumstance introduced even more uncertainty to an already inefficient protection against expropriation, for none of the available solutions on the treatment of foreign investors offered a reliable guide to practice.[65]

2.2 THE LAW OF EXPROPRIATION AT THE UN

The spread of communism after 1945, and the newly obtained sovereignty of several African and Asian states after the decolonisation process,[66] led to a globalisation of the long-standing conflict between the USA and Western Europe, and the Latin American states.[67] Capital-importing countries blamed the weakness of their national economies on foreign control over key industries and major natural resources, which were seen as vital for the welfare of the population and the security of the state. They concluded that their political independence was nothing but formal, and that the only way to achieve an authentic sovereignty was by gaining economic independence from developed states.[68] This meant, in practice, the extension of the public sector through the nationalisation of both industries and natural resources, and the establishment of state monopolies.[69]

The classical international law of expropriation was aimed at protecting physical persons from situations involving individual takings. It soon proved to be inadequate to solve the new problems posed by these expropriatory measures of a general character. Former European colonies claimed that the traditional rules of international law, in which formation they had taken no part, did not reflect their own cultural and legal traditions.[70] These new states rejected the international minimum standard and supported the doctrine developed in Latin America, under the name of Calvo.[71] In an effort to establish the concept of economic independence at an international level, capital-importing states challenged customary law at the UN, particularly at its General Assembly.[72]

2.2.1 Sovereignty and Natural Resources

Gaining control over natural resources was one of the main motives that drove European states like Portugal, Spain, the Netherlands, the UK, France, and later Germany and Italy, to colonise overseas territories throughout the world.[73] The exploitation of these resources was considered unlimited, and was left, almost exclusively, to the colonising state.[74] During this period, the flow of assets within imperial limits was sufficiently protected by the laws of the corresponding power. There was no need for an international law on foreign investment in these regions, and the making of these rules was restricted to the Latin American states' relations with the USA and European powers.[75] After the decolonisation process that took place in the second half of the 20th century, the world was divided into separate blocks. As Thomas Waelde recalls 't]he rich and exploitative "North"', on one side, and 'the underdeveloped and striving "South", and the sympathetic socialist countries', on the other.[76] It was only a matter of time until the newly independent states of Asia and Africa would espouse their claim to permanent sovereignty over natural resources to that of communist and Latin American countries.[77] The reliance of capital-exporting states on property rights and the sanctity of contracts was thus challenged by capital-importing countries, who considered the right of economic self-determination of a state to outweigh any other. Claiming that full compensation in cases of expropriation would render any major restructuring of a national economy impossible, communist, Latin American and the new states of Asia and Africa questioned classical international law and tried to establish customary rules of expropriation through UN General Assembly resolutions.[78]

The first of these attempts was Resolution 523 (VI) of 1952. Although there was no express mention of the issue of expropriation, it emphasised that 'under-developed countries have the right to determine freely the use of their natural resources'.[79] That year, the General Assembly expressly declared in Resolution 626 (VII) that 'the right of peoples freely to use and exploit their natural wealth and resources is inherent in their sovereignty and is in accordance with the Purposes and Principles of the Charter of the United Nations'.[80] Two years later, based on the right of self-determination, the permanent sovereignty over natural wealth and resources was established by Resolution 837 (IX).[81]

In 1958, the General Assembly established the Commission on Permanent Sovereignty over Natural Resources by Resolution 1314 (XIII).[82] Following its report, Resolution 1803 (XVII) was adopted in 1962.[83] Known as the Resolution on Permanent Sovereignty over Natural Resources, the General Assembly declared in it the inalienable right of all states to freely dispose of their natural wealth and resources in accordance with their national interests. This right was linked to the principles of sovereign equality of states, self-determination and economic independence. Resolution 1803 (XVII) of 1962 further recognised some of the requirements of a lawful taking advanced by capital-exporting states, but in a weaker form:

> Nationalization, expropriation or requisitioning shall be based on grounds or reasons of public utility, security or the national interest which are recognized as overriding purely individual or private interests, both domestic and foreign.

> In such cases the owner shall be paid appropriate compensation, in accordance with the rules in force in the State taking such measures in the exercise of its sovereignty and in accordance with international law. In any case where the question of compensation gives rise to a controversy, the national jurisdiction of the State taking such measures shall be exhausted. However, upon agreement by sovereign States and other parties concerned, settlement of the dispute should be made through arbitration or international adjudication.[84]

Besides the international minimum standard, this resolution reaffirmed the principle of *pacta sunt servanda*, stating that '[f]oreign investment agreements freely entered into by or between sovereign states shall be observed in good faith [...]'.[85]

Resolution 1803 (XVII) of 1962 was adopted by 87 votes to 2, with 12 abstentions. France and South Africa voted no, and the communist-bloc abstained, along with Ghana and Burma. The USA voted in favour, but stated – for the record – that according to Resolution 1803 (XVII) 'the owner shall be paid' meant that the payment of compensation was not discretionary but an obligation of the state, and that 'appropriate compensation' would be interpreted as meaning under international law, prompt, adequate and effective compensation.[86] This resolution recognises the power of the state to take private property, a principle already mentioned by Grotius,[87] and the rule of *pacta sunt servanda*, dating back to Cicero and Ulpian.[88] Since both principles conform to the notion of sovereignty, their recognition by Resolution 1803 (XVII) was easily considered to evidence customary international law.[89] This was, for instance, the position adopted by René-Jean Dupuy, the sole arbitrator in the *TOPCO/CALASIATIC* case.[90]

Due to the consensus achieved by the contending group of states in 1962, even the payment of an 'appropriate' compensation was acknowledged for many years a customary status.[91] Andreas Lowenfeld explains that Resolution 1803 (XVII) was fairly regarded to:

> [...] constitute a consensus of sorts between developed and less developed countries, around four basic principles:
>
> - that compensation must be paid in the event of taking of alien property;
> - that such compensation must be paid in accordance with international law;
> - that investment agreements between states and private parties have a binding effect; and
> - that arbitration agreements between states and private parties have a binding effect.[92]

The General Assembly addressed the issue of permanent sovereignty over natural resources again in 1966, when Resolution 2158 (XXI) recognised, in order to improve its exercise:

> [...] the right of all countries, and in particular of the developing countries, to secure and increase their share in the administration of enterprises which are fully or partly operated by foreign capital and to have a greater share in the advantages and profits derived therefrom on an equitable basis, with due regard to development needs and objectives of the peoples concerned and to mutually acceptable contractual practices.[93]

One hundred and four countries voted in favour of this resolution, while six states abstained, including the USA, who criticised its lack of clarity on the problem of expropriation.[94] That same year, the right of permanent sovereignty over natural resources was included in Article 1 paragraph 2 of the International Covenant on Economic, Social and Cultural Rights.[95] After reaffirming this right in Resolutions 2386 (XXIII) of 1968,[96] 2692 (XXV) of 1970,[97] and 3016 (XXVII) of 1972,[98] the General Assembly went a step further in 1973, when its Resolution 3171 (XXVIII) plainly stated an exclusive national treatment standard in the following terms:

> [...] the application of the principle of nationalization carried out by States, as an expression of their sovereignty in order to safeguard their natural resources, implies that each State is entitled to determine the amount of possible compensation and the mode of payment, and that any disputes which might arise should be settled in accordance with the national legislation of each State carrying out such measures.[99]

This declaration was founded on the principles of self-determination and sovereign equality of states, as recognised in Resolution 2625 (XXV) of 1970, which contains the Declaration on Principles of International Law concerning Friendly Relations and Co-operation among States in accordance with the Charter of the UN.[100] The replacement of an 'appropriate' compensation, for only a 'possible' one, and the fact that its determination was left solely to the domestic legislation of the expropriating state, led to the adoption of Resolution 3171 (XXVIII) in 1973 by 108 votes in favour to 1, with 16 abstentions, including 10 Western European countries and the USA.[101] These abstentions certainly reduced the legal weight of the resolution. The opposition of developed countries to the adoption of the so-called Charter of Economic Rights and Duties of States, would confirm almost a year later the lack of *opinio iuris* of this new approach on the issue of compensation.

2.2.2 International Economic Orders

Seeking greater sympathy for their particular interests in the international economic system, and expecting to neutralise the 1947 General Agreement on Tariffs and Trade (GATT), developing countries decidedly encouraged the creation in 1964 of the United Nations Conference on Trade and Development (UNCTAD) as their institutional spokesperson in the field of international economic relations.[102] By the beginning of the 1970s, however, capital-importing states had given up on their intention of reforming the international economic order. The idea of its replacement by a new and different one strongly emerged in these years.[103] The success of the Organization of the Petroleum Exporting Countries (OPEC) in substantially increasing the prices of this natural resource in 1973 served as a catalyst that brought together developing countries in support of a call for a NIEO. Communist states declared themselves immune from most of the demands that this order involved. Nevertheless, they supported the third world as part of their strategy of political and economic competition with Western states.[104] Designed to better represent the interests of Latin American and newly decolonised countries, the NIEO was defined by Christian Tomuschat:

> as a body of general legal, political and economic principles, outlined in various resolutions and declarations of the United Nations, which, as a whole, intended to provide a blueprint for an alternative international economic system, the overriding objective of which [was] an international redistribution of wealth to the advantage of developing States and to be achieved by systematic preferential treatment of this group of States on all levels of international economic relations.[105]

In 1974, the Sixth Special Session of the UN General Assembly adopted the Declaration on the Establishment of the NIEO. Reaffirming once more the sovereign equality of states and self-determination, the resolution confirmed the:

> [f]ull permanent sovereignty of every State over its natural resources and all economic activities. In order to safeguard these resources, each State is entitled to exercise effective control over them and their exploitation with means suitable to its own situation, including the right to nationalization or transfer of ownership to its nationals, this right being an expression of the full permanent sovereignty of the State.[106]

This declaration was supplemented by the Programme of Action on the Establishment of a NIEO, included in UN General Assembly Resolution 3202 (S-VI) of the same year.[107] Both resolutions were adopted by consensus, notwithstanding the reservations registered by developed states.[108] Inspired by them, the most important document encompassing the principles of NIEO was the Charter of Economic Rights and Duties of States, adopted by the UN General Assembly Resolution 3281 (XXIX) of 1974.[109] Twelve years after Resolution 1803 (XVII) of 1962, and less in conformance with the position of developed countries, the General Assembly declared this time that each state has the right:

> [t]o nationalize, expropriate or transfer ownership of foreign property, in which case appropriate compensation should be paid by the State adopting such measures, taking into account its relevant laws and regulations and all circumstances that the State considers pertinent. In any case where the question of compensation gives rise to a controversy, it shall be settled under the domestic law of the nationalizing State and by its tribunals, unless it is freely and mutually agreed by all States concerned that other peaceful means be sought on the basis of the sovereign equality of States and in accordance with the principle of free choice of means.[110]

Belgium, Denmark, the Federal Republic of Germany, Luxembourg, the UK, and the USA voted against this resolution. Austria, Canada, France, Israel, Italy, Japan, the Netherlands, Norway, and Spain abstained.[111] With 120 votes in favour to 6 against, and 10 abstentions, this resolution confirmed to a very large extent the Mexican doctrine set forth in the diplomatic exchange with the USA of 1938. In fact, it was no other than the president of Mexico who first suggested the idea of a legally binding Charter of Economic Rights and Duties of States, and it was this country that officially introduced in the Second Committee of the General Assembly a draft Charter that would be voted and adopted as Resolution 3281 (XXIX) in 1974.[112] Again, the standard of compensation was typified as 'appropriate' and its determination was left exclusively to the domestic laws of the nationalising or expropriating state. As with Resolution 3171 (XXVIII) of 1973, all the major capital-exporting states either opposed or abstained from the 1974 Charter and its national treatment standard.[113] This circumstance minimised the legal impact of the Charter, limiting its relevance to the political sphere.[114] According to Ernst-Ulrich Petersmann, the drafting history and the voting of the resolution deprived its content of the character of *opinio iuris*, 'at least on the part of [its] dissenters and abstainers, which included the main addressees of many of the Charter demands'.[115] In the *TOPCO/CALASIATIC* case, René-Jean Dupuy considered the Charter to have nothing more than a *lege ferenda* value and only for those states that adopted it. For those countries voting against it, Dupuy even concluded that this resolution was *contra legem*.[116] Lowenfeld recalls that, in its historical context:

> [a]t minimum, the Charter of the Rights and Duties of States was a concerted effort by the developing countries to repudiate a system of law in whose creation they played little or no part. [...] Viewed more than a quarter century later, the Charter [...] seems less significant than it appeared at the time. If there was indeed an effort to divorce international investment from international law, that effort did not succeed, [n]early all the capital-exporting states either voted against [it] or abstained, so that the consensus attributed to Resolution 1803 of 1962 [...] could not be attributed to the Charter.[117]

Against this background, the UN General Assembly abandoned the practice of advocating a NIEO in its resolutions on international economic cooperation. In some cases, it has even expressly endorsed the old or traditional economic order.[118] Several reasons explain the collapse of the NIEO. According to Waelde, the concept was politically and commercially unworkable, for '[i]t was not possible to direct or regulate international business by resolutions at diplomatic conferences'.[119] Duncan French adds that '[u]ltimately, the NIEO suffered not only for appearing partisan but also for being overly-radical'.[120] Third-world governments eventually realised that international trade and foreign investment were not responsible for underdevelopment. As a result, open market-economies were established in these countries, and the inward-orientation of national policies was replaced by their outward-orientation.[121] Furthermore, the statist model of development was seriously discredited due to corruption practices in third-world states, and the fall of communism or its transformation[122] left those countries supporting the NIEO without an alternative model to capitalism. In all, the very notion of a third world, with its own characteristics and interests, disappeared after the other two blocks (*i.e.*, the first and second worlds) faded away with the end of the Cold War.[123]

2.3 CHANGES IN ECONOMY, POLITICS AND TREATY LAW

The political and economic background that explained the 20th-century nationalisation process, and the ensuing debate on compensation at the General Assembly, have been essentially transformed in the last decades. Politically, permanent sovereignty over natural resources is no longer a priority for those states that gained control over these elements. Moreover, the favourable scenario that had given capital-importing countries a unity of purpose, and consequently a considerable diplomatic weight, has been substantially modified by the recovery of the developed states from the 1970s oil crisis and the collapse of communism at the end of the 1980s. Economically, foreign investment is no longer focused exclusively on the area of natural resources. Other sectors like manufacturing, services and high-end technology are increasingly attracting foreign investors today. These changes in international politics and economics led to a withdrawal of the state from the direction of business worldwide. Deregulation and privatisation became key topics in the governmental agendas of most states, whether developed or developing. By the end of the last century, foreign investors had returned to former second- and third-world countries, encouraged by the liberalisation of investment conditions and economic growth.[124]

The mixture of fear and desire that foreign investment represented to developing states is largely part of the past. In a globalised world, based on deep and extended links between national societies, it is no longer perceived as negative.[125] Property rights and market-oriented policies have been increasingly recognised. State-run enterprises have become privatised companies that need foreign investment to operate and thrive in profitable regulated sectors of the economy. In this context, the old hesitation between restricting or facilitating foreign investment is gone, even in those states that supported the Charter of Economic Rights and Duties of States in 1974.[126] It was not only the decline and fall of the Soviet Union and its satellites that made them change their mind. It was also the economic stagnation of most of Africa and Latin America, which sharply contrasted with the rapid economic development of the East Asian states that had welcomed foreign investment and free-market policies, like Hong Kong, Singapore, South Korea, Taiwan and Thailand. In the end, even those countries that did not reject foreign investors, but did not encourage them either, realised that an attractive investment climate was needed if they were to profit from foreign capital in their development process.[127]

2.3.1 Investment Protection at the Turn of a Century

Following the debt crisis of the 1980s, foreign direct investment (FDI)[128] is now perceived as more attractive by host-states than foreign indirect or portfolio investment.[129] The main reasons for this new approach towards FDI are that it is easily available, it does not burden the capital-importing country with debt, and it brings additional contributions to the host-state, for example, in terms of know-how, technology and skills.[130] Numerous other benefits of FDI for the host country can be mentioned. Those highlighted by Noah Rubins are worth recalling: 'wage increases, reduced unemployment, increased demand for local goods, inflow of foreign capital, opening of markets, improved balance of payments, [...] increased tax revenues, and improved infrastructure'.[131]

Developing countries, eager to regulate and attract foreign investment, have committed themselves to its encouragement and protection through national laws, known as investment codes, enacted to deal specifically and solely with the issue in one piece of legislation.[132] Despite being the result of different social, economic and legal traditions, these codes display extensive similarities and even uniformity on particular topics. Examples of investment codes are the Korean Foreign Capital Inducement Act of 1966; the Chilean Statute of Foreign Investment of 1974; the Namibian Foreign Investment Act of 1990; and the Polish Foreign Investment Law of 1991. The primary purpose of investment codes is the promotion of FDI, and to that effect they regulate its admission and standards of treatment.[133] These standards include national and most-favoured-nation (MFN) treatment; sometimes fair and equitable treatment (FET); the free transfer of capital and profits; the protection against expropriation; and a dispute settlement mechanism.

Treaties dealing with the promotion and protection of foreign investment have come to confirm and supplement domestic policies and provisions favourable to it. By the end of 2010, UNCTAD had identified over 6000 international investment agreements (IIAs) concluded worldwide.[134] BITs started to be signed and ratified in the second half of the 20th century by developed and developing countries, not only to encourage foreign investment, but also to protect it.[135] This second aspect of BITs explains their spread. Host-states compete to offer potential investors a credible protection of foreign property mostly by concluding BITs. These treaties allow governments to make clear commitments which explicitly involve two states, not just private parties and governmental officials. A mandatory dispute-settlement mechanism enhances the enforcement of those commitments.[136] The first BIT was entered into by Germany and Pakistan in 1959.[137] The number of agreements concluded since then has increased substantially. By the end of 2012, more than 2800 BITs had been signed, most of them after 1990.[138] Several of them have been concluded between developing countries.[139] Occasionally, BITs have even been signed between developed states.[140]

Bilateral, trilateral and plurilateral EIAs currently complement the international law of foreign investment.[141] One example is the 1992 NAFTA between Canada, Mexico and the USA.[142] Notwithstanding its sectorial character, the multilateral 1994 Energy Charter Treaty (ECT) also includes important investment provisions.[143] There are other examples too. The Common Market of the South, commonly referred to as MERCOSUR, is a customs union between Argentina, Brazil, Paraguay, Uruguay and Venezuela.[144] The investment of aliens and related issues are addressed in its 1994 Colonia and Buenos Aires Investment Protocols.[145] The Colonia Protocol covers foreign investments from nationals of member-states in the territory of any other member-state, and includes in its Article 4 a protection against expropriation which resembles that of NAFTA. Article 1 defines investment in traditional broad terms, comprising tangibles and intangibles, and Article 9 gives the investor the option of having an investment dispute with the host-state settled by arbitration under the rules of the International Centre for Settlement of Investment Disputes (ICSID), or the UN Commission on International Trade Law (UNCITRAL). The Buenos Aires Protocol covers foreign investments from nationals of non-member states in the territory of any member-state, and provides the same protections as the Colonia Protocol, including the settlement of investor-to-state disputes through international arbitration. Neither of the two MERSOCUR protocols is, however, in force today.[146] The natural reluctance of Brazil towards the international protection of foreign investment, the numerous BIT arbitrations initiated against Argentina, and the entrance of Venezuela as a member to the customs union in 2005, considerably reduce the chances of obtaining the necessary number of ratifications for these instruments. But this situation does not change the overall picture of international investment law, for the total number of EIAs that contain a commitment to liberalise, promote and protect foreign investment was more than 300 by the end of 2012.[147]

BITs, and the corresponding chapters of EIAs, re-established and developed the pre-NIEO standard of treatment.[148] The impressive network formed by these treaties is mainly aimed at facilitating trade and investment flows. The promotion and protection of foreign investment is achieved through provisions in its admission, general standards of treatment and mechanisms for the settlement of investment disputes.[149] Among these standards are, for instance, FET, full protection and security, non-discrimination, observance of specific undertakings, national and MFN treatment, and free transfer of funds. Although BITs and EIAs do not follow a uniform design, they tend to establish the international adjudication of investor-to-state disputes and corroborate the customary requirements of a lawful expropriation with an extraordinary homogeneity.[150] The wide conclusion of BITs and EIAs in Latin America only came to confirm the abandonment of the NIEO, even in the region of its birth.[151] The settlement of investor-to-state disputes through international arbitration, as well as the Hull formula, has been included in the treaties concluded by the country of Carlos Calvo (Argentina); by the state that advanced the concept of adequate or appropriate compensation (Mexico); and by the first country to call for a NIEO in 1952, during the debate of the draft of the International Covenant on Human Rights (Chile).[152] Many Latin American states have also become members of the Multilateral Investment Guarantee Agency (MIGA).[153] More importantly, most of them have become a party to the 1965 Convention on the Settlement of Investment Disputes between States and Nationals of Other States (Washington Convention).[154] Following the predominant NIEO approach in the region during the 1960s and the 1970s, these states had stayed out of this treaty. While only some Latin American countries became parties to the Washington Convention in the 1980s, most had done so by the 1990s.[155]

Nevertheless, things change quickly in volatile regions. Argentina is currently the country with the highest number of investment claims lodged against it before ICSID: 52, by the end of 2012.[156] The amounts awarded by arbitral panels to claimants in investment-treaty arbitrations are normally large and sometimes extremely large, particularly for a developing country like Argentina. Its government might face a hard choice: paying and mortgaging its future development, or not paying and being shunned by the powerful group of open-market, trade-oriented, pro-investment states. If forced into this choice, the Argentinian authorities have already showed their reluctance to follow the first path.[157] The withdrawal of Bolivia, Ecuador and Venezuela from the Washington Convention in 2008, 2009 and 2012, respectively, and the termination of BITs by these countries leave open the question of whether this growing opposition to the international minimum standard will affect what, until recently, appeared to be a clear trend towards foreign investment and free-market rules not only in Latin America, but also in the other regions of the globe.[158]

2.3.2 A Shift in the International Debate

The customary nature of the rights of permanent sovereignty over natural resources and nationalisation can be traced back to the UN General Assembly Resolution 1803 (XVII) of 1962. It has now been confirmed by the expropriation provisions of BITs and some EIAs.[159] In recent years, the permanent sovereignty over natural resources has been interpreted and applied as a source of duties, as well as rights, with respect to the treatment of foreign investors.[160] According to Nico Schrijver, this means that:

> Assertions of economic sovereignty of host States now include recognitions of obligations, for example to respect international law, to observe in good faith contractual and treaty obligations and to provide fair treatment to foreign investors, including appeal possibilities and recourse to international dispute-settlement mechanisms [...].[161]

On the specific problem of compensation, international treaties typically refer to a 'prompt, adequate and effective' compensation[162] or to other formulas, such as 'just' compensation, followed by requirements that make them similar in practice to the former.[163] The conventional adoption of the capital-exporting countries' view on this issue indicates a deflection from the appropriate compensation standard and a return to the Hull or comparable formulas, so stubbornly rejected by capital-importing states in the diplomatic forum.[164] This is noteworthy, considering that the payment of an appropriate compensation in conformance with international law was generally regarded as an international legal custom, applicable in case of expropriation or nationalisation, after the adoption by the General Assembly in 1962 of Resolution 1803 (XVII).

Prior to the recent nationalisation wave in Latin America, particularly in Argentina, Bolivia, Ecuador and Venezuela, the last major expropriation of a general kind had taken place in Libya, in 1973. This concept still haunts the political debate from time to time, not only in developing countries, but even in developed ones like the UK. Although nationalisation is, under certain conditions, a legal option for the state, it is no longer the central issue in the international law of expropriation. Takings are currently more likely to be aimed at individual properties or enterprises, and to assume a more subtle character – an indirect form. Among the reasons for the fall of the use of outright seizures as a policy tool, Andrew Guzman mentions:

> the success of [least developed countries (LDCs)] in removing control of property from the hands of former colonial powers and their citizens, a fall in the popularity of state ownership, a desire to attract new investment, a belief among LDCs that they can benefit from investment as long as it is regulated, improvement in the managerial and administrative expertise of LDC governments, changed international economic conditions, and changed behavior on the part of investors who have adopted investment strategies that are less vulnerable (e.g., joint ventures, structures that leave certain important operations outside of the host country, strategically placed management from the home country without whom the value of assets fall substantially, and so on).[165]

Two categories of costs face a country that chooses to directly expropriate a foreign investor. Not only may the government be far less competent to run the enterprise than the original owner, but also the country's international reputation will be damaged in the opinion of other states and potential investors.[166] Max Gutbrod and Steffen Hindelang agree with Guzman, and add that:

> States which wish to import capital do not like to be associated with posing a permanent, non-calculable threat to foreign-owned property but prefer to present themselves as places with very stable, reliable and orderly regulatory environments.[167]

At present, identifying the boundaries between non-compensable state measures and compensable indirect takings is the main question of the international law of expropriation.[168] Veijo Heiskanen, quoting Rudolf Dolzer, describes the new scenario as follows:

> the focus of debate in international investment law has shifted from the standard of compensation to the definition of expropriation. As a result of this shift, which has taken place in the context of the ongoing economic globalization and the global adoption of neo-liberal policies, the key issue in the field is no longer whether full or only 'appropriate' compensation should be paid, but rather whether any expropriation has occurred in the first place. As the State increasingly withdraws from its role as an economic actor – owner or manager of enterprises – to the role of a regulator, the tools it employs also change. In this new context, where nationalizations of enterprises or entire industries become less common, if not extinct, and are replaced by regulatory interventions, 'the single most important development in state practice has become the issue of indirect expropriations'.[169]

The need to answer the threshold question is compounded by the fact that unlike nationalisation programmes, which are adopted and implemented under exceptional circumstances, the regulation of vital areas of public interest is now part of the state's routine.[170] BITs and the investment chapters of EIAs address the issue of takings by speaking not only of 'expropriation' or 'nationalisation', but also of 'direct' or 'indirect'[171] nationalisation or expropriation, and measures 'equivalent'[172] or 'tantamount'[173] to these. The problem is that BITs and EIAs merely mention such concepts without defining any of them. This is not an issue which is exclusive to the protection against expropriation. Investment treaties, for instance, do not provide a concept of FET or full protection and security. Even though direct expropriations are normally easy to recognise, indirect takings are not. A common notion is surely lacking. Or at least, reliable guidelines to help decision and policy-makers distinguish non-compensable measures from indirect expropriations.

2.4 CONCLUSION

Before the 1917 Russian revolution and Mexican constitution, takings were identified with individual expropriations. Two positions could be clearly distinguished back then. On one hand, acknowledging the interest of all states in the proper treatment of their nationals abroad, capital-exporting countries upheld the international minimum standard and the principle of diplomatic protection. On the other, affirming the complete and exclusive jurisdiction over persons and events in their territory, capital-importing countries endorsed the national treatment standard and the principle of territorial sovereignty represented by the Calvo doctrine. The extensive nationalisation process, the subsequent conclusion of lump-sum agreements, and the General-Assembly debate over well-established legal concepts such as sovereignty, self-determination, equality of states, *pacta sunt servanda*, non-intervention and the peaceful settlement of disputes, brought further uncertainty to a handful of already controversial rules of customary international law. Changes in the international politics and economy of the last half of the 20th century have strongly undermined this enduring dispute between capital-exporting and capital-importing countries. Today, developing states no longer protect themselves from FDI, but compete for it, offering legal protection to those aliens investing abroad. To this effect, BITs and EIAs have been widely concluded across the world in terms that only confirm the failure of an exclusive national treatment standard and a NIEO.

In the domestic sphere, the liberalisation and development of national and international politics and economy, conveying the recognition of property rights and the enactment of investment codes, have also led to the expansion of the scope of state regulation. Health, planning and land use, antitrust, securities, consumer and environmental protection, amongst others, have joined traditional areas of public policy like taxation and labour. This situation and the conventional incorporation of the Hull formula, along with the undefined concepts of direct and indirect expropriations and nationalisations, have reoriented the debate in the international law of takings. It is no longer the problem of compensation, but that of indirect takings which demands the attention of states, foreign investors and decision-makers, as well as scholars and NGOs. Even though the challenge to the regulatory powers of the host-state is not restricted to indirect takings, for the violation of any investment protection will trigger the international responsibility of the wrongdoing state, expropriation is still the main risk that anyone investing abroad faces. However, the answer to the threshold question is not only important to international investment law. Regional human rights conventions also protect the right of property, and the case-law of the European and Inter-American systems is as relevant to the international law of expropriation as is the jurisprudence of the Iran–US CT and investment treaty arbitrations.

NOTES

1. *See* M Sornarajah, 'Power and Justice in International Law', (1997) 1/I *SJICL* 28, at 54–5; A Newcombe and L Paradell, *Law and Practice of Investment Treaties: Standards of Treatment* (2009), 10–11; and M Sornarajah, *The International Law on Foreign Investment* (2010), 19–20. *See also* F González de Cossío, *Arbitraje de inversión* (2009), 18–19.
2. Vattel had already advocated this principle in the 18th century. Sornarajah (2010), note 54 at 19. *See* González de Cossío (2009), 18–19; and Newcombe and Paradell (2009), 4.
3. This principle can be traced back to the works of Vitoria in the 16th century. Sornarajah (2010), 19. *See* González de Cossío (2009), 18–19.
4. *See* A Cassese, *International Law* (2005), 243–4.
5. *See* R Higgins, *Problems & Process. International Law and How We Use It* (1994), 159; P Malanczuk, *Akehurst's Modern Introduction to International Law* (1997), 256; Cassese (2005), 121; Newcombe and Paradell (2009), 11; S Schill, *The Multilateralization of International Investment Law* (2009), 27–8; and J Crawford, *Brownlie's Principles of Public International Law* (2012), 612–14.
6. *See* Malanczuk (1997), 256–7; and J Salacuse, *The Law of International Investment Treaties* (2010), 48–9.
7. Classical international law refers to the body of rules that existed before the Second World War. Those created in the ensuing years constitute contemporary international law. J-A Pastor Ridruejo, *Curso de derecho internacional y organizaciones internacionales* (2009), 59–64.
8. *Harry Roberts (USA) v. United Mexican States*, US–Mexican General Claims Commission, Decision, 2 November 1926, (1926) 4 *RIAA* 77, para. 8. The following part of the decision on the *Neer* case, of the same claims commission and of the same year, has normally been considered to indicate the content of the minimum standard:

    > [...] the treatment of an alien, in order to constitute an international delinquency, should amount to an outrage, to bad faith, to wilful neglect of duty, or to an insufficiency of governmental action so far short of international standards that every reasonable and impartial man would readily recognize its insufficiency. (*L.F.E. Neer and Pauline E. Neer (USA) v. United Mexican States*, US–Mexican General Claims Commission, Decision, 15 October 1926, (1926) 4 *RIAA* 60, para. 4.)

    Nevertheless, the description in *Neer* was made for a case of denial of justice, and should only be applicable to similar situations. In other cases, particularly in those referring to the responsibility of the state for the conduct of the executive or legislative powers, the elements of the *Neer* decision might be considered aggravating circumstances, but are not necessary to constitute an internationally wrongful act. J Paulsson and G Petrochilos, 'Neer-ly Misled?', (2007) 22/2 *ICSID Rev.* 242, at 242–7 & 253–7. *See* S Montt, *State Liability in Investment Treaty Arbitration: Global Constitutional and Administrative Law in the BIT Generation* (2009), 18–9 & 152–3.

9. D Vagts, 'Minimum Standard', in R Bernhardt (ed.), *EPIL* (1997), Vol. 3, 408. *See* A Falsafi, 'The International Minimum Standard of Treatment of Foreign Investor's Property: A Contingent Standard', (2007) 30/1 *Suff. TLR* 317, at 318–24; Newcombe and Paradell (2009), 11–12 & 14–15; and Schill (2009), 25–6.
10. *See* R Dolzer, 'New Foundations of the Law of Expropriation of Alien Property', (1981) 75/3 *AJIL* 553, at 557–8; P Norton, 'A Law of the Future or a Law of the Past? Modern Tribunals and the International Law of Expropriation', (1991) 85/3 *AJIL* 474, at 475–6; and A Cassese, *International Law in a Divided World* (1994), 317–320.
11. *See* C Amerasinghe, *Diplomatic Protection* (2008), 8–16. *Cf.* Newcombe and Paradell (2009), 5.
12. *See* D Shea, *The Calvo Clause: A Problem of Inter-American and International Law and Diplomacy* (1955), 4–5 & 9–11; and D Quataert, *The Ottoman Empire 1700–1922* (2006), 78–9. *See also* Newcombe and Paradell (2009), 11; and Sornarajah (2010), 366.
13. *See* Shea (1955), 20.
14. *See generally* C Calvo, *Le droit international théorique et pratique* (1896). The doctrine was first stated in the 1868 Spanish version of this treatise. M Garcia-Mora, 'The Calvo Clause in Latin American Constitutions and International Law', (1950) 33/4 *Marq. LR* 205, at 205–6. *See* Shea (1955), 16–21; González de Cossío (2009), 23–4; Newcombe and Paradell (2009), 13–14; and Salacuse (2010), 49 & 65–8.
15. *See* F Francioni, 'Compensation for Nationalisation of Foreign Property: The Borderline between Law and Equity', (1975) 24/2 *ICLQ* 255, at 269.
16. *See* N Schrijver, *Sovereignty over Natural Resources. Balancing Rights and Duties* (1997), 178. *See also* R Bishop, J Crawford and M Reisman, *Foreign Investment Disputes. Cases, Materials and Commentary* (2005), 3; and J Paulsson, *Denial of Justice in International Law* (2005), 20–1.
17. Montt (2009), 40–1.
18. *See* Montt (2009), 41–5. *See generally* A Bello, *Principios de derecho de jentes* (1832). The doctrine was later developed in the 1844 edition of his treatise, titled *Principios de derecho internacional.*
19. *See* Amerasinghe (2008), 11–12, and A Guzmán Brito, *Vida y obra de Andrés Bello especialmente considerado como jurista* (2008), 77–9. *See generally* E Vattel, *Les droits des gens ou principes de la loi naturelle* (1758).
20. Sornarajah (2010), 126.
21. *Ibid.*
22. *See generally* M Silagi, 'Preferential Claims against Venezuela Arbitration', in R Bernhardt (ed.), *EPIL* (1997), Vol. 3. For more examples of gunboat diplomacy in Latin America, *see* Montt (2009), 37.
23. *See* K Lipstein, 'The Place of the Calvo Clause in International Law', (1945) 22 *BYIL* 130, at 130; Shea (1955), 11–16; F Garcia-Amador, 'Calvo Doctrine, Calvo Clause', in R Bernhardt (ed.), *EPIL* (1992), Vol. 1, 521; and Amerasinghe (2008), 191–2.
24. *See* Lipstein (1945), 130–4; Garcia-Mora (1950), 206; Garcia-Amador (1992), 522; Cassese (1994), 50; González de Cossío (2009), 24; and Salacuse (2010), 65.
25. *See* Shea (1955), 5–6; Amerasinghe (2008), 192; and N Blackaby et al, *Redfern & Hunter on International Arbitration* (2009), 465–6.
26. *See* Montt (2009), 45–6.

27. FCNS are generally available at http://avalon.law.yale.edu (last visited 30 June 2013). *See* Garcia-Amador (1992), 521; and Newcombe and Paradell (2009), 17–18.
28. Cited in Paulsson (2005), 22.
29. Available in Spanish at http://www.oas.org/juridico/spanish/tratados/a-42.html (last visited 30 June 2013). For more examples of Calvo clauses, *see* Montt (2009), 46–8; and Salacuse (2010), 65–6.
30. Shea (1955), 6–7.
31. *See* Shea (1955), 20–1; F Graham, 'The Calvo Clause: Its Current Status as a Contractual Renunciation of Diplomatic Protection', (1970) 6/2 *Tex. ILF* 289, at 295–7; and Schrijver (1997), 178–80.
32. *See Mavrommatis Palestine Concessions* (Greece v. UK), PCIJ, Judgment, 30 August 1924 (1924) *PCIJ Rep.* Series B No 3.
33. *See North American Dredging Company of Texas (USA) v. United Mexican States*, US–Mexican General Claims Commission, Decision, (1926) 4 *RIAA* 26. *See also* Shea, (1955), 198–211; Graham (1970), 296–7; Paulsson (2005), 29–32; and Salacuse (2010), 66–7.
34. According to Chittharanjan Amerasinghe it may even 'trump a provision in a compromise waiving the requirement that local remedies should be exhausted'. Amerasinghe (2008), 194–5. *See ibid.* 203–4 & 210–11. *See also* Shea (1955), 260.
35. Cassese (1994), 50. *See* Graham (1970), 296; and Schrijver (1997), 179–80. On the possible interpretations of the Calvo clause, following the *North American Dredging Co.* case, *see* Amerasinghe (2008), 194–6.
36. Report of the ILC, Fifty-eighth Session (1 May–9 June and 3 July–11 August 2006), Official Records of the UNGA, Sixty-first Session, Supplement No. 10 (A/61/10), at 26. Available at http://www.un.org/law/ilc (last visited 30 June 2013).
37. Report of the ILC, Fifty-eighth Session (1 May–9 June and 3 July–11 August 2006), Official Records of the UNGA, Sixty-first Session, Supplement No. 10 (A/61/10), at 73–4.
38. Schrijver (1997), 181. *See* Paulsson (2005), 27–9. *See* Chapters 5 & 6 below.
39. Report of the ILC, Fifty-eighth Session (1 May–9 June and 3 July–11 August 2006), Official Records of the UNGA, Sixty-first Session, Supplement No. 10 (A/61/10), at 73–4.
40. Sometimes called 'socialisations'. I Brownlie, *Principles of Public International Law* (2008), 537.
41. R Dolzer, 'Expropriation and Nationalization', in R Bernhardt (ed.), *EPIL* (1995), Vol. 2, 320; A Lowenfeld, *International Economic Law* (2008), 470–1; and Salacuse (2010), 62–5. *See* B Wortley, *Expropriation in Public International Law* (1959), 61–2.
42. Lowenfeld (2008), 471–2.
43. *See* F Dunn, 'International Law and Private Property Rights', (1928) 28/2 *Colum. LR* 166, at 168–9.
44. Available in Spanish at http://constitucion.presidencia.gob.mx/index.php?idseccion =210 (last visited 30 June 2013).
45. R Higgins, 'The Taking of Property by the State: Recent Developments in International Law', (1982) 176/3 *RCADI* 261, at 274–5.
46. Lowenfeld (2008), 472.
47. *See generally* the diplomatic exchange between the US Secretary of State, Cordell Hull, and the Mexican Minister of Foreign Affairs, Eduardo Hay, published in (1938) 32 *AJIL Sup* 181.
48. *Ibid.*, 182.
49. *Ibid.*, 193.
50. *Ibid.*, 191, 193, 195–6 & 199.
51. *See* Chapter 5 below.

52. *See* diplomatic exchange between USA and Mexico (1938), 184, 191 & 194.
53. *See* Cassese (2005), 523; and Newcombe and Paradell (2009), 18.
54. Lowenfeld (2008), 480. *See* Vandevelde (2010), 283–4.
55. Dolzer (1995), 320; and Vagts (1997), 409. *See* J Herz, 'Expropriation of Foreign Property', (1941) 35/2 *AJIL* 243, at 258; and Wortley (1959), 64–6.
56. *See* Comeaux and Kinsella (1996), 63–4. *See also* Doak, Crawford and Reisman (2005), 4; and Newcombe and Paradell (2009), 18–9.
57. *See* Lowenfeld (2008), 483–4. *See also* Doak, Crawford and Reisman (2005), 5; and K Vandevelde, *Bilateral Investment Treaties: History, Policy, and Interpretation* (2010), 42–3 & 46–7.
58. Lowenfeld (2008), 484.
59. Cassese (2005), 525.
60. R Lillich, 'Lump Sum Agreements', in R Bernhardt (ed.), *EPIL* (1997), Vol. 3, 269. *See* Newcombe and Paradell (2009), 34–5.
61. Lowenfeld (2008), 484.
62. *Ibid.*, 485.
63. *Texas Overseas Petroleum Co. & California Asiatic Oil Co.* (TOPCO/CALASIATIC) *v. Libyan Arab Republic*, Dupuy, sole arbitrator, Award, 19 January 1977, (1978) 17/1 *ILM* 1, para 69.
64. *See* A Mouri, *The International Law of Expropriation as Reflected in the Work of the Iran–U.S. Claims Tribunal* (1994), 354–7.
65. Lowenfeld (2008), 485. *See* G Sacerdoti, 'Bilateral Treaties and Multilateral Instruments on Investment Protection', (1997) 269 *RCADI* 251, at 391; and Sornarajah (2010), 21.
66. Along with some small countries in the Americas, like Barbados, Belize, Guyana, Jamaica, Surinam, and Trinidad and Tobago, amongst others.
67. *See* Sornarajah (1997), 50 & 54.
68. *See* Doak, Crawford and Reisman (2005), 3; and Newcombe and Paradell (2009), 26. *See also* D French, 'From Seoul with Love – the Continuing Relevance of the 1986 Seoul ILA Declaration on Progressive Development of Principles of Public International Law Relating to a New International Economic Order', (2008) 55/1 *Neth. ILR* 3, at 6–7.
69. *See* UNCTAD, *International Investment Agreements: Key Issues* (2004), Vol. 1, at 7; and Cassese (2005), 524.
70. Norton (1991), 478. *See* Salacuse (2010), 68.
71. Sornarajah (2010), 37, 122–3 & 127.
72. Technically, the resolutions of this organ of the UN do not constitute a source of international law. Nevertheless, by reflecting the views of the states voting for them, General Assembly resolutions can evidence customary norms. *See Advisory Opinion on the Legality or the Threat or Use of Nuclear Weapons*, ICJ, 8 July 1996, (1996) 35/4 *ILM* 814, para. 70.
73. B Brower, 'Natural Resources, Sovereignty over', in R Bernhardt (ed.), *EPIL* (1997), Vol. 3, 520.
74. *See generally* M Hartwig, 'Colonies and Colonial Régime', in R Bernhardt (ed.), *EPIL* (1992), Vol. 1.
75. Sornarajah (1997), 54.
76. T Waelde, 'Requiem for New International Economic Order', in G Hafner et al (eds.), *Liber Amicorum I. Seidl-Hohenveldern* (1998), 774. Such rhetoric can still be heard in certain academic and political circles, particularly in Latin America.
77. The theoretical link between the communist and developing countries' position was based on the right of self-determination, first referred by the Marxist-Leninist Declaration of Rights of the Operative and Exploited People of 10 July, 1918, which was central to the decolonisation process and the notion of permanent sovereignty

over natural resources. *See* Hartwig (1992), 663.

On the nationalist and Marxist approach to foreign investment, *see* K Vandevelde, 'Sustainable Liberalism and the International Investment Regime', (1998) 19/2 *Mich. JIL* 373, at 377–8; K Vandevelde, 'The Political Economy of a Bilateral Investment Treaty', (1998) 92/4 *AJIL* 621, at 621–7; and Vandevelde (2010), 75–7 & 87–90.

78. *See* Comeaux and Kinsella (1996), 65. *See generally* Brower (1997).
79. 1952 UNGA Res. 523 (VI), Preamble. UN General Assembly resolutions are available at http://www.un.org/documents/resga.htm (last visited 30 June 2013).
80. 1952 UNGA Res. 626 (VII), Preamble.
81. *See* 1954 UNGA Res. 837 (IX).
82. *See* 1958 UNGA Res. 1314 (XIII).
83. Before this resolution, the General Assembly had recommended the respect of the sovereign right of every state to dispose of its wealth and its natural resources, in conformity with the rights and duties of States under international law. *See* 1960 Res. 1515 (XV).
84. 1962 UNGA Res. 1803 (XVII), para 4.
85. *Ibid.*, para 8.
86. *See* Lowenfeld (2008), 486–9; and Salacuse (2010), 70.
87. *See* F Mann, 'Outlines of a History of Expropriation', (1959) 75/2 *LQR* 188, at 192.
88. *See* M Lachs, 'Pacta Sunt Servanda', in R Bernhardt (ed.), *EPIL* (1997), Vol. 3, at 847.
89. *See* M Pellonpää and M Fitzmaurice, 'Taking of Property in the Practice of the Iran–United States Claims Tribunal', (1988) 19 *Neth. YIL* 53, at 61, note 30; Mouri (1994), note 197 at 65 & 359–62; Comeaux and Kinsella (1996), 68; Y Dinstein, 'Deprivation of Property of Foreigners under International Law', in N Ando et al (eds.), *Liber Amicorum Judge Shigeru Oda* (2002), 851; Brownlie (2008), 543; and Schill (2009), 38. *See also* F Beveridge, *The Treatment and Taxation of Foreign Investment under International Law* (2000), 7, 21 & 24.
90. *See Texas Overseas Petroleum*, Award, 19 January 1977, paras. 86–7.
91. *See* J Dugard, *International Law. A South African Perspective* (2000), 228.
92. Lowenfeld (2008), 489. *See* French (2008), 7; and Salacuse (2010), 70.
93. 1966 UNGA Res. 2158 (XXI), para. 5.
94. Lowenfeld (2008), 490.
95. Art. 1 para. 2 of this treaty provides that:

    > All peoples may, for their own ends, freely dispose of their natural wealth and resources without prejudice to any obligations arising out of international economic co-operation, based upon the principle of mutual benefit, and international law. [...] (1966 UNGA Res. 2200A (XXI))

    The International Covenant on Economic, Social and Cultural Rights entered into force in 1976.
96. *See* 1968 UNGA Res. 2386 (XXIII).
97. *See* 1970 UNGA Res. 2692 (XXV).
98. *See* 1972 UNGA Res. 3016 (XXVII).
99. 1973 UNGA Res. 3171 (XXVIII), para. 3.
100. *See* 1970 UNGA Res. 2625 (XXV).
101. Lowenfeld (2008), 491.
102. C Tomuschat, 'New International Economic Order', in R Bernhardt (ed.), *EPIL* (1997), Vol. 3, 579.
103. *Ibid.*
104. Waelde (1998), 782.
105. Tomuschat (1997), 578. *See also* French (2008), 4 & 6–11.

106. 1974 UNGA Res. 3201 (S-VI), para. 4(e).
107. *See* 1974 UNGA Res. 3202 (S-VI).
108. E-U Petersmann, 'Charter of Economic Rights and Duties of States', in R Bernhardt (ed.), *EPIL* (1992), Vol. 1, 562.
109. These three 1974 resolutions – UNGA Res. 3201 (S-VI), 3202 (S-VI) and 3281 (XXIX) – have been described as 'probably […] the most important, comprehensive, far-reaching – and controversial – resolutions of the General Assembly in economic matters'. Waelde (1998), 772.
110. 1974 UNGA Res. 3281 (XXIX), Art. 2.2(c).
111. *See* Lowenfeld (2008), 493; and Salacuse (2010), 71.
112. *See* Petersmann (1992), 561–2.
113. Norton (1991), 478; and Petersmann (1992), 562.
114. *See* Lowenfeld (2008), 492–3. *See also* M Pellonpää and M Fitzmaurice, 'Taking of Property in the Practice of the Iran–United States Claims Tribunal', (1988) 19 *Neth. YIL* 53, 61, note 30; Petersmann (1992), 562; and I Seidl-Hohenveldern, 'Aliens, Property', in R Bernhardt (ed.), *EPIL* (1992), Vol. 1, at 118; Mouri (1994), 359–62; Comeaux and Kinsella (1996), 68; Brownlie (2008), 542–3; and Salacuse (2010), 74–5.
115. Petersmann (1992), 564.
116. *Texas Overseas Petroleum*, Award, 19 January 1977, paras. 87–8.
117. Lowenfeld (2008), 492–3. *See* Dinstein (2002), 851.
118. Tomuschat (1997), 581.
119. Waelde (1998), 778.
120. French (2008), 8.
121. Waelde (1998), 779–80.
122. As in China and Vietnam.
123. *See* Waelde (1998), 780–2.
124. *See* K Vandevelde, 'Investment Liberalization and Economic Development: The Role of Bilateral Investment Treaties', (1998) 36/3 *Colum. JTL* 501, at 502, and Waelde (1998), 783–4. *See also* Vandevelde (2010), 59–64.
125. *See* Doak, Crawford and Reisman (2005), 7–8; K Vandevelde, 'A Brief History of International Investment Agreements', (2006) 12/1 *UC-Davis JILP* 157, at 177–9; and Schill (2009), 43–4.
126. *See* Comeaux and Kinsella (1996), xxi–iii; Waelde (1998), 783–5; and G Gagné, 'The U.S. Policy on the Protection of Foreign Investment: From the NAFTA to the U.S.–Korea FTA', (2011) 12/5 *JWIT* 807, at 807.
127. *See* A Lowenfeld, 'Investment Agreements and International Law', (2003) 42/1 *Colum. JTL* 123, at 126–7. *See also* Vandevelde, (1998), 502.
128. That is, when the manager holds control of the company. FDI may take the form of a new venture or the acquisition of an existing one. S Riesenfeld, 'Foreign Investments', in R Bernhardt (ed.), *EPIL* (1995), Vol. 2, at 435.
129. That is, when the management and control of the company are dissociated. Portfolio investment normally takes the form of a movement of money, aimed at buying shares in a foreign company or other security instruments by which capital is raised abroad for ventures. Sornarajah (2010), 8. *See* González de Cossío (2009), 5; and Salacuse (2010), 20–2 & 29–31.
130. UNCTAD (2004), 12.
131. N Rubins, 'The Notion of "Investment" in International Investment Arbitration', in N Horn (ed.), *Arbitrating Foreign Investment Disputes. Procedural and Substantive Legal Aspects* (2004), 286 note 1
132. R Buxbaum and S Riesenfeld, 'Investment Codes', in R Bernhardt (ed.), *EPIL* (1995), Vol. 2, 1440; and A Parra, 'Principles Governing Foreign Investment, as Reflected in National Investment Codes', (1992) 7/2 *ICSID Rev.* 428, at 428. *See* E

Schlemmer, 'Investment, Investor, Nationality, and Shareholders', in P Muchlinski, F Ortino and C Schreuer (eds.), *The Oxford Handbook of International Investment Law* (2008), 52–5.

133. *See* P Bernardini, 'Investment Protection under Bilateral Investment Treaties and Investment Contracts', (2001) 2/2 *JWIT* 235, at 238–9, and UNCTAD (2004), 14–16.
134. These include double taxation treaties. UNCTAD, *World Investment Report* (2011), x & 100–1.
135. *See* Dolzer (1995), 351, UNCTAD (2004), 2–4, 13 & 18–20; and Blackaby et al (2009), 467–9. *See* Chapter 5 below.
136. *See generally* Z Elkins, A Guzman and B Simmons, 'Competing for Capital: The Diffusion of Bilateral Investment Treaties, 1960–2000', (2008) 1 *U.Ill. LR* 265. *See also* Newcombe and Paradell (2009), 41–9.
137. *See* Salacuse (2010), 91–2. This treaty was only replaced in 2009 by another BIT, which entered into force in 2011.
138. *See* UNCTAD, *World Investment Report* (2013), xix & 101. *See also* UNCTAD (2004), 18; UNCTAD, *Recent Developments in International Investment Agreements 2008–June 2009* (2009), 2; Montt (2009), 1, 83, 110–12 & 116–18; Schill (2009), 41–2; and Vandevelde (2010), 59 & 64. The total number of BITs in force was more than 1800 by the end of 2005. UNCTAD, *The Entry into Force of Bilateral Investment Treaties* (2006), 2.
139. *See e.g.* the 1997 Argentina–Costa Rica BIT. By the end of 2004, one-fourth of the total number of BITs concluded worldwide corresponded to treaties between developing states. B Kishaiyian, 'The Utility of Bilateral Investment Treaties in the Formulation of Customary International Law', (1994) 14/2 *Nw JILB* 327, at 327; Schrijver (1997), 191; UNCTAD (2004), 19; Vandevelde (2006), 183; Schill (2009), 42; and Salacuse (2010), 96.

    According to UNCTAD, this number 'reflects a greater emphasis in recent development strategies on South–South cooperation on investment, as well as the emergence of some developing countries firms as global players'. UNCTAD, *Recent Developments in International Investment Agreements* (2005), 3–4. *See also* J Zhan, 'The Spread of BITs and their Changing Face', (2009) 24/2 *ICSID Rev.* 339, at 342–3.
140. *See e.g.* the 1975 Singapore–UK BIT.
141. *See* UNCTAD (2004), 13 & 17–18; and Blackaby et al (2009), 469. *See* Chapter 6 below.
142. *See* Chapter 11 on Investment of NAFTA.
143. *See* Part III and V of ECT.
144. For more on this international organisation, *see* http://www.mercosur.int (last visited 30 June 2013).
145. The Colonia Protocol for the Reciprocal Promotion and Protection of Investments in MERCOSUR was approved by Common Market Council Decision No. 11/93 of 17 January 1994. Available in Spanish at http://www.sice.oas.org/Trade/MRCSR/colonia/pcolonia_s.asp (last visited 30 June 2013).

    The Buenos Aires Protocol on the Promotion and Protection of Investments in MERCOSUR from Non-Member Countries was approved by Common Market Council Decision No. 11/94 of 5 August 1994. Available in Spanish at http://www.senado.gov.py/archivos/leyes/1382593.doc (last visited 30 June 2013).
146. *See* Salacuse (2010), 99. A comparison between both instruments is available in Spanish at http://www.ftaa-alca.org/ngroups/ngin/publications/spanish99/cint_mer.asp (last visited 30 June 2013).
147. UNCTAD, *World Investment Report* (2013), xix & 101.

148. *See* Montt (2009), 34–5, 62–3, 66–7 & 73. In fact, these treaties were one of the unwanted results of the NIEO. *See ibid.*, 63 & 73. *See also* S Schwebel, 'A BIT about ICSID', (2008) 23/1 *ICSID Rev*. 1, at 1–5; and Vandevelde (2010), 75–80, 90–3 & 108–112.
149. *See* Comeaux and Kinsella (1996), 101–4 & 115–25; UNCTAD (2005), 11–13; Lowenfeld (2008), 554–72; and Blackaby et al (2009), 488–508. *See also* Vandevelde (2010), 4–11.
150. *See e.g.* Chapter 10 of the 2003 FTA between Chile and USA, in relation to ECT's Arts. 10 to 17 of Part III and Art. 26 of Part V.
151. *See* Amerasinghe (2008), 206–9. *See also* Newcombe and Paradell (2009), 50–1; and R Dolzer and C Schreuer, *Principles of International Investment Law* (2012), 5.
152. *See e.g.* Arts. 5 and 8 of the 1990 Argentina–Italy BIT; Arts. 5 and 11 of the 2001 Austria–Mexico BIT; and Arts. 5 and 8 of the 2003 Chile–Iceland BIT. *See also* Mouri (1994), 360; and O Garcia-Bolívar, 'Sovereignty vs. Investment Protection: Back to Calvo?', (2009) 24/2 *ICSID Rev*. 464, at 467–8.
153. *See* C Dalrymple, 'Politics and Foreign Direct Investment: The Multilateral Investment Guarantee Agency and the Calvo Clause', (1996) 29/1 *Corn. ILJ* 161. *See* Chapter 7 below.
154. The Washington Convention entered into force on 14 October 1966 and is available at http://www.worldbank.org/icsid/basicdoc/CRR_English-final.pdf (last visited 30 June 2013).
155. For a list of the contracting states to the Washington Convention, *see* http://www.worldbank.org/icsid/constate/c-states-en.htm (last visited 30 June 2013).
156. Venezuela, Ecuador and Mexico followed with 34, 23 and 21 cases, respectively. UNCTAD, *Recent Developments in Investor–State Dispute Settlement* (2013), 4.
157. *See e.g.* S Sornarajah, 'A Coming Crisis: Expansionary Trends in Investment Treaty Arbitration', in K Sauvant (ed.), *Appeals Mechanism in International Investment Disputes* (2008), 42.
158. On Argentina, Bolivia, Ecuador and Venezuela, *see* Garcia-Bolívar (2009), 468–81; González de Cossío (2009), 300–2; A Kaushal, 'Revisiting History: How the Past Matters for the Present Backlash against the Foreign Investment Regime', (2009) 50/2 *Harv. ILJ* 491, at 492–3; and S Subedi, *International Investment Law: Reconciling Policy and Principle* (2012), 186–7.

See also Newcombe and Paradell (2009), note 316 at 51; B Kingsbury and S Schill, 'Public Law Concepts to Balance Investors' Rights with State Regulatory Actions in the Public Interest – the Concept of Proportionality', in S Schill (ed.), *International Investment Law and Comparative Public Law* (2010), note 3 at 75; S Schill, 'International Investment Law and Comparative Public Law', in S Schill (ed.), *International Investment Law and Comparative Public Law* (2010), note 8 at 6; S Spears, 'The Quest for Policy Space in a New Generation of International Investment Agreements', (2010) 13/4 *JIEL* 1037, notes 24 & 25 at 1043; Vandevelde (2010), 74; and S Schill, 'Enhancing International Investment Law's Legitimacy: Conceptual and Methodological Foundations of a New Public Law Approach', (2011) 52/1 *Virg. JIL* 57, note 22 at 64.

Regarding the problems posed by the unilateral termination of the Washington Convention and BITs, *see e.g.* C Schreuer, 'Denunciation of the ICSID Convention and Consent to Arbitration', in M Waibel et al, *The Backlash against Investment Arbitration: Perceptions and Reality* (2010); UNCTAD, *Denunciation of the ICSID Convention and BITs: Impact on Investor–State Claims* (2010); and C Schreuer, 'The Future of Investment Arbitration', in M Arsanjani et al (eds.), *Looking at the Future: Essays on International Law in Honor of W. Michael Reisman* (2011), 793–5.

159. *See e.g.* Art. 5 of the 1993 Algeria–France BIT; and Art. 1110 of NAFTA. Article 13 of the 1978 Vienna Convention on State Succession in Respect of Treaties, in force since 1996, also refers expressly to the 'permanent sovereignty over natural wealth and resources'. Available at http://www.un.org/law/ilc/texts/treasucc.htm (last visited 30 June 2013). In the area of energy law, ECT also includes an express recognition of this right in its Article 18, titled 'Sovereignty over Energy Resources'.
160. Schrijver (1997), 171.
161. *Ibid.*, 251.
162. *E.g.*, Art. 8 of the 1997 Armenia–Canada BIT; and Art. 13 of ECT.
163. For instance, a specific method of valuation. *See e.g.* Art. 5 of the 1980 Philippines–UK BIT. *See* Dolzer (1996), 108–9 & 114–17; Sacerdoti (1997), 394–5; and UNCTAD (2004), 235 & 243–5. *See* Chapters 5 & 6 below.
164. Lowenfeld (2008), 569–70.
165. A Guzman, 'Why LDCs Sign Treaties That Hurt Them: Explaining the Popularity of Bilateral Investment Treaties', (1998) 38/4 *Virginia JIL* 639, note 23 at 647.
166. *See* Guzman (1998), 663–4.
167. M Gutbrod and S Hindelang, 'Externalization of Effective Legal Protection against Indirect Expropriation. Can the Legal Order of Developing Countries Live up to the Standards Required by International Investment Agreements? A Disenchanting Comparative Analysis', (2006) 7/1 *JWIT* 59, at 59. *See* M Reisman and R Sloane, 'Indirect Expropriation and Its Valuation in the BIT Generation', (2003) 74 *BYIL* 115, at 118; A Hoffmann, 'Indirect Expropriation', in A Reinisch (ed.), *Standards of Investment Protection* (2008), 151; and Dolzer and Schreuer (2012), 101.
168. *See e.g.* T Waelde and A Kolo, 'Environmental Regulation, Investment Protection and "Regulatory Taking" in International Law', (2001) 50/4 *ICLQ* 811; R Dolzer, 'Indirect Expropriations: New Developments?', (2003) 11/1 *NYU ELJ* 64, at 64–5; R Dolzer and F Bloch, 'Indirect Expropriation: Conceptual Realigments?', (2003) 5/3 *FORUM* 155, at 155; V Heiskanen, 'The Contribution of the Iran–United States Claims Tribunal to the Development of the Doctrine of Indirect Expropriation', (2003) 5/3 *FORUM* 176, at 176; UNCTAD (2004), 237; C Schreuer, 'The Concept of Expropriation under the ECT and other Investment Protection Treaties', in C Ribeiro (ed.), *Investment Arbitration and the Energy Charter Treaty* (2006), 111; Hoffmann (2008), 152; A Reinisch, 'Legality of Expropriations', in A Reinisch (ed.), *Standards of Investment Protection* (2008), 171; Salacuse (2010), 287; Sornarajah (2010), 363–4; Vandevelde (2010), 279; and Dolzer and Schreuer (2012), 102.
169. V Heiskanen, 'The Doctrine of Indirect Expropriation in Light of the Practice of the Iran–United States Claims Tribunal', (2007) 8/2 *JWIT* 215, at 215.
170. U Kriebaum, 'Regulatory Takings: Balancing the Interests of the Investor and the State', (2007) 8/5 *JWIT* 717, at 718. On the regulatory state, *see* Montt (2009), 6–9.
171. *E.g.*, Art. 6 of the 2004 Uruguay USA BIT.
172. *E.g.*, Art. 13 of ECT.
173. *E.g.*, Art 1110 of NAFTA.

3. Expropriation in human rights law

Property is not only at the centre of the protection of aliens, and of international investment law: it is also a human right under international law. Although property was included in the 1948 Universal Declaration of Human Rights, it was not considered within those rights listed in the 1966 International Covenants of the UN on Civil and Political Rights, and on Economic, Social and Cultural Rights. At the regional level, property has been a part of the European, American and African systems since 1952, 1969 and 1981, respectively. Article 21 of the American Convention on Human Rights, and Article 14 of the African Charter on Human and Peoples' Rights, protect property against eventual deprivations, or encroachments on it. Neither of these provisions, however, have been interpreted and applied extensively. The most complex and influential case-law on the issue is the one derived from Article 1 of the First Optional Protocol of the European Convention on Human Rights, which has been developed by the European Commission and the Court of Human Rights, far from the ideological debate at the UN between capital-importing and capital-exporting states, and the emergence of international investment law.

According to Article 1 of the European Convention, as construed by these institutions, the state is not prevented from interfering with the use of property. A measure that produces this result is justified when the correspondent authorities observe a fair balance between individual and community interests. For this purpose, the state is given a wide margin of appreciation. The European Commission and Court have recognised three related rules in this provision: interferences to the peaceful enjoyment of possessions, the deprivation of property, and the control on its use. Each rule is found, in the first sentence of Article 1, in the second sentence of the same paragraph, and in its second paragraph. Distinguishing among these rules is not easy in practice. The European Court has given a restrictive interpretation to the concept of expropriation, and a broad one to the notion of control on the use of property. In this context, the tribunal will consider other interferences only when it is not able to establish a deprivation or control on the use. From the three forms of interference that comprise Article 1, only deprivations require compensation to be considered lawful. In this respect, the state will enjoy a wide margin of appreciation at the moment of establishing the sum due, especially in cases of nationalisation. As a general rule, the European Court requires an amount reasonably related to the property taken. Full compensation, however, is not guaranteed for every taking.

This chapter is about property and its deprivation in international human rights law. It centres on the protection of this right in the Americas, Africa and Europe. The relevance of the decisions of the European Commission and Court explains the focus given to the practice of these institutions regarding not only the deprivation of property, but also the control on its use and other interferences. The case-law on Article 1 of the First Protocol is addressed in detail. The chapter ends with the study of the meaning given by these institutions to certain concepts included in the second rule on deprivation: public interest, conditions provided by municipal law, and those stipulated by general principles of international law.

3.1 A DEBATED RIGHT AND ITS TAKING

Article 17 of the 1948 Universal Declaration of Human Rights states that '(1) Everyone has the right to own property alone as well as in association with others', and '(2) No one shall be arbitrarily deprived of his property'.[1] Adopted as a UN General Assembly resolution,[2] the Universal Declaration was the result of a collective effort of an international society that included, for the first time in the history of international law, states with important differences in their political, social, economic and cultural backgrounds. As Antonio Cassese explains, its object was to find the lowest common denominator in the conception of basic human rights, and the relationship between state and individual.[3] This legally non-binding instrument focused on civil and political rights, rather than on economic, social, and cultural rights.[4] Even though it reflected a developed states' view of human rights, the Universal Declaration is today an essential instrument to this area of law.[5] It forbade arbitrary deprivations of property and, therefore, acknowledged the right to expropriate by implication.[6] The two legally binding 1966 multilateral treaties, known as the UN Covenants, were based on the Universal Declaration.[7] However, neither the covenant on civil and political rights, nor the one on economic, social and cultural rights, included the right of property.[8] This omission reveals a second and third world approach to human rights, aimed at undermining international customary norms which in the past had protected the property of aliens from expropriation through the Hull formula.[9] The right to own property was only reasserted by the UN in 1986, in a General Assembly resolution.[10] Meanwhile, two regional human-rights treaties had followed in the footsteps of the Universal Declaration and acknowledged the state's right of expropriation by implication in Europe and the Americas during the 1950s and 1960s. A couple of decades later, another regional human-rights treaty recognised this right in Africa.

3.1.1 Protecting Property in the Americas

Article XXIII of the 1948 American Declaration of the Rights and Duties of Man expressly established that '[e]very person has a right to own such private property as meets the essential needs of decent living and helps to maintain the dignity of the individual and of the home'.[11] Originally, the American Declaration was a legally non-binding instrument adopted within the context of the Organization of American States (OAS). It came to be considered by the Inter-American Commission on Human Rights and the Inter-American Court of Human Rights as incorporated into the OAS Charter, only after the amendment of the latter in 1967 and 1970.[12] The Inter-American Commission even considered the American Declaration in the 1990s to establish 'universal and regional rules which have become rules of customary international law and, as such [...] obligatory in [...] international law'.[13] By then, the Inter-American human rights system had established a more detailed regulation of the right of property in another legally binding instrument. Article 21 of the 1969 American Convention on Human Rights, also known as the Pact of San José de Costa Rica,[14] contains a protection against expropriation.[15] Consequently, it recognises the correspondent right of the state to expropriate by implication, following certain requirements which constitute a minimum standard of treatment applicable not only to foreigners, but also to nationals of the state adopting the respective measure. Article 21 provides:

1. Everyone has the right to the use and enjoyment of his property. The law may subordinate such use and enjoyment to the interest of society.
2. No one shall be deprived of his property except upon payment of just compensation, for reasons of public utility or social interest, and in the cases and according to the forms established by law.
3. Usury and any other form of exploitation of man by man shall be prohibited by law.[16]

Property was one of the most debated rights during the preparatory stage of the American Convention. Some delegations even tried to remove any reference to it from the treaty, but in the end the right to property and its social function were included in the approved text of the Convention.[17] Because the implementation of the Inter-American system has been mostly a Latin American affair, focused in a long and difficult struggle against military regimes, the human-rights community has considered the protection of property in the Americas as something sophisticated, even frivolous.[18] Even though the Inter-American Commission has considered Article 21 as a rule of customary international law,[19] the endemic mistrust towards foreign investment in Latin America has made both the Commission and Court somehow reluctant at the moment of interpreting and applying this right.[20]

As construed by the Inter-American Court, Article 21 refers to property in the traditional wider sense attached to the word, comprising tangible and intangible assets.[21] This is a rather broad interpretation, which includes the private and communal property of indigenous peoples.[22] *Ivcher* was the first claim of indirect expropriation settled by the Court.[23] It involved a naturalised Peruvian citizen who owned a television network, on which he had been denouncing serious violations of human rights and acts of corruption. In conformity with a domestic statute, owners of telecommunications media companies in Perú must be of Peruvian nationality. Based on this norm, the Peruvian state annulled Mr. Ivcher's nationality in order to remove him from the editorial control of his television network. As a consequence, a judicial resolution suspended the exercise of the applicant's rights in the company and revoked his appointment as a director and chairman. Mr. Ivcher was prevented from transferring his shares and receiving dividends, and from taking part in board meetings, where the minority shareholders took important decisions, like increasing the company's capital. This judicial measure even prevented Mr. Ivcher's wife, co-owner of the shares, from enforcing her rights.[24] The case was submitted to the Inter-American Court by the Commission, following the two-tier procedure established in the Convention. Implicitly endorsing the concept of indirect expropriation, and quoting the case-law of the European Court of Human Rights, the Inter-American Court said:

> To determine whether Mr. Ivcher was deprived of his property, the Court should not restrict itself to evaluating whether a formal dispossession or expropriation took place, but should look beyond mere appearances and establish the real situation behind the situation that was denounced.[25]

The tribunal found no evidence of public utility or social interest in the domestic judicial decision that prevented Mr. Ivcher from exercising his property rights. Moreover, the tribunal found no indication that the applicant received compensation for the deprivation of the enjoyment and use of his property, or that the measure that affected him was adopted satisfying the minimum requirements of due process of law.[26] Mr. Ivcher's deprivation of property was thus considered inappropriate, arbitrary and in breach of Article 21 of the American Convention.[27] In the words of Francisco Orrego:

> It was [...] held that although the claimant was not deprived of his property of company shares, he was in fact deprived by judicial decision of the fundamental rights associated with such property, namely the right to vote in the company and to receive dividends.[28]

3.1.2 Deprivations and Encroachments

The Inter-American Court dealt again with a dispute involving a taking in *Salvador*.[29] Although this case referred mostly to the payment of just compensation, it is important for the link expressly made by the Court between the notions of expropriation and fair balance or proportionality. *Salvador* was submitted by the Commission against Ecuador, and referred to the situation of two of its nationals: a sister acting on behalf of her dead brother. Both had inherited land from their father in Quito. The municipal authorities of the city declared its expropriation for public utility, and occupied the property. The Salvador brothers presented several claims before state authorities against this measure, asking for a just compensation in conformity with Ecuadorian law and the American Convention of Human Rights, to no avail.[30] In its judgment, the Inter-American Court started by recognising the broad notion of property in Article 21, comprising tangibles and intangibles.[31] It then related the protection of this right with the concept of proportionality, as developed in the case-law of the European Court of Human Rights. According to the Inter-American Court:

> The right to property must be understood within the context of a democratic society, where there must be proportional measures that guarantee individual rights, if the public welfare and collective rights are to prevail. The social function of property is a fundamental element for its functioning. For this reason, the State can limit or restrict the right to property to guarantee other fundamental rights of vital relevance in a specific society, always respecting Article 21 of the Convention, and the general principles of international law.[32]

The Court was clear in this point. There must be a fair balance between the interests of the society and those of the individual. For that purpose, the state has to employ proportional means.[33] Quoting the European Court of Human Rights, the tribunal insisted on the notion of lawfulness, by which the legislation that regulates a deprivation of the right to property must be clear, specific and foreseeable.[34] For the Inter-American Court, a law depriving or restricting property must respect the essential content of this right.[35]

In *Salvador*, there was no conflict between the parties regarding the 'public utility or social interest' that had motivated the municipal authorities of Quito to expropriate the claimants' land. The state wanted to create a metropolitan park, aimed at the recreation and ecological protection of the city.[36] Regarding this point, the Court emphasised that:

> […] in relation to the deprivation of the right to property […] a legitimate or general interest based on the protection of the environment as the one seen in this case, represents a cause of legitimate public use.[37]

In this respect, the Inter-American Court equated the concepts of 'public utility or social interest' used in Article 21 of the Convention to that of common good, understood as:

> a concept that must be interpreted as an integral element of the public order of a democratic state, the main purpose of which is [in conformity with the American Declaration of the Rights and Duties of Man] 'the protection of the essential rights of man and the creation of circumstances that will permit him to achieve spiritual and material progress and attain happiness'.[38]

The conflict in *Salvador* had to do with the payment of a just compensation. The Court considered this requirement to be a derivation of the need to balance the social and the individual interests. It described the compensation requirement as 'prompt, adequate and effective', quoting the case-law of the Iran–US CT (*INA*).[39] In the end, the Inter-American Court concluded that, even though the aim of the expropriation was legitimate, Ecuador did not respect the requirements established in the American Convention, thus not complying with the principle of lawfulness. As a consequence, the expropriatory process was considered arbitrary.[40] The Court concluded that Article 21 had been violated by Ecuador.[41]

In his concurring vote, Judge Manuel Ventura further developed the notion of fair balance between the interests of the society and the individual. He considered this notion to be useful for 'the determination of a violation of the right to property, resulting from the lack of proportionality of the means used by the state to restrict such rights', on one hand, and for 'the appraisal of a fair compensation in the specific case', on the other.[42] In his opinion, the state should use the less costly means to the right to property every time it decides to limit it.[43] Quoting the European Court of Human Rights, he added that:

> [a]ll limitation, necessarily must entail a reasonable relation of proportionality between the means employed and the aim sought to be realized by any measures applied by the State, including measures designed to control the use of the individual's property.[44]

Outside the Americas, Article 14 of the 1981 African Charter on Human and Peoples' Rights also establishes the right of expropriation by implication.[45] The terms of this provision are broad. In conformity with it, not only '[t]he right to property shall be guaranteed', but also '[i]t may only be encroached upon in the interest of public need or in the general interest of the community and in accordance with the provisions of appropriate laws'.[46] Like Article 1 of the First Optional Protocol to the European Convention, and contrary to Article 21 of the American Convention, Article 14 does not refer explicitly to the payment of compensation in any form. The few pronouncements of the African Commission on Human and Peoples' Rights regarding this provision relate to the state's sealing up of premises of publications.[47] In *Media Rights Agenda*, the African Commission found a violation to the right protected by Article 14 in these terms:

> The right of property necessarily includes a right to have access to property of one's own and the right that one's property not be removed. The decrees which enabled these premises to be sealed up and for publications to be seized cannot be said to be 'appropriate' or in the interest of the public or the community in general. [...] In addition, the seizure of the magazines for reasons that have not been shown to be in the public need or interest also violates the right to property.[48]

This view was reaffirmed in *Constitutional Rights Project*, where the African Commission declared:

> The government did not offer any explanation for the sealing up of the premises of many publications, but maintained the seizure in violation of direct court orders. [...] The right to property necessarily includes a right to have access to one's property and the right not to have one's property invaded or encroached upon. The Decrees which permitted the newspapers' premises

> to be sealed up and publications to be seized cannot be said to be 'appropriate' or in the interest of the public or the community in general. The Commission finds a violation of Article 14.[49]

3.2 THE EUROPEAN CONVENTION AND PROPERTY

The right of property has been dubbed the problem child of the European family of rights and freedoms.[50] The earliest list of basic civil and political rights considered by the first drafting committee of the European Convention on Human Rights included it, but was later deleted on the suggestion that the right of property was not a fundamental requirement of a democratic society.[51] According to Robertson and Merrills, it was then clear that the inclusion of property would only be acceptable to Western socialist governments if the relevant provision would not prevent states from nationalising private property.[52] The Council of Europe decided not to defer the signature of the Convention until an agreement on an acceptable wording for this right, and those of education and to free elections, would be reached.[53] The right of property was, therefore, not included in the 1950 Convention for the Protection of Human Rights and Fundamental Freedoms.[54] The aim of this treaty was to encourage a cohesive democratic bloc of states that would serve as a buttress against communism and the resurgence of national-socialism.[55] The Convention had to be endorsed as a minimum standard of treatment, and for that it had to reflect the views of the members of the Council of Europe, which ranged from capitalist to socialist states. For this purpose, its drafters tried to include those core values that create and maintain a democratic society, while at the same time respecting the political, social and economic differences of the parties, present at the moment of its signature.[56]

Two years later, however, an agreement on the wording of the protection of property was reached. Incorporated in Article 1 of the First Optional Protocol to the European Convention, it said:

> Every natural or legal person is entitled to the peaceful enjoyment of his possessions. No one shall be deprived of his possessions except in the public interest and subject to the conditions provided for by law and by the general principles of international law.
>
> The preceding provisions shall not, however, in any way impair the right of a State to enforce such laws as it deems necessary to control the use of property in accordance with the general interest or to secure the payment of taxes or other contributions or penalties.[57]

This provision contains a minimum standard of treatment and a general commitment to the rule of law.[58] The difficulties that surrounded the introduction of the right of property, among those protected by the European Convention, explain the fact that Article 1 neither mentions expropriation as such, nor expressly includes the right to be compensated. This right is only implied in the reference to general principles of international law regarding deprivations of property, a formula adopted as a compromise between those states in favour of mentioning compensation and those against it.[59] Despite all these difficulties, the problem child did come of age: Article 1 is, at present, the second most frequently invoked guarantee of the European Convention on Human Rights.[60]

3.2.1 Interferences with a Right

After its adoption, Article 1 was soon criticised in doctrine as an inadequate and excessively weak provision, establishing an economic and social entitlement rather than a proper right.[61] The European Court of Human Rights, however, has not shared this vision. According to it, by recognising the right to the peaceful enjoyment of possessions, Article 1 is in substance guaranteeing the right of property of both tangible and intangible assets. The wording of the other official version of the European Convention confirms the conclusion of the Court. In the French text, the first paragraph of Article 1 talks about '*biens*' and '*propriété*', instead of 'possessions'.[62] In this context, the European Commission and Court have interpreted this last word to include, for instance, contractual rights,[63] company shares,[64] goodwill in a business,[65] fishing rights,[66] patents,[67] and planning permissions.[68] As Luigi Condorelli explains, neither the Commission nor the Court has identified with precision the contours of the right of property, thus allowing the progressive enlargement of this legal concept according to the needs of an evolving society.[69] But such an approach is not limitless. The European Court, for example, has not considered the enjoyment of aesthetic or environmental qualities of possessions as guaranteed under Article 1.[70] The right to acquire property is also not protected by the Convention.[71]

The meaning given by the European Court to the term possessions is an autonomous one.[72] As a consequence, the determination of its existence in a specific situation is not affected by the non-recognition of an interest as a right or its legal qualification, when recognised, under the relevant municipal law.[73] Nevertheless, the correspondent applicant must demonstrate that his or her interest has an economic value. That is to say, what Richard Clayton and Hugh Tomlinson call a legal right to some benefit, even if is contingent upon satisfaction of certain conditions.[74]

Expectations are generally not regarded as possessions because they lack the necessary degree of certainty or concreteness.[75] In some cases, the European Court has considered them within this concept if they have a sufficient basis in national law.[76] Legitimate expectations must be of a nature more concrete than a mere hope.[77] As stated in *Lelas*:

> The Court considers that an individual acting in good faith is, in principle, entitled to rely on statements made by state or public officials who appear to have the requisite authority to do so, and that internal rules and procedures were complied with, unless it clearly follows from publicly accessible documents (including primary or subordinate legislation), or an individual was otherwise aware, or should have been aware, that a certain official lacked the authority to legally bind the State. It should not be incumbent on an individual to ensure that the state authorities are adhering to their own internal rules and procedures inaccessible to the public and which are primarily designed to ensure accountability and efficiency within a state authority. A State whose authorities failed to observe their own internal rules and procedures should not be allowed to profit from their wrongdoing and escape their obligations. In other words, the risk of any mistake made by state authorities must be borne by the State and the errors must not be remedied at the expense of the individual concerned, especially where no other conflicting private interest is at stake.[78]

Licences to serve alcoholic beverages[79] or to extract gravel,[80] among others, are considered to be included in Article 1 only if their lasting nature can reasonably be expected by the licence-holder.[81] From this perspective, claims can also be considered possessions.[82] This is, for instance, how the European Court construed in *Pressos Compania Naviera* the legitimate expectation that an unresolved claim will be decided in accordance with the general law.[83] Not surprisingly, pensions are considered within the notion of possessions every time an individual satisfies the corresponding requirements for such a benefit.[84] In sum, as the European Court observed in *Kopecky*:

> 'Possessions' can be either 'existing possessions' or assets, including claims, in respect of which the applicant can argue that he or she has at least a 'legitimate expectation' of obtaining effective enjoyment of a property right. By way of contrast, the hope of recognition of a property right which it has been impossible to exercise effectively cannot be considered a 'possession' within the meaning of Article 1 of Protocol No. 1, nor can a conditional claim which lapses as a result of the non-fulfilment of the condition.[85]

It took some time before the first case on Article 1 was decided by the European Court.[86] The increasingly complex regulations, derived from the market-oriented policies favoured in the continent during the last decades, and the establishment of the individual right of petition before the Court by Protocol 11 of the European Convention,[87] prompted a large and authoritative case-law on Article 1.[88] In conformity with this provision, state measures can interfere with the peaceful enjoyment of possessions in three different degrees. Deprivations, controls on the use of property, and other interferences have been identified by the European Court of Human Rights as distinct, but somehow connected rules.[89] The fact that these rules are related explains the general approach of the European Court when considering cases under Article 1. Because the second and third rules (deprivations and controls on the use) are particular instances of the first rule (other interferences),[90] the tribunal will start by establishing whether a deprivation or a control on the use of property has taken place.[91] Only if neither has occurred, will it study whether the state has interfered with this right in any other way.[92]

The European Court has recently stated that 'the genuine, effective exercise of the right protected by Article 1 of Protocol No. 1 does not depend merely on the State's duty not to interfere, but may give rise to positive obligations'.[93] In this sense, governments must act 'in an appropriate manner and with utmost consistency' so that their measures are implemented 'with reasonable clarity and coherence, in order to avoid, in so far as possible, legal uncertainty and ambiguity for the persons concerned by [them]'.[94] As the Court has expressly recognised, these positive duties of the state comprise a larger obligation: good governance.[95]

3.2.2 Proportionality and Deprivations

Under Article 1, the state can justify interferences with the right of property 'in the public interest', in relation to the second rule, and 'in the general interest', in relation to the third rule. It is unlikely that any particular distinction was intended between public and general interest. The European Court has not attempted to distinguish them either.[96] Moreover, the tribunal has applied a single test for the three rules at the moment of establishing whether an interference is justified or not. Each will require the achievement of a fair balance between the interests of the community and those of the affected person.[97] For this purpose, the objectives of the correspondent measure must be proportional to the means actually used for their fulfilment. The idea is to avoid an excessive burden on the protected persons.[98] According to the tribunal, '[t]he issue of whether a fair balance has been struck becomes relevant only once it has been established that the interference in question satisfied the requirement of lawfulness and was not arbitrary'.[99] In this regard, the Court explained in *Forminster* that:

> [...] the character of interference, the aim pursued, the nature of property rights interfered with, and the behaviour of the applicant and the interfering State authorities are among the principle factors material to the assessment whether the contested measure respects the requisite fair balance and, notably, whether it imposes a disproportionate burden on the applicants.[100]

In the application of this test, the state has consistently been given a wide margin of appreciation or discretion – not only to identify the public or general interest involved, but also to assess the means chosen and their consequences or effects.[101] The Court has declared that 'regional planning and environmental conservation policies, where the community's general interest is pre-eminent, confer on the State a margin of appreciation that is greater than when exclusively civil rights are at stake'.[102] However wide the margin, the European Court has expressly said that it is not limitless – otherwise, the protection embodied in Article 1 would become illusory.[103] The margin, therefore, has to be construed – in the wording of this tribunal – 'so as to guarantee to individuals that the essence of their rights is protected'.[104] The payment of compensation will generally play an important role in the determination of the proportionality of an interference with property.[105] The European Court openly declared so in *James*:

> Clearly, compensation terms are material to the assessment whether the contested legislation respects a fair balance between the various interests at stake and, notably, whether it does not impose a disproportionate burden on the applicants.[106]

Given the common analytical approach adopted by this tribunal to all interventions with property, the practical relevance of the distinction among deprivations, controls on use, and other interferences lies in the payment of compensation.[107] According to the case-law of the European Commission and Court, controls on the use of property and other interferences do not create a right to compensation. If these are considered unlawful, however, the Court has repeatedly stated that they should be repaired, 'putting the applicant [...] in the position in which it would have been had the violation not occurred'.[108] Only exceptionally will the European Court conclude that a total lack of compensation is justifiable.[109] In cases of deprivation, the Commission and the Court have considered that the protection of Article 1 would be ineffective in the absence of a compensatory principle equivalent to that of European comparative law.[110] Full compensation is, nevertheless, not guaranteed in all circumstances.[111]

Expropriations are not mentioned as such in Article 1. In conformity with the second sentence of this provision, deprivations of property are permitted if the respective state measure is adopted in the public interest, subject to the conditions provided by national law, and by the general principles of international law. The European Court has considered the notion of deprivation to cover not only direct takings of property, but also measures that amount to them.[112] The tribunal explained in *Sporrong and Lönnroth* that:

> In the absence of a formal expropriation, that is to say a transfer of ownership, the Court [...] must look behind the appearances and investigate the realities of the situation complained of [...]. Since the Convention is intended to guarantee rights that are 'practical and effective' [...], it has to be ascertained whether that situation amounted to a de facto expropriation [...].[113]

According to Clare Ovey and Robin White, the extinction of the rights of the owner will be the main criterion at the moment of determining whether a deprivation has taken place.[114] Ursula Kriebaum points to a more accurate factor: there must not be any possible use or economic value of the property remaining.[115] However, not all acts producing this result will necessarily constitute an expropriation, for they may be treated as a control on the use of property.[116] Within this context, the destruction of property will be tantamount to a deprivation.[117] Temporary seizures of property will merely amount to a control on the use.[118] In any case, a deprivation requires the taking of the whole bundle of rights. If only some of these are taken, the Court's analysis will fall under the third and first rules: *i.e.*, as controls on the use, or other interferences.[119] The European Court has been cautious in finding that a measure amounts to a deprivation, when there is no formal extinction of legal rights, because the second rule requires a substantial interference with the enjoyment of possessions.[120] For this reason, a restriction of rights will not constitute an expropriation, though it might be considered another interference, under the residual category of Article 1.[121] In *Moskal*, the Court expressly related the concept of deprivation with that of good governance. The tribunal defined the latter as a principle that 'requires that where an issue in the general interest is at stake it is incumbent on the public authorities to act in good time, in an appropriate manner and with utmost consistency'.[122] The European Court went on to state that:

> [i]t is desirable that public authorities act with the utmost scrupulousness, in particular when dealing with matters of vital importance to individuals, such

as welfare benefits and other property rights. In the instant case, the Court considers that having discovered their mistake the authorities failed in their duty to act in good time and in an appropriate and consistent manner.[123]

3.3 NOT ONLY EXPROPRIATIONS

Directly related with the fair balance test is the notion of public interest. In conformity with the second sentence of Article 1, the measure resulting in a deprivation must be aimed at this objective. Although there is no conventional definition of such a term, the European Court of Human Rights has considered it to be similar to that of general interest, known in international law as public purpose.[124] This condition will require a balancing of the individual and collective concerns.[125] As Rosalyn Higgins notes, the object of the test is to differentiate takings for purely private gain on the part of the ruler, from those adopted for reasons related to the economic and social preferences of the country concerned.[126] The second sentence of Article 1 adds that an expropriatory measure must be subject to the conditions established in municipal law. This means that any taking in breach of domestic norms amounts to a violation of Article 1:[127] the act of deprivation adopted by the state must have a basis in municipal rules. The European Court has considered this condition not merely to refer back to domestic norms, but also to the quality of these rules, 'requiring it to be compatible with the rule of law, which is expressly mentioned in the preamble to the Convention'.[128]

Besides expropriations, Article 1 comprises two more rules. The second paragraph of this provision refers to state measures that fall short of deprivation, but interfere with the right of property to a higher degree than those established in the first sentence of this provision. The power of the state to enforce those laws that are necessary to control the use, enjoyment or disposition of property in conformity with the general interest,[129] or to secure the payment of taxes, is wide. So is its margin of appreciation to judge the necessity of the measure adopted, from the standpoint of the principle of fair balance.[130] The European Court will focus on the establishment of a reasonable relationship of proportionality between the means employed and the aim sought to be realised by the respective state, applying a lax standard to controls on the use, thus allowing national authorities a wider margin of appreciation than for deprivations of property.[131] The distinction between deprivations and controls on the use is not always easy. According to Pieter van Dijk, Fried van Hoof and Arjen van Rijn, when property is clearly affected by a state measure and it is not possible to identify a deprivation or a control on its use, the European Court will decide the respective case in conformity with the rule laid down in the first sentence of Article 1.[132] Other interferences are, therefore, a residual category in this provision.[133]

3.3.1 Public Interest and Lawfulness

The European Court has given the state great autonomy when adopting measures that interfere with the right of property. For the tribunal there is almost a presumption that a national measure is in the public interest.[134] This explains its reluctance to review the identification of the collective interest involved made by the state adopting the respective measure.[135] In early cases related to takings of property, the European Commission and Court held that states had an unlimited right to determine the necessity of such deprivation.[136] This almost absolute right has been replaced by the wide margin of appreciation illustrated in *James*.[137] The applicants were trustees, acting under a will, of an area in central London where a large estate was developed. A leasehold law conferred rights of acquisition to the occupants of the estate. A number of them exercised this right and deprived the trustees of their ownership in a number of properties. The applicants claimed that this compulsory transfer gave rise to a violation of Article 1. In essence, the applicants were complaining against the terms and conditions of the contested legislation, not against the manner of execution of the law by a state authority.[138] From this perspective, the European Court started its analysis of the situation by declaring that:

> a deprivation of property effected for no reason other than to confer a private benefit on a private party cannot be 'in the public interest'. Nonetheless, the compulsory transfer of property from one individual to another may, depending upon the circumstances, constitute a legitimate means for promoting the public interest.[139]

The Court declared in *James* that a taking of property, in pursuance of a policy calculated to enhance social justice within the community, can be properly described as being in the public interest. It even stated that an expropriation adopted in pursuance of a legitimate policy may be in such an interest, even if the community at large has no direct use or enjoyment of the property taken.[140] The Court's general view on the margin of appreciation was clearly expressed in this case. It provides a guideline on how to approach other cases involving deprivations of property for public purpose:

> Because of their direct knowledge of their society and its needs, the national authorities are in principle better placed than the international judge to

appreciate what is 'in the public interest'. Under the system of protection established by the Convention, it is thus for the national authorities to make the initial assessment both of the existence of a problem of public concern warranting measures of deprivation of property and of the remedial action to be taken […].

Furthermore, the notion of 'public interest' is necessarily extensive. In particular, as the Commission noted, the decision to enact laws expropriating property will commonly involve consideration of political, economic and social issues on which opinions within a democratic society may reasonably differ widely. The Court, finding it natural that the margin of appreciation available to the legislature in implementing social and economic policies should be a wide one, will respect the legislature's judgment as to what is 'in the public interest' unless that judgment be manifestly without reasonable foundation.[141]

In other words, national authorities know the needs of their societies better.[142] This extensive conception of public purpose makes it difficult for a tribunal to deny the general interest claimed by the state adopting a measure that deprives someone of his/her/its property.[143] On this basis, for instance, the European Court found that the leasehold law involved in *James* was compatible with Article 1. This margin, although considerable, is not without restrictions. As the European Court declared in *Broniowski*, 'the exercise of the State's discretion, even in the context of the most complex reform of the State, cannot entail consequences at variance with Convention standards'.[144] Hélène Ruiz Fabri concludes that:

[t]he Court's review is limited in practice to verifying whether, in the abstract, the deprivation of property has pursued a legitimate aim in the public interest. This means that any probing judicial review will focus on other criteria.[145]

Article 1 not only requires deprivation be in the public interest, but also subject to the conditions provided for by law and by the general principles of international law. As a consequence, national law should be adequately accessible and sufficiently precise.[146] In addition, it must have foreseeable consequences, and the taking itself should be surrounded by basic procedural safeguards.[147] Whether the deprivation is subject to the conditions provided by municipal law requires a case-by-case analysis, where the European Court will only look for manifest violations of domestic norms.[148] However, it will not examine the correct application of national law. In this respect, the European Court will refer to the judgment of the relevant domestic court in order not to function as a 'fourth instance'.[149] In *Guiso-Gallisay*, the European Court reiterated its views on lawfulness. It declared that this principle 'presupposes that the provisions of domestic law are sufficiently accessible, precise and foreseeable in their application'.[150] The tribunal considered legal certainty as an element of the rule of law.[151]

As to the general principles of international law mentioned in the second sentence of Article 1, these entitle non-nationals to protection against arbitrary expropriations by the host-state in the form of compensation for the loss of their property.[152] Ruiz Fabri explains that a special reference to those principles was the result of a compromise between states which refused any mention of compensation, and states which desired such a mention.[153] The case-law of the Court generally describes a form of protection that is very close to the requirements of the principles of international law.[154] Nevertheless, the standard of compensation is only incorporated for cases of deprivation, not for those related to controls on the use or other interferences with property.[155] As a consequence, Article 1 would strongly imply that there is no such duty for normal state regulation.[156] Unjustified expropriations, however, should be compensated.[157]

The European Court has concluded that a reference to the general principles of international law does not entitle nationals of the expropriating state to this protection.[158] While such an approach conforms to the minimum standard enjoyed by foreigners under international law, it contradicts the equal application of human rights law in the host-state.[159] It also runs counter to the European Convention itself, for Article 14 expressly prohibits discrimination in the enjoyment of its substantive rights on grounds of national origin. The reason for this position was explained in *James*, in the following terms:

> Especially as regards a taking of property effected in the context of a social reform, there may well be good grounds for drawing a distinction between nationals and non-nationals as far as compensation is concerned. To begin with, non-nationals are more vulnerable to domestic legislation: unlike nationals, they will generally have played no part in the election or designation of its authors nor have been consulted on its adoption. Secondly, although a taking of property must always be effected in the public interest, different considerations may apply to nationals and non-nationals and there may well be legitimate reason for requiring nationals to bear a greater burden in the public interest than non-nationals.[160]

The tribunal confirmed their exclusion from Article 1 by referring to the *travaux préparatoires* of the Protocol.[161] Consequently, there would be no compensation for the deprivations of the property of nationals of the host-state: at least, in theory. But due to the application of the fair balance test, their position is rarely (if ever) less favourable than that of non-nationals.[162] The sum paid as compensation is part of the proportionality assessment of the state measure.[163] As the European Court declared in *Holy Monasteries*:

> the taking of property without payment of an amount reasonably related to its value will normally constitute a disproportionate interference and a total lack of compensation can be considered justifiable under Article 1 only under exceptional circumstances.[164]

Regarding the standard of compensation in case of deprivation, the Court has not followed international law. While according to the latter, the alien is entitled to a prompt, adequate and effective compensation of the value of his/her/its property taken, Article 1 requires neither this standard nor the same level of compensation for every category of deprivation.[165] In principle, the corresponding amount must be reasonably related to the value of the property taken.[166] Nevertheless, the European Court will give the state a wide margin of appreciation when it comes to this. That is to say, it will respect the judgment of the domestic authorities on the terms and conditions of the compensation, unless it is manifestly without reasonable foundation.[167] For this purpose, the European Court will distinguish between nationalisations and other forms of takings, as the state's margin of appreciation appears to be wider in the former. The tribunal explained its view on the subject in *Lithgow*:

> Article 1 (P1-1) does not [...] guarantee a right to full compensation in all circumstances, since legitimate objectives of 'public interest', such as pursued in measures of economic reform or measures designed to achieve greater social justice, may call for less than reimbursement of the full market value.[168]

The proportionality test is not used in European human rights law to decide whether an expropriation has occurred, but to establish a fair balance between the interests of the state and the affected person. As a result, the application of this test can lead to the payment of an amount which is less than the fair market value of the respective property.[169] In any case, compensation must be adequate. That is, it should take into account the damage arising from the length of the deprivation, and be paid within a reasonable time.[170] Excessive delays in receipt of final compensation by those deprived of their property will amount to a breach of the fair balance requirement.[171]

3.3.2 Controls on the Use, other Interferences

The second paragraph of Article 1 refers to controls on the use, which are not always compensable. The availability of this compensation, however, will be one of the factors taken into account in the assessment of the balance test, and its payment should normally support a finding of non-violation of Article 1.[172] This criterion of fair balance is flexible: a measure will be disproportionate when the public interest could have been satisfied without imposing an excessive burden on someone. In practice, the European Court will not easily conclude that a fair balance between the individual and community interest was lacking.[173] *Chassagnou*, *Immobiliare Saffi*, *Hutten-Czapska*, *Saliba* and *Lindheim* are rare examples of cases in which the Court found state authorities to fail the proportionality test when controlling the use of property.[174] Even though Article 1 does not expressly require controls on the use to be in conformity with law, the European Court has considered itself competent to review the lawfulness of these measures.[175] According to the Court:

> [...] a norm cannot be regarded as a 'law' within the meaning of the Convention unless it is formulated with sufficient precision to enable the citizen to regulate his conduct; an individual must be able – if need be with appropriate advice – to foresee, to a degree that is reasonable in the circumstances, the consequences which a given action may entail. [...] A law may still satisfy the requirement of foreseeability even if the person concerned has to take appropriate legal advice to assess, to a degree that is reasonable in the circumstances, the[se] consequences [...].[176]

This requirement of lawfulness presupposes, among other things, the existence of procedural guarantees affording the individual or legal entity a reasonable opportunity to challenge the respective measure before an independent body.[177] The tribunal will respect the legislature's judgment on the general interest involved in cases of control on the use, unless that appraisal is manifestly not in accordance with domestic law[178] or without reasonable foundation.[179] In this context, purposes considered to be in the general interest are, for instance, social and economic policies related to town planning;[180] alcohol consumption;[181] housing;[182] the protection of nature[183] and the environment;[184] and the combat of international drugs trafficking.[185] Regarding taxes, contributions, and penalties, the European Commission has declared that taxation measures will adversely affect the guarantee established in the second paragraph of Article 1 only if they place an excessive burden on the person concerned or fundamentally interfere with his or her financial position.[186] In relation to measures taken by the state to enforce tax obligations, the European Court has held that it will respect the authorities' assessment unless it is devoid of reasonable foundation.[187] As a result, the second paragraph of Article 1 allows national authorities an almost unlimited power to impose restrictions on the use of property in accordance with the general interest.[188]

In contrast with the narrow reading given by the European Court to the notion of deprivation, the concept of control on the use of property has received a wider one. Clayton and Tomlinson point out that the elimination of one of the bundle of rights comprising ownership, for instance, will usually not be enough to deprive someone of his or her ownership, but this infringement may amount to a control on the use of property.[189] However, not all interferences short of deprivation will necessarily be considered such an act by the European Court.[190] A state may control the use of property by requiring certain actions or imposing certain restrictions on the activities of individuals and legal entities.[191] The European Court has a longstanding tendency to classify as controls on use, measures that by most ordinary standards would be considered deprivations.[192] The seizure of obscene publications;[193] refusal to register as certified accountants;[194] withdrawal of licences;[195] rent controls;[196] planning restrictions;[197] temporary seizure of property in criminal proceedings;[198] temporary seizure of an aircraft for drugs enforcement;[199] retrospective tax legislation;[200] and a sequestration measure,[201] are all examples of control on the use of property. Under the second paragraph of Article 1, states are even entitled to adopt measures which affect the execution of contracts in force.[202]

Besides controls on the use, the European Court of Human Rights has identified a third possibility within Article 1: other interferences with the right of property. The Court first distinguished them, as different from deprivations or controls on its use, in the most widely cited judgment under Article 1 of the Protocol.[203] In *Sporrong and Lönnroth*, the Swedish government had granted long-term expropriation permits to the city of Stockholm.[204] Although not depriving the applicants' rights by themselves, these permits gave the authorities the power to do so in the future. The city of Stockholm then adopted prohibitions on construction on the applicants' properties. After being in force for twenty-three and eight years, respectively, Mr. Sporrong and Mr. Lönnroth complained that these permits made it impossible to sell or build anything in these properties, and difficult to invest or obtain mortgages for them. The applicants argued that this situation amounted to an interference with their right to a peaceful enjoyment of their possessions. The European Commission of Human Rights found no violation of Article 1, and concluded that the measures were enforced in the general interest and were thus justifiable.[205] The approach of the European Court in this case was both different and novel. Before *Sporrong*, it was generally assumed that claims related to Article 1 should take the form of either a deprivation or a control on the use of property. In this case, the European Court declared that the state can interfere with the peaceful enjoyment of possessions by measures that do not amount to deprivations or controls on its use. Applying the fair balance test between the individual and community interests, the Court concluded that a violation of the rule established in the first sentence of Article 1 had taken place.[206] *Loizidou*, *Stretch* and *Broniowski* are other examples of findings on this rule.[207]

Although the condition of public or general interest is not expressly mentioned in the first sentence of Article 1, the European Court has considered it applicable to any interference by the host-state within this provision. In *Beyeler*, the tribunal declared that:

> The principle of a 'fair balance' inherent in Article 1 of Protocol No. 1 itself presupposes the existence of a general interest of the community. [...] it should be reiterated that the various rules incorporated in Article 1 are not distinct in the sense of being unconnected and that the second and third rules are concerned only with particular instances [...]. One of the effects of this is that the existence of a 'public interest' required under the second sentence, or the 'general interest' referred to in the second paragraph, are in fact corollaries of the principle set forth in the first sentence, so that an interference with the exercise of the right to the peaceful enjoyment of possessions within the meaning of the first sentence of Article 1 must also pursue an aim in the public interest.[208]

The Court has adopted a broad approach to the notion of the control on the use of property, leaving comparatively few cases to be considered under the residual category of Article 1. The European Commission and Court had found violations to this rule, for instance, in the refusal of a housing licence to an applicant to live in his own house;[209] the provisional transfer of the applicants' land to other landowners as part of a consolidation plan;[210] the annulment by law of an arbitration award in favour of the applicants;[211] an urban development scheme which impeded the development of the applicant's property for many years;[212] and public interest declarations, issued as a preliminary expropriation, and prohibitions to build or change the use of certain parcels of land.[213] More recently, cases dealing with governmental and administrative partiality and arbitrariness have been solved in conformity with the first rule.[214] In all, David Anderson observes that other interferences:

> [have] been applied to both restrictions which are consistent with Article 1 and might just as well have been characterised as controls of use, and to particularly blatant interferences which could easily have been described as deprivations.[215]

3.4 CONCLUSION

The right of property of tangible and intangible assets is protected, primarily, by regional instruments of human rights. Among these norms, the European Convention stands out as the main source for the study of expropriation in this area of international law. Article 1 of the First Optional Protocol to this treaty protects property against interferences with it, particularly against those that do not respect a fair balance between community and individual interests. To this end, the objectives of the respective measure must be proportional to the means employed in their completion. In that way, the burden suffered by the affected person will not be excessive. According to the European Court of Human Rights, Article 1 includes three different rules: deprivations of property, controls on its use, and other interferences. In all of them, the state enjoys a wide margin of appreciation with regards to the fair balance test and the application of the requirement of public or general interest. A measure that interferes with the right of property to a higher degree than the residual category, but falls short of a deprivation, is a control on the use. The state may exercise this control by requiring certain actions or imposing certain restrictions in the activities of persons. In this respect, the power of the state is almost unlimited. As with other interferences, the control on the use of property does not create a right to compensation for those affected by the respective measure, as long as the interference is not considered unlawful.

Regarding expropriations, Article 1 recognises an international minimum standard: non-nationals affected by the measure adopted by the respective state are entitled to compensation. In practice, both nationals and foreigners are compensated for deprivations. As a general rule, the amount required by this provision should be reasonably related to the value of the taken property. Deprivations include indirect takings, which require a substantial interference with the right of property. The effects doctrine is not found in Article 1 or in its interpretation by the European Court. Facts that would normally be classified as deprivations might be given the category of controls on use by this tribunal, even of other interferences. This situation and the lack of an absolute standard of compensation for the deprivation of property allows the European Court to take into account not only the interests of the aliens, but also those of the host-state, without having to resort to the effects doctrine's counterpart in cases of interference with the rights of property: the police-powers theory.

At present, this fair balance approach is not only restricted to the European system. The Inter-American Court has referred to notions such as proportionality and lawfulness in its meagre case-law on indirect takings. It has also described the concept of good governance, without mentioning it expressly. That the host-state's regulation must be clear, specific and foreseeable is a requirement not unknown in the European Court's case-law. This tribunal has referred explicitly to the notion of good governance in relation to Article 1. According to the European Court, this obligation of the state involves certain positive duties, such as acting in a timely fashion with reasonable clarity and utmost consistency. Its aim is to avoid, as far as possible, legal uncertainty and ambiguity. To this effect, domestic laws must be sufficiently accessible, precise and foreseeable in their application, and state measures must be implemented with coherence. In the European Court's view, good governance is an essential element of the rule of law.

NOTES

1. Available at http://www.un.org/rights/50/decla.htm (last visited 30 June 2013).
2. 1948 UNGA Res. 217 (III).
3. A Cassese, *International Law in a Divided World* (1994), 299.
4. *Ibid.*.
5. The Universal Declaration has been considered by some to evidence customary international law. *See* F Tschofen, 'Multilateral Approaches to the Treatment of Foreign Investment' (1992) 7/2 *ICSID Review – Foreign Investment Law Journal* 384, at 388. *See also Filartiga v. Peña-Irala*, US Circuit Court of Appeals, 2nd Circuit, 30 June, 1980, Opinion by Circuit Judge Kaufman. Available at http://www.icrc.org/ihl-nat.nsf/0/27721c1b47e7ca90c1256d18002a2565?OpenDocument (last visited 30 June 2013).

   See generally H Charlesworth, 'Universal Declaration of Human Rights (1948)', in R Wolfrum (ed.), *EPIL* online edition, available at http://www.mpepil.com/sample_article?id=/epil/entries/law-9780199231690-e887&recno=24& (last visited 30 June 2013).
6. Tschofen (1992), 407–8.
7. Tschofen (1992), 388. The International Covenant on Civil and Political Rights and its first Optional Protocol, and the International Covenant on Economic, Social and Cultural Rights, were opened for signature, ratification and accession by UN General Assembly Res. 2200 A (XXI), adopted on 16 December, 1966. Both treaties entered into force in 1976.
8. Cassese (1994), 303. *See* A Robertson and J Merrills, *Human Rights in the World* (1996), 37 & 276. This exclusion was apparently due to differences on the content of the concept. J Waincymer, 'Balancing Property Rights and Human Rights in

Expropriation', in P Dupuy, F Francioni and E Petersmann (eds.), *Human Rights in International Investment Law and Arbitration* (2009), 279. *See* C Tomuschat, 'The European Court of Human Rights and Investment Protection', in C Binder et al (eds.), *International Investment Law for the 21st Century: Essays in Honour of Christoph Schreuer* (2009), 638.

9. Cassese (1994), 303.
10. 1986 UNGA Res. 41/132. *See* I Seidl-Hohenveldern, *International Economic Law* (1992), 132.
11. The American Declaration was approved by the Ninth International Conference of American States held in Bogotá, Colombia, in 1948. Available at http://www.cidh.oas.org/Basicos/basic2.htm (last visited 30 June 2013).
12. *See* Res. No. 23/81, Case 2141 (USA), 6 March 1981, Annual Report of the I/A Commission HR 1980–1981; and Res. No. 3/87, Case 9647 (USA), 22 September 1987, Annual Report of the I/A Commission HR 1986–1987. The annual reports of I/A Commission HR are available at http://www.cidh.oas.org/annual.eng.htm (last visited 30 June 2013). *See also* S Davidson, *The Inter-American Human Rights System* (1997), 23–30.
13. 'Report on Nicaragua', Annual Report of the I/A Commission HR 1993. *See* S Davidson, 'The Civil and Political Rights Protected in the Inter-American Human Rights System', in D Harris and S Livingstone (eds.), *The Inter-American System of Human Rights* (1998), 276. Finally, *see* Advisory Opinion OC-10/89 of the I/A Court HR, 14 July 1989, on the Interpretation of the American Declaration of the Rights and Duties of Man within the Framework of Article 64 of the American Convention on Human Rights. The advisory opinions of the I/A Court HR are available in Spanish at http://www.corteidh.or.cr/opiniones.cfm (last visited 30 June 2013).
14. In force since 1978.
15. On the two instruments that form the current Inter-American system of human rights, *see* P Nikken, 'Balancing of Human Rights and Investment Law in the Inter-American System of Human Rights' in P Dupuy et al (2009), 246.
16. Available at http://www.oas.org/juridico/english/Treaties/b-32.htm (last visited 30 June 2013).
17. *See Comunidad Mayagna (Sumo) Awas Tingni c. Nicaragua*, I/A Court HR, Series C No. 79, Judgment, 31 August 2001, para. 145. All judgments of the I/A Court HR are available in Spanish at http://www.corteidh.or.cr/casos.cfm (last visited 30 June 2013).
18. Nikken (2009), 247. *See* Tomuschat (2009), 639–40.
19. 'Report on Nicaragua', Annual Report of the I/A Commission HR 1993. *See* Davidson (1998), 276.
20. Nikken (2009), 247.
21. *See Baruch Ivcher Bronstein c. Perú*, I/A Court HR, Series C No. 74, Judgment, 6 February 2001, para. 122; *Comunidad Mayagna*, Judgment, 31 August 2001, para. 144; *Cinco pensionistas c. Perú*, I/A Court HR, Series C No. 98, Judgment, 28 February 2003, para. 103; *Comunidad indígena Yakye Axa c. Paraguay*, I/A Court HR, Series C No. 125, Judgment, 17 June 2005, para. 137; *Humberto Palamara Iribarne c. Chile*, I/A Court HR, Series C No. 135, Judgment, 22 November 2005, para. 102; *Comunidad indígena Sawhoyamaxa c. Paraguay*, I/A Court HR, Series C No. 146, Judgment, 29 March 2006, para. 121; *Familia Barrios c. Venezuela*, I/A Court HR, Series C No. 237, Judgment, 24 November 2011, para. 148; and *Alicia Barbani Duarte y otros c. Uruguay*, I/A Court HR, Series C No. 234, Judgment, 13 October 2011, para. 237.
22. *See Comunidad Mayagna*, Judgment, 31 August 2001, paras. 148–9 & 151; *Comunidad Moiwana c. Suriname*, I/A Court HR, Series C No. 124, Judgment, 15

June 2005, paras. 129–34; *Comunidad Yakye Axa*, Judgment, 17 June 2005, paras. 135–7; *Comunidad Sawhoyamaxa*, Judgment, 29 March 2006, paras. 118–21; *Comunidad indígena Xákmok Kásek c. Paraguay*, I/A Court HR, Series C No. 214, Judgment, 24 August 2010, paras. 85–7 & 109–13; and *Pueblo indígena Kichwa de Sarayaku c. Ecuador*, I/A Court HR, Series C No. 245, Judgment, 27 June 2012, paras. 145–8 & 171.

On the relation between private property and the communal property of indigenous peoples, *see Comunidad Yakye Axa*, Judgment, 17 June 2005, paras. 143–51; *Comunidad Sawhoyamaxa*, Judgment, 29 March 2006, paras. 126–41; and *Comunidad Xákmok Kásek*, Judgment, 24 August 2010, paras. 110–13. *See also* Nikken (2009), 261–5. *See generally* J Anaya and R Williams, 'The Protection of Indigenous Peoples' Rights over Lands and Natural Resources under the Inter-American Human Rights System', (2001) 14 *Harv. HRJ* 33; M del Toro, 'El derecho de propiedad colectiva de los miembros de comunidades y pueblos indígenas en la jurisprudencia de la Corte Interamericana de Derechos Humanos', (2010) 10 *AMDI* 49; and F Forero, 'Conectividad: alcances del derecho a la propiedad aborigen y tribal en la jurisprudencia de la Corte Interamericana de Derechos Humanos', (2010) 16 *IL-RCDI* 177.

23. *See Ivcher Bronstein*, I/A Court HR, Judgment, 6 February 2001.
24. *Ibid.*, paras, 125–7.
25. *Ivcher Bronstein*, I/A Court HR, Judgment, 6 February 2001, para, 124. The Inter-American Court made reference to *Belvedere Albergheria S.R.L. v. Italy*, Eur. Court HR, Reports of Judgments and Decisions 2000-VI, Judgment, 30 May 2000, para. 53.
26. *Ivcher Bronstein*, I/A Court HR, Judgment, 6 February 2001, para, 130.
27. *Ibid.*, paras, 130–1.
28. F Orrego Vicuña, 'Carlos Calvo, Honorary NAFTA Citizen', (2002) 11/1 *NYU ELJ* 19, at 22.
29. *See María y Julio Guillermo Salvador Chiriboga c. Ecuador*, I/A Court HR, Series C No. 179, Judgment, 6 May 2008.
30. *Ibid.*, paras. 1–4, 6 & 50.
31. *Ibid.*, para. 55.
32. *Salvador Chiriboga*, I/A Court HR, Judgment, 6 May 2008, para. 60. *See Comunidad Yakye Axa*, Judgment, 17 June 2005, paras. 144–5; and *Comunidad Sawhoyamaxa*, Judgment, 29 March 2006, para. 212.
33. *Salvador Chiriboga*, I/A Court HR, Judgment, 6 May 2008, paras. 63 & 75.
34. *Salvador Chiriboga*, I/A Court HR, Judgment, 6 May 2008, para. 64. The Inter-American Court cited the following cases: *Beyeler v. Italy*, Eur. Court HR, Reports of Judgments and Decisions 2000-I, Judgment, 5 January 2000, paras. 108–9; *Carbonara and Ventura v. Italy*, Eur. Court HR, Reports of Judgments and Decisions 2000-VI, Judgment, 30 May 2000, para. 65; *Belvedere*, Eur. Court HR, Judgment, 30 May 2000, para. 58; and *Velikovi and Others v. Bulgaria*, Eur. Court HR, Judgment, 15 March 2007, para. 166.
35. *Salvador Chiriboga*, I/A Court HR, Judgment, 6 May 2008, para. 65.
36. *Ibid.*, paras. 67 & 76.
37. *Ibid.*, para. 76.
38. *Ibid.*, para. 74.
39. *Salvador Chiriboga*, I/A Court HR, Judgment, 6 May 2008, para. 96. *See INA Corporation, v. The Government of the Islamic Republic of Iran*, Iran–US CT, Award No. 184-161-1, 13 August 1985, (1987) 8 *Iran–US CTR* 373. *See* Chapter 4 below.
40. *Salvador Chiriboga*, I/A Court HR, Judgment, 6 May 2008, paras. 113 & 116–17.
41. *Ibid.*, paras. 114 & 118.

42. *Salvador Chiriboga*, I/A Court HR, Judgment, 6 May 2008, Concurring Vote of Judge Ventura, para. 3.
43. *Ibid.*, para. 6.
44. *Salvador Chiriboga*, I/A Court HR, Judgment, 6 May 2008, Concurring Vote of Judge Ventura, para. 8. Judge Ventura made reference to *Hutten-Czapska v. Poland*, Eur. Court HR, Judgment, 22 February 2005, para. 93. In his concurring vote, Judge Ventura also cited the following cases of the European Court: *Sporrong and Lönnroth v. Sweden*, Eur. Court HR, Series A No. 52, Judgment, 23 September 1982; *James and Others v. United Kingdom*, Eur. Court HR, Series A No. 98, Judgment, 21 February 1986; *Papamichalopoulos and Others v. Greece*, Eur. Court HR, Series A No. 260-B, Judgment, 24 June 1993; *Matos e Silva Lda. and Others v. Portugal*, Eur. Court HR, Reports of Judgments and Decisions 1996-IV, Judgment, 16 September 1996; *Belvedere*, Eur. Court HR, Judgment, 30 May 2000; and *Jahn and Others v. Germany*, Eur. Court HR, Judgment, 30 June 2005.
45. This treaty has been in force since 1986.
46. Art. 14 of the African Charter on Human and Peoples' Rights is available at http://www1.umn.edu/humanrts/instree/z1afchar.htm (last visited 30 June 2013).
47. *See* C Heyns, 'Civil and Political Rights in the African Charter', in M Evans and R Murray (eds.), *The African Charter on Human and Peoples' Rights: The System in Practice, 1986–2000* (2002), 174–5. *See also* K Olaniyan, 'Civil and Political Rights in the African Charter: Articles 8–14', in M Evans and R Murray (eds.), *The African Charter on Human and Peoples' Rights: The System in Practice, 1986–2006* (2010), 238–41. On the problems of the African system of human rights, *see* Tomuschat (2009), 640.
48. Communications 105/93, 128/94, 130/94 and 152/96, *Media Rights Agenda and Constitutional Rights Project v. Nigeria*, African Commission HPR, 12th Activity Report 1998–99, Annex V, para. 77, in R Murray and M Evans (ed), *Documents of the African Commission on Human and Peoples' Rights* (2001), at 727.
49. Communications 140/94, 141/94 and 145/95, *Constitutional Rights Project, Civil Liberties Organisation and Media Rights Agenda v. Nigeria*, African Commission HPR, 13th Activity Report 1999–2000, Annex V, para. 54, as quoted in M Evans and R Murray (2002), 175.
50. D Anderson, 'Compensation for Interference with Property', (1999) 4/6 *Eur. HRLR* 543, at 545.
51. *See* A Robertson and J Merrills, *Human Rights in Europe. A Study of the European Convention on Human Rights* (2001), 7–9; D Harris, M O'Boyle, C Warbrick and E. Bates, *Law of the European Convention on Human Rights* (2009), 655; and Tomuschat (2009), 638.
52. Robertson and Merrills (2001), 12. *See* T Allen, *Property and The Human Rights Act 1998* (2005), 17–28; and T Allen, 'Compensation for Property under the European Convention of Human Rights', (2007) 28/2 *Mich. JIL* 287, at 291.
53. *See ibid.*, 12–13.
54. This treaty entered into force in 1953.
55. H Mountfield, 'Regulatory Expropriations in Europe: The Approach of the European Court of Human Rights', (2003) 11/1 *NYU ELJ* 136, at 138.
56. *See ibid.*, 138–9.
57. Signed in 1952, the First Protocol came into force in 1954. The European Convention and all its protocols are available at http://www.echr.coe.int/NR/rdonlyres/D5CC24A7-DC13-4318-B457-5C9014916D7A/0/EnglishAnglais.pdf (last visited 30 June 2013).
58. *See* Y Arai-Takahashi, *The Margin of Appreciation Doctrine and the Principle of Proportionality in the Jurisprudence of the ECHR* (2002), 3 & 152–3; and Allen (2007), 292–4.

59. H Ruiz Fabri, 'The Approach Taken by the European Court of Human Rights to the Assessment of Compensation for "Regulatory Expropriations" of the Property of Foreign Investors', (2003) 11/1 *NYU ELJ* 148, at 151.
60. After Art. 6, concerning the right to a fair hearing. L Wildhaber and I Wildhaber, 'Recent Case Law on the Protection of Property in the European Convention on Human Rights', in C Binder et al (eds.), *International Investment Law for the 21st Century: Essays in Honour of Christoph Schreuer* (2009), 657.
61. Mountfield (2003), 139–40. *See* Anderson (1999), 545; and R Clayton and H Tomlinson, *The Law of Human Rights* (2000), 1302.
62. *See* E Schwelb, 'The Protection of the Right of Property of Nationals under the First Protocol to the European Convention on Human Rights', (1964) 13/4 *AJCL* 518, at 519–20; B Wortley, 'Some Early but Basic Theories of Expropriation', (1977) 20 *GYIL* 236, at 238; and G Gretton, 'The Protection of Property Rights', in A Boyle et al (eds.), *Human Rights and Scots Law* (2002), 276–7.
63. *See A, B and Company AS v. Federal Republic of Germany,* Eur. Commission HR, No. 7742/76, (1978) 14 Decisions and Reports 146.
64. *See Bramelid & Malmstrom v. Sweden*, Eur. Commission HR, Nos. 8588/79 and 8589/79, (1982) 29 Decisions and Reports 64.
65. *See Van Marle and Others v. Netherlands*, Eur. Court HR, Series A No. 101, Judgment, 26 June 1986.
66. *See Baner v. Sweden*, Eur. Commission HR, No. 11763/85, (1989) 60 Decisions and Reports 128.
67. *See Smith Kline and French Laboratories Ltd v. Netherlands*, Eur. Commission HR, No. 12633/87, (1990) 66 Decisions and Reports 70.
68. *See Pine Valley Developments Ltd and Others v. Ireland*, Eur. Court HR, Series A No. 222, Judgment, 29 November 1991. *See also* Clayton and Tomlinson (2000), 1305–7; M Ruffert, 'The Protection of Foreign Direct Investment by the European Convention on Human Rights', (2000) 43 *GYIL* 116, at 222–3; Harris et al (2009), 656–62; Tomuschat (2009), 646–7; Wildhaber and Wildhaber (2009), 659–64; and R White and C Ovey, *Jacobs, White and Ovey: The European Convention on Human Rights* (2010), 481–8.
69. L Condorelli, 'Premier Protocole Additionnel. Article 1', in L-E Pettiti, E Decaux and P-H Imbert (eds.), *La Convention Européenne des Droits de l'Homme* (1999), 975. *See* U Kriebaum, 'Is the European Court of Human Rights an Alternative to Investor-State Arbitration?', in P Dupuy et al (2009), 232–3.
70. Clayton and Tomlinson (2000), 1307. *See* P van Dijk, F van Hoof, A van Rijn and L Zwaak (eds.), *Theory and Practice of the European Convention on Human Rights* (2006), 865–6.
71. *See Marckx v. Belgium*, Eur. Court HR, Series A No. 31, Judgment, 13 June 1979, para. 63. *See also Moskal v. Poland*, Eur. Court HR, Judgment, 15 September 2009, para. 38; and *Valkov and Others v. Bulgaria*, Eur. Court HR, Judgment, 25 October 2011, para. 84. All judgments of the European Court are available at http://www.echr.coe.int/ECHR/EN/hudoc/ (last visited 30 June 2013).
72. *Gasus Dosier- und Fordertechnik GmbH v. Netherlands*, Eur. Court HR, Series A No. 306-B, Judgment, 23 February 1995, para. 53. *See Broniowski v. Poland*, Eur. Court HR, Reports of Judgments and Decisions 2004-V, Judgment, 22 June 2004, para. 129.
73. *See* Clayton and Tomlinson (2000), 1304; Ruiz Fabri (2003), 153; van Dijk et al (2006), 865–6; Harris et al (2009), 658; Kriebaum (2009), 233; and Wildhaber and Wildhaber (2009), 658.
74. Clayton and Tomlinson (2000), 1305. *See* Kriebaum (2009), 233.
75. Harris et al (2009), 657–8.
76. *Depalle v. France*, Eur. Court HR, Judgment, 29 March 2010, para. 63.

77. *Sierpinski v. Poland*, Eur. Court HR, Judgment, 3 November 2009, para. 65.
78. *Lelas v. Croatia*, Eur. Court HR, Judgment, 20 May 2010, para. 74.
79. *See Tre Traktörer Aktiebolag v. Sweden*, Eur. Court HR, Series A No. 159, Judgment, 7 July 1989.
80. *See Fredin v. Sweden*, Eur. Court HR, Series A No. 192, Judgment, 18 February 1991.
81. Clayton and Tomlinson (2000), 1305.
82. *See e.g. Stran Greek Refineries and Stratis Andreadis v. Greece*, Eur. Court HR, Series A No. 301-B, Judgment, 9 December 1994, para. 62; *Gratzinger and Gratzingerova v. Czech Republic*, Eur. Court HR, Admissibility decision, 10 July, 2002, para. 69; and *Stretch v. United Kingdom*, Eur. Court HR, Judgment, 24 June 2003, para. 32. In any case, the respective claim must be sufficiently established to be enforceable, and must have a basis in national law. *See e.g. OAO Plodovaya Kompaniya v. Russia*, Eur. Court HR, Judgment, 7 June 2007, para. 27; *Lelas*, Judgment, 20 May 2010, para. 56; and *Maggio and Others v. Italy*, Eur. Court HR, Judgment, 3 May 2011, para. 54.
83. *See Pressos Compania Naviera S.A. and Others v. Belgium*, Eur. Court HR, Series A No. 332, Judgment, 20 November 1995. *See also* Anderson (1999), 546.
84. *Iwaszkiewicz v. Poland*, Eur. Court HR, Judgment, 26 June 2011, para. 41. *See Grudić v. Serbia*, Eur. Court HR, Judgment, 14 April 2012, para. 72.
85. *Kopecky v. Slovakia*, Eur. Court HR, Reports of Judgments and Decisions 2004-IX, Judgment, 28 September 2004, para. 35. *See Viaşu c. Roumanie*, Eur. Court HR, Judgment, 9 December 2008, para. 58; and *Bulves AD v. Bulgaria*, Eur. Court HR, Judgment, 22 January 2009, para. 53 & 57.

    On legitimate expectations and the European Court, *see* U Kriebaum, 'Regulatory Takings: Balancing the Interests of the Investor and the State', (2007) 8/5 *JWIT* 717, note 65 at 734; P De Sena, 'Economic and Non-Economic Values in the Case Law of the European Court of Human Rights', in P Dupuy et al (2009), 210; and Wildhaber and Wildhaber (2009), 661–2.
86. *See Handyside v. United Kingdom*, Eur. Court HR, Series A No. 24, Judgment, 7 December 1976. The first case decided by the European Court concerning an interference with the property of a foreigner was *AGOSI*. *See AGOSI v. United Kingdom*, Eur. Court HR, Series A No. 108, Judgment, 24 October 1986. *See also* Kriebaum (2009), 217.
87. In force since 1998.
88. *See* Gretton (2002), 291.
89. This test was first applied by the European Court in 1982. *See Sporrong and Lönnroth*, Eur. Court HR, Judgment, 23 September 1982, para. 61. *See also Holy Monasteries v. Greece*, Eur. Court HR, Series A No. 301-A, Judgment, 9 December 1994, para. 56; *Carbonara and Ventura*, Eur. Court HR, Judgment, 30 May 2000, para. 58; and *Jahn and Others v. Germany*, Eur. Court HR, Judgment, 30 June 2005, para. 78. *See* Clayton and Tomlinson (2000), 1302; Ruffert (2000), 120–1; Merrills and Robertson (2001), 235; Ruiz Fabri (2003), 152; van Dijk et al (2006), 864; Harris et al (2009), 666; Wildhaber and Wildhaber (2009), 658; and White and Ovey (2010), 478.
90. *See e.g. AGOSI*, Judgment, 24 October 1986, para. 48. *See also James*, Eur. Court HR, Judgment, 21 February 1986, para. 37. More recently, *see Adzhigovich v. Russia*, Eur. Court HR, Judgment, 8 October 2009, para. 25. Deprivations and controls on use – the second and third rules – cover the three main legislative powers: the taking of private property for public use, the regulation of its use, and taxation. Clayton and Tomlinson (2000), 1303.
91. In both cases there has to be a reasonable and foreseeable national legal basis for the measure. Mountfield (2003), 141.

92. *See* Allen (2005), 110–12; and White and Ovey (2010), 347.
93. *Sierpinski*, Eur. Court HR, Judgment, 3 November 2009, para. 68. *See Malysh and Others v. Russia*, Eur. Court HR, Judgment, 11 February 2010, para. 74.
94. *Sierpinski*, Judgment, 3 November 2009, paras. 65–6.
95. *See Moskal*, Eur. Court HR, Judgment, 15 September 2009, paras. 51 & 72; *Rysovskyy v. Ukraine*, Eur. Court HR, Judgment, 10 October 2011, paras. 70–1; and *Kapel v. Poland*, Eur. Court HR, Judgment, 2 October 2012, para. 75; and *Zofia Sikora v. Poland*, Eur. Court HR, Judgment, 4 December 2012, para. 62.
96. Gretton (2002), 281.
97. *See* Allen (2007), 294–8 & 305. *See e.g. Sporrong and Lönnroth*, Eur. Court HR, Judgment, 23 September 1982, para. 69; *Holy Monasteries*, Eur. Court HR, Judgment, 9 December 1994, para. 70; and *Velosa Barreto v. Portugal*, Eur. Court HR, Series A No. 334, Judgment, 21 November 1995, para. 36.
98. S Montt, *State Liability in Investment Treaty Arbitration: Global Constitutional and Administrative Law in the BIT Generation* (2009), 220. This author, however, only considers the fair balance test to be applicable to the first and third rules: *i.e.*, to other interferences and controls on the use. *See ibid.* 200 & 220.
99. *Seryavin and Others v. Russia*, Eur. Court HR, Judgment, 10 January 2011, para. 107. *See Beyeler*, Judgment, 5 January 2000, para. 107.
100. *Forminster Enterprises Limited v. Czech Republic*, Eur. Court HR, Judgment, 9 October 2008.
101. Clayton and Tomlinson (2000), 1314; and Arai-Takahashi (2002), 156–7. On the margin of appreciation, *see generally* H Yourow, *The Margin of Appreciation Doctrine in the Dynamics of European Human Rights Jurisprudence* (1995); Arai-Takahashi (2002); J García Roca, *El margen de apreciación nacional en la interpretación del Convenio Europeo de Derechos Humanos: soberanía e integración* (2010); and A Legg, *The Margin of Appreciation in International Human Rights Law: Deference and Proportionality* (2012).
102. *Depalle*, Eur. Court HR, Judgment, 29 March 2010, para. 84.
103. *Družstevni Zálažna Pria and Others v. Czech Republic*, Eur. Court HR, Judgment, 31 July 2008, para. 93.
104. *Ibid.*
105. Anderson (1999), 548; and Ruffert (2000), 129. *See* Allen (2007), 298–300; and Tomuschat (2009), 652–3.
106. *James*, Eur. Court HR, Judgment, 21 February 1986, para. 54. *See Perdigão v. Portugal*, Eur. Court HR, Judgment, 16 November 2010, para. 68. *See also Curmi v. Malta*, Eur. Court HR, Judgment, 22 November 2011, paras. 42 & 48–9.
107. Anderson (1999), 554.
108. *Zlínsat, Spol SRO v. Bulgaria*, Eur. Court HR, Judgment, 10 January 2008, para. 39. *See* Kriebaum (2009), 243. According to the European Court, the finding of a violation constitutes in itself sufficient just satisfaction for any non-pecuniary damage sustained by an applicant. *See e.g. Hentrich v. France*, Eur. Court HR, Series A No. 296-A, Judgment, 22 September 1994; and *Bulves*, Eur. Court HR, Judgment, 22 January 2009.
109. Wildhaber and Wildhaber (2009), 659. *Cf.* Tomuschat (2009), 654.
110. *See e.g. Lithgow and Others v. United Kingdom*, Eur. Court HR, Series A No. 102, Judgment 8 July 1986, para. 120; *Baner*, Eur. Commission HR (1989); and *Pinnacle Meat Processors v. United Kingdom*, Eur. Commission HR, No. 33298/96, Admissibility decision, 21 October 1998, (1998) 27 *Eur. HR Rep. CD* 217.

    See also R Higgins, 'The Taking of Property by the State: Recent Developments in International Law', (1982) 176/3 *RCADI* 259, at 360; Clayton and Tomlinson (2000), 1311–13; Ruffert (2000), 129 & 134–6; Mountfield (2003) 141–2; and M Perkams, 'The Concept of Indirect Expropriation in Comparative Public Law –

Searching for Light in the Dark', in S Schill (ed.), *International Investment Law and Comparative Public Law* (2010), 112–13. *See generally* Allen (2007).

111. *See e.g. Holy Monasteries*, Eur. Court HR, Judgment, 9 December, 1994, para. 71; *J.A. Pye (Oxford) Ltd. and J.A. Pye (Oxford) Land Ltd. v. United Kingdom*, Eur. Court HR, Judgment, 30 August 2007, para. 54; and *Curmi*, Judgment, 22 November 2011, para. 41. *See also* Ruffert (2000), 129–30 & 136–8; and Wildhaber and Wildhaber (2009), 659.
112. *Fredin*, Eur. Court HR, Judgment, 18 February 1991, para. 42.
113. *Sporrong and Lönnroth*, Eur. Court HR, Judgment, 23 September 1982, para. 63. This is the first description of an indirect taking given by the European Court. Wildhaber and Wildhaber (2009), 667.
114. White and Ovey (2010), 488.
115. Kriebaum (2009), 238–9.
116. Clayton and Tomlinson (2000), 1308.
117. *See e.g. Akdivar and Others v. Turkey*, Eur. Court HR, Reports of Judgments and Decisions 1996-IV, Judgment, 16 September 1996, para. 88.
118. *See e.g. Handyside*, Eur. Court HR, Judgment, 7 December 1976, para. 63.
119. Wildhaber and Wildhaber (2009), 659.
120. Clayton and Tomlinson (2000), 1308. The approach of the European Court of Justice to the problem of indirect takings has been similar to that of the European Court of Human Rights. *See* Allen (2005), 15–16; UNCTAD, *Investment Provisions in Economic Integration Agreements* (2006), 109–10; B De Witte, 'Balancing of Economic Law and Human Rights by the European Court of Human Rights', in P Dupuy et al (2009), 199–201; and Perkams (2010), 138–47.

    See also e.g. J Nold, Kohlen-und Baustoffgroßhandlung v. Commission of the European Communities, ECJ, Case 4-73, Judgment, 14 May, 1974; *Liselotte Hauer v. Land RheinlandPfalz*, ECJ, Case 44/79, Judgment 13 December, 1979; *SA Biovilac NV v. European Economic Community*, ECJ, Case 59/83, Judgment, 6 December 1984; and *Hubert Wachauf v. Bundesamt für Ernährung und Forstwirtschaft*, ECJ, Case 5/88, Judgment, 13 July 1989. These judgments are available at http://eur-lex.europa.eu/en/index.htm (last visited 30 June 2013).
121. *See e.g. Matos e Silva Lda. and Others v. Portugal*, Eur. Court HR, Reports of Judgments and Decisions 1996-IV, Judgment, 16 September 1996, paras. 79 & 85. *Papamichalopoulos*, *Hentrich*, *Pressos Compania Naviera*, and *Guiso-Gallisay* are good examples of cases in which the European Court of Human Rights found a deprivation of property, in the form of an indirect expropriation. *See Papamichalopoulos and Others v. Greece*, Eur. Court HR, Series A No. 260-B, Judgment, 24 June 1993; *Hentrich*, Eur. Court HR, Judgment, 22 September 1994; *Pressos*, Eur. Court HR, Judgment, 20 November 1995; and *Guiso-Gallisay v. Italy*, Eur. Court HR, Judgment, 8 December 2005.
122. *Moskal*, Eur. Court HR, Judgment, 15 September 2009, para. 51.
123. *Ibid.*, para.72.
124. Ruiz Fabri (2003), 158. *See* Higgins (1982), 371; Anderson (1999), 547; and De Sena (2009), 212.
125. White and Ovey (2010), 491.
126. Higgins (1982), 371.
127. White and Ovey (2010), 491.
128. *Malone v. United Kingdom*, Eur. Court HR, Series A No. 82, Judgment, 2 August 1984, para. 67.
129. *See* Allen (2005), 119.
130. Clayton and Tomlinson (2000), 1317.
131. Arai-Takahashi (2002), 151–2. *See* Clayton and Tomlinson (2000), 1303 & 1314. *See e.g. AGOSI*, Eur. Court HR, Judgment, 24 October 1986, para. 52; *Allan*

Jacobsson v. Sweden, Eur. Court HR, Series A No. 163, Judgment, 25 October 1989, para. 55; *Mellacher and Others v. Austria*, Eur. Court HR, Series A No. 169, Judgment, 19 December 1989, para. 48; and *Spadea and Scalabrino v. Italy*, Eur. Court HR, Series A No. 315-B, Judgment, 28 September 1995, para. 33.

132. van Dijk et al (2006), 873; and A Mowbray, *Cases and Materials on the European Convention on Human Rights* (2007), 924.
133. Anderson (1999), 546; and Gretton (2002), 278.
134. White and Ovey (2010), 492.
135. *See* Clayton and Tomlinson (2000), 1315; Arai-Takahashi (2002), 157–8; Mountfield (2003), 140; van Dijk et al (2006), 879–81; Harris et al (2009), 667; and White and Ovey (2010), 492.
136. Ruiz Fabri (2003), note 48 at 158.
137. *James*, Eur. Court HR, Judgment, 21 February 1986.
138. *Ibid.*, para. 36.
139. *Ibid.*, para. 40.
140. *Ibid.*, paras. 41 & 45.
141. *Ibid.*, para. 46.
142. Ruiz Fabri (2003), 158.
143. *Ibid.*, 159.
144. *Broniowski*, Eur. Court HR, Judgment, 22 June 2004, para 183.
145. Ruiz Fabri (2003), 159.
146. *Lithgow*, Eur. Court HR, Judgment, 8 July 1986, para. 110.
147. *Hentrich*, Eur. Court HR, Judgment 22 September 1994, para. 42. *E.g.*, the availability of procedural remedies to prevent the arbitrary adoption and exercise of state measures. *See* De Sena (2009), 215–16.
148. Ruiz Fabri (2003), note 57 at 159. *See* Allen (2005), 95.
149. van Dijk et al (2006), 885.
150. *Guiso-Gallisay v. Italy*, Eur. Court HR, Judgment, 8 December 2005, para 82.
151. *See Guiso-Gallisay v. Italy*, Eur. Court HR, Judgment, 8 December 2005, paras. 82 & 93. *See also Minsayan and Semerjyan v. Armenia*, Eur. Court HR, Judgment, 23 June 2009, paras. 66–7; and *Malysh*, Judgment, 11 February 2010, para. 82; *Seryavin*, Judgment, 10 January 2011, para. 40.
152. *See* White and Ovey (2010), 492. *See also Anheuser-Busch, Inc. v. Portugal*, Eur. Court HR, Judgment, 11 January 2007, Dissenting Opinion of Judges Caflisch and Cabral Barreto, para. 9.
153. Ruiz Fabri (2003), 151.
154. *Ibid.*, 173.
155. *See* Higgins (1982), 360; Clayton and Tomlinson (2000), 1313; and Mountfield (2003), 141–2.
156. K Yannaca-Small, 'Indirect Expropriation and the Right to Regulate: How to Draw the Line?', in K Yannaca-Small (ed), *Arbitration under International Investment Agreements: A Guide to the Key Issues* (2010), 452.
157. Kriebaum (2009), 240.
158. *See* Anderson (1999), 549.
159. *See e.g.* Schwelb (1964), 520–32 & 541.
160. *James*, Eur. Court HR, Judgment, 21 February 1986, para. 63. *See Lithgow*, Eur. Court HR, Judgment 8 July 1986, paras. 111–19. Interestingly enough, the European Court had not found an expropriation of a foreigner by 2009. *See* Kriebaum (2009), 241–2.
161. *James*, Eur. Court HR, Judgment, 21 February 1986, para. 64. *Cf.* Schwelb (1964), 532–41.
162. Anderson (1999), 549; De Sena (2009), 214 & 217; and Tomuschat (2009), 652–3.
163. Kriebaum (2009), 240–1. *See* Wildhaber and Wildhaber (2009), 672–3.

164. *Holy Monasteries*, Eur. Court HR, Judgment, 9 December 1994, para. 71.
165. Harris et al (2009), 681.
166. Kriebaum (2009), 240.
167. Ruiz Fabri (2003), 166.
168. *Lithgow*, Eur. Court HR, Judgment 8 July 1986, para. 121. *See* Ruiz Fabri (2003), 166 & 170; and Harris et al (2009), 682.
169. *See* Kriebaum (2009), 241.
170. *See Guillemin v. France*, Eur. Court HR, Reports of Judgments and Decisions 1997-I, Judgment, 21 February 1997, para. 54.
171. *Almeida Garrett, Mascarenhas Falcão and Others v. Portugal*, Eur. Court HR, Reports of Judgments and Decisions 2000-I, Judgment, 11 January 2000, para. 54.
172. Nevertheless, in several cases the European Commission and Court have concluded that the challenged measure was proportionate, notwithstanding the failure to compensate the affected applicant for the reduction in the value of his property. Anderson (1999), 550–1.
173. Allen (2005), 119; and van Dijk et al (2006), 888–9.
174. *See Chassagnou and Others v. France*, Eur. Court HR, Reports of Judgments and Decisions 1999-III, Judgment, 29 April 1999; *Immobiliare Saffi v. Italy*, Eur. Court HR, Reports of Judgments and Decisions 1999-V, Judgment 28 July 1999; *Hutten-Czapska*, Eur. Court HR, Judgment, 22 February 2005; *Saliba and Others v. Malta*, Eur. Court HR, Judgment, 22 November 2011; and *Lindheim and Others v. Norway*, Eur. Court HR, Judgment, 12 June 2012. *See also Schneider c. Luxembourg*, Eur. Court HR, Judgment, 10 July 2007; and *Hermann v. Germany*, Eur. Court HR, Judgment, 26 June 2012.
175. van Dijk et al (2006), 890–1.
176. *Forminster*, Eur. Court HR, Judgment, 9 October 2008, para. 65. *See Sun v. Russia*, Eur. Court HR, Judgment, 5 February 2009, para. 27.
177. *Družstevni*, Eur. Court HR, Judgment 31 July, 2008.
178. *Tre Traktörer*, Eur. Court HR, Judgment, 7 July 1989, para. 58.
179. *Mellacher*, Eur. Court HR, Judgment, 19 December 1989, para. 45.
180. *See Allan Jacobsson*, Eur. Court HR, Judgment, 25 October 1989, para. 55.
181. *See Tre Traktörer*, Eur. Court HR, Judgment, 7 July 1989, para. 58.
182. *See Mellacher*, Eur. Court HR, Judgment, 19 December 1989, para. 45.
183. *See Fredin*, Eur. Court HR, Judgment, 18 February 1991.
184. *See Pine Valley*, European Court, Judgment, 29 November 1991.
185. *See Air Canada v. United Kingdom*, Eur. Court HR, Series A No. 316-A, Judgment, 5 May 1995.
186. *See Svenska Managementgruppen v. Sweden*, Eur. Commission HR No 11036/84, (1985) 45 Decisions and Reports 211, *Wasa Liv Omsesidigt v. Sweden*, Eur. Commission HR, No. 13013/87, (1988) 58 Decisions and Reports 163; and *Travers and 27 Others v. Italy*, Eur. Commission HR, No. 15117/89, (1995) 80 Decisions and Reports 5.
187. *Gasus Dosier*, Eur. Court HR, Judgment, 23 February 1995, para. 60.
188. van Dijk et al (2006), 887.
189. Clayton and Tomlinson (2000), 1309.
190. Harris et al (2009), 686.
191. *See* Clayton and Tomlinson (2000), 1309; and Harris et al (2009), 687.
192. Anderson (1999), 553.
193. *See Handyside*, Eur. Court HR, Judgment, 7 December 1976.
194. *See Van Marle*, Eur. Court HR, Judgment, 26 June 1986.
195. *See Tre Traktörer*, Eur. Court HR, Judgment, 7 July 1989. *See also Fredin*, Eur. Court HR, Judgment, 18 February 1991.
196. *See Mellacher*, Eur. Court HR, Judgment, 19 December 1989.

197. *See Pine Valley*, Eur. Court HR, Judgment, 29 November 1991.
198. *See Raimondo v. Italy*, Eur. Court HR, Series A No. 281-A, Judgment, 22 February 1994.
199. *See Air Canada*, Eur. Court HR, Judgment, 5 May 1995.
200. *See The National & Provincial Building Society, the Leeds Permanent Building Society and the Yorkshire Building Society v. United Kingdom*, Eur. Court HR, Reports of Judgments and Decisions 1997-VII, Judgment, 23 October 1997.
201. *See Ismayilov v. Russia*, Eur. Court HR, Judgment, 6 November 2008, para. 30, 33 & 35; and *Sun*, Eur. Court HR, Judgment, 5 February 2009, paras. 24–5.
202. *Mellacher*, Eur. Court HR, Judgment, 19 December 1989, para. 51.
203. Yannaca-Small (2010), 463. *See Sporrong and Lönnroth*, Eur. Court HR, Judgment, 23 September 1982.
204. Under the 1972 Expropriation Act.
205. *See* Higgins (1982), 344.
206. *See Sporrong and Lönnroth*, Eur. Court HR, Judgment, 23 September 1982, paras. 56–75.
207. *See Loizidou v. Turkey*, Eur. Court HR, Reports of Judgments and Decisions 1996-VI, Judgment, 18 December 1996; *Stretch*, Eur. Court HR, Judgment, 24 June 2003; and *Broniowski*, Eur. Court HR, Judgment, 22 June 2004.
208. *Beyeler*, Eur. Court HR, Judgment, 5 January 2000, para. 111. *See e.g. Viaşu*, Eur. Court HR, Judgment, 9 December 2008, para. 73.
209. *See Wiggins v. United Kingdom*, Eur. Commission HR, No. 7456/76, (1979) 13 Decisions and Reports 40.
210. *See Ekner and Hofauer v. Austria*, Eur. Court HR, Judgment, 23 April 1987.
211. *See Stran Greek Refineries*, Eur. Court HR, Judgment, 9 December 1994.
212. In fact, more than 16 years. *See Phocas v. France*, Eur. Court HR, Reports of Judgments and Decisions 1996-II, Judgment, 23 April 1996.
213. *See Matos*, Eur. Court HR, Judgment, 16 September 1996.
214. Wildhaber and Wildhaber (2009), 674–6. *See Intersplav v. Ukraine*, Eur. Court HR, Judgment, 9 January 2007; and *Smirnov v. Russia*, Eur. Court HR, Judgment, 7 June 2007.
215. Anderson (1999), 551–2.

4. The approach of the Iran–US Claims Tribunal

The Iran–US CT was set up in 1981 as part of a political compromise reached by the Iranian and US governments. In conformity with its constitutive treaty, the tribunal was established to settle disputes between the nationals of both states arising out of interferences with an international minimum standard of treatment, which protected them against expropriations and other measures affecting property rights. No definition was given in this instrument to property. The Iran–US CT chose the traditional wider notion of foreign investment, comprising tangibles and intangibles. It interpreted expropriation as covering both *de jure* and *de facto* takings, the latter derived not only from acts but also from omissions. Before the establishment of the Iran–US CT, only a handful of decisions given by claims commissions, the PCIJ, arbitral tribunals and the ICJ, had referred to the expropriation of aliens. The judgments of the Iran–US CT formed the first clear and detailed international case-law on this issue. The link between expropriation, taking and deprivation was thus established in a generally coherent jurisprudence, which illustrates when an act is expropriatory, and when it is not.

The tribunal recognised and developed the protection against expropriation included in the minimum standard of customary international law, without losing sight of the jurisdiction given in its constitutive treaty. The Iran–US CT did not hesitate to solve the thorny issue of the state's intent at the moment of taking the property of an alien. Adopting an effects approach in most of the cases brought before it, the Iran–US CT awarded compensation when there was a non-ephemeral and unreasonable interference of the state with the enjoyment of the constituent elements of the right of property: that is to say, with the use or control of the property and of the economic benefits derived from it. The tribunal also construed and applied the notion of other measures affecting property rights, within its jurisdiction. Through the application of this concept the Iran–US CT was able to award compensation in those situations where the deprivation was not tantamount to a taking. To this effect, the tribunal relied on the interpretation given by the European Court of Human Rights to the notion of other interferences with the peaceful enjoyment of possessions.

In conformity with Article 32 of the Tribunal Rules of Procedure of 3 May 1983, the jurisprudence of the Iran–US CT is publicly available, and expressly reasoned. For this reason, the work of the tribunal constitutes an indispensable guide for decision-makers confronted with the difficult problem of establishing the boundaries of compensable and non-compensable state measures. The present chapter studies this case-law, profusely quoted and referred to by international arbitral tribunals in investor-to-state disputes. It deals with the Iran–US CT's definition of property and expropriation, as well as with its views on those acts that constitute a taking, and those that do not. The notion of other measures affecting property rights, as developed in the case-law of this tribunal, is analysed too. Finally, the traditional requirements of public purpose, non-discrimination and compensation are seen from the standpoint of the Iran–US CT.

4.1 TAKINGS IN AN *AD HOC* FORUM

The 1979 Iranian revolution, which replaced the constitutional monarchy under the *Shah*[1] by an Islamic Republic under the Rahbar,[2] gave rise to most of the expropriation claims presented to the Iran–US CT.[3] In the context of a strong anti-Western rhetoric that led to political and civil unrest, US business dependents and representatives were gradually repatriated or forced to depart the country. The new Iranian government wanted complete control of vital sectors of the economy, like banks, insurance companies, heavy and oil industries, all of which were nationalised in 1979 and 1980. Besides direct expropriations, Iran also implemented other measures that affected foreign investors. For example, it encouraged the formation of workers' councils to manage their businesses, and replaced those managers and directors designated by the respective company for those appointed by the Iranian authorities. In 1979, when the US embassy in Tehran was seized, and nationals of the sending state were taken hostage, all existing business contacts between Iran and the USA were brought to an end.

Iran failed to comply with the orders to release the hostages issued by the ICJ in the *United States Diplomatic and Consular Staff in Tehran* case.[4] The USA launched an unsuccessful rescue operation, and adopted internal measures to exert economic pressure on the new government in Iran, the most important of which was the freezing of Iranian assets. Negotiations finally took place between the two states during 1980, under the good offices of the Algerian government.[5] The crisis was settled in

1981 through a group of treaties known as the 'Algiers Accords'. The Claims Settlement Declaration that established the Iran–US CT was one of them.[6]

4.1.1 Defining Property and Expropriation

Most cases brought before the Iran–US CT were related to the injury of aliens caused in the context of the Iranian revolution. For this reason, the Iran–US CT can fairly be considered a contemporary version of the claims commissions or mixed tribunals established at the beginning of the 20th century.[7] According to Article II paragraph 1 of the Claims Settlement Declaration, the Iran–US CT was set up to resolve disputes between nationals of both countries arising, among other things, out of 'expropriations and other measures affecting property rights'. Individuals were allowed to present their claims directly to the tribunal, without having to resort to diplomatic protection, or having to exhaust local remedies.[8] The disputes mentioned in Article II paragraph 1 had to be resolved in conformity with Article V of the same treaty. This is:

> on the basis of respect for law, applying such choice of law rules and principles of commercial and international law as the Tribunal determines to be applicable, taking into account relevant usages of the trade, contract provisions and changed circumstances.[9]

Although Article II paragraph 1 did not define 'property rights', the tribunal followed the general approach in international legal practice and opted for a broad notion of property, including both tangibles and intangibles. This solution followed those adopted by the 1922 *Norwegian Shipowner's* claim, the 1926 *Chorzow Factory* case, and the 1934 *Oscar Chinn* case.[10] In the interlocutory award of *Starrett Housing*, the Iran–US CT declared that property must be deemed to comprise physical assets as well as contract rights.[11] This wide concept was confirmed in the final award of the same case, where the tribunal stated that '[i]t is a well-settled rule of customary international law that a taking of one property right may also involve a taking of a closely connected ancillary right'.[12] In conformity with this broad notion of property, management rights,[13] the right to receive dividend payments,[14] and other shareholders' rights and interests[15] – *inter alia* – would be included within the Claims Settlement Declaration. The partial award of *Amoco International Finance* gave a concept of takings that illustrates the wide scope of its object:

> [e]xpropriation, which can be defined as a compulsory transfer of property rights, may extend to any rights which can be the object of a commercial transaction, i.e. freely sold and bought, and thus has a monetary value.[16]

This scope was, nonetheless, not unlimited. The tribunal excluded, for instance, claims that sought compensation for personal injuries.[17]

The Iran–US CT considered expropriation and taking to be synonyms. According to Allahyar Mouri, a distinction appears to have been made between these concepts and deprivation. As he explains, in the tribunal's case-law 'expropriation always results in a deprivation of the owner of that property or right', but 'the converse is not always true: deprivation is not in all circumstances an act of expropriation'.[18] In most cases where a deprivation was found, however, the tribunal did conclude that it amounted to a taking.[19] Judge Charles Brower declared in *Eastman Kodak* that an expropriation usually implies 'that the State involved has itself acquired the benefit of the affected alien's property or at least has been the instrument of its redistribution'.[20] Acknowledging that this might not always be the case, in *Tippets, Abbett, McCarthy, Stratton* (*TAMS*) the tribunal preferred to use 'deprivation' over 'taking', because 'the latter may be understood to imply that the Government has acquired something of value, which is not required'.[21] In the same award, nonetheless, the Iran–US CT declared that both:

> A deprivation or taking of property may occur under international law through interference by a state in the use of that property or with the enjoyment of its benefits, even where legal title to the property is not affected.[22]

As illustrated in this last paragraph, the Iran–US CT construed the term 'expropriation' used in the Claims Settlement Declaration to cover not only *de jure*, but also *de facto* takings.[23] The tribunal dealt with few claims of direct expropriation, and it had no problems finding that a taking took place when there was an Iranian law expressly nationalising an industry or a particular entity.[24] The majority of the cases brought before the tribunal were related to claims of indirect expropriation, in which there was either a *de facto* seizure of property without any formal declaration announcing the taking, or in which there was such a formal declaration, but a *de facto* taking had allegedly occurred at an earlier date.[25] Both acts and omissions were included in the tribunal's case-law on indirect expropriation. The Iran–US CT generally required an affirmative action from the government that adopted the challenged measure before finding that a taking attributable to that state had occurred.[26]

The tribunal further distinguished the term 'taking' or 'expropriation' from 'appropriation', the latter being not an act of the state, but of a private person (like the party to a contract) that results in the owner's deprivation.[27] Charles Brower and Jason Brueschke point out that the tribunal's awards often seem 'somewhat lax' when keeping strict conceptual distinctions between acts constituting 'expropriation', 'deprivation', or 'appropriation'. According to these authors, the main reason for this attitude was the fact that a decision of the tribunal was 'immediately and automatically satisfied from the Security Account, regardless of [its] theoretical basis'.[28]

Establishing the date of the taking was a difficult task for the judges. Most of the indirect expropriation cases presented before the tribunal corresponded to claims of creeping or constructive takings. This date was important not only in relation to the jurisdictional deadline fixed in the constitutive treaty of the Iran–US CT,[29] but also for the valuation of the property taken, the determination of the exchange rate of the currency in which the compensation was to be paid, and the moment from which the interest was to run on the award.[30] *International Technical Products* gave a solution to this problem in the following terms:

> Where the alleged expropriation is carried out by way of a series of interferences in the enjoyment of the property, the breach forming the cause of action is deemed to take place on the day when the interference has ripened into more or less irreversible deprivation of the property rather than on the beginning date of the events. The point at which interference ripens into a taking depends on the circumstances of the case and does not require that legal title has been transferred.[31]

In this case, the Iran–US CT considered expropriation claims to be outstanding 'on the date of the taking of property'.[32] Several other awards later followed this standard.[33]

4.1.2 Other Measures Affecting Property Rights

The international minimum standard, applicable under the Claims Settlement Declaration, offered Iranian and US nationals a protection that went beyond that traditionally offered by the international law of expropriation. The Declaration gave the Iran–US CT jurisdiction over disputes arising not only out of takings, but also out of 'other measures affecting property rights'. The tribunal found deprivations that fitted this description in a number of cases where the level of the interference did not amount to an actual taking.[34] The phrase was given a broad meaning, and a variety of measures – whether actions or omissions, and irrespective of their form of execution – were considered to be able to affect the property of Iranian or US nationals. Even the failure to exert due diligence in the protection of foreign investors, or a tortious act affecting their property, were exceptionally accepted as included in this phrase.[35] According to Mouri, in general:

> the Tribunal's awards based on the phrase 'other measures affecting property rights' required a threshold showing that the State committed serious, specific, and unreasonable acts of interference with the actual use and benefit of a particular property or with the fundamental property rights of a given claimant, with irreversible deprivative consequence similar to that arising from expropriation.[36]

Veijo Heiskanen points out that the Iran–US CT resorted to 'other measures' exceptionally, and that only a few of the claims were resolved solely on this basis, while the bulk of them involved takings.[37] The tribunal found the Iranian authorities liable for subjecting the claimant to 'other measures' in *TAMS*.[38] An equally owned entity called TAMS-AFFA had been created in 1975 by a US partnership (TAMS) and an Iranian firm (AFFA),[39] for the sole purpose of performing engineering and architectural services on the Tehran International Airport. TAMS-AFFA's articles of partnership established joint control of the entity by its partners. This meant that any decision required the consent of at least one member appointed by TAMS and one member appointed by AFFA, and that the authority to sign documents creating obligations for TAMS-AFFA was vested in two individuals, one appointed by each partner. At the beginning of 1979, the Tehran International Airport project almost completely stopped as a result of the Iranian revolution. The government of Iran appointed a temporary manager for AFFA, who also assumed the role of manager of TAMS-AFFA and started to sign cheques by himself on its behalf, as well as making personnel and other decisions without consulting TAMS. Negotiations took place during 1979 between the US company and the manager of TAMS-AFFA with some success. This trend was reversed after the hostage crisis occurred at the end of the same year, and TAMS-AFFA stopped reporting to the foreign investor and responding to its letters and faxes. The Iran–US CT considered TAMS to be deprived of its property interests in TAMS-AFFA from this moment. No taking, however, was found. The tribunal concluded that Iran was responsible for 'other measures' affecting the claimant's rights.[40]

Foremost Tehran is another example of a lesser interference with the property of a foreign investor – that is to say, one that did not amount to an expropriation.[41] In this case, a US group of companies (Foremost) owned a percentage in an Iranian joint stock company (Pak Dairy).[42] After expatriating its personnel in Iran, Pak Dairy declared dividends in

1979, 1980 and 1981, and paid them to Iranian stockholders, while refusing to pay them to the foreign investor.[43] One of Foremost's main representatives in Iran was ousted from the board of directors by the government and replaced by an Iranian national acting on the instructions of his state. Finally, Pak Dairy's board informed Foremost of its decision to make no payments to foreign shareholders. The US group claimed before the Iran–US CT that a taking of its interest in the company had occurred as a 'cumulative result of a number of instances of interference with the exercise of its rights as a shareholder'.[44] The tribunal established that the non-payment of dividends to Foremost was an interference with its rights, compensable under the rubric of 'other measures affecting property rights'. The Iran–US CT supported its conclusion by reference to the *Sporrong and Lönnroth* case, decided by the European Court of Human Rights in 1982.[45] In that case, a violation of Article 1 of the First Optional Protocol of the European Convention on Human Rights was found in the form of the residual category of other interference with the protected peaceful enjoyment of possessions.[46]

In *Eastman Kodak*, a US investor established a corporation in Iran to act as distributor of its products and to operate a finishing photo laboratory called Rangiran.[47] With the advent of the Iranian revolution in 1978, Eastman Kodak's expatriate management personnel left the country. Rangiran continued functioning with Iranian nationals, appointed by the foreign investor, who were later joined by a couple of US nationals that had returned to assume management functions in Iran. After the hostage crisis in 1979, these last remaining expatriate officers left the country, and Rangiran's accounts in Iranian banks were frozen by order of the government of Iran. A worker's council formed by employees of the company was then instructed to assume the supervision of Rangiran, and an Iranian national was appointed as its manager by the state. The shareholders of the company decided in 1980 to place it in liquidation. Although the worker's council accepted this decision, Iran sealed Rangiran's office building, preventing the personnel from working until the company appointed a liquidator acceptable to the government. The board of liquidators appointed by the shareholders of the company declared Rangiran bankrupt, an action that was later confirmed by a court in Tehran. The Iran–US CT found no expropriation in its partial award, mostly because 'the Claimant, as majority shareholder, was able effectively to decide to liquidate and to declare Rangiran bankrupt'.[48] Expressly following the *Sporrong* case and the award in *Foremost*, the tribunal was nevertheless satisfied that Eastman Kodak's claim for expropriation 'must be taken to include a claim for a lesser degree of interference with its property rights', and concluded that Iran's actions amounted to 'other measures'.[49]

Rouhollah Karubian is yet another award based on 'other measures affecting property rights'.[50] In this proceeding, the Iranian state enacted land-reform acts in 1979 and 1982 by which certain undeveloped plots should become government property. The implementation and enforcement of these norms remained contingent upon the determination that the respective immovables were in fact undeveloped. No such action was taken regarding Mr. Karubian's properties. The uncertainty as to the status of these plots produced doubts over the ownership of the lands, since the correspondent title deeds were susceptible to cancellation at any time. Quoting both *Foremost* and *Eastman Kodak*, the Iran–US CT found no expropriation resulting from the Iranian legislation. Nonetheless, the tribunal also concluded that the uncertainty surrounding the ownership of the properties made it difficult for the claimant to find a buyer for his plots. According to the Iran–US CT, this situation represented an impairment of the right to dispose of them, adversely affecting Karubian's property under the Claims Settlement Declaration.[51] The facts of this award bring to mind those of *Sporrong*, the leading case in the jurisprudence of the European Court of Human Rights on other interferences with the peaceful enjoyment of possessions. It comes as no surprise that the Iran–US CT found that the state's legislation did not amount to an expropriation in *Karubian*, but to 'other measures affecting property rights'.

4.2 THE PROBLEM OF INDIRECT TAKINGS

The findings on expropriation of the Iran–US CT depended on the circumstances that surrounded the respective claim and the type of property that was taken.[52] In almost all of these cases the tribunal applied customary international law.[53] In *Harza Engineering*, the Iran–US CT agreed with the claimant's assertion 'that a taking of property may occur under international law, even in the absence of a formal nationalization or expropriation, if a government has interfered unreasonably with the use of property'.[54] Other cases in which this standard was followed include *Ataollah Golpira* and *International Technical Products*.[55] The description of the standard was different in other decisions. For instance, in the interlocutory award of *Starrett*, the Iran–US CT stated that under international law 'measures taken by a State can interfere with property rights to such an extent that these rights are rendered so useless that they must be deemed to have been expropriated'.[56] *TAMS*, on the other hand, considered a taking to occur 'whenever events demonstrate that the owner was deprived of fundamental rights of ownership and it appears that this deprivation is not merely ephemeral'.[57] According to Brower and Brueschke, this requirement 'is somewhat ambiguous but generally should be taken to mean that the deprivation is not of such a temporary or short duration that compensation should not be awarded'.[58] In *Constantine Gianoplus,* the Iran–US CT came out with yet another description, when it declared that '[u]nder appropriate circumstances government interference depriving an owner of effective use and control of property may give rise to a claim for expropriation'.[59] This standard of effective deprivation had already been used by the PCIJ in the *Chorzow Factory* and *Oscar Chinn* cases.[60]

4.2.1 Constitutive Acts

Nuances in the tribunal's wording might suggest that there was more than one applicable standard. However, the Iran–US CT focused on the impact of the alleged taking rather than on semantics. In Brower's view, the standard applied explicitly and implicitly by the tribunal required an unreasonable interference with the foreigner's property caused by actions attributable to the host-state.[61] What in fact constituted this unreasonable interference varied, depending on the circumstances of the respective case. Because of this, Brower and Brueschke affirm that it is impossible to discern in Iran–US CT's case-law a single standard for determining when an expropriation has occurred.[62] In this context, Hassan Sedigh concludes that 'the boundary between regulation and expropriation becomes the unreasonableness of an interference, and the unreasonableness of an interference would depend on the nature of the affected property and the means used'.[63] Such a conclusion would imply that the Iran–US CT adopted a police-powers solution, when in fact it applied an effects rule in most expropriation claims. For this reason, it is more accurate to say that the tribunal's answer to the threshold question called for something more than just an unreasonable interference.

The finding of a formal or informal expropriation by the Iran–US CT required the establishment of two facts by the claimant: first, a taking of possession, a transfer of property, or its distribution by the state; and, second, the denial of its use to the owner.[64] The Iran–US CT applied both requirements to cases involving the indirect taking of physical properties and business operations.[65] In those cases involving the seizure of tangible objects, the tribunal had no difficulties in finding a taking from the date that the owner's access to his property was obstructed, if the correspondent act was attributable to the Iranian government.[66] In this respect, even acts performed by the judiciary were considered to be susceptible of producing expropriatory effects.[67] The tribunal's conclusion in *Dames & Moore*, that a 'unilateral taking of possession of property and the denial of its use to the rightful owners may amount to an expropriation even without a formal decree regarding title to the property',[68] is an example of the application of these conditions to a particular claim of this type.[69] Concerning companies and business operations, the Iran–US CT replaced the first requirement (*i.e.*, the taking of possession, transfer or distribution of the property by the state) with that of irreversible control by the state over the business or company, and the second requirement (the denial of the property's use to the owner) with that of deprivative consequences of such control over virtually all of the value of the owner's property.[70] In *ITT Industries*, Judge George Aldrich held that:

> while assumption of control over property by a government does not automatically and immediately justify a conclusion that the property has been taken by the government, thus requiring compensation under international law, such a conclusion is warranted whenever events demonstrate that the owner was deprived of fundamental rights of ownership and it appears that this deprivation is not merely ephemeral.[71]

This rule was followed by the Iran–US CT in other awards.[72] The tribunal assessed the appointment of managers and supervisors by the Iranian state pursuant to newly enacted legislation as an 'important', 'significant', or 'relevant' factor, but not conclusive at the moment of establishing whether an expropriation had occurred.[73] The decisive element for this determination was, as Aldrich explains, the non-transitory character of the deprivation of property produced as a consequence of the respective measure.[74] In the words of the interlocutory award of *SEDCO*, when there is 'no reasonable prospect of return of control, a taking should conclusively be found to have occurred as of that date'.[75] According to Charles Brower and Jason Brueschke:

> given the factual nature of the Tribunal's inquiry its decisions have never fixed on a mechanical standard for determining whether or when the appointment of managers has effected a taking. It has considered many factors, including whether the owner has been excluded from the ordinary dissemination of financial information and income distributions, as well as the scope of functions assumed by the Government-appointed managers.[76]

The Iran–US CT often declared that an ephemeral interruption of control would not constitute by itself an expropriation.[77] However, with the exception of *Motorola*, the tribunal generally considered the correspondent assumption by the government-appointed individual to be definitive or permanent rather than provisional or temporary, as labelled by the Iranian state.[78] George Aldrich points out that:

> by the time the first claims for expropriation or other takings of property began to be decided by the Tribunal in late 1983, the interference with property rights had endured for at least three years or more, and the continuation of strained relations between Iran and the United States gave the Tribunal little reason to believe that such interference would soon end. Consequently, the often difficult question of when allegedly temporary interference with the rights of property owners should be considered to have ripened into a compensable taking or deprivation of those rights rarely troubled the Iran-United States Claims Tribunal.[79]

In most cases involving the interference of the control over property, the tribunal came to the conclusion that the respective expropriation occurred precisely at this moment, *i.e.* when the manager or supervisor assumed his duties.[80]

Besides the physical seizure of property or its deprivation through the appointment of managers or supervisors, the Iran–US CT found expropriations in cases involving, for instance, involuntary or forced transactions;[81] the refusal of the Iranian government to return property subject to a lease;[82] the loss of goods left with that state;[83] and its failure to grant a re-export permit for equipment in Iran.[84]

4.2.2 Claims That Were Rejected

In a number of cases, no taking was found by the Iran–US CT. Expropriation claims were rejected, for example, when the challenged act was not attributable to the Iranian state.[85] As Veijo Heiskanen recalls:

> The adoption of the effects doctrine did not mean that the Tribunal automatically attributed all irregularities that occurred in Iran during the Islamic Revolution to the Government of Iran. The Tribunal stressed that the key issue in drawing the line between the deprivation of a property right and the materialization of a political risk was the attributability of the loss to the Government; if the loss could not be attributed to the Government, there could be no liability.[86]

In this regard, the Iran–US CT followed the traditional requirements of state responsibility in international law; today included in Article 2 of the Articles on Responsibility of States for Internationally Wrongful Acts, adopted by the ILC in 2001.[87] Various failures of proof also prevented some claimants from obtaining a finding in their favour.[88] In certain cases, they were not the owners of the allegedly taken properties;[89] in others, the claimant retained some control over the property.[90] The tribunal further refused to conclude that the nationalisation of the property of the majority shareholders caused the indirect taking of the investment of the minority shareholders.[91] A similar situation was found in relation to the nationalisation of the banking institutions in Iran. The mere assumption of control over these entities was not considered a taking of the funds in the respective bank accounts or an interference with the banking transactions normally provided by them.[92] Exceptionally, the tribunal held the Iranian state responsible for a taking when it found that a specific measure adopted by the government-controlled bank had a serious deprivative impact on the claimant.[93]

Regarding the expropriatory effect of state regulations, the Iran–US CT declared in the interlocutory award of *SEDCO* that it is 'an accepted principle of international law that a State is not liable for economic injury which is a consequence of bona fide "regulation" within the accepted police powers of States'.[94] At first sight, this might seem a police-powers solution. Nevertheless, in the same case the tribunal acknowledged that the duty to compensate will arise if this regulation damages the property to a 'substantial or excessive degree'.[95] This is a clear effects approach. The only claim rejected by the Iran–US CT on grounds of police-powers was *Emanuel Too*.[96] In this proceeding, an Iranian national owned an insured motel and restaurant in Turlock, California. In 1980, the motel-restaurant was destroyed by fire, the cause of which was identified as arson. Mr. Too contended that he had been the victim of 'unknown prejudiced Americans', who had previously threatened him.[97] The police and fire departments in Turlock investigated the incident without arriving at any final conclusion. The insurance company did not pay out the proceeds of the respective policy to the claimant, and the motel-restaurant was subject to a forced sale. The Internal Revenue Service of the USA (IRS) sold the liquor permit held by Mr. Too at public auction, and used the proceeds to pay part of the claimant's overdue employment taxes. The claimant was also the owner of a cold-storage trailer, found in the state of Arizona, that he argued was wrongfully expropriated by the USA. The authorities of Arizona had made efforts to inform Mr. Too about this trailer and the impending auction for abandoned property. The claimant did not try to recover the trailer, and it was sold at auction by the State of Arizona. In a wording reminiscent of that in *SEDCO*, the Iran–US CT quoted the American Law Institute's Third Restatement of the Foreign Relations Law of the United States, and declared that:

> a State is not responsible for loss of property or for other economic disadvantage resulting from bona fide general taxation or any other action that is commonly accepted as within the police power of States, provided it is not discriminatory and is not designed to cause the alien to abandon the property to the State or to sell it at a distress price.[98]

According to the tribunal, the IRS's action was not aimed at Mr. Too because he was an Iranian, nor was it 'deliberately intended to cause him to abandon the property to the State or to sell it at a distress price'.[99] The action of the IRS was the result of Mr. Too's failure to pay taxes withheld by him from his employees' salaries: a lawful levy for overdue taxes, for which there is no state responsibility. As for the cold-storage trailer left in Arizona, the Iran–US CT said: '[t]here is no question that the disposition of abandoned property is commonly accepted as a lawful action within the police powers of States, again provided that such a disposition does not discriminate against aliens'.[100]

Exchange control restrictions were a problem related to that of state regulations. In several cases it was claimed that these measures constituted an expropriation.[101] The Iran–US CT did not preclude the possibility of characterising them as a taking, but subjected this determination to their harmony with the International Monetary Fund's Articles of Agreement. The tribunal found no disharmony with these articles in its awards.[102]

4.3 CONDITIONS OF LEGALITY AND THEIR CONSEQUENCE

The Iran–US CT judged the legality of an expropriation by reference to international law.[103] Even though it recognized the three traditional requirements of a lawful taking (*i.e.*, public purpose, non-discrimination and compensation), it generally did not support due process of law as an independent condition of legality.[104] The tribunal's interpretation of public purpose and non-discrimination clearly favoured the economic sovereignty of the state. The national authorities' assertion that the expropriatory measure was adopted in conformity with these conditions, created a strong presumption for the Iran–US CT that they had been duly fulfilled.[105] This wide margin of appreciation resembles that given to the state in the case-law of the European Court of Human Rights concerning Article 1 of the First Optional Protocol to the Convention for the Protection of Human Rights and Fundamental Freedoms.[106] It was best illustrated in *Amoco*, where the Iran–US CT declared that:

> [a] precise definition of the 'public purpose' for which an expropriation may be lawfully decided has neither been agreed upon in international law nor even suggested. It is clear that, as a result of the modern acceptance of the right to nationalize, this term is broadly interpreted, and that States, in practice, are granted extensive discretion.[107]

In fact, there was virtually no award in which a taking was found unlawful for lacking a public purpose.[108] For example, in *Amoco* the Iran–US CT stated that the nationalisation of foreign properties, aimed at obtaining revenues from the exploitation of natural resources for the development of a country, 'has not generally been denounced as unlawful and illegitimate'.[109] Even though the discretion given by the tribunal to national authorities was wide, it was not absolute. The Iran–US CT explicitly declared that a state has no right to expropriate an alien only for financial purposes.[110] It also noted that a taking exclusively aimed at avoiding contractual obligations of a state or a state-controlled entity is unlawful under international norms, because it would be contrary to the principle of good faith and to the 'well-settled rule that a State has the right to commit itself by contract to foreign corporations'.[111] For this conclusion, the Iran–US CT referred to *American Independent Oil* (AMINOIL), the arbitration against Kuwait settled a year before by an *ad hoc* tribunal.[112] In *Amoco*, the Iran–US CT further declared that:

> [c]onformity with domestic law is not usually cited as a condition for an internationally lawful nationalization, and the Treaty specifies no such condition. It is therefore doubtful whether it is one of the requisites of international law. The case law on this point is not very helpful. Violation of domestic law, when invoked, is most often analyzed as evidence of the lack of fulfilment of one of the conditions imposed by international law, such as the existence of a public purpose.[113]

4.3.1 The Effect or Impact of the Measure

The state is liable to pay compensation for a taking. According to Matti Pellonpää and Malgosia Fitzmaurice, if some indication of it was made at the time of the taking, its non-payment did not render the expropriation illegal in the case-law of the Iran–US CT.[114] For this tribunal, the duty to compensate is based on the loss or damages suffered by the foreign investor as a result of the corresponding measure, not on the doctrines of acquired rights, *pacta sunt servanda* or unjust enrichment.[115] Regarding this last theory, however, the tribunal did acknowledge in *Sea-Land Service* that it 'is widely accepted as having been assimilated into the catalogue of general principles of law available to be applied by international tribunals', for '[t]he concept of unjust enrichment had its origins in Roman Law, where it emerged as an equitable device "to cover those cases in which a general action for damages was not available"', and '[...] is codified or judicially recognised in the great majority of the municipal legal systems of the world'.[116] The Iran–US CT quoted the *Lena Goldfields* arbitration on the issue.[117]

Concerning the problem of intent, the tribunal adopted an effects solution. It generally found that worthy economic or social objectives motivating an expropriation did not exempt the host-state from the obligation to pay compensation. In this approach, the tribunal was apparently influenced by the decisions of the *Chorzow Factory* case and the *Norwegian Shipowners'* claim.[118] As George Aldrich points out, Article II paragraph 1 of the Claims Settlement Declaration:

> explicitly gave the Tribunal jurisdiction over claims that arose out of both 'expropriations' and 'other measures affecting property rights', thereby suggesting clearly that neither the terminology nor the intent of actions attributable to either Government would affect the Tribunal's jurisdiction to award compensation if the actions had adversely affected a claimant's property rights.[119]

Already in the 1983 *ITT* case, Judge Aldrich had declared that '[t]he intent of the government is less important than the effects of the measures on the owner, and the form of [these] measures [...] is less important than the reality of their impact'.[120] A couple of months later, the Iran–US CT affirmed in *Starrett* that state measures rendering property-rights useless must be deemed expropriatory under international law, even though the state did not purport to take them.[121] In 1984, the tribunal came to the opposite conclusion in *Sea-Land*.[122] The claimant was a US corporation engaged in international transportation by water of containerised cargo. Since 1978, Sea-Land encountered increasing difficulties in the continued use of a cargo facility built and operated by it in the port of Bandar Abbas, Iran, due to the unexplained absence of government officials in charge of customs, immigration, health, etc. These difficulties led to the suspension and eventual termination of its operations. In this case, the Iran–US CT concluded that the country was in a state of upheaval following the 1979 revolution, and that nothing suggested a policy of intentional disruption or non-cooperation with Sea-Land from the Iranian authorities. According to the tribunal, a finding of expropriation would require, at the very least, a deliberate governmental interference with the foreign investor depriving it of the use and benefit of its investment.[123] No intentional course of conduct directed against Sea-Land was found, so the expropriation claim was dismissed. The Iran–US CT quoted *Oscar Chinn* in support of its decision.[124] Judge Howard Holtzmann disagreed with this conclusion and expressly declared that:

> the critical question is the objective effect of a government's acts, not its subjective intentions. Acts by a government which have the effect of depriving an alien of his property are considered expropriatory in international law, whatever the government's intentions.[125]

The police-powers finding in *Sea-Land* obtained no support in subsequent awards.[126] In *TAMS* and in *Thomas Payne* the tribunal repeated the effects statement of Judge Aldrich in *ITT*: *i.e.*, that the intent of the government is less important than the effects of the measures on the owner, and that the form of the measures of control or interference is less important than the reality of their impact.[127] *Phillips Petroleum* was no exception. The Iran–US CT again declared that 'a government's liability to compensate for expropriation of alien property does not depend on proof that the expropriation was intentional'.[128] The interlocutory award in *SEDCO* and the award in *Phelps Dodge* also followed Judge Aldrich's reasoning.[129] Phelps Dodge was a US corporation that had invested in an Iranian company established to manufacture and sell various wire and cable products. During 1979 and 1980, there was a progressive erosion of the claimant's ability to exercise its ownership rights. At the end of 1980, the management of the company was transferred to agencies of the Iranian government and the control of its factory was directly assumed by these authorities. The Iran–US CT found that, from this moment, Phelps Dodge was deprived of virtually all of the factory's value.[130] It also stated:

> The Tribunal fully understands the reasons why the Respondent felt compelled to protect its interests through this transfer of management, and the Tribunal understands the financial, economic and social concerns that inspired the law pursuant to which it acted, but those reasons and concerns cannot relieve the Respondent of the obligation to compensate Phelps Dodge for its loss.[131]

The Iran–US CT confirmed this view in *Harold Birnbaum*.[132] This case settled the claim of a US national who was alleged to have been expropriated of his ownership interest in an Iranian architectural and engineering partnership named AFFA,[133] which had been liquidated by the state of Iran. The tribunal found that the ownership interests of Mr. Birnbaum were taken on the date the provisional manager appointed by the Iran authorities effectively took control of the company. The Iran–US CT explicitly declared that '[t]he Respondent's reasons and concerns for taking control of AFFA cannot relieve it from responsibility to compensate the Claimant for the taking', and that 'a government cannot avoid liability for compensation by showing that its actions were taken legitimately pursuant to its own laws'.[134]

4.3.2 Compensation and its Standard

Before the establishment of the Iran–US CT, *Sapphire International Petroleum* had recognised a full compensation standard comprising the loss suffered (*damnum emergens*) and the profit lost (*lucrum cessans*).[135] This distinction has been rightly criticised in doctrine, for the concepts of *damnum emergens* and *lucrum cessans* stem from the law of damages, and not from the law of expropriation.[136] For the Iran–US CT, the distinction between lawful and unlawful takings was relevant in relation to the restitution of the expropriated property.[137] The tribunal, however, could not ensure specific performance, and was therefore normally reluctant to grant this remedy to the affected claimant.[138] This reluctance also reflected, as Brower and Brueschke explain, 'the customary practice that restitution is generally available only where the taking is found to be unlawful and the fact that the Tribunal [...] never found Iran's taking of American property to have been unlawful'.[139] The 1955 Iran–US Treaty of Amity, Economic Relations, and Consular Rights (Iran–USA FCN) established the applicable standard of compensation for lawful takings of nationals of either country, in the territory of the other. In a clear reference to the Hull Formula, Article IV paragraph 2 of this treaty provided that the property of these nationals:

> shall not be taken except for a public purpose, nor shall it be taken without the prompt payment of just compensation. Such compensation shall be in an effectively realizable form and shall represent the full equivalent of the property taken; and adequate provision shall have been made at or prior to the time of taking for the determination and payment thereof.[140]

The tribunal did not restrict its analysis to this provision. Numerous awards and separate opinions of several judges also addressed the issue of the standard of compensation in customary international law. John Westberg points out that one of the reasons for this situation was the Iranian challenge to the validity of the treaty in some early disputes:

> Choosing in these cases to avoid the question of the Treaty's status, the Tribunal ruled the question irrelevant on reasoning that the treaty provisions

on compensation were synonymous with the requirements of customary international law.[141]

The first award to do so was *ITT*. Judge Aldrich's concurring opinion to this decision concluded that the applicable rules of customary international law were not significantly different from those of the treaty: '[i]n either case, a taking of property must be accompanied by the prompt payment of just compensation which is effective and adequate to compensate fully for the value of the property taken'.[142] Judge Aldrich made express reference to the *Norwegian Shipowners* claim and *Chorzow Factory* case. His position was later confirmed by *American International*, *TAMS, Phelps Dodge, SEDCO, Sola Tiles* and *Petrolane*.[143] The standard of appropriate compensation was only applied exceptionally by the Iran–US CT in *Ebrahimi*.[144] But even in this case, the amount actually awarded to the claimants could reasonably be considered full compensation.[145]

The duty to compensate both expropriations and nationalisations was explicitly acknowledged in the *INA* case. In this award, the tribunal affirmed that nationalisations 'are not *per se* unlawful' and that a lawful one would also 'impose on the government concerned the obligation to pay compensation'.[146] The tribunal then applied the treaty standard, which it considered to be similar to that of customary international norms. The Iran–US CT went on to declare *obiter* that, regarding lawful large-scale nationalisations, international law had undergone a 'gradual reappraisal, the effect of which may be to undermine the doctrinal value of any "full" or "adequate" (when used as identical to "full") compensation standard'.[147] This declaration triggered separate opinions by Judges Gunnar Lagergren and Howard Holtzmann. The former argued that international law recognised a flexible standard allowing for partial compensation in cases of large-scale nationalisations; the latter was emphatic in denying this change in the law.[148] *INA*'s approach was not followed by other decisions.[149]

In conformity with the case-law of the Iran–US CT, the standard of full compensation was generally applicable not only for expropriations and nationalisations, but also for lawful and unlawful takings.[150] Regarding expropriations that involved contract rights, the tribunal found that the valuation should also take into account the legitimate expectations of the foreign investor.[151] Moral damage was excluded from the tribunal's jurisdiction, limited *ratione materiae* to strictly economic loss.[152] The tribunal did not award punitive damages, not even when the expropriation was considered unlawful under customary international law.[153] *Amoco* was the sole award of the Iran–US CT to depart from the otherwise uniformly applied principle of full compensation.[154] In this case, the tribunal concluded that the taking was lawful and that the Iran–USA FCN's requirement of compensation was applicable. Nevertheless, it sought the aid of customary rules for interpreting and implementing this condition, and embarked on an extensive analysis of the *Chorzow Factory* case. The analysis led the Iran–US CT to conclude that compensation for a lawful taking only includes the value of the expropriated property – in other words, *damnum emergens*, but not *lucrum cessans*. An unlawful taking, on the other hand, would require both.[155]

According to Pellonpää and Fitzmaurice, the tribunal in *Amoco* equated *damnum emergens* to the going concern value of the company taken, with 'a somewhat broad meaning, also encompassing elements (notably "commercial prospects") which also might be argued to fall under *lucrum cessans*'.[156] In his concurring opinion to this award, Judge Brower considered the tribunal's finding to be 'a misreading of *Chorzow Factory* and a misunderstanding of economics'.[157] He argued that the PCIJ's case presented a simple scheme: lawful takings would entitle the claimant to *damnum emergens* and *lucrum cessans*, while unlawful expropriations to restitution of the property taken or, if this is impossible or impracticable, to damages equal to *damnum emergens* and *lucrum cessans*, plus any consequential damages.[158] *Amoco*'s conclusions were rejected implicitly in *Starrett* and explicitly in *Phillips*.[159] In this last case, the tribunal declared that the distinction between lawful and unlawful expropriation under customary international law, as evidenced in the *Chorzow Factory* case:

> is relevant only to two possible issues: whether restitution of the property can be awarded and whether compensation can be awarded for any increase in the value of the property between the date of taking and the date of the judicial or arbitral decision awarding compensation. The Chorzow decision provides no basis for any assertion that a lawful taking requires less compensation than that which is equal to the value of the property on the date of taking.[160]

For cases involving other measures affecting property rights, the Iran–US CT followed the standard established in *Amoco* for lawful expropriations. This is, *damnum emergens*, but not *lucrum cessans*.[161] Full compensation was, thus, not applied in these cases.[162] The different standard established for 'other measures' allowed the Iran–US CT to find an interference with the foreign investor's right of property in those cases where its members were reluctant to grant the claimant full compensation. As Aldrich explains, it was questionable:

> whether either the Foremost or the Kodak award would have rejected liability for a taking or deprivation of property rights if the Claims Settlement Declaration had not permitted the Tribunal to give the claimants partial compensation under the guise of compensation for 'other measures affecting property rights'.[163]

He then adds:

> Certainly, it was my impression that Judges Lagergren and Virally, the chairmen of the Tribunal chambers for Foremost and Kodak, respectively, generally sought what they considered to be equitable results and were not always comfortable with the full compensation standard that the 1955 Treaty of Amity between the United States and Iran made applicable to all takings of property rights.[164]

4.4 CONCLUSION

The Iran–US CT's interpretation of the protection against expropriation and other measures affecting property rights, established in its constitutive treaty, acknowledges the traditional international minimum standard of treatment. It is not unusual to find references in the tribunal's decisions to customary international law and statements of international claims commissions, the PCIJ, arbitral tribunals and the ICJ, regarding the expropriation of foreign property. The Iran–US CT recognised the three conditions for a lawful taking. The broad interpretation given to the requirements of public purpose and non-discrimination gave host-states a wide margin of appreciation at the moment of adopting regulatory measures, similar to that enjoyed by the parties of the European Convention on Human Rights. The Iran–US CT presumed that these two conditions had been fulfilled every time the correspondent government asserted that the respective measure was adopted in the general interest of the national community, on a non-discriminatory basis. As to other measures affecting property rights, the tribunal considered this phrase to include not only measures within the scope of the concept of expropriation, but also other acts and omissions that seriously and unreasonably interfered with the property of an alien. Irreversible deprivative consequences, similar to those arising out of a taking, were generally required. The Iran–US CT supported its 'other measures' findings on the notion of other interferences found in Article 1 of the First Optional Protocol to the European Convention on Human Rights.

Most of the cases brought before the Iran–US CT involved claims of creeping or constructive expropriations. This situation made the determination of the date of the taking difficult. The tribunal's solution consisted in establishing, on a case-by-case basis, the moment at which the interference had ripened into a more or less irreversible deprivation of property. A finding on expropriation also depended on the circumstances that surrounded the respective claim. The threshold applied by the tribunal was that of a non-ephemeral and unreasonable interference, depriving the owner of the effective use and control of his/her/its property. In other words, the moment when the foreign investor's fundamental rights of ownership were rendered so useless that they must be deemed to have been taken. According to the tribunal, any expropriation – whether formal or informal – required the determination that a taking, transfer or distribution of the property by the host-state had occurred, and that the owner had been denied the use of its investment. In cases of expropriation of companies and business operations, these conditions were replaced by the host-state's irreversible control of the respective entity and the deprivative consequences of this control over the property of the foreigner. Almost without exception, the Iran–US CT upheld the effects rule and concluded that the intention of the state is less important than the consequence of the measure. National authorities are therefore liable to compensate an expropriated foreign investor whether the respective measure was motivated by worthy economic or social objectives or not. The tribunal occasionally recognised a police-powers exception, but from an effects perspective. It acknowledged that a state is not liable for economic injury as a consequence of *bona fide* regulation, within their accepted regulatory powers. However, if this regulation damages the alien's property to a substantial and excessive degree, then the host-state will have to pay compensation.

In the case-law of the Iran–US CT, only unlawful takings required the restitution of property. The term 'just compensation' of the Iran–USA FCN was generally understood as equivalent to the full value of the expropriated property. The Iran–US CT found this standard of full compensation to be similar to that of customary international law, and applied it in a majority of the cases of expropriations and nationalisations, either lawful or unlawful. Aliens affected by other measures received a lower amount. This different standard enabled the tribunal to compensate a foreign investor for a lesser interference, in those situations where the measure was not tantamount to a taking. In this way, the Iran–US CT was able to fulfil its purpose, within its jurisdiction: to successfully settle cases involving expropriation and other measures affecting property rights of Iranian and US nationals.

NOTES

1. Persian for 'monarch', the title of former Iranian rulers.
2. Persian for 'supreme leader', currently the highest political and religious authority in Iran.
3. G Aldrich, *The Jurisprudence of the Iran–United States Claims Tribunal* (1996), 171. *See* C Brower, 'Current Developments in the Law of Expropriation and Compensation: A Preliminary Survey of Awards of the Iran–United States Claims Tribunal', (1987) 21/3 *IL* 639, at 641–3; or Brower and Brueschke (1998), 369–72.
4. *See* S Riesenfeld and D Caron, 'United States–Iran Agreement of January 19, 1981 (Hostages and Financial Agreements)', in R Bernhardt (ed.), *EPIL* (2000), Vol. 4, at 1218–19. *See also United States Diplomatic and Consular Staff in Tehran case* (USA v. Iran), ICJ, Provisional Measures, 15 December 1979, (1979) *ICJ Rep.* 7; and *United States Diplomatic and Consular Staff in Tehran case* (USA v. Iran), ICJ, Judgment, 24 May 1980, (1980) *ICJ Rep.* 3.
5. *See* Riesenfeld and Caron (2000), 1218–19.
6. Declaration of the Government of the Democratic and Popular Republic of Algeria concerning the Settlement of Claims by the Government of the United States of America and the Government of the Islamic Republic of Iran, (1983) 1 *Iran–US CTR 9*, or (1981) 20 *ILM* 231. Also available at http://www.iusct.org/claims-settlement.pdf (last visited 30 June 2013). Besides the Claims Settlement Declaration, the Algiers Accords consisted of three political agreements and two technical ones. *See* Brower (1987), 640; and Riesenfeld and Caron (2000), 1219.
7. D Müller, 'Other Specific Regimes of Responsibility: The Iran–US Claims Tribunal', in J Crawford, A Pellet and S Olleson (eds.), *The Law of International Responsibility* (2010), 844.
8. Müller (2010), 844.
9. J Westberg, 'Applicable Law, Expropriatory Takings and Compensations in Cases of Expropriation: ICSID and Iran – United States Claims Tribunal Case Law Compared', (1993) 8/1 *ICSID Rev.* 1, at 5–6 & 8–10.
10. *See Norwegian Shipowners* (Norway v. USA), Anderson, Vogt and Valloton, arbitrators, Award, 13 October, 1922, (1922) 1 *RIAA* 307, at 325; *Factory at Chorzow case* (Germany v. Poland), PCIJ, Judgment, 25 May 1926, (1926) *PCIJ Rep.* Series A No 7, at 44; and *Oscar Chinn* (UK v. Belgium), PCIJ, Judgment, 12 December, 1934, (1934) *PCIJ Rep.* Series A/B No 63, at 88. *See also* A Reinisch, 'Expropriation', in P Muchlinski, F Ortino and C Schreuer (eds.), *The Oxford Handbook of International Investment Law* (2008), 411–14.
11. *Starrett Housing Corporation, Starrett Systems, Inc., Starrett Housing International, Inc., v. The Government of the Islamic Republic of Iran et al*, Iran–US CT, Interlocutory Award No. ITL 32-24-1, 19 December 1983, (1985) 4 *Iran–US CTR* 122, at 156–7.
12. *Starrett Housing Corporation, Starrett Systems, Inc., Starrett Housing International, Inc., v. The Government of the Islamic Republic of Iran et al*, Iran–US CT, Final Award No. ITL 314-24-1, 14 August 1987, (1988) 16 *Iran–US CTR* 122, at 230. *See also Phillips Petroleum Company Iran v. The Islamic Republic of Iran and The National Iranian Oil Company*, Iran–US CT, Award No. 425-39-2, 29 June 1989, (1990) 21 *Iran–US CTR* 79, at 115.
13. *See SEDCO, Inc., and Sediran Drilling Company v. National Iranian Oil Company, and The Islamic Republic of Iran*, Iran–US CT, First Interlocutory Award No ITL 55-129-3, 28 October 1985, (1987) 9 *Iran–US CTR* 248, at 277.

14. *See Foremost Tehran, Inc. et al v. The Government of the Islamic Republic of Iran et al*, Iran–US CT, Award No. 220-37/231-1, 11 April 1986, (1987) 10 *Iran–US CTR* 228, at 244–50.
15. *See Thomas Earl Payne v. The Government of the Islamic Republic of Iran*, Iran–US CT, Award No. 245-335-2, 8 August 1986, (1988) 12 *Iran–US CTR* 3, at 7–11. *See also* Brower and Brueschke (1998), 374–5.
16. *Amoco International Finance Corporation v. The Government of the Islamic Republic of Iran et al*, Iran–US CT, Partial Award No. 310-56-3, 14 July 1987, (1988) 15 *Iran–US CTR* 189, at 220.
17. *See Manuchehr Haddadi v. The United States of America*, Iran–US CT, Award No 162-763-3, 31 January 1985, (1987) 8 *Iran–US CTR* 20, at 22. *See also Jack Rankin v. The Islamic Republic of Iran*, Iran–US CT, Award No 326-10913-2, 3 November 1987, (1988) 17 *Iran–US CTR* 135, at 148.
18. A Mouri, *The International Law of Expropriation as Reflected in the Work of the Iran-U.S. Claims Tribunal* (1994), 88. *See ibid.*, 66–9.
19. Westberg, (1993), 15; and G Aldrich, 'What Constitutes a Compensable Taking: The Decisions of the Iran–United States Claims Tribunal', (1994) 88/4 *AJIL* 585, at 589; or Aldrich (1996), 178.
20. *Eastman Kodak Company, Eastman Kodak International Sales Co., and Kodak Inc. v. The Government of Iran et al*, Iran–US CT, Partial Award No. 329-227/12384-3, 11 November 1987, Concurring and Dissenting Opinion of Judge Brower, (1988) 17 *Iran–US CTR* 153, at 173 & 181.
21. *Tippets, Abbett, McCarthy, Stratton* (TAMS) *v. TAMS-AFFA Consulting Engineers of Iran, The Government of the Islamic Republic of Iran et al,* Iran–US CT, Award No. 141-7-2, 29 June 1984, (1986) 6 *Iran–US CTR* 219, at 225.
22. *TAMS,* Iran–US CT, Award, 29 June 1984, at 225.
23. *See* Mouri (1994), 70–99; and Brower and Brueschke (1998), 376–83.
24. *See e.g. American International Group, Inc. and American Life Insurance Company v. Islamic Republic of Iran and Central Insurance of Iran*, Iran–US CT, Award No 93-2-3, 19 December 1983, (1985) 4 *Iran–US CTR* 96; or *Amoco International Finance Corporation v. The Government of the Islamic Republic of Iran et al*, Iran–US CT, Partial Award No 310-56-3, 14 July 1987, (1988) 15 *Iran–US CTR* 189.
25. *See* Brower and Brueschke (1998), 377–8. *See also* M Brunetti, 'The Iran-United States Claims Tribunal, NAFTA Chapter 11, and the Doctrine of Indirect Expropriation', (2001) 2/1 *Chic. JIL* 203, at 205.
26. Brower and Brueschke (1998), 383.
27. Mouri (1994), 172–4. *See e.g. SEDCO, Inc., v. National Iranian Oil Company and The Islamic Republic of Iran*, Iran–US CT, Award No. 309-129-3, 7 July 1987, (1988) 15 *Iran–US CTR* 23, at 29; and *Component Builders, Inc., Wood Components Co. and Moshofsky Enterprises v. The Islamic Republic of Iran, Bank Maskan Iran and Insurance Company of Iran*, Iran–US CT, Award No. 431-395-3, 10 August 1989, (1991) 23 *Iran–US CTR* 3, at 25–7.
28. Brower and Brueschke (1998), 380.
29. The tribunal had jurisdiction over claims and counterclaims that were outstanding on 19 January 1981. Art. II, para. 1, of the Claims Settlement Declaration.
30. Brower and Brueschke (1998), 430–1.
31. *International Technical Products Corporation and ITP Export Corporation v. The Government of Islamic Republic of Iran et al*, Iran–US CT, Award No. 196-302-3, 24 October 1985, (1987) 9 *Iran–US CTR* 206, at 240–1.
32. *Ibid.*, at 240.
33. *See e.g. International Systems & Controls Corporation v. The Islamic Republic of Iran et al*, Iran–US CT, Award No. 256-439-2, 26 September 1986, (1988) 12

Iran–US CTR 239, at 263; and *Reza Said Malek v. The Government of the Islamic Republic of Iran*, Iran–US CT, Award No. 534-193-3, 11 August 1992, (1996) 28 *Iran–US CTR* 246, at 288–9.
34. Mouri (1994), 67–8; and Brower and Brueschke (1998), 379. *See* S Montt, *State Liability in Investment Treaty Arbitration: Global Constitutional and Administrative Law in the BIT Generation* (2009), 200.
35. *See e.g. Schering Corporation v. The Islamic Republic of Iran*, Iran–US CT, Award No. 122-38-3, 16 April 1984, (1985) 5 *Iran–US CTR* 361, at 367; and *Alfred L.W. Short v. The Islamic Republic of Iran*, Iran–US CT, Award No. 312-11135-3, 14 July 1987, (1988) 16 *Iran–US CTR* 76, at 78–9. *Cf. Lillian Byrdine Grimm v. The Islamic Republic of Iran*, Iran–US CT, Award No. 25-71-1, 22 February 1983, (1984) 2 *Iran–US CTR* 78, at 79; and *International Systems & Controls Corporation v. The Islamic Republic of Iran et al*, Iran–US CT, Award No. 256-439-2, 26 September 1986, (1988) 12 *Iran–US CTR* 239, at 263–4. *See* Mouri (1994), 119–29.
36. Mouri (1994), 129.
37. V Heiskanen, 'The Contribution of the Iran–United States Claims Tribunal to the Development of the Doctrine of Indirect Expropriation', (2003) 5/3 *FORUM* 176, at 179; and V Heiskanen, 'The Doctrine of Indirect Expropriation in Light of the Practice of the Iran-United States Claims Tribunal', (2007) 8/2 *JWIT* 215, at 219.
38. *See TAMS*, Iran–US CT, Award, 29 June 1984.
39. Aziz Farmanfarmaian & Associates.
40. *TAMS*, Iran–US CT, Award, 29 June 1984, at 225.
41. *See Foremost Tehran, Inc. et al v. The Government of the Islamic Republic of Iran et al*, Iran–US CT, Award No. 220-37/231-1, 11 April 1986, (1987) 10 *Iran–US CTR* 228.
42. Sherkat Sahami Labaniat Pasteurize Pak.
43. Exceptionally, the stock dividend declared in 1980 was distributed to Foremost too.
44. *Foremost Tehran*, Iran–US CT, Award, 11 April 1986, at 224.
45. *See ibid.*, at 251–2.
46. *See Sporrong and Lönnroth v. Sweden*, Eur. Court HR, Series A No. 52, Judgment, 23 September 1982.
47. Rangiran Photographic Services Co. *See Eastman Kodak Company, Eastman Kodak International Sales Co. and Kodak (Near East) Inc. v. The Government of Iran et al*, Iran–US CT, Partial Award No. 329-227/12384-3, 11 November 1987, (1988) 17 *Iran–US. CTR* 153.
48. *Eastman Kodak*, Iran–US CT, Partial Award, 11 November 1987, at 169.
49. *Ibid.*
50. *See Rouhollah Karubian v. The Government of the Islamic Republic of Iran*, Iran–US CT, Award No. 569-419-2, 6 March 1996, (1996) 32 *Iran–US CTR* 3.
51. *Ibid.*, paras. 137 & 140–5.
52. *See* Brower and Brueschke (1998), 378–9.
53. Brunetti (2001), 205.
54. *Harza Engineering Company v. The Islamic Republic of Iran,* Iran–US CT, Award No. 19-98-2, 30 December 1982, (1983) 1 *Iran–US CTR* 499, at 504.
55. *Ataollah Golpira v. The Islamic Republic of Iran*, Iran–US CT, Award No. 32-211-2, 29 March 1983, (1984) 2 *Iran–US CTR* 171, at 177; and *International Technical Products Corporation and ITP Export Corporation v. The Government of Islamic Republic of Iran et al*, Iran–US CT, Award No. 196-302-3, 24 October, 1985, (1987) 9 *Iran–US CTR* 206, at 238–9.
56. *Starrett Housing Corporation, Starrett Systems, Inc., Starrett Housing International, Inc., v. The Government of the Islamic Republic of Iran et al*, Iran–US CT, Interlocutory Award No. ITL 32-24-1, 19 December 1983, (1985) 4 *Iran–US CTR* 122, at 154. *See Foremost Tehran, Inc. et al v. The Government of the Islamic*

Republic of Iran et al, Iran–US CT, Award No. 220-37/231-1, 11 April 1986, (1987) 10 *Iran–US CTR* 228, at 244.
57. *TAMS*, Iran–US CT, Award, 29 June 1984, at 225. *See Phelps Dodge Corp. and Overseas Private Investment Corp. v. The Islamic Republic of Iran*, Iran–US CT, Award No. 217-99-2, 19 March 1986, (1987) 10 *Iran–US CTR* 121, at 130.
58. Brower and Brueschke (1998), 378.
59. *Constantine A. Gianoplus v. The Government of the Islamic Republic of Iran*, Iran–US CT, Award No. 237-314-1, 20 June 1986, (1988) 11 *Iran–US CTR* 217, at 221. *See Starrett Housing Corporation, Starrett Systems, Inc., Starrett Housing International, Inc., v. The Government of the Islamic Republic of Iran et al*, Iran–US CT, Interlocutory Award No. ITL 32-24-1, 19 December 1983, (1985) 4 *Iran–US CTR* 122, at 156.
60. *See* H Sedigh, 'What Level of Host State Interference Amounts to a Taking under Contemporary International Law', (2001) 2/2 *JWIT* 631, at 644–6.
61. Brower (1987), 644.
62. Brower and Brueschke (1998), 440. *See* M Pellonpää and M Fitzmaurice, 'Taking of Property in the Practice of the Iran–United States Claims Tribunal', (1988) 19 *Neth. YIL* 53, at 85.
63. Sedigh (2001), 682.
64. Mouri (1994), 88.
65. *See ibid*., 89–99.
66. Pellonpää and Fitzmaurice (1988) 86; and Brower and Brueschke (1998), 434. *See American Bell International, Inc., v. The Islamic Republic of Iran et al*, Iran–US CT, Award No. 255-48-3, 19 September 1986, (1988) 12 *Iran–US CTR* 170, at 214–15; and *Kenneth P. Yeager v. The Islamic Republic of Iran*, Iran–US CT, Partial Award No. 324-10199-1, 2 November 1987, (1988) 17 *Iran–US CTR* 92, at 108–9. *See also* Brower and Brueschke (1998), 384–91.
67. *See Oil Field of Texas, Inc., v. The Government of the Islamic Republic of Iran and National Iranian Oil Company*, Iran–US CT, Award No. 258-43-1, 8 October 1986, (1988) 12 *Iran–US CTR* 308, at 318.
68. *Dames & Moore v. The Islamic Republic of Iran et al*, Iran–US CT, Award No. 97-54-3, 20 December 1983, (1985) 4 *Iran–US CTR* 212, at 223.
69. *See William L. Pereira Associates v. Islamic Republic of Iran*, Iran–US CT, Award No. 116-1-3, 19 March 1984, (1985) 5 *Iran–US CTR* 198; *Computer Sciences Corporation v. The Government of the Islamic Republic of Iran et al*, Iran–US CT, Award No. 221-65-1, 16 April 1986, (1987) 10 *Iran–US CTR* 269; *Sola Tiles, Inc., v. The Government of the Islamic Republic of Iran*, Iran–US CT, Award No. 298-317-1, 22 April 1987, (1988) 14 *Iran–US CTR* 223; and *Leonard and Mavis Daley v. The Islamic Republic of Iran*, Iran–US CT, Award No. 360-10514-1, 20 April 1988, (1989) 18 *Iran–US CTR* 232.
70. Mouri (1994), 94. *See* Brower and Brueschke (1998), 394–410.
71. *ITT Industries, Inc., v. The Islamic Republic of Iran and The Organisation of Nationalised Industries of Iran*, Iran US CT, Award on Agreed Terms No. 47-156-2, 26 May 1983, Concurring Opinion of Judge Aldrich, (1984) 2 *Iran–US CTR* 348, at 351–2.
72. *See e.g. TAMS*, Iran–US CT, Award, 29 June 1984, at 225.
73. *See Thomas Earl Payne v. The Government of the Islamic Republic of Iran*, Iran–US CT, Award No. 245-335-2, 8 August 1986, (1988) 12 *Iran–US CTR* 3, at 11; *Motorola, Inc., v. Iranian National Airlines Corporation and the Government of the Islamic Republic of Iran*, Iran–US CT, Award No. 373-481-3, 28 June 1988, (1989) 19 *Iran–US CTR* 73, at 85; and *James M. Saghi, Michael R. Saghi and Allan J.*

Saghi v. The Islamic Republic of Iran, Iran–US CT, Award No. 544-298-2, 22 January 1993, (2000) 29 *Iran–US CTR* 20, at 41 & 44–5. *See also* Sedigh (2001), 648–9.

74. Aldrich (1994), 592.
75. *SEDCO, Inc., and Sediran Drilling Company v. National Iranian Oil Company, and The Islamic Republic of Iran*, Iran–US CT, First Interlocutory Award No ITL 55-129-3, 28 October 1985, (1987) 9 *Iran–US CTR* 248, at 276–9.
76. Brower and Brueschke (1998), 398.
77. Aldrich (1996), 187.
78. *See Motorola, Inc., v. Iranian National Airlines Corporation and the Government of the Islamic Republic of Iran*, Iran–US CT, Award No. 373-481-3, 28 June 1988, (1989) 19 *Iran–US CTR* 73, at 85.
79. Aldrich (1996), 172.
80. Aldrich (1994), 589. *See e.g. Harold Birnbaum v. The Islamic Republic of Iran*, Iran–US CT, Award No. 549-967-2, 6 July 1993, (2000) 29 *Iran–US CTR* 260.
81. *See American Bell International, Inc., v. The Islamic Republic of Iran et al*, Iran–US CT, Award No. 255-48-3, 19 September 1986, (1988) 12 *Iran–US CTR* 170.
82. *See Oil Field of Texas, Inc., v. The Government of the Islamic Republic of Iran and National Iranian Oil Company*, Iran–US CT, Award No. 258-43-1, 8 October 1986, (1988) 12 *Iran–US CTR* 308, at 319.
83. *See United Painting, Inc., v. The Islamic Republic of Iran*, Iran–US CT, Award No. 458-11286-3, 20 December 1989, (1991) 23 *Iran–US CTR* 351.
84. *See Petrolane, Inc., Eastman Whipstock Manufacturing, Inc., and Seahorse Fleet, Inc., v. The Government of the Islamic Republic of Iran et al*, Iran–US CT, Award No. 518-131-2, 14 August, 1991, (1992) 27 *Iran–US CTR* 64.
85. *See Flexi-Van Leasing, Inc., v. The Government of the Islamic Republic of Iran*, Iran–US CT, Award No. 259-36-1, 13 October 1986, (1988) 12 *Iran–US CTR* 335.
86. Heiskanen, (2007), 224.
87. According to this provision:

    There is an internationally wrongful act of a State when conduct consisting of an action or omission:
    (a) is attributable to the State under international law; and
    (b) constitutes a breach of an international obligation of the State.

    On the question of attributability in the case-law of the Iran–US CT, *see* Brower (1987), 652–6; Pellonpää and Fitzmaurice (1988), 72–85; Aldrich (1994), 604–5; Aldrich (1996), 197–200 & 207–8; Brower and Brueschke (1998), 442–71; and Sedigh (2001), at 666–76.
88. *See e.g. Verney Rodney Pointon and Mary Lou Pointon v. The Government of the Islamic Republic of Iran*, Iran–US CT, Award No. 516-322-1, 23 July 1991, (1992) 27 *Iran–US CTR* 49.
89. *See Esahak Sabbonchian v. The Islamic Republic of Iran*, Iran–US CT, Award No. 524-313-2, 15 November 1991, (1992) 27 *Iran–US CTR* 248.
90. *See Seismograph Service Corporation and Compagnie Française de Prospection Sismique v. National Iranian Oil Company and The Islamic Republic of Iran*, Iran–US CT, Award No. 420-443-3, 31 March 1989, (1990) 22 *Iran–US CTR* 3. In this type of situation, the Iran–US CT sometimes awarded partial compensation under other measures affecting property rights.
91. *See Ataollah Golpira v. The Islamic Republic of Iran*, Iran–US CT, Award No. 32-211-2, 29 March 1983, (1984) 2 *Iran–US CTR* 171.
92. *See William L. Pereira Associates v. Islamic Republic of Iran*, Iran–US CT, Award No. 116-1-3, 19 March 1984, (1985) 5 *Iran–US CTR* 198.
93. Mouri (1994), 147.

94. *SEDCO, Inc., and Sediran Drilling Company v. National Iranian Oil Company, and The Islamic Republic of Iran*, Iran–US CT, First Interlocutory Award No ITL 55-129-3, 28 October 1985, (1987) 9 *Iran–US CTR* 248, at 275.
95. *Ibid.*, note 25 at 275.
96. *See Emanuel Too v. Greater Modesto Insurance Associates and the United States of America*, Iran–US CT, Award No. 460-880-2, 29 December 1989, (1991) 23 *Iran–US CTR* 378.
97. *Ibid.*, at 379.
98. *Emanuel Too*, Iran–US CT, Award, 29 December 1989, at 387. On the Third Restatement of the Foreign Relations Law of the United States, *see* Chapter 6 below.
99. *Emanuel Too*, Iran–US CT, Award, 29 December, 1989, at 387–8.
100. *Ibid.*, at 388.
101. *See Hood Corporation v. The Islamic Republic of Iran, Bank Markazi Iran and Bank Mellat*, Iran–US CT, Award No. 142-100-3, 13 July 1984, (1986) 7 *Iran–US CTR* 36.
102. Mouri (1994), 148.
103. *See* Brower and Brueschke (1998), 502–3.
104. *See* Pellonpää and Fitzmaurice (1988), 60–72; and Mouri (1994), 320–47.
105. *See e.g. American International Group, Inc., and American Life Insurance Company v. Islamic Republic of Iran and Central Insurance of Iran*, Iran–US CT, Award No 93-2-3, 19 December 1983, (1985) 4 *Iran–US CTR* 96, at 105.
106. *See* Chapter 3 above.
107. *Amoco International Finance Corporation v. The Government of the Islamic Republic of Iran et al*, Iran–US CT, Partial Award No 310-56-3, 14 July 1987, (1988) 15 *Iran–US CTR* 189, at 233.
108. Mouri (1994), note 968 at 325.
109. *Amoco*, Iran–US CT, Partial Award, 14 July 1987, at 233.
110. *Ibid.*
111. *Ibid.*
112. *American Independent Oil Co.* (AMINOIL) *v. Kuwait*, Reuter, Sultan and Fitzmaurice, arbitrators, Award, 24 March 1982, (1982) 21/4 *ILM* 976.
113. *Amoco*, Iran–US CT, Partial Award, 14 July 1987, at 225.
114. Pellonpää and Fitzmaurice (1988), 70.
115. *See* Mouri (1994), 311–19.
116. *Sea-Land Service, Inc., v. The Government of the Islamic Republic of Iran and Ports and Shipping Organization*, Iran–US CT, Award No 135-33-1, 22 June 1984, (1986) 6 *Iran–US CTR* 149, at 168.
117. *See Lena Goldfields, Ltd. v. Union of Soviet Socialist Republics*, Stutzer and Scott arbitrators, Award, 3 September 1930, reprinted in A Nussbaum, 'The Arbitration between the Lena Goldfields, Ltd. and the Soviet Government', (1950) *Corn. LQ* 31. *See* Mouri (1994), 315–19.
118. *See* Mouri (1994), 258–9.
119. Aldrich (1996), 173.
120. *ITT Industries, Inc., v. The Islamic Republic of Iran and The Organisation of Nationalised Industries of Iran*, Iran–US CT, Award on Agreed Terms No. 47-156-2, 26 May 1983, Concurring Opinion of Judge Aldrich, (1984) 2 *Iran–US CTR* 348, at 352.
121. *Starrett Housing Corporation, Starrett Systems, Inc., Starrett Housing International, Inc., v. The Government of the Islamic Republic of Iran et al*, Iran–US CT, Interlocutory Award No. ITL 32-24-1, 19 December 1983, (1985) 4 *Iran–US CTR* 122, at 154.

122. *See Sea-Land Service, Inc., v. The Government of the Islamic Republic of Iran and Ports and Shipping Organization*, Iran–US CT, Award No 135-33-1, 22 June 1984, (1986) 6 *Iran–US CTR* 149.
123. *Ibid.*, at 166.
124. *Oscar Chinn* (UK v. Belgium), PCIJ, Judgment, 12 December 1934, (1934) *PCIJ Rep.* Series A/B No 63, at 86.
125. *Sea-Land Service, Inc., v. The Government of the Islamic Republic of Iran and Ports and Shipping Organization*, Iran–US CT, Award No 135-33-1, 22 June 1984, Opinion of Judge Holtzmann, (1986) 6 *Iran–US CTR* 149, at 207.
126. Aldrich (1994), 603; or Aldrich (1996), 206–7.
127. *TAMS*, Iran–US CT, Award, 29 June 1984, at 225–6; and *Thomas Earl Payne v. The Government of the Islamic Republic of Iran*, Iran–US CT, Award No. 245-335-2, 8 August 1986, (1988) 12 *Iran–US CTR* 3, at 10–11.
128. *Phillips Petroleum Company Iran v. The Islamic Republic of Iran and The National Iranian Oil Company*, Iran–US CT, Award No. 425-39-2, 29 June 1989, (1990) 21 *Iran–US CTR* 79, at 115.
129. *See SEDCO, Inc., and Sediran Drilling Company v. National Iranian Oil Company, and The Islamic Republic of Iran*, Iran–US CT, First Interlocutory Award No ITL 55-129-3, 28 October 1985, (1987) 9 *Iran–US CTR* 248, at 274–5; and *Phelps Dodge Corp. and Overseas Private Investment Corp. v. The Islamic Republic of Iran*, Iran–US CT, Award No. 217-99-2, 19 March 1986, (1987) 10 *Iran–US CTR* 121, at 130.
130. *Phelps Dodge*, Iran–US CT, Award, 19 March 1986, at 130.
131. *Ibid.*
132. *See Harold Birnbaum v. The Islamic Republic of Iran*, Iran–US CT, Award No. 549-967-2, 6 July 1993, (2000) 29 *Iran–US CTR* 260.
133. Abdolaziz Farmanfarmaian & Associates.
134. *Harold Birnbaum*, Iran–US CT, Award, 6 July 1993, at 270.
135. *See Sapphire International Petroleum Ltd. v. National Iranian Oil Company*, Cavin, sole arbitrator, Award, 15 March 1963, (1967) 35 *ILR* 136. This was an arbitration between a Canadian firm and the National Iranian Oil Company, regarding the nationalisation of Iran's oil industry in 1952.
136. I Marboe, 'Compensation and Damages in International Law. The Limits of the "Fair Market Value"', (2006) 7/5 *JWIT* 723, at 728. *See* Chapter 5 below.
137. *Phillips Petroleum Company Iran v. The Islamic Republic of Iran and The National Iranian Oil Company*, Iran–US CT, Award No. 425-39-2, 29 June 1989, (1990) 21 *Iran–US CTR* 79, at 122.
138. Brower and Brueschke (1998), 476.
139. *Ibid.*, 476–7.
140. Available at http://www.parstimes.com/law/iran_us_treaty.html (last visited 30 June 2013).
141. J Westberg, 'Compensation in Cases of Expropriation and Nationalization: Awards of the Iran–United States Claims Tribunal', (1990) 5/2 *ICSID Rev.* 256, note 68 at 271.
142. *ITT Industries, Inc., v. The Islamic Republic of Iran and The Organisation of Nationalised Industries of Iran*, Iran–US CT, Award on Agreed Terms No. 47-156-2, 26 May 1983, Concurring Opinion of Judge Aldrich, (1984) 2 *Iran–US CTR* 348, at 354.
143. *See American International Group, Inc. and American Life Insurance Company v. Islamic Republic of Iran and Central Insurance of Iran*, Iran–US CT, Award No 93-2-3, 19 December 1983, (1985) 4 *Iran–US CTR* 96, at 102–6; *TAMS*, Iran–US CT, Award, 29 June 1984, at 225; *Phelps Dodge Corp. and Overseas Private Investment Corp. v. The Islamic Republic of Iran*, Iran–US CT, Award No. 217-99-2,

19 March 1986, (1987) 10 *Iran–US CTR* 121, at 132; *SEDCO, Inc., v. National Iranian Oil Company, and The Islamic Republic of Iran*, Iran–US CT, Second Interlocutory Award No ITL 59-129-3, 27 March 1986, (1987) 10 *Iran–US CTR* 180, at 189; *Sola Tiles, Inc., v. The Government of the Islamic Republic of Iran*, Iran–US CT, Award No. 298-317-1, 22 April 1987, (1988) 14 *Iran–US CTR* 223, at 234–7; and *Petrolane, Inc., Eastman Whipstock Manufacturing, Inc., and Seahorse Fleet, Inc., v. The Government of the Islamic Republic of Iran et al*, Iran–US CT, Award No. 518-131-2, 14 August 1991, (1992) 27 *Iran–US CTR* 64, at 99.

144. *See Shahin Shaine Ebrahimi, Cecilia Radene Ebrahimi and Christina Tandis Ebrahimi v. The Government of the Islamic Republic of Iran and National Iranian Oil Company*, Iran–US CT, Award No. 560-44/46/47-3, 12 October 1994, (1994) 30 *Iran–US CTR* 180, at 197–202.
145. Aldrich (1996), 238. *See* Brower and Brueschke (1998), 536; and Westberg, (1993), 15 & 16–18.
146. *INA Corporation, v. The Government of the Islamic Republic of Iran*, Iran–US CT, Award No. 184-161-1, 13 August 1985, (1987) 8 *Iran–US CTR* 373, at 378.
147. *INA Corporation*, Iran–US CT, Award, 13 August 1985, at 378.
148. *See* Westberg (1990), 273–5.
149. *See* Brower and Brueschke (1998), note 2326 at 491.
150. *See* Pellonpää and Fitzmaurice (1988), 126–7.
151. *See Mobil Oil Iran, Inc. et al v. The Islamic Republic of Iran and The National Iranian Oil Company*, Iran–US CT, Award No. 311-74/76/ 81/150-3, 14 July 1987, (1988) 16 *Iran–US CTR* 3; and *Phillips Petroleum Company Iran v. The Islamic Republic of Iran and The National Iranian Oil Company*, Iran–US CT, Award No. 425-39-2, 29 June 1989, (1990) 21 *Iran–US CTR* 79. *See also* Mouri (1994), 399–403
152. Müller (2010), 848.
153. *See e.g. Amoco International Finance Corporation v. The Government of the Islamic Republic of Iran et al*, Iran–US CT, Partial Award No. 310-56-3, 14 July 1987, (1988) 15 *Iran–US CTR* 189, at 248. *See also* Brower and Brueschke (1998), 477.
154. See *Amoco*, Iran–US CT, Partial Award, 14 July 1987.
155. *See ibid.*, at 214, 222–4, 244 & 246–52.
156. Pellonpää and Fitzmaurice (1988), 125.
157. *Amoco*, Iran–US CT, Partial Award, 14 July 1987, Concurring Opinion of Judge Brower, at 300.
158. *Ibid.*, at 300–1.
159. *See Starrett Housing Corporation, Starrett Systems, Inc., Starrett Housing International, Inc., v. The Government of the Islamic Republic of Iran et al*, Iran–US CT, Final Award No. ITL 314-24-1, 14 August 1987, (1988) 16 *Iran–US CTR* 122; and *Phillips Petroleum Company Iran v. The Islamic Republic of Iran and The National Iranian Oil Company*, Iran–US CT, Award No. 425-39-2, 29 June 1989, (1990) 21 *Iran US CTR* 79. *See also* Westberg (1990), 265–6; and Brower and Brueschke (1998), 506 & 512.
160. *Phillips Petroleum Company Iran v. The Islamic Republic of Iran and The National Iranian Oil Company*, Iran–US CT, Award No. 425-39-2, 29 June 1989, (1990) 21 *Iran–US CTR* 79, at 122.
161. Mouri (1994), 390.
162. *See* Aldrich (1994), 591; and Mouri (1994), 390.
163. Aldrich (1994), 591.
164. *Ibid.*.

5. Bilateral treaties and international awards

The first treaties to protect the property of aliens were FCNs, replaced in the late 1950s by BITs. A positive approach towards private property and foreign investment in third- and former second-world states during the last decades of the 20th century, led to the gradual establishment of a wide network of these treaties, originally concluded between developed and developing countries that needed funds or materials to boost their economies. BITs provide for an international minimum standard, comprising a protection against takings, fair and equitable treatment, full protection and security, most-favoured-nation treatment, and national treatment, among other commitments. This wide network of treaties includes today most of the formerly reluctant Latin American states, commonly associated with the Calvo doctrine, the principle of permanent sovereignty over natural resources, and the now dated NIEO.

BITs follow the three traditional conditions of a lawful expropriation – *i.e.*, public purpose, non-discrimination and compensation – normally adding a fourth requirement, due process of law. Property is called investment, and is broadly defined in these treaties. The conventional concept of investment is essential to the takings provision, for anything within its contours will be protected against deprivations. BITs mention direct and indirect expropriations as such, but give no definition of them, leaving the development of these notions to the case-law of international arbitral tribunals, established under the dispute settlement mechanism of these treaties. ICSID, UNCITRAL and *ad hoc* panels generally refer in their awards to other judicial decisions. The jurisprudence of the Iran–US CT is frequently relied upon, as well as that of international arbitral panels established under the dispute settlement provisions of investment codes, investment agreements, BITs and investment chapters of EIAs. Panels in investment treaty arbitration also refer to international human rights tribunals, particularly the European Court's case-law on deprivations of property. This process of mutual reference decisively shapes the judicial interpretation of BITs, affecting state practice as well.

The following pages analyse the protection against expropriation in bilateral treaties, as construed by international arbitral tribunals. It deals with FCNs and BITs, focusing on the latter. The conventional notions of investment and lawful expropriation are discussed in this chapter, which identifies and explains the substantial and permanent interference standard applied by arbitral panels in investment disputes to claims of indirect takings, generally from an effects standpoint. BIT arbitrations like *Wena Hotels*, *Middle East Cement*, *TECMED*, *Eureko*, *Saluka*, *ADC*, *Siemens*, *Aguas del Aconquija*, *Biwater Gauff*, *Rumeli*, *Saipem*, *Alpha Projektholding*, *Tza* and *Unglaube,* among others, are studied below.

5.1 FCN'S FAILURE, BIT'S SUCCESS

The 1785 Treaty of Amity and Commerce between Prussia and the USA, and the 1955 Treaty of Amity, Economic Relations and Consular Rights between Iran and the USA, are FCNs: the forerunners of BITs.[1] As these titles suggest, FCNs were mainly aimed at promoting trade and shipping, and only exceptionally included provisions protecting the property of aliens. This type of treaty was especially favoured by the USA, which concluded FCNs for almost two hundred years.[2] Throughout this time, the US government established a vast network of bilateral treaties with European and Latin American states, at first, and with countries of Asia and Africa, after the decolonisation process.

The investment provisions of early FCNs were limited to an absolute standard of treatment that guaranteed a 'special protection to the persons and property'[3] or a 'full and perfect protection for [...] persons and property'[4] of each contracting party. The first expropriation provisions of FCNs appeared in the late 19th century. They forbade the seizure of 'vessels, cargoes, merchandise and effects', belonging to nationals of the other party, without payment of 'equitable and sufficient compensation'.[5] This guarantee was later broadened to property in general.[6] During the first half of the 20th century, the requirement of due process was expressly included in the takings provision of FCNs.[7]

After the Second World War, the USA negotiated and concluded a new wave of FCNs aimed mainly at the protection of foreign investment. These treaties featured a detailed expropriation provision that guaranteed prompt, adequate and effective compensation.[8] By then, however, developing countries were no longer open to accepting the international minimum standard requested for US nationals abroad. A new bilateral treaty protecting investment was needed, and Europe would provide a blueprint for it.

5.1.1 *Ad Hoc* Investment Treaties

The Resolution on International Investment for Economic Development, adopted in 1955 by the parties to the General Agreement on Tariffs and Trade (GATT), urged for the conclusion of bilateral treaties providing for the protection and security of the property of aliens.[9] Following this resolution, Western European countries started to negotiate and conclude a new type of international agreement, dealing exclusively with foreign investment.[10] The theory of economic development behind BITs was different from that of FCNs. The latter relied on a simple idea, summarised by Michael Reisman and Robert Sloane in these terms:

> Merely put foreign investment into an underdeveloped economy, and, provided the host state refrains from expropriating the investment, it will generate a reasonable profit while the host state will experience the benefits of the multiplier effect.[11]

BITs require from the host-state much more than just refraining from taking the property of aliens. As Kenneth Vandevelde concludes, the purpose of this kind of international agreement is to reduce political risk by stabilising the favourable investment policy that exists in the respective state, at the time it enters into the corresponding treaty.[12] In other words, the aim of BITs is to develop a basic legal and administrative framework that promotes and protects aliens in host-states.[13] That is to say, to provide good governance for foreigners investing abroad.[14] The success of BITs was gradual, and the reason for their positive reception is not entirely clear. According to Jeswald Salacuse:

> it may lie in the fact that the European countries were less demanding than was the United States with respect to guarantees on such matters as free convertibility of local currency, abolition of performance requirements, and protection against expropriation. Moreover, the special relationship between European countries and their former colonies may have predisposed some newly independent nations to look favorably on concluding investment treaties with their previous colonial rulers.[15]

The good results of the European experience encouraged the USA to launch its own BIT programme in 1977.[16] Today, these treaties are one of the most important instruments for US investment abroad.[17] Vandevelde rightly notes:

> Whereas the FCN agreements had been concerned principally with establishing economic relations, the BITs were a defensive reaction to past expropriations of existing investments without payment of fair market value. In the

> United States in particular, the decision to negotiate BITs was very much motivated by a desire to create a network of treaties adopting the standard of prompt, adequate and effective compensation for expropriation, a standard that, among other things, required payment of fair market value. Indeed, the United States hoped that the conclusion of a sufficiently large network of treaties embracing that standard would provide evidence that the standard was a norm of customary international law and thus applied to expropriations even in the absence of a treaty. The United States therefore refused to conclude any BITs unless it adopted that standard explicitly. Establishing the principle of prompt, adequate and effective compensation was more important to the United States than obtaining protection for any specific asset of foreign investment.[18]

The starting point of BITs are models, prototypes or draft treaties designed by a developed state, generally on the basis of the failed 1967 Draft Convention on the Protection of Foreign Property, undertaken by the Organisation for Economic Co-operation and Development (OECD).[19] This explains the homogeneity of BITs. Besides takings, both the European and US models cover the same areas in similar terms: admission, treatment and dispute settlement.[20] The US model contains, however, more detailed rules than the European version. For example, unlike the latter, the treatment provisions of the US version cover the pre-establishment phase of the investment as well.[21] These differences are due to the fact that the US model has included, since its first version, a mixture of provisions taken from modern FCNs and European BITs.[22]

The titles in most BITs openly declare a duality of purposes that illustrates the complementary interests of capital-exporting and capital-importing states: the reciprocal encouragement or promotion of investments, and their protection.[23] The first objective was originally pursued by developing states. Since many third- and former second-world countries had poor records concerning the respect of the right of private property, BITs were an unambiguous sign addressed to the international society revealing a crucial transformation of the respective state's policy towards foreign investment.[24] Whether this goal has been achieved in practice is open to question.[25] The second purpose answered initially to the concerns of developed countries, who wanted to protect their investors from eventual abuses by host-states. An impartial device to settle controversies is an essential part of the protective purpose of BITs. Almost all of them include provisions regulating not only conflicts between the parties over the interpretation or application of the respective treaty, but also those disagreements between the foreign investor and the host-state over the observance of its provisions, known as investment disputes.

BITs normally refer these disputes to pre-existing arbitration rules, after a period of consultation between the parties.[26] The majority of these treaties make a reference to ICSID, an autonomous international organisation within the World Bank group that facilitates the settlement of investment disputes through conciliation and arbitration. The applicable procedural rules for these cases are those contained in its constitutive treaty, the 1965 Washington Convention.[27] Some BITs refer to arbitration under the rules of UNCITRAL, or to the Court of Arbitration of the International Chamber of Commerce (ICC).[28] *Ad hoc* arbitration is also a possibility, in certain situations.[29] All these mechanisms for the settlement of investment disputes are now available on the basis of the host-state's unilateral promise contained in treaties, and not on previous contracts with the aliens.[30] This is one of the biggest innovations in contemporary international law, but one that took some time before it was exercised by its main beneficiary: the foreign investor.[31]

Most BIT provisions are aimed at protecting investment, rather than promoting it. In these treaties, investment promotion is mainly a consequence of its protection.[32] Clear legal rules designed not only to replace local legislation and institutions, but also to prevent controversial international customs from arising, are regularly included in BITs as part of their protective purpose.[33] Ultimately aimed at guiding the interpretation of treaty provisions by arbitral panels, these rules have been included by traditional capital-exporting countries. As Vandevelde recalls, one of the main objectives of the US programme was to counter historical challenges to the Hull formula, which had gained momentum in the 1960s and 1970s.[34] More recently, following the experience of NAFTA and recent BIT arbitrations, the new US model has implicitly rejected the effects rule, allowing arbitral panels to apply a police-powers solution or even a proportionality test to expropriation claims.

This illustrates the ironic fate of bilateral treaties designed to protect foreign investors abroad. Notwithstanding their differences, FCNs and BITs share a common characteristic: unexpected consequences, in practice, for the interests of the capital-exporting state that supported their conclusion. While an FCN allowed the USA to exercise diplomatic protection on behalf of its nationals and bring an action against Italy before the ICJ in the *ELSI* case,[35] and another one provided the standard of compensation under which the expropriation claims were assessed in the Iran–US CT,[36] the FCN with Japan helped this country to gain access to the internal market and basic exemptions in the USA,[37] a further one was the basis of an action brought against the USA before the ICJ in the *Nicaragua* case,[38] and the FCN with Iran allowed this country to bring a claim against the USA before the ICJ in the *Oil Platforms* case.[39] As to

BITs, the same provisions designed to protect the investment of nationals of developed states in developing countries have been used to challenge sovereign regulatory measures adopted by the former, even by foreign investors of the latter.[40]

5.1.2 Lawful Takings under BITs

From the alien's point of view, the most important protection is the expropriation provision. All BITs contain an article on takings in a similar, if not identical, wording.[41] A lawful expropriation – one that is consistent with the treaty – requires a public purpose, a non-discriminatory basis, the payment of compensation to the deprived investor, and due process of law in the exercise of the host-state's expropriatory powers. The first BIT already considered these four conditions in its takings provision;[42] the latest have not been innovative on this issue.[43] Unfortunately, the distinction between lawful and unlawful expropriations is meaningless in practice – the same standard of compensation is applicable for both types of takings. The Iran–US CT generally made no difference between them at the moment of awarding compensation.[44] Neither do investment-dispute tribunals, who apply the Hull formula or similar standards, whether there is a breach of the respective treaty or not.[45]

BITs refer to the first requirement of a lawful taking as public 'purpose',[46] 'policy'[47] or 'interest',[48] among other denominations.[49] This undefined condition is aimed at preventing the host-state from adopting measures only for private reasons, not for the collective good.[50] Non-discrimination, the second requirement of a lawful expropriation, is normally included in BITs with no further qualification.[51] Both conditions may overlap at times, as Allahyar Mouri explains, since 'a taking which is not for a public purpose is to some extent discriminatory'.[52] In accordance with the Third Restatement of the Foreign Relations of the United States, the discrimination prohibited by international law implies unreasonable distinction.[53] This circumstance may be difficult to establish in practice. The crucial test will rest in the good faith of the state adopting the challenged measure.[54] Applied to expropriations, the rule on non-discrimination forbids a state from taking the property of nationals of a specific country or giving the deprived foreigner a differential treatment regarding the procedure and the amount of compensation.[55] The national and most-favoured-nation (MFN) treatment clauses in BITs, as well as the FET provision, reiterate this requirement of non-discrimination. Rudolf Dolzer and Margrete Stevens point out that the inclusion of this standard in the expropriation provision is 'presumably justified by the assumption that the treatment clauses refer to subsisting investments and that therefore these general clauses might no longer be applicable once an expropriatory measure has taken effect'.[56]

The third requirement of a lawful taking refers to the payment of compensation. The uncertainty over this standard in customary international law, derived from the long dispute between traditional capital-exporting and capital-importing states, led BITs to address the issue expressly.[57] A majority of these treaties subscribe to the Hull formula.[58] Almost all BITs concluded by Latin American states, for example, implicitly reject the 'appropriate' standard by incorporating a provision that requires the payment of compensation in terms of this formula.[59] The adoption of such a solution is done either by referring expressly to a 'prompt, adequate and effective' compensation;[60] by describing the compensation due in cases of expropriation in conformance with the meaning of this set of words;[61] or by including a different formula, like 'just' compensation, accompanied by a specific method of valuation that makes it similar, in practice, to Hull's.[62] There is no different standard for nationalisations than for expropriations.

Prompt does not mean immediate, but it does mean with no delay.[63] This term is generally used in BITs to resolve disputes on the amount of the compensation due. By adding this word, interests are considered implicitly included in its payment, accruing from the date of the taking.[64] Adequate is normally defined as 'market' or 'fair market' value before the expropriation took place.[65] 'Just', 'full', 'genuine' or 'real' are usually considered to indicate the same standard.[66] BITs hardly ever include an express regulation on the methods of calculation of this value.[67] Effective means in a form usable by the foreign investor, *i.e.* in a freely convertible currency with no restrictions regarding its transfer.[68] In sum, the Hull standard requires the quick payment ('prompt') of the fair market value of the expropriated asset ('adequate'), in a convertible currency ('effective').[69]

The fourth requirement of a lawful taking is due process, a concept which derives from the Fifth and Fourteenth Amendments to the 1778 Constitution of the USA,[70] but is used in BITs of other countries as well: in fact, nearly all of these treaties include the requirement.[71] Due process of law refers to the expropriation procedure, and imports an *obligation de moyens*, rather than an *obligation de résultat*, thus requiring the host-state to adopt a particular course of conduct.[72] As Andrew Newcombe and Lluís Paradell indicate, this condition may be breached in a variety of ways, which include the failure of prior notice or a fair hearing before the taking occurs.[73] Some BITs add that the expropriatory measures should be taken 'under domestic legal procedures' or 'in a legally established manner'.[74] According to Dolzer and Stevens, due process also suggests that the measure must be adopted by an unbiased official after a reasonable period of time.[75] In some BITs, this requirement involves the availability of judicial review for the expropriation.[76]

Against the background of a large number of homogenous treaties, the question of the influence of BITs on the customary law of expropriation has been asked several times. In doctrine, the positions range from those considering BITs to evidence international customs,[77] to those denying these treaties any evidentiary character of customary law.[78] The geographical scope of BITs, comprising both developed and developing states, strongly supports the first of these views today. EIAs, widely concluded in the last years, corroborate this conclusion.[79] Apparently, developed states have been successful in confirming a general distinction between lawful and unlawful expropriations based in at least three requirements – public purpose, non-discrimination, and the payment of compensation in conformity with the Hull formula. Outside international investment law, the 'appropriate' compensation standard is still relevant, for example in the case-law of the European Court of Human Rights on nationalisations.[80]

5.2 AIMING AT THE CASE-LAW

The investment and expropriation provisions necessarily interact with each other. A measure may or may not amount to a taking, depending on how property is defined in the corresponding treaty. BITs normally include a general definition of investment, followed by an open-ended list of examples that acknowledges the dynamic nature of the concept of property in international law.[81] These treaties have recognised, since the early 1960s, the well-accepted principle of law that an expropriation may materialise in a direct or indirect form.[82] Treaty-law often refers to takings as 'expropriations', 'nationalisations' or state actions that have an 'effect equivalent to'[83] or are 'tantamount to'[84] an expropriation or a nationalisation. Phrases like these help in construing the respective provision on the problem of intent.[85] Occasionally, BITs refer to takings as 'deprivations' or 'dispossessions', and of a 'direct or indirect' character.[86]

The notion of property identifies the tangibles and intangibles to which the respective treaty applies. Lately, the uncertainty created by open-ended definitions of investment in BITs has prompted the USA and Canada to attach long and detailed lists of examples to their recent treaties.[87] Regarding the takings provision, the lack of a conventional concept of expropriation or nationalisation, and the general effect-approach to the question of intent in international case-law, have led last-generation US and Canadian BITs to outline the expropriatory measures included in this article, and their exceptions. A police-powers solution, not available in former versions of these treaties, is now implicitly suggested to those decision-makers called to settle investment disputes under the newest versions.[88]

5.2.1 The Expropriation of Investments

In the past, indirect or portfolio investment was not protected by customary international law. Any risk related to it was regarded as commercial, leaving the alien as solely responsible for the respective contingency. International legal customs, however, did protect FDI. Potential state interferences with it were considered political risks, enabling the state of the injured alien to claim the international responsibility of the wrongdoing state via diplomatic protection.[89] Today, BITs cover both portfolio investment and FDI. The ideologically charged notion of property, rarely mentioned in the sources of international law, is now referred to as investment in a large network of treaties, and defined in them.[90]

The concept of investment is found in those articles related to the scope of application of the BIT.[91] A general definition is normally followed by an exemplary list that includes movable and immovable property; interests in companies, such as shares, stocks and debentures; claims to money and titles to performance; intellectual property rights; and business concessions and similar rights.[92] The fact that the definition of investment in BITs is broad does not imply that foreign investors have an absolute right of entry under these treaties. Many BITs limit the benefits of their provisions to investments approved by their parties.[93] Others specify that an investment is covered only if it is made in accordance with the laws and regulations of the host-state.[94] Old treaties included a further qualification, referring to the moment of the investment.[95] Recent BITs offer protection to investments made after their entry into force, as well as those made before that time.[96]

The latest US BITs, for example, have an elaborate definition of investment: every asset that an alien owns or controls, directly or indirectly, which has characteristics such as the commitment of capital or other resources, the expectation of gain or profit, or the assumption of risk.[97] According to the exemplary list of these treaties, property may take the form of FDI or portfolio investment. This list includes a number of contracts, rights, authorisations, licenses or permits, the breach or withdrawal of which would constitute an expropriation. The same provision contains an explanatory footnote clarifying that the characterisation of licenses, permits or similar instruments as investments depends on the rights of the holder under domestic law.[98] This and other declarations are the result of the now abundant case-law on investment disputes.[99]

The state has a right to expropriate foreign investments, following certain conditions. What is not clear is when a regulatory measure becomes a compensable taking under international law. The tests applied by international tribunals to this question are inconsistent. The severity of the impact of the measure; the duration of the interference; the character of the governmental action; the respect for legitimate expectations; and the proportionality of the measure uneasily coexist in the case-law on expropriation.[100] In general, arbitral panels established under investment codes, investment agreements and BITs have applied the substantial and permanent interference standard, which excludes mere temporal restrictions on the alien's property from the concept of indirect takings. Some arbitral panels have privileged a legal approach in this respect, while others have focused on the economic result of the corresponding measure.[101]

The legal view relates to the state's interference with the ability of a foreign investor to use, enjoy and dispose of his/her/its property.[102] As the tribunal in *Biwater Gauff* said: '[a] substantial interference with rights may well occur without actually causing any economic damage which can be quantified in terms of due compensation'.[103] Why? Because 'the absence of economic loss or damage is primarily a matter of causation and quantum – rather than a necessary ingredient in the cause of action of expropriation itself'.[104] Several tribunals have complemented this rather theoretical approach with a more pragmatic solution, which stresses the economic effects of the measure. It is for this reason that the panels in *CME*; *Middle East Cement*; *Occidental*; *Telenor*; *Aguas del Aconquija*; *Parkerings-Compagniet*; *Tokios Tokelés*; *Alpha Projektholding*; *Nations Energy*'; and *Tza* referred to the impact of the challenged interference in the value of the claimant's investment.[105]

Normally, international arbitral panels will focus on the results of the respective measure and not on the intent of the government adopting it.[106] A police-powers solution has only exceptionally been endorsed in NAFTA and BIT arbitrations. The application of the effects rule has led the USA to add the following declaration in an annex to its latest BITs:

1. [The takings provision] is intended to reflect customary international law concerning the obligation of States with respect to expropriation.
2. An action or a series of actions by a Party cannot constitute an expropriation unless it interferes with a tangible or intangible property right or property interest in an investment.
3. [The takings provision] addresses two situations. The first is known as direct expropriation, where an investment is nationalized or otherwise directly expropriated through formal transfer of title or outright seizure.
4. The second situation addressed by [the takings provision] is known as indirect expropriation, where an action or series of actions by a Party has an effect equivalent to direct expropriation without formal transfer of title or outright seizure.
   (a) The determination of whether an action or series of actions by a Party, in a specific fact situation, constitutes an indirect expropriation, requires a case-by-case, fact-based inquiry that considers, among other factors:
      (i) the economic impact of the government action, although the fact that an action or series of actions by a Party has an adverse effect on the economic value of an investment, standing alone, does not establish that an indirect expropriation has occurred;
      (ii) the extent to which the government action interferes with distinct, reasonable investment-backed expectations; and
      (iii) the character of the government action.
   (b) Except in rare circumstances, non-discriminatory regulatory actions by a Party that are designed and applied to protect legitimate public welfare objectives, such as public health, safety, and the environment, do not constitute indirect expropriations.[107]

This annex confirms the broad concept of property normally found in treaty-law, and tries to avoid the type of debate that arose in NAFTA arbitrations in relation to the meaning of measures 'tantamount to nationalization or expropriation'.[108] By expressly declaring that the takings provision reflects customary international law, US drafters aim at more conservative interpretations in potential investment disputes. More important, this annex gives the international standard of treatment a particular national content: that developed by the US regulatory takings doctrine. It names the three factors put forward by the US Supreme Court in the *Penn Central* case for the determination of an indirect expropriation.[109] These factors are the economic impact of the measure, the interference with the investor's legitimate expectations, and the character of the governmental action.[110]

Even though US treaties refer to the economic impact of the measure, they expressly reject an effects solution. In fact, they openly adopt a wide police-powers exception for non-discriminatory regulatory measures aimed at public purposes, which can easily be interpreted as a police-powers rule.[111] The latest Canadian model follows the US approach in similar terms,[112] but not the newest British, Mexican or Swiss versions, to name just a few.[113] For instance, the Bahrain-Germany BIT explains its takings provision from a clear effects approach: '[a] claim of compensation shall [...] exist when, as a result of State intervention in the enterprise in which the investment is made, its economic substance is severely impaired'.[114] So far, only exceptionally have countries other than the USA and Canada included the declaration of the former in their treaties.[115]

5.2.2 Early Claims before Arbitral Panels

Investment disputes generally confirm the customary minimum standard of treatment which protects aliens from unlawful expropriations. Following the case-law of the PCIJ, the European Court of Human Rights, and the Iran–US CT, these awards adopt a traditional definition of property, including tangibles as well as intangibles.[116] According to investment arbitrations, both actions and omissions can lead to a finding of indirect expropriation. This conforms to the 2001 ILC's Articles on State Responsibility.[117] Early disputes, based on the settlement provisions of investment agreements concluded between a host-state and a foreigner, illustrate the nature of expropriatory measures and the interaction between the concepts of property and indirect takings. In *Benvenuti et Bonfant*, a series of actions and omissions of the Congolese authorities were considered to have the cumulative effect of a *de facto* expropriation of an Italian investor.[118] *Biloune* involved the development of a hotel resort complex in the city of Accra, Ghana, by the joint venture of a Syrian national and a governmental entity.[119] The tribunal concluded that the combination of the host-state's order to stop the work on the complex and its demolition, along with the arrest, detention and deportation of Mr. Biloune without the possibility of re-entry, prevented the foreign investor from pursuing an approved project, thus constituting a constructive expropriation of the foreign investor's contractual rights and the taking of the value of his interest in the joint venture.[120]

SPP is an early example of the application of an effects solution to an expropriation claim.[121] A Hong Kong corporation, owning a joint venture with the Egyptian authorities, wanted to develop two tourist complexes: one at the Pyramids area near Cairo, and another at Ras El Hekma, on the Mediterranean coast of Egypt. The Pyramids project encountered political opposition in Egypt, on the grounds that it posed a threat to undiscovered antiquities. As a result of a series of governmental decrees and resolutions, this project was cancelled. SPP initiated an arbitration before the ICC, relying on the dispute settlement clause of the investment agreement concluded with the host-state. The tribunal established Egypt's obligation to pay compensation to the claimant. The Egyptian authorities appealed the ICC award to the French *Cour d'Appel*, which annulled it for jurisdictional reasons. SPP then commenced arbitral proceedings under the Washington Convention relying on the dispute settlement provision of the Egyptian investment code. In its award, the ICSID tribunal recognised that the host-state's cancellation of the project to protect antiquities 'constituted a lawful exercise of the right of eminent domain'.[122] It added, nevertheless, that the rules of Egyptian and international law governing the exercise of this right impose an obligation to indemnify those affected by it, an obligation that 'applies equally where antiquities are involved'.[123] SPP was therefore granted compensation for the taking of its contractual rights in the joint venture as a consequence of the cancellation by the Egyptian authorities of the Pyramids project.[124]

Early BIT arbitrations relied on the international minimum standard of treatment as well, construing the relevant treaty provision from customary law. In *Goetz*, the panel concluded that the revocation of the French national's free zone benefits by the government of Burundi completely deprived the claimant of the utility of his investment, thus amounting to a measure having an effect similar to a taking.[125] A year later, the tribunal in *Wena Hotels* decided that the physical seizure of the assets of a British investor, by an Egyptian public company, amounted to a *de facto* expropriation.[126] Quoting the Iran–US CT (*TAMS*),[127] this panel found Egypt responsible for the 'non-ephemeral' deprivation of the alien's 'fundamental rights of ownership' derived from this seizure.[128] The tribunal agreed with *AMCO*'s assertion that 'a case of expropriation exists not only when a state takes over private property, but also when the expropriating state transfers ownership to another legal or natural person', and that a taking 'also exists merely by the state withdrawing the protection of its courts from the owner expropriated, and tacitly allowing a *de facto* possessor to remain in possession of the thing seized'.[129]

Although the transfer of property to the state adopting the measure has not been generally considered a necessary condition for finding an indirect taking, its appropriation constitutes *prima facie* proof of an expropriation.[130] Divergent interpretations of the concept of property can lead different tribunals to opposed findings, even when the awards are issued almost at the same time. This was the case in *Lauder* and *CME*.[131] Applying a restrictive view of the rights attached to property, the panel in *Lauder* found no taking.[132] Conversely, the tribunal in *CME* opted for a broad notion of investment, which included the income-producing potential of property rights, equating the destruction of the commercial value of the corresponding property to its deprivation.[133] *CME*'s solution is normally favoured in investment disputes. According to Jan Paulsson and Zachary Douglas, it exposes 'the limitations of a purely legal or formalistic concept of property [common in direct takings case-law] that is not sensitive to the economic rights or expectations associated with the property'.[134]

Middle East Cement is another early BIT arbitration where an indirect taking was found.[135] In this case, a Greek investor was allowed by decree to import and store cement in a quay near the El-Abadia Port in Suez, and to pack and dispatch it within the country. After some time, another decree of the Egyptian authorities prohibited certain imports of cement, directly affecting the alien's activity. The applicable BIT mentioned 'business concessions conferred by law or under contract' within its definition of investment. The tribunal had no doubt that licenses were included in this phrase, and had no problems in finding that the measure adopted by Egypt deprived the foreign investor of the use and benefit of its investment, even though it retained nominal ownership of the respective rights.[136]

5.3 THE QUESTION OF INTENT

Most panels in investment treaty arbitrations have followed the effects rule, awarding compensation for the effective deprivation of the foreign investor. In conformity with the case-law of these tribunals, host-states enjoy a wide margin of appreciation, similar to that recognised by the European Court of Human Rights and the Iran–US CT.[137] Arbitral panels will normally refrain from challenging the motives of national authorities. *Goetz*, for instance, stated that in the absence of manifest error, an international tribunal should not substitute its own judgment for the host-state's discretionary evaluation of the public purpose involved in the adoption of a particular measure.[138] Contradictions on this issue, however, are not uncommon, and they may even appear within a single judicial decision. In *Biloune*, the panel expressly declared that '[t]he motivations for the actions and omissions of Ghanaian governmental authorities are not clear[,] [b]ut the Tribunal need not establish those motivations to come to a conclusion in the case'.[139] Few lines later, the same panel implicitly refuted this effects approach by recognising a police-powers rule in the form of a broad exception worded in these terms:

> such prevention of [the foreign investor] from pursuing its approved project would constitute constructive expropriation of [the alien's] contractual rights in the project and, accordingly, the expropriation of the value of Mr Biloune's interest in [the company], unless the Respondents can establish by persuasive evidence sufficient justification for these events.[140]

Recently, some international tribunals established under BITs have decided to assess the public purpose claimed by the host-state. This tendency reflects the debate in the context of NAFTA, following a number of claims filed mostly against the USA and Canada. It also jeopardises the dominance of the effects rule in investment treaty arbitration.

5.3.1 Exceptions to an Approach

The clearest statement of the effects rule is found in *Santa Elena*, one of the few arbitrations that have dealt with a direct expropriation claim in recent years.[141] In this case, the tribunal made the following declaration:

> While an expropriation or taking for environmental reasons may be classified as a taking for a public purpose, and thus may be legitimate, the fact that the Property was taken for this reason does not affect either the nature or the measure of the compensation to be paid for the taking. That is, the purpose of protecting the environment for which the Property was taken does not alter the legal character of the taking for which adequate compensation must be paid. The international source of the obligation to protect the environment makes no difference.
>
> Expropriatory environmental measures – no matter how laudable and beneficial to society as a whole – are, in this respect, similar to any other expropriatory measures that a state may take in order to implement its policies: where property is expropriated, even for environmental purposes, whether domestic or international, the state's obligation to pay compensation remains.[142]

The tribunal referred to the Iran–US CT (*TAMS*) in support of this view.[143] A year later, the *ad hoc* panel in *CME* expressly acknowledged the police-powers exception of the effects rule established in the Convention Establishing the Multilateral Investment Guarantee Agency (MIGA).[144] According to this tribunal, non-discriminatory measures of general application, which governments normally take for the purpose of regulating economic activity in their territories, do not constitute a taking.[145] Not long after this statement was issued, *Generation Ukraine* quoted the Iran–US CT (*TAMS*) and *Santa Elena*, expressly stating that the intent of the government is less important than the effects of the measures on the owner, and that the form of the measures of control or interference is less important than the reality of their impact.[146] Predictability and the respect for legitimate expectations were stressed as elements of the protection against expropriation.[147] That same year, another ICSID panel initially endorsed the effects rule, only to refute it implicitly afterwards.

TECMED involved a Spanish investor that bought a controlled landfill of hazardous industrial waste in Mexico.[148] Even though the local authorities granted a renewable license to operate it, the Mexican state rejected TECMED's application for renewal, and requested the closure of the landfill. This measure moved the foreign investor to institute arbitral proceedings under the applicable BIT. The tribunal started its analysis of the expropriation claim from the standpoint of the effects doctrine. Quoting a NAFTA arbitration (*Metalclad*),[149] the panel understood takings to materialise 'through actions or conduct, which do not explicitly express the purpose of depriving one of rights or assets, but actually have that effect'.[150] In the tribunal's view, to establish whether the Mexican state's measure was equivalent to an expropriation under the terms of the BIT, it should be first determined that the claimant was, due to this measure, 'radically deprived of the economical use and enjoyment of its investments, as if the rights related thereto – such as the income or benefits related to the Landfill or to its exploitation – had ceased to exist'.[151] According to the panel:

> This determination is important because it is one of the main elements to distinguish, from the point of view of an international tribunal, between a regulatory measure, which is an ordinary expression of the exercise of the state's police power that entails a decrease in assets or rights, and a *de facto* expropriation that deprives those assets and rights of any real substance.[152]

The tribunal found support for this view in the wording of the BIT, covering expropriations, nationalisations or 'any other measure with similar characteristics or effects'.[153] With quotes on the case-law of the Inter-American Court of Human Rights (*Ivcher*),[154] the European Court of Human Rights (*Matos*)[155] and the Iran–US CT (*TAMS* and *Phelps Dodge*),[156] the panel reasoned that in an indirect taking claim the decision-maker should not restrict itself to the evaluation of whether a formal dispossession occurred, but should look beyond mere appearances and determine the reality behind the situation that was denounced, for:

> it is understood that the measures adopted by a State, whether regulatory or not, are an indirect *de facto* expropriation if they are irreversible and permanent and if the assets or rights subject to such measure have been affected in such a way that '… any form of exploitation thereof …' has disappeared; i.e. the economic value of the use, enjoyment or disposition of the assets or rights affected by the administrative action or decision have been neutralized or destroyed. Under international law, the owner is also deprived of property where the use or enjoyment of benefits related thereto is exacted or interfered with to a similar extent, even where legal ownership over the assets in question is not affected, and so long as the deprivation is not temporary. The government's intention is less important than the effects of the measures on the owner of the assets or on the benefits arising from such assets affected by the measures; and the form of the deprivation measure is less important than its actual effects.[157]

The arbitral panel in *TECMED* concluded that the measure adopted by Mexico fulfilled these characteristics. Surprisingly, it then decided to approach the claim from a police-powers perspective, using the fair balance test developed by the European Court of Human Rights, and at least two of the three factors of the US *Penn Central* case for this purpose.[158] The tribunal declared that a state measure is expropriatory if it has a negative financial impact and is proportional to the public interest protected.[159] It recognised that due deference is owed to the host-state's definition and implementation of its public policy. The panel considered, however, that this circumstance did not prevent it from establishing whether such measures were reasonable 'with respect to their goals, the deprivation of economic rights and the legitimate expectations of who suffered such deprivation'.[160] Only the third factor of the *Penn Central* case was missing from this assessment, *i.e.* the character of the governmental action. In a direct reference to the case-law of the European Court, the tribunal added that there must be a balance between the charge or weight imposed on the foreign investor and the aim sought to be realised by the conduct of the state, and '[t]o value such charge or weight, it is very important to measure the size of the ownership deprivation caused by the actions of the state and whether such deprivation was compensated or not'.[161] The panel reviewed the motives of Mexico's measure – that is to say, its public purpose – not to determine if it was legally issued, but to establish if the BIT was violated. It concluded that the measure was adopted solely on political considerations.[162] Because no justification was found, the tribunal awarded TECMED compensation for the taking of its property.[163]

Other tribunals have adopted *TECMED*'s proportionality approach. In *Azurix*, the panel complemented the effects rule with the proportionality and the legitimate expectations principles.[164] *LG&E* confirmed the applicability of the fair balance test to investment arbitrations,[165] quoting the Iran–US CT (*Emanuel Too*)[166] and the Third Restatement of the Foreign Relations Law of the United States.[167] So did the award in *Continental Casualty*, with a reference to European human rights law.[168] No taking was found in any of these BIT arbitrations.[169] *Tza* did not openly apply the proportionality test, nor directly follow the effects rule. Instead, it mixed both standards in a somewhat original and not altogether clear approach.[170]

To establish whether Peru had expropriated the Chinese investor, the tribunal studied four elements in *Tza*. The first of these was the impact and duration of the measures adopted by the host-state.[171] Applying the substantial and permanent deprivation standard, the panel concluded that Mr. Tza's investment had been expropriated unlawfully, because he had not been compensated.[172] Then the tribunal analysed a second element, which combined the requirements of public purpose and non-discrimination, as a possible exemption of responsibility.[173] From this perspective, the panel reached the conclusion that the measures adopted by Peru were not justified.[174] The third element studied by the tribunal was the efficacy of the conduct by the host-state, concluding that it had an overwhelming negative result for the investor.[175] Finally, the panel analysed the availability of legal remedies, as a condition of due process in the adoption of these measures.[176] This last conclusion was also against Peru, and in favour of Mr. Tza.[177]

5.3.2 Conforming to a Trend?

CCL is a rare example of an award relying exclusively on the intention of the host-state to establish an indirect expropriation.[178] Normally, BIT arbitrators focus on the effects of the state's measures, applying the standard of substantial and permanent interference, first used in the context of investment disputes by a NAFTA case (*Pope & Talbot*).[179] This standard had already been applied by the Iran–US CT, with a different wording – *i.e.*, as a non-ephemeral unreasonable interference, which deprives the owner of his/her/its property.[180] For instance, the BIT panel in *Occidental* concluded that 'there has been no deprivation of the use or reasonably expected economic benefit of the investment, let alone measures affecting a significant part of the investment'.[181] The tribunal in *CMS* defined indirect taking as measures that do not involve an overt expropriation, but that effectively neutralise the enjoyment of the property.[182] It rejected the US investor's claim of expropriation from the effects standpoint advanced by the Iran–US CT (*TAMS*),[183] NAFTA's *Metalclad*[184] and *CME*.[185] That same year, an *ad hoc* tribunal held that certain acts and omissions of the Polish authorities did amount to a deprivation of the claimant's investment. *Eureko* referred to the failed privatisation of a wholly state-owned insurance company.[186] The panel considered that, though the Dutch investor was not deprived of its shares in the company or of its dividends, the refusal of the authorities to conduct the agreed public offering of shares was discriminatory and in blunt violation of its expectations.[187] *TECMED* and *CME* were mentioned in support for the tribunal's finding that Eureko was indirectly deprived of its contractual rights by the host-state, in breach of the Netherlands–Poland BIT. *Metalclad* was also mentioned in this regard.[188]

The question of intent was directly and controversially addressed in *Saluka*, a BIT arbitration that endorsed the police-powers solution adopted months before in another NAFTA case: *Methanex*.[189] In *Saluka*, the panel expressly declared that:

> It is now established in international law that States are not liable to pay compensation to a foreign investor when, in the normal exercise of their regulatory powers, they adopt in a non-discriminatory manner *bona fide* regulations that are aimed at the general welfare.[190]

In other words, 'certain takings or deprivations are non-compensable'.[191] According to this tribunal, international law has yet to draw:

> a bright and easily distinguishable line between non-compensable regulations on the one hand and, on the other, measures that have the effect of depriving foreign investors of their investment and are thus unlawful and compensable in international law.[192]

The problem with *Saluka*'s solution is that it forgets an important aspect of the international law of expropriation: compensation is not just a consequence of the breach of an international obligation; it is also a requirement of a lawful taking. The panel reached this conclusion from a police-powers approach, even though the provision of the applicable BIT was worded on the traditional terms of the international law of expropriation, establishing the four conditions for a lawful taking: public purpose, non-discrimination, payment of compensation and due process.[193] Without further reasoning, the tribunal in *Saluka* decided that the Czech Republic had not crossed the line that separates permissible regulatory action from expropriation. As a result, the host-state was not held responsible for breaching the treaty.[194] Except for *El Paso*, where the tribunal stated that 'in principle, general non-discriminatory regulatory measures, adopted in accordance with the rules of good faith and due process, do not entail a duty of compensation', this view has not been followed in later BIT arbitrations.[195]

In *Telenor*, the tribunal openly avoided giving its view on the problem of intent, and concluded that it lacked jurisdiction over the expropriation claim on the basis of the standard of substantial deprivation.[196] This BIT panel, however, expressly declared that to answer the threshold question 'the determinative factors are the intensity and duration of the economic deprivation suffered by the investor as the result of them'.[197] A month later, the arbitral tribunal in *ADC* awarded compensation to the claimant for the breach by the host-state of the requirements of a lawful taking.[198] This panel declared that a just compensation in case of deprivation is within the legitimate and reasonable expectations of a foreign investor. In a rather uncommon approach in investment disputes, the panel decided to assess the requirement of public purpose claimed by Hungary. The tribunal reasoned that this condition requires some proven genuine general interest, for the mere reference to public purpose does not 'magically put such interest into existence'.[199] No public purpose appeared from the conduct of the Hungarian authorities. Furthermore, no due process of law was found in their conduct.[200] For these reasons, compensation was awarded in favour of the foreign investor.

Another BIT-based panel approached the requirement of public purpose in the same way as *ADC*, followed the effects rule, and decided that the claimant was subject to an indirect taking. *Siemens* involved a German investor in Argentina.[201] The tribunal concluded that the host-state interfered with the execution of the contract signed with Siemens through governmental action that amounted to a creeping expropriation, in 'effect and permanence'.[202] The panel quoted the *Norwegian Shipowners'* claim and confirmed the traditional effects rule by recalling that:

> The Treaty refers to measures that have the effect of an expropriation; it does not refer to the intent of the State to expropriate. [...] A different matter is the purpose of the expropriation, but that is one of the requirements for determining whether the expropriation is in accordance with the terms of the Treaty and not for determining whether an expropriation has occurred.[203]

The tribunal analysed the public purpose claimed by the Argentinian authorities and found no such requirement in the uncompensated measures adopted by it.[204] In *Aguas del Aconquija*, the panel concluded that Argentina was responsible for expropriating the French investor, quoting profusely the case-law of other international tribunals to support its choice on the problems of intention and degree of interference.[205] The tribunal said:

> it is not infrequent in cases of indirect expropriation that the investor suffers a substantial deprivation of value of its investment. Numerous tribunals have looked at the diminution of the value of the investment to determine whether the contested measure is expropriatory. The weight of authority [...] appears to draw a distinction between only a partial deprivation of value (not an expropriation) and a complete or near complete deprivation of value (expropriation).[206]

On the question of intent, *Aguas del Aconquija* adopted the effects rule, as understood by the Iran–US CT (*TAMS* and *Phillips Petroleum*),[207] and NAFTA arbitrations (*Pope & Talbot* and *Metalclad*);[208]

> There is extensive authority for the proposition that the state's intent, or its subjective motives are at most a secondary consideration. While intent will weigh in favour of showing a measure to be expropriatory, it is not a requirement, because the effect of the measure on the investor, not the state's intent, is the critical factor. [...]
>
> Also, the structure of Article 5(2) of the Treaty directs the Tribunal first to consider whether the challenged measures are expropriatory, and only then to ask whether they can comply with certain conditions, *ie* public purpose, non-discriminatory, specific commitments, et cetera. If we conclude that the challenged measures are expropriatory, there will be violation of Article 5(2) of the Treaty, even if the measures might be for a public purpose and non-discriminatory, because no compensation has been paid.[209]

In *BC Group*, the panel was asked to interpret the phrase 'measures having effect equivalent to [...] expropriation' of the 1990 Argentina–UK BIT.[210] For this purpose, the panel distinguished non-expropriatory interferences from indirect takings. With references to the Iran–US CT (*Starrett Housing*),[211] NAFTA arbitrations (*Lauder* and *Pope & Talbot*)[212] and *LG&E*, this tribunal applied the standard of substantial and permanent deprivation, and concluded that the British investor had not been expropriated by Argentina.[213] Not long after this award, *Biwater Gauff* gave a traditional definition of indirect takings, relied on *Siemens*'s concept of creeping expropriations, and openly recognised that 'many tribunals in other cases have tested governmental conduct in the context of indirect expropriation claims by reference to the effect of relevant acts, rather than the intention behind them'.[214] The tribunal added that '[i]n general terms, a substantial deprivation of rights, for at least a meaningful period of time, is required'.[215] It concluded that the British investor had been expropriated, as a result of the cumulative effect of Tanzania's conduct.[216] *Tokios Tokelés*, *Sempra*, *Metalpar*, *LESI*, *Nations Energy* and other BIT arbitrations where no indirect expropriation was found have also followed an effects approach, whether explicitly or implicitly.[217]

Quoting *Oil Field of Texas* of the Iran–US CT, the tribunal in *Rumeli* confirmed that judicial decisions may also amount to a taking in international law.[218] With a further reference to the jurisprudence of the Iran–US CT (*Phillips Petroleum*), the panel declared: 'the intent of the State is relevant to, but is not decisive of the question whether there has been an expropriation'.[219] In this case, the tribunal concluded that Kazakhstan had taken the Turkish investor's property, in the form of a creeping expropriation.[220] *Saipem* involved judicial decisions as well, this time from Bangladeshi courts. This BIT panel expressly endorsed the effects doctrine, centred its analysis on the illegality of the conduct of the judiciary, and concluded that the respondent state had expropriated the Italian claimant.[221] The case-law of the Iran–US CT (*Starrett*) was also quoted in *Alpha Projektholding*. Applying the effects rule, this panel concluded that the Austrian investor had been deprived of its property by Ukraine.[222] Recently, the panel in *Unglaube* again followed an effects approach, quoting *Santa Elena* with approval, and concluded that the claimants had been subject to a *de facto* expropriation.[223] According to this BIT-based tribunal:

> while there can be no question concerning the right of the government of Costa Rica to expropriate property for a *bona fide* public purpose, pursuant to law, and in a manner which is neither arbitrary or discriminatory, the expropriatory measure must be accompanied by compensation for the fair market value of the investment.[224]

5.4 CONCLUSION

BITs have transformed the protection of aliens into one of the most active fields in international law. Countries in Europe, the Americas, Asia, Africa and Oceania have concluded these treaties, accepting the international minimum standard recognised in them. Most BITs are currently in force, and the breadth of state practice is now such that the basic takings provisions included in most treaties, can be fairly considered to evidence customary international law. The dispute settlement clauses of BITs have allowed international arbitral panels to construe the protection against expropriation in a relatively coherent case-law. Based on these clauses, foreign investors have questioned state conduct that interferes with their property, not just in developing countries. For this reason, the USA and Canada have modified their BIT models to guide the interpretation of decision-makers in subsequent claims of indirect expropriation directed against them.

Arbitral tribunals in investment disputes adopt a broad concept of property and apply different tests to answer the threshold question, focusing mostly on the impact and the duration of the challenged measure. From this perspective, a successful claim of indirect taking will normally require proving a substantial interference, which effectively and permanently deprives the foreign investor of his/hers/its property. This deprivation can be the result of either actions or omissions of the host-state, or both. *Generation Ukraine*, *TECMED*, *Occidental*, *Eureko*, *Azurix* and *ADC* highlight the role of the foreign investor's legitimate expectations in that determination. Arbitral panels have generally granted the host-state a wide margin of discretion in the assessment of the requirement of public purpose, one which resembles that of the European Court of Human Rights and the Iran–US CT. As a consequence, international tribunals will generally refrain from challenging the fulfilment of this condition by the corresponding state. *Siemens*, *ADC* and *Tza* have departed from this otherwise general trend, analysing the public purpose claimed by the host-state, to judge the legality of the respective expropriation. In *Saluka*, the objective was different: to decide whether there had been a compensable taking at all.

On the whole, the effects rule is still dominant in investment arbitration. *SPP*, *Goetz*, *Santa Elena*, *Lauder*, *Generation Ukraine*, *CMS*, *Eureko*, *ADC*, *Siemens*, *Aguas del Aconquija*, *BC Group*, *Biwater Gauff*, *Rumeli*, *Saipem*, *Alpha Projektholding* and *Unglaube* have applied it. The most prominent exceptions to this trend are found in *TECMED* and *Saluka*. While the proportionality or fair balance test of *TECMED* has been somehow followed by *Azurix*, *LG&E*, *Continental Casualty* and *Tza*, the police-powers solution of *Saluka* has only received an implicit support in *El Paso*.

NOTES

1. On FCNs, *see* K Vandevelde, 'The Bilateral Investment Treaty Program of the United States', (1988) 21/2 *Cornell ILJ* 201, at 203–8; J Salacuse, 'BIT by BIT:

The Growth of Bilateral Investment Treaties and Their Impact on Foreign Investment in Developing Countries', (1990) 24/3 *IL* 655, at 656–7; K Vandevelde, 'U.S. Bilateral Investment Treaties: The Second Wave', (1993) 14/4 *Mich. JIL* 621, at 624–5; R Dolzer and M Stevens *Bilateral Investment Treaties* (1995), 3–4; A Guzman, 'Why LDCs Sign Treaties That Hurt Them: Explaining the Popularity of Bilateral Investment Treaties', (1998) 38/4 *Virg. JIL* 639, at 652–3; D Blumemwitz, 'Treaties of Friendship, Commerce and Navigation', in R Bernhardt (ed.), *EPIL* (2000), Vol. 4; S Schill, *The Multilateralization of International Investment Law* (2009), 29–30; J Salacuse, *The Law of International Investment Treaties* (2010), 83–6 & 88–90; and M Sornarajah, *The International Law on Foreign Investment* (2010), 180–2.

2. Vandevelde (1988), 204. The first FCN was the 1778 Treaty of Amity and Commerce between France and the USA. FCNs are generally available at http://avalon.law.yale.edu (last visited 30 June 2013).
3. Art. XIII of the 1858 Treaty of Peace, Friendship, Commerce and Navigation between Bolivia and the USA.
4. Art. IX, para. 3, of the 1859 Treaty of Friendship, Commerce and Navigation between Paraguay and the USA.
5. Art. VIII of the 1870 General Treaty of Amity, Commerce and Consular Privileges between El Salvador and the USA; and Art. VIII of the 1846 General Treaty of Peace, Amity, Navigation and Commerce between New Granada and the USA.
6. Vandevelde (1988), 205. *See* K Vandevelde, *Bilateral Investment Treaties: History, Policy, and Interpretation* (2010), 23–4 & 282.
7. *See* Art. I, para. 6, of the 1928 Treaty of Friendship, Commerce and Consular Rights between Austria and the USA.
8. An example of this new model was Art. IV, para. 2, of the 1955 Iran–USA FCN. *See* Chapter 4 above.
9. L Loppacher and W Kerr, 'Investment Rules. The U.S. Agenda in Bilateral Trade Agreements', (2006) 7/1 *JWIT* 39, at 45. This area was not covered by GATT. Guzman (1998), 653. GATT was a draft multilateral treaty containing general principles of trade, completed in 1947 during one of the conferences held to negotiate an international organisation on this issue. As the negotiations of its constitutive treaty lagged on, a Protocol of Provisional Application was adopted by 23 states. Its object was to apply GATT from 1948 onwards, without having to wait for the Charter for an International Trade Organization to be enforceable. M Matsushita, T Schoenbaum and P Mavroidis, *The World Trade Organization: Law, Practice, and Policy* (2006), 2. *See* Chapter 6 below.
10. *See* Salacuse (2010), 91–3.
11. M Reisman and R Sloane, 'Indirect Expropriation and Its Valuation in the BIT Generation', (2003) 74 *BYIL* 115, at 116.
12. *See* K Vandevelde, 'Investment Liberalization and Economic Development: The Role of Bilateral Investment Treaties', (1998) 36/3 *Colum. JTL* 501, at 522–5.
13. Reisman and Sloane (2003), at 117–8.
14. *See* Salacuse (2010), 6–9, 109–11 & 114; and Vandevelde (2010), 2–4.
15. Salacuse (1990), at 657. *See* Salacuse (2010), 95.
16. The last FCNs were the 1966 Treaties of Amity and Economic Relations with Togo, and with Thailand. The first US BIT was that with Egypt, concluded in 1982. *See* Vandevelde (1988), 208–11; Vandevelde (1993), 624–7; and Vandevelde (2010), 56–7.
17. Loppacher and Kerr (2006), at 46.
18. K Vandevelde, 'A Brief History of International Investment Agreements', (2006) 12/1 *UC-Davis JILP* 157, at 171.

19. *See* Salacuse (1990) 662–4; Dolzer and Stevens (1992), 1–3 & 13; G Sacerdoti, 'Bilateral Treaties and Multilateral Instruments on Investment Protection', (1997) 269 *RCADI* 251, at 300–1; P Juillard, 'MAI: A European View', (1998) 31/3 *Corn. ILJ* 477, at 477; M Clodfelter, 'The Adaptation of States to the Changing World of Investment Protection through Model BITs', (2009) 24/1 *ICSID Rev.* 165, at 166; Schill (2009), 39–40 & 90–2; and S Schill, 'International Investment Law and Comparative Public Law', in S Schill (ed.), *International Investment Law and Comparative Public Law* (2010), 31. *See* Chapter 6 below. The OECD is an international organisation with 30 member states at present, 'sharing a commitment to democratic government and the market economy'. *See* http://www.oecd.org (last visited 30 June 2013).
20. On European BITs, *see generally* R Dolzer, 'The European Approach to BITs', (2009) 24/2 *ICSID Rev.* 368.
21. OECD, *Working Papers on International Investment* (2004), Nr. 1, at 4.
22. *See* Vandevelde (1993), 626. *See also* Clodfelter (2009), 166.
23. *See e.g.* the 1968 Denmark–Indonesia BIT, called 'Agreement concerning the encouragement and reciprocal protection of investments'; and the 1994 Estonia–Israel BIT titled 'Agreement […] for the promotion and reciprocal protection of investments'.
24. Sornarajah (2010), 185. *See* Dolzer and Stevens (1995), 12; Vandevelde (1998), 503–4; V Been and J Beauvais, 'The Global Fifth Amendment: NAFTA's Investment Protection and the Misguided Quest for an International "Regulatory Takings" Doctrine', (2003) 78/1 *NYU LR* 30, at 118–20 & 126; Reisman and Sloane (2003), 116; and Salacuse (2010), 110–11. On an original and plausible explanation to the problem of why do developing states conclude BITs, *see* Montt (2009), 83–123.
25. Some authors have concluded that BITs have little positive effect on the FDI that flows to developing countries. *See e.g.* M Hallward-Driemeier, 'Do Bilateral Investment Treaties Attract Foreign Direct Investment? Only a Bit … and They Could Bite', (2003) 3121 *World Bank Policy Research Working Paper*; J Tobin and S Rose-Ackerman, 'Foreign Direct Investment and the Business Environment in Developing Countries: The Impact of Bilateral Investment Treaties', (2004) 293 *Yale Law and Economics Research Paper*; or J Tobin and S Rose-Ackerman, 'When BITs have some bite', (2006) *Yale Law School Draft Working Paper*.

    See also Been and Beauvais (2003), 123–4. Others are of the opinion that BITs help to raise the FDI flows to developing countries. *See e.g.* E Neumayer and L Spess, 'Do Bilateral Investment Treaties Increase Foreign Direct Investment to Developing Countries?, (2005) *LSE Res. On.*; J Salacuse and N Sullivan, 'Do BITs Really Work: An Evaluation of Bilateral Investment Treaties and Their Grand Bargain', (2005) 46/1 *Harv. ILJ* 67; and D Swenson, 'Why Do Developing Countries Sign BITs?', (2006) 12/1 *UC-Davis JILP* 131. *See also* Vandevelde (2010), 116–19.
26. Dolzer and Stevens (1995), 119.
27. An example of this type of dispute settlement provision is Art. 8 of the 1990 France–Nigeria BIT. *See also* Art. 9 of the 1994 Lithuania–Netherlands BIT.
28. Dolzer and Stevens (1995), 129. *E.g.* Art. 8 of the 1993 Ukraine–UK BIT. *See also* Art. 9 of the 1999 Albania–Finland BIT; or Art. 9 of the 2002 Bahrain–Thailand BIT.
29. *See e.g.* Annex B to the 1998 Australia–Lithuania BIT.
30. *See* J Paulsson, 'Arbitration without Privity', (1995) 10/2 *ICSID Rev.* 232. *See also* Schill (2010), 15–16. These mechanisms are sometimes available under investment codes too.
31. The first claim under the dispute settlement provisions of a BIT was only filed in 1987. *See Asian Agricultural Products Ltd* (AAPL) *v. Republic of Sri Lanka*, ICSID

case No. ARB/87/3, Award, 27 June 1990. *See also* N Blackaby et al, *Redfern & Hunter on International Arbitration* (2009), 468.
32. Vandevelde (2010), 4–5. *See* Salacuse (2010), 8–9 & 109–11.
33. Salacuse (1990), 661.
34. Vandevelde (1993), 625. *See* Montt (2009), 66.
35. *See Elettronica Sicula, S.p.A.* (ELSI) (US v. Italy), International Court of Justice, Judgment, 20 July1989, (1989) 28/5 *ILM* 1111.
36. *See* Chapter 4 above.
37. M Sornarajah, 'Power and Justice in International Law', (1997) 1/1 *SJICL* 28, at 57.
38. *See Military and Paramilitary Activities In and Against Nicaragua* (Nicaragua v. USA), International Court of Justice, Judgment, 27 June 1986, (1986) 25/5 *ILM* 1023.
39. *See Oil Platforms* (Iran v. USA), International Court of Justice, Judgment, 6 November 2003, (2003) 42/6 *ILM* 1334.
40. *See e.g. Emilio Agustin Maffezini v. The Kingdom of Spain*, ICSID case No. ARB/97/7, Award, 13 November 2000.
41. A Lowenfeld, *International Economic Law* (2008), 559.
42. *See* Art. 3, para. 2, of the 1959 Germany–Pakistan BIT.
43. *See e.g.* Art. 13, para. 1, of the 2006 Canada–Perú BIT.
44. *See* Y Dinstein, 'Deprivation of Property of Foreigners under International Law', in N Ando et al (eds.), *Liber Amicorum Judge Shigeru Oda* (2002), 864. *See* Chapter 4 above.
45. Exceptionally, the tribunal in *ADC* distinguished between a conventional and a customary standard – *i.e.*, between compensation and damages. According to this panel, the customary standard would be the one described by the PCIJ in the *Chorzow Factory* case: 'payment of a sum corresponding to the value which a restitution in kind would bear; the award, if need be, of damages for loss sustained which would not be covered by restitution in kind or payment in place of it'. *ADC Affiliate Limited and ADC & ADMC Management Limited v. The Republic of Hungary*, ICSID case No. ARB/03/16, Award, 2 October 2006, para. 485. *See ibid.*, paras. 479–94. *See also Factory at Chorzow* (Germany v. Poland), PCIJ, Judgment, 13 September 1928. (1928) PCIJ Rep. Series A No 17. This solution has been criticised in doctrine. *See e.g.* Montt (2009), 285–6; and Salacuse (2010), 327–8.
46. *See e.g.* Art. 5, para. 1, of the 1982 Cameroon–UK BIT.
47. *See e.g.* Art. 3, para. 2, of the 1978 Benin–Germany BIT.
48. *See e.g,* Art 5, para. 1, of the 1982 Belgium–Sri Lanka BIT.
49. A Reinisch, 'Legality of Expropriations', in A Reinisch (ed.), *Standards of Investment Protection* (2008), 178–9; and Newcombe and Paradell (2009), 370.
50. Dolzer and Stevens (1992), 104–5. *See* Newcombe and Paradell (2009), 370–1; and Vandevelde (2010), 272.
51. Sacerdoti (1997), 389. *See e.g.* Art. 5, para. 2, of the 1993 Algeria–France BIT. *See also* Art. 6, para. 1, of the 2004 Iceland–Lebanon BIT.
52. Mouri (1994), 328.
53. American Law Institute, *Restatement of the Law Third. The Foreign Relations Law of the United States* (1987), 200. *See* Chapter 6 below.
54. A Maniruzzaman, 'Expropriation of Alien Property and the Principle of Non-Discrimination in International Law of Foreign Investment: An Overview', (1998) 8/1 *JTLP* 57, at 67.
55. Sacerdoti (1997), 388. *See* Reinisch, 'Legality of Expropriations' (2008), 186–7; Newcombe and Paradell (2009), 373–4; and Vandevelde (2010), 273.
56. Dolzer and Stevens (1995), 106.
57. *Ibid.*, 108–9.

58. *See e.g.* R Higgins, 'The Taking of Property by the State: Recent Developments in International Law', (1982) 176/3 *RCADI* 259, at 315; Dolzer and Stevens (1995) 97; Sacerdoti (1997) 395; M Ruffert, 'The Protection of Foreign Direct Investment by the European Convention on Human Rights', (2000) 43 *GYIL* 116, at 134–6; Reisman and Sloane (2003), 135; UNCTAD, *International Investment Agreements: Key Issues* (2004), Vol. 1, at 245; Reinisch, 'Legality of Expropriations' (2008), 176; T Waelde and B Sabahi, 'Compensation, Damages, and Valuation', in P Muchlinski, F Ortino and C Schreuer (eds.), *The Oxford Handbook of International Investment Law* (2008), 1069; Clodfelter (2009), 171 & 175; Salacuse (2010), 323–5; Vandevelde (2010), 273–4; K Yannaca-Small, 'Indirect Expropriation and the Right to Regulate: How to Draw the Line?', in K Yannaca-Small (ed.), *Arbitration under International Investment Agreements: A Guide to the Key Issues* (2010), 445–6; R Dolzer and C Schreuer, *Principles of International Investment Law* (2012), 5 & 100; and S Subedi, *International Investment Law: Reconciling Policy and Principle* (2012), 91–2. *See also* Newcombe and Paradell (2009), 373–4.
59. *See* A Escobar, 'Introductory Note on Bilateral Investment Treaties Recently Concluded by Latin American States', (1996) 11/1 *ICSID Rev.* 86, at 90.
60. *See e.g.* Art. 5, para. 1, of the 1993 Finland–Korea BIT. *See also* Art. V, para. 1, of the 1996 Chile–Ecuador BIT.
61. *See e.g,* Art VI, paras. 1 & 2, of the 1991 Hungary–Norway BIT.
62. *See e.g.* Art. 4 of the 1987 Netherlands–Oman BIT. *See* Chapter 2 above. The non-binding 1992 World Bank Guidelines on the Treatment of Foreign Direct Investment, designed to complement BITs, provides for appropriate compensation, but then immediately adds that it will be deemed as such 'if it is adequate, effective and prompt'. Guideline IV, Sections 1 and 2, available at http://ita.law.uvic.ca/documents/WorldBank.pdf (last visited 30 June 2013). *See* Chapter 6 below.
63. Vandevelde (2010), 274.
64. Lowenfeld (2008), 565. *See e.g.* Art. VI, para. 2, of the 2000 Chile–Colombia BIT. *Cf.* Vandevelde (2010), 275–6.
65. *See e.g* Art. 6, para.1, of the 2004 Uruguay–USA BIT.
66. Blackaby et al (2009), 508; and Vandevelde (2010), 274.
67. Dolzer and Stevens (1995) 110; and Sacerdoti (1997) 398. *See* Vandevelde (2010), 274–5. For this reason, the 1992 World Bank Guidelines on the Treatment of Foreign Direct Investment suggests that for a going concern, with a proven record of profitability, the valuation should be made on the basis of the discounted cash flow value, used for establishing the present value of the expected future earnings of the business. For a non-going concern with lack of profitability, it should be made on the basis of the liquidation value. And for other assets, on the basis of the replacement value or the book value, in case such value has been recently assessed or has been determined as of the date of the taking. 'Going concern', 'discounted cash flow value', 'liquidation value', 'replacement value', and 'book value' are all defined in this provision. *See* Guideline IV, Section 6. *See* Chapter 6 below. Not even last generation BITs include such methods expressly. *E.g.*, Art. 13, para. 2, of the 2006 Canada–Perú BIT only says that the '[v]aluation criteria shall include going concern value, asset value including declared tax value of tangible property, and other criteria, as appropriate, to determine fair market value'.
68. Lowenfeld (2008), 565. *See e.g.* Art. 5, para. 1, of the 1997 Czech Republic–Ireland BIT. *See also* Vandevelde (2010), 276–7.
69. Blackaby et al (2009), 502. *See* G Sacerdoti, 'The Admission and Treatment of Foreign Investment under Recent Bilateral and Regional Treaties', (2000) 1/1 *JWIT* 105, at 123.
70. *See* UNCTAD (2004), 245; and G Fletcher and S Sheppard, *American Law in a Global Context: The Basics* (2005), 59–60. *See also* H Muir Watt, 'Globalization

and Comparative Law', in M Reimann and R Zimmermann (eds.), *The Oxford Handbook of Comparative Law* (2006), 587.

71. *See e.g.* Art. 7, para 1, of the 1991 Australia–Vietnam BIT. *See also* Art. 5, para. 1, of the 1998 China–Swaziland BIT.
72. Newcombe and Paradell (2009), 375–6. *See ibid.* note 90 at 249.
73. Newcombe and Paradell (2009), 375. *See* Dolzer and Stevens (1995), 106; and Vandevelde (2010), 273.
74. *See e.g.* Art. 6, para. 1, of the 1995 Norway–Perú BIT. *See also* Art. 5, para. 1, of the 1998 Japan–Russia BIT.
75. Dolzer and Stevens (1995), 106.
76. *See e.g.* Art. 5, para 1, of the 1975 Singapore–UK BIT. *See also* Art. 5, para. 1, of the 1995 Denmark–Mongolia BIT.
77. *See e.g.* F Mann, 'British Treaties for the Promotion and Protection of Investments', (1981) 52 *BYIL* 241, at 249–50; Dolzer and Stevens (1995), 117; A Lowenfeld, 'Investment Agreements and International Law', (2003) 42/1 *Colum. JTL* 123, at 128; Reisman and Sloane (2003), note 158 at 150; S Hindelang, 'Bilateral Investment Treaties, Custom and a Healthy Investment Climate – the Question of Whether BITs Influence Customary International Law Revisited', (2004) 5/5 *JWIT* 769, at 798–809; S Schwebel, 'The Influence of Bilateral Investment Treaties on Customary International Law, (2004) 98 *ASIL Proc.* 27, at 27 & 29–30; Salacuse and Sullivan (2005), 112–15; I Brownlie, *Principles of Public International Law* (2008), 544; Lowenfeld (2008), 586; Schill (2009), 84; and Vandevelde (2010), 272.
78. *See e.g.* B Kishaiyian, 'The Utility of Bilateral Investment Treaties in the Formulation of Customary International Law', (1994) 14/2 *Nw JILB* 327, at 329 & 372–5; Sacerdoti (1997) 395–7; Guzman (1998), 643–4, 666–9, 678–80 & 684–7; A Cassese, *International Law* (2005), 524–5; M Sornarajah, 'A Coming Crisis: Expansionary Trends in Investment Treaty Arbitration', in K Sauvant (ed.), *Appeals Mechanism in International Investment Disputes* (2008), 45–8; and Sornarajah (2010), 175–7.
79. *See* Chapter 6 below.
80. *See* Chapter 3 above.
81. Salacuse (1990), 664. The lack of a definition of investment in the 1965 Convention on the Settlement of Investment Disputes between States and Nationals of Other States also recognises the non-static character of this notion, giving BIT and EIA draftsmen a great degree of flexibility. Blackaby et al (2009), 474.
82. Sacerdoti (1997) 382. *See e.g.* Art. 3 of the 1961 Switzerland–Tunisia BIT.
83. *See e.g.* Art. 6 of the 1988 Italy–Malaysia BIT. *See also* Art. 4, para. 2, of the 1997 Brazil–Cuba BIT.
84. *See e.g.* Art. 4, para. 2, of the 1981 Germany–Somalia BIT. *See also* Art. 5, para. 1, of the 1997 Jordan–USA BIT.
85. U Kriebaum, 'Regulatory Takings: Balancing the Interests of the Investor and the State', (2007) 8/5 *JWIT* 717, at 722.
86. *See e.g.* Art. 4 of the 1987 Belgium–Malta BIT. *See also* Art. 4, para. 1, of the 1995 Albania–Sweden BIT; and Art. 6 of the 1998 Netherlands–Zimbabwe BIT.
87. *See e.g.* Art. 1 of the 2004 Uruguay–USA BIT; and Art. 1 of the 2006 Canada–Perú BIT.
88. *See e.g.* Annex B of the 2004 Uruguay–USA BIT; Annex B.13 (1) of the 2006 Canada–Perú BIT; Annex B of the 2008 Rwanda–USA BIT; Annex B of the 2009 Canada–Latvia BIT; and Annex A of the 2010 Canada–Slovakia BIT. *See also* Kriebaum, (2007) 8/5 *JWIT* 717, at 722–3.
89. Sornarajah (2010), 9. *See* F González de Cossío, *Arbitraje de inversión* (2009), 5.
90. According to Rudolf Dolzer and Christoph Schreuer, the reason for using 'investment' in BITs and EIAs, rather than 'property', is because these treaties are not

meant to cover all types of property rights and interests, but only those included in the corresponding definition. Dolzer and Schreuer (2012), 60.

91. On the interaction between the international and the domestic notions of investment, *see* Montt (2009), 243–53; and Newcombe and Paradell (2009), 351–2.

92. *See* Salacuse (1990), 664; Dolzer and Stevens (1995), 26; N Rubins, 'The Notion of "Investment" in International Investment Arbitration', in N Horn (ed.), *Arbitrating Foreign Investment Disputes. Procedural and Substantive Legal Aspects* (2004), 292–3; E Schlemmer, 'Investment, Investor, Nationality, and Shareholders', in P Muchlinski et al (2008), 55–6; González de Cossío (2009), 84–6; Newcombe and Paradell (2009), 65–6; and Salacuse (2010), 160–2; K Yannaca-Small, 'Definition of 'Investment': An Open-ended Search for a Balanced Approach', in K Yannaca-Small (ed.), *Arbitration under International Investment Agreements: A Guide to the Key Issues* (2010), 246–8; and Dolzer and Schreuer (2012), 63. *See e.g.* Art. 8, para. 1, of the 1966 Germany–Uganda BIT; Art. 1, para. 3, of the 1973 Egypt–Switzerland BIT; Art. 1 (a) of the 1976 Indonesia–UK BIT; and Art. 1, para. 1, of the 1989 Bulgaria–France BIT.

Exceptionally, BITs cover FDI, but not portfolio investment. *E.g.*, Art. 1, para. 1, of the 1991 Denmark–Poland BIT, after giving a general definition of investment and the corresponding exemplary list, adds that it:

> shall refer [...] to all investments in companies made for the purpose of establishing lasting economic relations between the investor and the company and giving the investor the possibility of exercising significant influence on the management of the company concerned.

93. *See e.g.* Art. 1, para. 3, of the 1971 Malaysia–Netherlands BIT.
94. *See e.g.* Art. 1, para. 1, of the 1991 China–Czech Republic BIT.
95. *See e.g.* Art. 9 of the 1959 Germany–Pakistan BIT.
96. Dolzer and Stevens (1995) 45–6. *See e.g.* Art. 1, para. 1, of the 1994 Italy–Lithuania BIT.
97. *See* Art. 1 of the 2004 Uruguay–USA BIT. *See also* Art. 1 of the 2008 Rwanda–USA BIT. On the 2012 US model BIT and earlier treaties, *see generally* M Kantor, 'Little Has Changed in the New US Model Bilateral Investment Treaty', (2012) 27/2 *ICSID Rev*. 335.
98. *See* note 3 to Art. 1 of the 2004 Uruguay–USA BIT.
99. The cumulative number of treaty-based investor-to-state claims, including NAFTA arbitrations, was 518 by the end of 2012: 314 have been brought before ICSID tribunals, and 204 before other arbitral panels. 245 claims have been concluded: approximately 42 per cent were decided in favour of the host-state, and 31 per cent in favour of the foreign investor. Approximately 27 per cent of these cases were settled. UNCTAD, *Recent Developments in Investor-State Dispute Settlement* (2013), 3–5. *See also* UNCTAD, *World Investment Report* (2012), 86–8; and UNCTAD, *World Investment Report* (2013), xxi & 110–11.
100. *See e.g.* Salacuse (2010), 307–18; and Yannaca-Small (2010), 460–76.
101. *See* Montt (2009), 261–5. *See also* B Kingsbury and S Schill, 'Public Law Concepts to Balance Investors' Rights with State Regulatory Actions in the Public Interest – the Concept of Proportionality', in S Schill (ed.), *International Investment Law and Comparative Public Law* (2010), 90.

Those explicitly and implicitly in favour of an economic approach include, *e.g.*, Waelde and Kolo (2001), 813, 825 & 846; Paulsson and Douglas (2004), 152–3; Kriebaum, (2007) 8/1 *JWIT* 69, at 71; U Kriebaum, 'Is the European Court of Human Rights an Alternative to Investor–State Arbitration?', in P Dupuy, F Francioni and E Petersmann (eds.), *Human Rights in International Investment Law and Arbitration* (2009), 237; S Robert-Cuendet, *Droits de l'investisseur étranger et protection de l'environnement: contribution à l'analyse de l'expropriation indirect* (2010), 147–50 & 160–1; Salacuse (2010), 308; Vandevelde (2010), 278–9 & 294; and Yannaca-Small (2010), 460. *See* Newcombe and Paradell (2009), 344–5.

These two approaches can also be found in the doctrine on expropriations under Article 1 of the First Optional Protocol of the European Convention of Human Rights. *E.g.*, Ursula Kriebaum favours an economic view, while Clare Ovey and Robin White support a legal one. *See* U Kriebaum, 'Is the European Court of Human Rights an Alternative to Investor–State Arbitration?', in P Dupuy et al (2009), 238–9; and R White and C Ovey, *Jacobs, White and Ovey: The European Convention on Human Rights* (2010), 488. *See also* T Allen, 'Compensation for Property under the European Convention of Human Rights', (2007) 28/2 *Mich. JIL* 287, at 305–27. *See* Chapter 3 above.

102. *See e.g. Wena Hotels Ltd. v. Arab Republic of Egypt*, ICSID case No. ARB/98/4, Award, 8 December 2000. (2002) 41/4 *ILM* 896, para. 99; *Ronald S. Lauder v. The Czech Republic*, UNCITRAL arbitration, Award, 3 September 2001, para. 200; *Generation Ukraine, Inc. v. Ukraine*, ICSID case No. ARB/00/9, Award, 16 September 2003, para. 20.32; *CMS Gas Transmission Company v. Republic of Argentina*, ICSID case No. ARB/01/8, Award, 12 May 2005, paras. 261 & 263; *Eureko B.V. v. Republic of Poland*, Ad hoc arbitration, Partial Award, 19 August 2005, para. 241; *Azurix Corp. v. The Argentine Republic*, ICSID case No. ARB/01/12, Award, 14 July 2006, para. 322; *BC Group Plc. v. Republic of Argentina*, UNCITRAL arbitration, Final Award, 24 December 2007, paras. 267–8; *Sempra Energy International v. Argentine Republic*, ICSID case No. ARB/02/16, Award, 28 September 2007, para. 284; *L.E.S.I. S.p.A. et ASTALDI S.p.A. c. République Algérienne Démocratique et Populaire*, ICSID case No. ARB/05/3, Award, 12 November 2008, paras. 130–2; and *Impregilo S.p.A. v. Argentine Republic*, ICSID case No. ARB/07/17, Award, 21 June 2011, para 270.

103. *Biwater Gauff (Tanzania) Ltd. v. United Republic of Tanzania*, ICSID case No. ARB/05/22, Award, 24 July 2008, para. 464.

104. *Biwater Gauff*, ICSID case No. ARB/05/22, Award, 24 July 2008, para. 465. 'In such circumstances', the tribunal added, 'there may still be scope for a non-compensatory remedy for the expropriation (e.g. injunctive, declaratory or restitutionary relief)'. *Ibid.*

105. *See CME Czech Republic B.V. v. The Czech Republic*, UNCITRAL arbitration, Partial Award, 13 September 2001, paras. 591, 604 & 606; *Middle East Cement Shipping and Handling Co. v. Arab Republic of Egypt*, ICSID case No. ARB/99/6, Award, 12 April 2002, para. 107; *Occidental Exploration and Production Co. (OEPC) v. The Republic of Ecuador*, UNCITRAL arbitration, Award, 1 July 2004, paras. 85 & 88–9; *Telenor Mobile Communications A.S. v. The Republic of Hungary*, ICSID case No. ARB/04/15, Award, 13 September 2006, paras. 63–7; *Compañía de Aguas del Aconquija S.A. and Vivendi Universal S.A. v. Argentine Republic (Vivendi II)*, ICSID case No. ARB/97/3, Award, 20 August 2007, paras. 7.5.11–17 & 7.5.24; *Parkerings-Compagniet AS v. Republic of Lithuania*, ICSID case No. ARB/05/8, Award, 11 September 2007, para. 455; *Tokios Tokelés v. Ukraine*, ICSID case No. ARB/02/18, Award, 26 July 2007, paras. 118 & 120; *Alpha Projektholding GmbH v. Ukraine*, ICSID case No. ARB/07/16, Award, 8 November 2010, paras. 408–10; *Nations Energy Inc., et al c. La República de Panamá*, ICSID case No. ARB/06/19, Award, 24 November 2010, paras. 684–5; and *Tza Yap Shum c. La República de Perú*, ICSID case No. ARB/07/6, Award, 7 July 2011, paras. 144, 151 & 158.

See also Técnicas Medioambientales TECMED S.A. v. The United Mexican States, ICSID case No. ARB (AF)/00/2, Award, 29 May 2003, paras. 115–16; *LG&E Energy Corp., LG&E Capital Corp., LG&E International Inc. v. Argentine*

Republic, ICSID case No. ARB/02/1, Decision on Liability, 3 October 2006, paras. 190–4; *Metalpar S.A. y Buen Aire S.A. c. República Argentina,* ICSID case No. ARB/03/5, Award, 6 June 2008, paras. 172–3; and *El Paso Energy International Company v. Argentine Republic*, ICSID case No. ARB/03/15, Award, 31 October 2011, paras. 245–56.

106. *See e.g.* B Kunoy, 'Developments in Indirect Expropriation Case Law in ICSID Transnational Arbitration', (2005) 6/3 *JWIT* 467, at 469; A Hoffmann, 'Indirect Expropriation', in A Reinisch (ed.), *Standards of Investment Protection* (2008), 156, 158–9 & 168; A Reinisch, 'Expropriation', in P Muchlinski et al (2008), 444–7; Montt (2009), 256; Newcombe and Paradell (2009), 325–7 & 341–8; S Puig and M Kinnear, 'NAFTA Chapter Eleven at Fifteen: Contributions to a Systemic Approach in Investment Arbitration', (2010) 25/2 *ICSID Rev.* 225, at 251; Salacuse (2010), 298 & 316–17; Vandevelde (2010), 289–302; M Porterfield, 'State Practice and the (Purported) Obligation under Customary International Law to Provide Compensation for Regulatory Expropriations', (2011) 37/1 *NC JILCR* 159, at 160, 163–5; Dolzer and Schreuer (2012), 112. *Cf.* Kingsbury and Schill (2010), 90–1; M Perkams, 'The Concept of Indirect Expropriation in Comparative Public Law – Searching for Light in the Dark', in S Schill (ed.), *International Investment Law and Comparative Public Law* (2010), 110–11; and Yannaca-Small (2010), 468.

107. Annex B of the 2004 Uruguay–USA BIT, and Annex B of the 2008 Rwanda–USA BIT.

108. *See* Chapter 6 below.

109. *See Penn Central Transportation Co. v. New York City*, (1978) 438 US 104.

110. *See* Chapters 6 & 7 below. Note 4 to Art. 1, of both the 2004 Uruguay–USA BIT and the 2008 Rwanda–USA BIT, provides that the term investment does not include an order or judgment entered in a judicial or administrative action. This declaration also follows the US regulatory takings doctrine, where judicial decisions cannot constitute expropriation. *See* Been and Beauvais (2003), 79.

111. Fortier and Drymer (2004), 317–19.

112. *See* Arts. 10 and 11, and Annex B.13 (1) of the 2006 Canada–Perú BIT; Art. XVII and Annex B of the 2009 Canada–Latvia BIT; and Art. IX and Annex A of the 2010 Canada–Slovakia BIT.

113. *See* the 2005 Afghanistan–Germany BIT; the 2006 Mexico–UK BIT; the 2007 Switzerland–Syria BIT; the 2008 Japan–Uzbekistan BIT; the 2009 Czech Republic–Saudi Arabia BIT; and the 2010 Chile–Uruguay BIT

114. Protocol to the 2007 Bahrein–Germany BIT.

115. *See e.g.* Art. 11 and Annex C of the 2007 Colombia–Perú BIT; and Art. 6 of the 2009 Colombia–India BIT. *Cf.* the 2005 Colombia–Spain BIT; the 2006 Colombia–Switzerland BIT; and the 2010 Colombia–UK BIT.

116. *See* Chapters 3 & 4 above.

117. *See* J Crawford, *The International Law Commission's Articles on State Responsibility. Introduction, Text and Commentaries* (2005), 77. *See also* Hoffmann (2008), 160; Reinisch, 'Expropriation' (2008), 431–2; and Newcombe and Paradell (2009), 337–8.

    Olguín is a rare example in which the tribunal refused to recognise omissions as constitutive of indirect expropriation. *Eudoro Armando Olguín c. República del Paraguay,* ICSID case No. ARB/98/5, Award, 26 July 2001, para. 84. *See* C McLachlan, L Shore and M Weiniger, *International Investment Arbitration: Substantive Principles* (2008), 291–2. *See also* S Nikièma, *L'expropriation indirecte en droit international des investissements* (2012), 121–9.

118. *See Ltd. Benvenuti et Bonfant srl. v. The Government of the People's Republic of the Congo*, ICSID case No. ARB/77/2, Award, 8 August 1980, (1982) 21/4 *ILM* 740.

119. *See Biloune and Marine Drive Complex Ltd v. Ghana Investments Centre and the Government of Ghana*, UNCITRAL arbitration, Award on Jurisdiction and Liability, 27 October 1989, (1994) 95 *ILR* 183.
120. *Ibid.*, at 209.
121. *See Southern Pacific Properties (Middle East) Limited (SPP) v. Arab Republic of Egypt*, ICSID case No. ARB/84/3, Award, 20 May 1992, (1993) 32/4 *ILM* 933.
122. *SPP*, Award, 20 May 1992, para. 158.
123. *Ibid.*, para. 159.
124. *See SPP*, Award, 20 May 1992, paras. 164, 169 & 172. The panel rejected the argument of the respondent that expropriation applies only to real property rights, quoting *Chorzow Factory*, *Amoco* and *Phillips Petroleum*. *See Factory at Chorzow*, Judgment, 13 September 1928; *Amoco International Finance Corporation v. The Government of the Islamic Republic of Iran et al*, Iran–US CT, Partial Award No. 310-56-3, 14 July 1987, (1988) 15 *Iran–US CTR* 189; and *Phillips Petroleum Company Iran v. The Islamic Republic of Iran and The National Iranian Oil Company*, Iran–US CT, Award No. 425-39-2, 29 June 1989, (1990) 21 *Iran–US CTR* 79.
125. *Antoine Goetz et consorts c. Republique du Burundi*, ICSID case No. ARB/95/3, Award, 10 February 1999, para. 124.
126. *See Wena Hotels*, Award, 8 December 2000.
127. *See Tippets, Abbett, McCarthy, Stratton (TAMS) v. TAMS-AFFA Consulting Engineers of Iran, The Government of the Islamic Republic of Iran et al*, Iran–US CT, Award No. 141-7-2, 29 June 1984, (1986) 6 *Iran–US CTR* 219. *See* Chapter 4 above.
128. *Wena Hotels*, Award, 8 December 2000, paras. 98–101.
129. *Wena Hotels*, Award, 8 December 2000, para. 97. In *AMCO*, however, the revocation of an investment licence was not considered a taking, but a breach of a *sui generis* legal relationship – comparable to a contract – between the alien and Indonesia. The arbitral panel found a violation by the host-state of a principle similar to that of *pacta sunt servanda* in international law, on one hand, and of the respect due for the acquired rights of the US investor, derived from that legal relationship, on the other. The proceedings in *AMCO* were instituted under the relevant settlement provision of an investment agreement between the foreign investor and the host-state, and the relevant provision of an investment code of Indonesia. *See AMCO Asia Corporation et al v. The Republic of Indonesia*, ICSID case No. ARB/81/1, Award, 21 November 1984, (1985) 24/4 *ILM* 1022, paras. 189, 244 & 248.
130. *See* A Newcombe, 'The Boundaries of Regulatory Expropriation in International Law', (2005) 20/1 *ICSID Rev.* 1, at 8. *See also* Vandevelde (2010), 301. *Olguín* and *Lauder* are exceptions to this general trend. *See Olguín*, Award, 26 July 2001, para. 84, and *Lauder*, Award, 3 September 2001, para. 203.
131. *See Lauder*, Award, 3 September 2001, and *CME*, Partial Award, 13 September 2001.
132. J Paulsson and Z Douglas, 'Indirect Expropriation in Investment Treaty Arbitrations', in N Horn (ed.), *Arbitrating Foreign Investment Disputes. Procedural and Substantive Legal Aspects* (2004), 150.
133. Paulsson and Douglas (2004), 150.
134. *Ibid.*, 152–3.
135. *See Middle East Cement Shipping and Handling Co. v. Arab Republic of Egypt*, ICSID case No. ARB/99/6, Award, 12 April 2002.
136. *Middle East Cement*, Award, 12 April 2002, paras. 100–1 & 107. Egypt was also found responsible for the administrative seizure and auction of a ship of the Greek investor, after the enactment of the decree that tacitly revoked its license. These

measures were considered by the tribunal to have effects 'tantamount to expropriation'. *Ibid.* para. 144.

137. *See* Chapters 3 & 4 above.
138. *Goetz*, Award, 10 February 1999, para. 126.
139. *Biloune*, Award on Jurisdiction and Liability, 27 October 1989, at 209.
140. *Ibid.*
141. *See Compañia del Desarrollo de Santa Elena, S.A. v. The Republic of Costa Rica*, ICSID case No. ARB/96/1, Award, 17 February 2000. This case was not based in a BIT and the dispute referred to the amount of compensation paid by Costa Rica to the US investor.

   Examples of BIT arbitrations involving direct takings are *Franz Sedelmayer v. The Russian Federation*, SCC arbitration, Award 7 July 1998; *Swembalt AB, Sweden v. The Republic of Latvia*, UNCITRAL arbitration, Award 23 October 2000; *ADC*, Award, 2 October 2006; *Bernardus Henricus Funnekotter and Others v. Republic of Zimbabwe*, ICSID case No. ARB/05/6, Award 22 April 2009; and *Waguih Elie George Siag and Clorinda Vecchi v. Arab Republic of Egypt*, ICSID case No. ARB/05/15, Award, 1 June 2009.
142. *Santa Elena*, Award, 17 February, 2000, para. 71.
143. *Santa Elena*, Award, 17 February 2000, para. 77. It also declared that:

   > [a] decree which heralds a process of administrative and judicial considerations of the issue in a manner that effectively freezes or blights the possibility for the owner reasonably to exploit the economic potential of the property, can, if the process thus triggered is not carried out within a reasonable time, properly be identified as the actual act of taking.

   Ibid., para. 76.
144. *See* Chapter 6 below.
145. *CME*, Partial Award, 13 September 2001, para. 321.
146. *Generation Ukraine*, Award, 16 September 2003, paras. 20.23–5.
147. *Generation Ukraine*, Award, 16 September 2003, paras. 20.29, 20.37 & 23. No taking was found in this case.
148. *See TECMED*, Award, 29 May, 2003.
149. *See Metalclad Corporation v. United Mexican States*, NAFTA, ICSID case No. ARB(AF)/97/1, Award, 30 August 2000. *See* Chapter 6 below.
150. *TECMED*, Award, 29 May, 2003, paras. 113–14.
151. *TECMED*, Award, 29 May 2003, para. 115. The tribunal referred to *Pope & Talbot* and the Third Restatement of the Foreign Relations Law of the United States, in this point. *See* Chapter 6 below.
152. *TECMED*, Award, 29 May 2003, para. 115.
153. *Ibid.*
154. *See Baruch Ivcher Bronstein v. Perú*, I/A Court HR, Series C No. 74, Judgment, 6 February 2001. *See* Chapter 3 above.
155. *See Matos e Silva Lda. and Others v. Portugal*, Eur. Court HR, Reports of Judgments and Decisions 1996-IV, Judgment, 16 September 1996. *See* Chapter 3 above.
156. *See Phelps Dodge Corp. and Overseas Private Investment Corp. v. The Islamic Republic of Iran*, Iran–US CT, Award No. 217-99-2, 19 March 1986, (1987) 10 *Iran–US CTR* 121. *See* Chapter 4 above.
157. *TECMED*, Award, 29 May 2003, para. 116.
158. *See* Newcombe (2005), 17–20. *See* Chapter 3 above & Chapter 6 below.
159. *TECMED*, Award, 29 May 2003, para. 122.
160. *Ibid.*

161. *TECMED*, Award, 29 May 2003, para. 122. The tribunal quoted profusely from the case-law of the European Court of Human Rights. *Matos*, *Mellacher*, *Pressos Compania Naviera* and *James* were mentioned in this regard. *See Mellacher and Others v. Austria*, Eur. Court HR, Series A No. 169, Judgment, 19 December 1989; *Pressos Compania Naviera S.A. and Others v. Belgium*, Eur. Court HR, Series A No. 332, Judgment, 20 November 1995; and *James and Others v. United Kingdom*, Eur. Court HR, Series A No. 98, Judgment, 21 February 1986. *See* Chapter 3 above.
162. *TECMED*, Award, 29 May 2003, paras. 129–32, 139, 144–5 & 148.
163. *Ibid.*, para. 151.
164. *Azurix*, Award, 14 July 2006, paras. 310–12.
165. *LG&E*, Decision on Liability, 3 October 2006, paras. 189 & 194–6.
166. *See Emanuel Too v. Greater Modesto Insurance Associates and the United States of America*, Iran–US CT, Award No. 460-880-2, 29 December 1989, (1991) 23 *Iran–US CTR* 378. *See* Chapter 4 above.
167. *See* Chapter 6 below.
168. *Continental Casualty Company v. Argentine Republic*, ICSID case No. ARB/03/9, Award, 5 September 2008, para. 276.
169. *Azurix*, Award, 14 July 2006, para. 322; *LG&E*, Decision on Liability, 3 October 2006, paras. 198–200; and *Continental Casualty*, Award, 5 September 2008, para. 283.
170. *See Tza*, Award, 7 July 2011.
171. *Ibid.*, paras. 152–70.
172. *Ibid.*, paras. 144, 156, 163 & 170.
173. *Ibid.*, paras. 171–218.
174. *Ibid.*, paras. 205 & 218.
175. *Ibid.*, paras. 219–22.
176. *Ibid.*, paras. 223–40.
177. *Ibid.*, para. 240.
178. *CCL v. Republic of Kazakhstan*, SCC case 122/2011, Final Award 2004, at 173. No taking was found in this case. *See* Hoffmann (2008), 162.
179. *See Pope & Talbot. Inc. v. The Government of Canada*, NAFTA, UNCITRAL arbitration, Interim Award, 26 June 2000. *See* Chapter 6 below.
180. *See* Chapter 4 above.
181. *Occidental*, Award, 1 July 2004, para. 89.
182. *CMS*, Award, 12 May, 2005, para. 261. *See CME*, Partial Award, 13 September 2001, para. 604.
183. *See* Chapter 4 above.
184. *See* Chapter 6 below.
185. No substantial and permanent deprivation was found by the tribunal, persuaded by Argentina's argument that after the measures adopted in response to the financial crisis in the country, CMS retained the full ownership and control of its investment. *CMS*, Award, 12 May 2005, para. 263.
186. *See Eureko,* Partial Award, 19 August 2005.
187. *Ibid.*, paras. 241–2.
188. *Eureko*, Partial Award, 19 August 2005, paras. 241 & 243. *See* Chapter 6 below.
189. *See Saluka Investments BV v. The Czech Republic*, UNCITRAL arbitration, Partial Award, 17 March 2006. *See also Methanex Corporation v. United States of America*, NAFTA, UNCITRAL arbitration, Final Award, 3 August 2005. *See* Chapter 6 below.
190. *Saluka*, Partial Award, 17 March 2006, para. 255.
191. *Ibid.*, para. 258.
192. *Ibid.*, para. 263.
193. *See ibid.*, para. 245.

194. *Ibid.*, para. 265.
195. *El Paso*, Award, 31 October 2011, para. 240. According to this panel, only unreasonable (*i.e.*, arbitrary or disproportionate) general regulations can amount to indirect expropriation if they neutralise the use of the corresponding investment. *See ibid.*, paras. 241–56.
196. *Telenor*, Award, 13 September 2006, paras. 65–7 & 79–80.
197. *Ibid.*, para. 70.
198. *See ADC*, Award, 2 October 2006.
199. *ADC*, Award, 2 October 2006, para. 432. Particularly damaging to Hungary's plea of public purpose was its subsequent privatisation of the airport, acquired by a company not related to the foreign investor.
200. *ADC*, Award, 2 October 2006, paras. 434–5.
201. *See Siemens A.G. v. The Argentine Republic*, ICSID case No. ARB/02/8, Award, 6 February 2007.
202. *Ibid.*, paras. 253, 260, 267 & 271.
203. *Siemens*, Award, 6 February 2007, para. 270. *See Norwegian Shipowners* (Norway v. USA), Anderson, Vogt and Valloton, arbitrators, Award, 13 October 1922. (1922) 1 *RIAA* 307.
204. *Siemens*, Award, 6 February 2007, para. 273.
205. *See Aguas del Aconquija*, Award, 20 August 2007.
206. *Aguas del Aconquija*, Award, 20 August 2007, para. 7.5.11. *See ibid.*, para. 7.5.24, 7.5.30 & 7.5.34.
207. *See* Chapter 4 above.
208. *See* Chapter 6 below.
209. *Aguas del Aconquija*, Award, 20 August 2007, paras. 7.5.20–1.
210. *BC Group*, Final Award, 24 December 2007, para. 259.
211. *See Starrett Housing Corporation, Starrett Systems, Inc., Starrett Housing International, Inc., v. The Government of the Islamic Republic of Iran et al*, Iran–US CT, Interlocutory Award No. ITL 32-24-1, 19 December 1983, (1985) 4 *Iran–US CTR* 122. *See* Chapter 4 above.
212. *See* Chapter 6 below.
213. *BC Group*, Final Award, 24 December 2007, paras. 260–72.
214. *Biwater Gauff*, Award, 24 July 2008, para. 452, 455–6 & 463.
215. *Ibid.*, para. 463.
216. *See ibid.*, paras. 485–519.
217. *See Tokios Tokelés*, Award, 26 July 2007, paras. 119–20; *Sempra*, Award, 28 September 2007, paras. 284–5; *Metalpar*, Award, 6 June 2008, paras. 172–4; *L.E.S.I.*, Award, 12 November 2008, paras. 130–1; and *Nations Energy*, Award, 24 November 2010, paras. 684–5.
218. *Rumeli Telekom A.S. and Telsim Mobil Telekomikasyon Hizmetleri A.S. v. Republic of Kazakhstan*, ICSID case No. ARB/05/16, Award, 29 July 2008, para. 702.
219. *Ibid.*, para. 700.
220. *See ibid.*, paras. 704–15.
221. *Saipem S.p.A. v. People's Republic of Bangladesh*, ICSID case No. ARB/05/7, Award, 30 June 2009, paras. 129, 132–4, 155–61, 167–70, 173 & 187.
222. *Alpha Projektholding*, Award, 8 November 2010, paras. 408–10.
223. *Marion Unglaube and Reinhard Unglaube v. Republic of Costa Rica*, ICSID cases No. ARB/08/1 and ARB/09/20, Award, 16 May 2012, paras. 209–21 & 223.
224. *Ibid.*, para. 205.

6. Takings in multilateral treaties

Different organisations have failed in their attempts to regulate the property of aliens in a multilateral treaty. The League of Nations and the ICC had a brief interest in the protection of foreign investment, during the first half of the 20th century. Before the decline of the NIEO, expropriation was highly debated at the UN General Assembly for at least two decades. In the 1960s, a failed multilateral treaty of the OECD played a leading role in the development of BITs, essential to what was later to become international investment law. In the 1990s, however, another unsuccessful attempt by the OECD to formulate a multilateral treaty on foreign investment ended up affecting this new area of law. The World Bank established in the 1960s and the 1980s two of the most important organisations in the history of international investment law: ICSID and MIGA. Additionally, it drafted a set of general guidelines for the treatment of aliens, which somehow filled the gap that had existed for a universal treaty regulating expropriation in international law.

In the meantime, a couple of institutions in the USA issued non-binding instruments, tackling the question of foreign investment from a domestic point of view. A fair number of mostly plurilateral treaties currently include investment provisions among their articles, repeating the protection against expropriation found in BITs. As a consequence, these treaties do not openly adopt a clear effects or police-powers solution. Arbitral tribunals established under NAFTA have construed its takings provision in a remarkably influential case-law, which construes the conventionally undefined notions of indirect expropriation and measures tantamount to it. Early NAFTA awards followed an effects approach, a convenient solution for the US government when other host-states were in the dock. When foreign investors started lodging expropriation claims against the USA, it became a threat and the reaction was swift. Rejecting a position defended for more than a hundred years in the international *fora*, the USA limited the protection of foreign investors to a national treatment standard equivalent to its domestic law, implicitly discarding the principle of international minimum treatment for aliens it had helped establish.

This chapter studies those instruments that emerged out of the failed efforts of international organisations and NGOs: from the Charter for an International Trade Organization (Havana Charter) to the Multilateral Agreement on Investment (MAI). It also explains the evolution of the expropriation clauses in EIAs, analysing the case-law of prominent treaties like NAFTA and ECT. The effects approach of *Pope & Talbot*, *Metalclad*, *S.D. Myers*, *GAMI*, *Glamis Gold*, *Cargill*, *Merrill & Ring* and *Grand River*, is contrasted with the police-powers solution adopted by *Methanex* and *Chemtura*. Awards not opting for a clear effects or police-powers position, like *Feldman*, *Waste Management 2*, *Fireman's Fund* and *Archer Daniels*, are also discussed. Outside of NAFTA, the following pages survey the answer given to the threshold question in *Nykomb*, *Petrobart*, *Plama*, *AES* and *RDC*.

6.1 DOCTRINE AND SOFT-LAW

One of the proposals of the 1944 conference on economic affairs held in Bretton Woods, New Hampshire, USA, was the creation of an international organisation focused on world trade. In the following years, negotiations on a constitutive treaty for this organisation took place within the UN Economic and Social Council (ECOSOC), during which the issue of expropriation of aliens was discussed. The second session of the ECOSOC Preparatory Committee, held at Geneva in 1947, concluded with a draft establishing that 'just compensation' should be paid in case of taking.[1] This provision was later deleted due to its lack of precision. The charter of the International Trade Organization (ITO), finally signed in Cuba's capital in 1948, included only generally-worded articles on the regulation of the property of aliens.[2]

Before the Havana Charter, two unsuccessful initiatives had been undertaken to regulate foreign investment at a multilateral level. In 1929, the League of Nations convened in Paris a diplomatic conference with the purpose of concluding an international convention on the treatment of aliens and foreign enterprises. A year later, the Hague Conference on the Codification of International Law included, among the issues under discussion, the responsibility of states for damage caused in their territory to the person or property of foreigners. Neither initiative achieved its objective, according to Peter Muchlinski 'due to the refusal of Latin American, East European and ex-colonial states to accept the traditional international minimum standards of treatment insisted upon by the capital-exporting states'.[3]

Following the demise of the Havana Charter, private-sector bodies in Europe and the USA, as well as international organisations, made several efforts to regulate foreign investment. The OECD and the World Bank group have been prominent in this, the former through its 1967 Draft Convention on the Protection of Foreign Property and 1998 MAI, and the latter through its 1965 ICSID or Washington Convention, 1985 MIGA Convention and 1995 Guidelines on the Treatment of Foreign Direct Investment.

6.1.1 First Attempts to Address Expropriation

Even though the Havana Charter was signed by 54 countries, a good number for the 1940s, it eventually failed to enter into force.[4] The investment articles of this treaty were reduced to two generally worded provisions, after the payment of just compensation for takings was excluded from its final version.[5] Article 11 established a broad protection of foreign investment, in the form of a negative obligation on the members of the ITO to avoid adopting unreasonable or unjustifiable measures within its territory, injurious to the rights or interests of nationals of other members. The importance of foreign investment in the promotion of economic development and social progress was recognised in Article 12, which required ITO members to stimulate the flow of capital from abroad, while acknowledging the right of the host-state to regulate its entry. Endorsing FCNs, the same provision encouraged the conclusion of bilateral and multilateral treaties for the promotion and protection of foreign investment among its members.

Due to its historical context, the Havana Charter required the support of the USA, to the point where other contracting countries decided to wait for its ratification in this state, before becoming a party to the treaty themselves. President Harry Truman submitted the Havana Charter to the US Congress in 1948. Two years later, his administration announced that it would no longer seek approval for the ITO.[6] For Andreas Lowenfeld, the treaty was abandoned in 1950 mainly for reasons unrelated to its investment provisions.[7] In his view, the US administration considered:

> that support for the Havana Charter might impair support for higher-priority issues of foreign affairs such as the Marshall Plan for the reconstruction of Europe […] and (from the summer of 1950 on) pursuit of the war in Korea.[8]

Not all authors agree with this position. Franziska Tschofen identifies the Havana Charter's 'unsatisfactory provisions on foreign investment' as one of the main reasons for its failure.[9] Muchlinski recalls that these provisions caused widespread opposition to the treaty among the business community in the USA.[10] Stefan Riesenfeld is of the same opinion. US businesses had particularly strong objections to Article 12, whose investment protection was considered to be 'too vague and too weak'.[11] Laura Loppacher and William Kerr add that the same countries that had pushed for investment to be included in the Havana Charter began to fear that the agreement negotiated did not provide adequate guarantees against expropriation.[12] Jeswald Salacuse confirms this. According to him, capital-exporting countries were not satisfied with the investment provisions of the Havana Charter.[13] Whatever the reason was, the abandonment of the Havana Charter in the USA led the other signatories to desist from securing its ratification in their respective states.

Meanwhile, a non-governmental organisation based in Paris had drafted an International Code of Fair Treatment for Foreign Investments. Among other protections, the 1949 ICC Code provided that the expropriation of the property of aliens should only be adopted with the appropriate legal procedure and fair compensation, determined prior to the taking in conformity with international law.[14] Designed as a model to be followed in the negotiation of bilateral and multilateral treaties, the ICC Code was presented to the UN for consideration by the governments and the ECOSOC, but was never adopted.[15] Almost ten years later, the Society to Advance the Protection of Foreign Investments – a private organisation based in Cologne, Germany – drew up the International Convention for the Mutual Protection of Private Property Rights in Foreign Countries. This draft was prepared under the guidance of Hermann Abs, chairperson of Deutsche Bank, and was combined in 1957 with another one prepared under the leadership of the UK's attorney-general, Lord Hartley Shawcross. Issued in 1959 as the Draft Convention on Investments Abroad (Abs/Shawcross Draft), this instrument did not expressly establish the right to expropriate, but acknowledged it by implication.[16] According to its authors, Article III of the draft was based on the idea that every state enjoys a sovereign right to nationalise or expropriate all property situated in its territory. In the case of alien property, this right may only be exercised under certain conditions.[17] Article III followed some of the requirements of a lawful expropriation:

> No Party shall take any measures against nationals of another Party to deprive them directly or indirectly of their property except under due process of law and provided that such measures are not discriminatory or contrary to undertakings given by that Party and are accompanied by the payment of just and effective compensation. Adequate provision shall have been made at or prior to the time of deprivation for the prompt determination and payment of

> such compensation, which shall represent the genuine value of the property affected, be made in transferable form, and be paid without undue delay.[18]

The comment on the Abs/Shawcross Draft explained that the purpose of this provision was to restate the international minimum standard.[19] In fact, the draft mentioned a just compensation which closely resembles the Hull formula. For its authors, this was the same standard applied in the *Norwegian Shipowners*' claim and the *Chorzow Factory* case, among other judicial decisions. The comment further recognised that the Abs/Shawcross Draft closely followed US FCNs. As Stanley Metzger notes, it was even more protective than these treaties or other multilateral efforts that foundered in the past.[20] From this perspective, as Georg Schwarzenberger rightly points out, the omission of the public interest requirement for lawful takings is surprising.[21] The Abs/Shawcross Draft was submitted by the Federal Republic of Germany to the OECD for 'consideration and appropriate action'.[22] Never concluded as a treaty, it was the basis of yet another unsuccessful attempt: the Draft Convention on the Protection of Foreign Property of the OECD. But before this, Harvard University professors Louis Sohn and Richard Baxter would revise and update, upon the request of the UN Secretariat, a draft convention on the international responsibility of states for injuries to aliens, prepared by Edward Borchard in 1929.

Sohn and Baxter presented their work to the ILC in 1961.[23] According to its authors, the Draft Convention on the International Responsibility of States for Injuries to Aliens (Harvard Draft) was based on the principle of an international minimum standard governing the treatment of aliens. Its purpose was not only 'to codify with some particularity the standards established by international law for the protection of aliens and thereby to obviate, as far as possible, the necessity of looking to customary international law', but also to develop these norms when necessary by the incorporation of 'international standards of the principles of law or of justice recognized by the principal legal systems of the world'.[24] The Harvard Draft was by far the most detailed instrument regulating the protection against expropriation in its time. The elements of a lawful taking included in Article 10 were public purpose, and payment of compensation in conformity with the Hull formula. According to this provision, the required public purpose had to be 'clearly recognized as such by a law of general application in effect at the time of the taking'.[25] The explanatory note on Article 10 pointed out that this qualification was intended to preclude *ad hoc* determinations of public purpose by government officials 'acting without any express authority in law'.[26] The same note observed that the content of this condition had never been defined with any degree of precision in comparative law, and that international tribunals had rarely embarked upon a survey of what in fact constitutes public purpose.[27]

Article 10 and its explanatory note described the second requirement of a lawful expropriation in Hull's terms.[28] If no compensation was paid, damages would provide proper reparation for the unlawful taking. In case of an expropriation adopted not for a public purpose or in violation of a treaty, restitution was the ordinary remedy. The owner would have no obligation to accept the compensation tendered, but if he did accept it, his claim to restitution of the property should be considered waived.[29] The requirement of compensation was applicable also for nationalisations. In this case, however, Article 10 allowed the host-state to pay it over a 'reasonable period of years', under certain conditions.[30] The Harvard Draft defined the concept of property applicable to this provision in broad terms, comprising tangibles and intangibles.[31] Article 10 explicitly included in its coverage not only outright takings, but also:

> any such unreasonable interference with the use, enjoyment, or disposal of property as to justify an inference that the owner thereof will not be able to use, enjoy, or dispose of the property within a reasonable period of time after the inception of such interference.[32]

Several examples of indirect takings were mentioned in the explanatory note: among others, blocking the entrance of a factory to make impossible its operation by the alien; denying entry visas for foreign technical personnel; the appointment of managers and inspectors interfering with the free use by the alien of its investment.[33] The case-law of the Iran–US CT and early *ad hoc* arbitrations dealt with some of these situations.[34] Although still possible, they seem rather dated today. Current investment-dispute claims are lodged generally to challenge highly sophisticated contractual and regulatory schemes. The note also added that whether an interference with property constituted an expropriation depends upon the duration of the interference. This determination might prove particularly difficult, considering that Article 10 expressly recognised the possibility of temporary takings.[35] Finally, the unreasonableness of the interference was to be determined in conformity with general principles of law.[36]

The Harvard Draft followed, to some extent, the US regulatory-takings doctrine.[37] Article 10 described certain non-compensable state regulations in such wide terms, that in practice it established a police-powers rule. According to its fifth paragraph, an uncompensated deprivation of property derived from: the execution of tax laws; the general change in the value of currency; the action of competent authorities in the maintenance of public order, health, or morality; the valid exercise of belligerent rights; or the normal operation of the laws of the state, was not considered wrongful if it complied with the following requirements: it did not amount to a clear and discriminatory violation of the host-state; it was not in breach of due process of law; it was not an 'unreasonable departure from the principles of justice recognized by the principal legal systems of the world'; and it was not a result of the abusive exercise of the regulatory powers of the host-state with the intention of depriving an alien of his or her property.[38] The explanatory note confirmed this approach by mentioning 'the requisite intent', necessary in the adoption of a measure that amounts to an expropriation.[39]

6.1.2 Guidelines for a Lack of Agreement

The OECD's Council approved the publication of its Draft Convention on the Protection of Foreign Property in 1967. Failing to gain sufficient international support, it was never opened to signature. The OECD only recommended the draft to its members as a model for investment protection treaties. In Muchlinski's view, the opposition of less developed southern-European OECD members prevented the convention from being adopted.[40] Rudolf Dolzer and Margrete Stevens add another reason for the failure of the Draft Convention: the fact that it was originally intended as a multilateral instrument applicable to all countries, and not only to OECD members.[41] An international organisation formed by developed states, negotiating a multilateral treaty aimed at the protection of foreign investments in mostly developing countries, was not a good idea. This circumstance would prove again to be fatal thirty years afterwards for MAI.

Article 3 of the OECD Draft Convention referred to expropriation, declaring that no party shall adopt any measure depriving directly or indirectly a national of another party of his property, unless the host-state complied with the conditions of a lawful taking: public interest, non-discrimination, payment of compensation, and due process of law. In conformity with its official commentary, Article 3 was meant to cover in particular 'creeping nationalisations', defined as measures otherwise lawful, applied in such a way as to 'deprive ultimately the alien of the enjoyment or value of his property', without any specific identifiable act of outright expropriation.[42] As examples of this type of taking, the commentary mentioned: excessive or arbitrary taxation; the prohibition of dividend distribution coupled with compulsory loans; the imposition of administrators; the prohibition of dismissal of staff; and the refusal of access to raw materials or of essential export or import licenses.[43] The same notes and comments stressed that '[t]he taking of property, within the meaning of the Article, must result in a loss of title or substance'.[44]

In this context, the police-powers solution adopted by the OECD in this draft is unexpected. Although nothing in the actual wording of Article 3 denoted such an approach, its commentary makes this solution explicit, by stating that the provision brought 'within its compass any measures taken with the intent of wrongfully depriving the national concerned of the substance of his rights and resulting in such loss'.[45] This is a confusing statement. The notes and comments on Article 3 had already acknowledged the right of the host-state to expropriate, that is to deprive the alien of his property, and expressly reconciled this right with its correspondent obligation to respect and protect foreign property, through the fulfilment of the four conditions of a lawful taking.[46] Why add 'with the intent of wrongfully depriving' then? This confusion still haunts the debate on indirect takings today.

As to other aspects of a taking, the official commentary followed the traditional rules of international law. For instance, it makes clear that whether the host-state's interference with property amounted to a deprivation depends 'on its extent and duration'.[47] In a position later adopted by the Iran–US CT, the notes and comments pointed out that though a measure may purport to be temporary, there comes a stage at which there is no immediate prospect that the owner will be able to resume the enjoyment of his property.[48] The commentary to Article 3 added that the requirement of public purpose implies that the expropriatory measures must be adopted in the interest of the state or any of its political subdivisions, not solely for private gain.[49] The notes and comments to this provision corroborate that the just compensation mentioned there conforms to the Hull formula.[50] The official commentary to Article 3 equated the requirement of due process with the concept of rule of law or *rechtsstaat*, containing both substantive and procedural elements present not only in the domestic law of the state concerned, but also in the principles of international law.[51] These notes and comments highlighted the availability of judicial review of the expropriatory measure, by an independent administrative or judicial tribunal, as an important safeguard included in this condition of due process.[52]

The American Law Institute, an NGO established in 1923 for the improvement of the law and the administration of justice, published its Third Restatement of the Foreign Relations Law of the United States in 1987. This instrument adopted a police-powers rule similar to that of Section 712 of the Harvard Draft, which dealt with state responsibility for economic injury to nationals of other states. The Third Restatement mentioned three requirements for a lawful taking: public purpose, non-discrimination – *i.e.*, no unreasonable distinction – and payment of just compensation, described in conformity with the Hull formula.[53] The commentary on Section 712 observed that although public purpose is reiterated in most formulations of the protection against expropriation, this condition has not figured prominently in international case-law 'perhaps because the concept [...] is broad and not subject to effective re-examination by other states'.[54] That direct and indirect takings are included in this provision is confirmed in another comment, which described the latter as an unreasonable interference, preventing or delaying the effective enjoyment of an alien's property.[55] Nonetheless, the same explanatory note added:

> A state is not responsible for loss of property or other economic disadvantage resulting from bona fide general taxation, regulation, forfeiture for crime, or other action of the kind that is commonly accepted as within the police powers of states, if it is not discriminatory.[56]

Not surprisingly, the reporters' notes to Section 712 of the Third Restatement explained that generally the line between compensable and non-compensable regulatory actions in international law is similar to that drawn in the US case-law on the Fifth Amendment.[57]

Three years after the publication of the Third Restatement, the UN abandoned its Draft Code of Conduct on Transnational Corporations (TNCs).[58] The legitimacy of the claims of capital-importing states for greater control over TNCs had been gradually accepted by international organisations in the second half of the 20th century, which began studying how to balance the interests of foreign investors and host-states in the 1970s.[59] It was against this background that the UN Code of Conduct was negotiated within the Commission on TNCs, established in 1974 by ECOSOC for the purpose of drafting this instrument. The last version available of the UN Draft Code is the text submitted in 1990 to ECOSOC by the chairman of the Commission on TNCs, reflecting the status of the negotiations as at 1986.[60] The UN Draft Code recognised the sovereign right to expropriate foreign property, directly or indirectly, in accordance with international law. In relation to the requirements of a lawful taking, the UN Draft Code mentioned not only public purpose, the payment of compensation and due process of law, but also respect for specific undertakings not to expropriate, adopted by contract or other agreement, already recognised in the Abs/Shawcross Draft. Compensation was described as prompt, adequate and effective – and as appropriate, in an alternative version. According to the UN Draft Code, expropriation claims should be settled under the domestic law of the host-state by its tribunals, respecting the international obligations freely undertaken by the authorities of this country.[61] In the end, the UN Draft Code was never adopted, due to strong disagreements between capital-importing and capital-exporting countries over an explicit reference to international minimum standards of treatment.[62] Nonetheless, it still informs issues of corporate responsibility, debated in the negotiation of investment treaties.[63]

It is in this context that the World Bank adopted its Guidelines on the Treatment of Foreign Direct Investment in 1992.[64] The Development Committee decided in 1991 to set up a working group consisting of lawyers from each of the institutions of the World Bank,[65] for the purpose of drafting a legal framework to FDI. This working group prepared a report, and submitted it a year later to the Development Committee. The report explained that the World Bank Group could not issue binding rules to states, and that although a multilateral treaty could be drawn and opened for signature, such a solution was not recommended, given the reluctance of states to commit themselves to this type of instrument in the area of foreign investment. Instead, the working group recommended the World Bank to issue non-binding guidelines, based on the general trends identified in the review of existing legal instruments, doctrine and available practice, and on the policies advocated by it in recent years. The resulting text was approved by the Development Committee for circulation among the member states of the World Bank group.[66]

The preamble of the Guidelines expressly stated their purpose and nature: to achieve a desirable overall framework of essential principles that would promote FDI in the common interest of all of the World Bank's members. As it declared, the Guidelines are 'not ultimate standards but an important step in the evolution of generally acceptable international standards which complement [BITs or EIAs]'.[67] There is no doubt that the Guidelines fit the description of soft-law found in the writings of some scholars,[68] *i.e.*, instruments which are normative in substance, but not in a legally binding form.[69] The Guidelines encouraged the admission of foreign investment, and at the same time recognised the right of the host-state to make regulations governing its admittance.[70] They also acknowledged the right of the state to expropriate 'or otherwise take' foreign investment, in whole or in part, or to adopt 'measures which have similar effects', following these conditions: 'in accordance with applicable legal procedures, in pursuance in good faith of a public purpose, without discrimination on the basis of nationality and against the payment of appropriate compensation'.[71] The latter is described in the terms of the Hull formula.[72] In case of nationalisation, the Guidelines recommended the determination of its compensation through negotiations between the host-state and the state of the expropriated foreigner; failing this, through international arbitration.[73]

6.2 INVESTMENT CHAPTERS OF EIAS AND THE FALL OF MAI

Not altogether far from Article 3 of the 1967 OECD Draft Convention on the Protection of Foreign Property, the 1980 Unified Agreement for the Investment of Arab Capital in the Arab States includes tangibles and intangibles in its notion of property, and allows host-states to:

> (a) Seize property for the public benefit in accordance with the authority vested in the State or its institutions to perform their functions in implementing public projects, provided that this is done on a non-discriminatory basis in return for fair compensation and according to general legal provisions regulating the seizure of property for the purposes of the public benefit.[74]

The 1985 MIGA Convention also adopts a traditional approach to the problem of indirect takings.[75] MIGA is an international organisation aimed at encouraging FDI and portfolio investment in developing states, mainly by providing insurance to foreign investors against political or non-commercial risks in these countries.[76] Its constitutive treaty describes expropriation and similar measures, as one of the covered risks, in these terms:

> any legislative action or administrative action or omission attributable to the host government which has the effect of depriving the holder of a guarantee of his ownership or control of, or a substantial benefit from, his investment, with the exception of non-discriminatory measures of general application which governments normally take for the purpose of regulating economic activity in their territories.[77]

This wording reveals an effects rule, undermined by an excessively broad police-powers exception.[78] In the years following the MIGA Convention, the issue of expropriation was addressed in another plurilateral treaty,[79] probably the most influential of them all: the 1992 NAFTA.[80]

The awards issued under the dispute settlement mechanism of this treaty have not only shaped recent BITs and EIAs of the USA and Canada, but of few other countries as well. NAFTA case-law even affected the OECD's MAI, which drowned partly due to the growing apprehension of developed countries and NGOs towards international claims directed against the host-state's exercise of its regulatory powers. This is a new scenario. In the past, the opposition to the international minimum standard came exclusively from second- and third-world countries. Now that most of them support it through investment treaties, countries like the USA and Canada endorse its counterpart, the principle of national treatment as a maximum standard, so strongly objected to by them for more than a hundred years. The reason? The treatment currently expected from developing countries with regard to foreign investors is demanded from developed states too. From this perspective, the chances for any future attempt to regulate investment universally in a multilateral treaty seem bleak.

6.2.1 NAFTA and other Plurilateral Treaties

NAFTA was an expansion to the earlier 1988 Canada–USA FTA, based on the US BIT model then available. While the Canada–USA FTA did not include the direct referral of investment disputes to international arbitration, NAFTA now provides for such a possibility.[81] Its Article 1120 gives the foreign investor the chance of opting among the Washington Convention, the ICSID Additional Facility Rules,[82] or the UNCITRAL Arbitration Rules,[83] following a period of consultation between the disputing parties. The expropriation provision of NAFTA is found in Chapter 11, sometimes called the investors' bill of rights.[84] The requirements of a lawful taking included in Article 1110 are public purpose, non-discrimination, payment of compensation, and due process of law. Compensation is described in detail according to the Hull formula. This article also adds another condition: the expropriatory measure must be adopted in accordance with FET and full protection and security. As to the investment protected by the international standard, NAFTA contains an innovative definition. Even though BITs normally provide an illustrative list of assets, Article 1139 establishes a closed or exhaustive one, with specific exclusions. In other words, what is not in this definition is not covered by the treaty. The list in NAFTA includes tangible and intangible property.[85]

Direct and indirect nationalisations and expropriations are expressly mentioned in Article 1110, as well as measures tantamount to them. Measure is defined in Article 201, paragraph 1, as any law, regulation, procedure, requirement or practice. Like other investment treaties, NAFTA gives no concept of expropriation and nationalisation, whether direct or indirect. This was a deliberate omission. The strategy of its drafters was to leave the solution to the problem of how to distinguish non-compensable regulation and indirect takings to arbitral panels. As one of the principal US negotiators in NAFTA recalls:

> If the United States Supreme Court and arbitral tribunals could not do it in over 200 years, it was unlikely that the negotiators were going to do it in a matter of weeks with one line in a treaty.[86]

No clear solution is found in the treaty on the problem of intent. In conformity with Article 1114, a general exception clause, nothing in Chapter 11 shall be construed to prevent a contracting party from adopting, maintaining or enforcing any measure otherwise consistent with it, that this party considers appropriate to ensure that the investment activity in its territory is undertaken in a manner sensitive to environmental concerns.[87] This provision might well be interpreted as a police-powers rule, or a police-powers exception from an effects perspective, depending on which provision is considered *lex specialis*: Article 1114 or Article 1110.

The interpretation of NAFTA's Chapter 11 given by arbitral panels established under its dispute-settlement provisions has strongly influenced subsequent US FTAs and BITs.[88] Last-generation investment treaties of the USA are drafted in conformity with the guidelines of the 2002 Trade Promotion Act, enacted in the wake of the award in *Metalclad*, while *Methanex* was still pending and other arbitrations threatening US interests loomed in the horizon. Section 2102 (b) (3) of this statute dealt with foreign investment, and declared:

> Recognizing that United States law on the whole provides a high level of protection for investment, consistent with or greater than the level required by international law, the principal negotiating objectives of the United States regarding foreign investment are to reduce or eliminate artificial or trade-distorting barriers to foreign investment, while ensuring that foreign investors in the United States are not accorded greater substantive rights with respect to investment protections than United States investors in the United States, and to secure for investors important rights comparable to those that would be available under United States legal principles and practice, by – (A) reducing or eliminating exceptions to the principle of national treatment; [...] (D) seeking to establish standards for expropriation and compensation for expropriation, consistent with United States legal principles and practice.[89]

This statement is remarkable. By giving foreign investors in the USA no greater substantive rights than its domestic investors, one of the main advocates of an absolute minimum standard of treatment in international law has adopted a relative maximum standard, linked to a specific national treatment. Such a limitation goes against the system of protection established at present in most BITs and EIAs, consisting in the complementary application of the international and national minimum standards.

Non-discrimination, as both a minimum and maximum standard of treatment, was developed in Latin America by the end of the 19th century.[90] The statement of the 2002 Trade Promotion Act is, in substance, identical to the national treatment standard adopted in 1890 by the First International Conference of American States, which Jan Paulsson identifies as one of the early formal recognitions of the Calvo doctrine in state practice.[91] The statement of the Trade Promotion Act is also similar to Article 9, paragraph 2, of the 1934 Montevideo Convention on the Rights and Duties of States, singled out by Francisco Garcia Amador as one of the most prominent examples of the Calvo doctrine in treaty-law.[92] It is even close to the Calvo clause interpreted in *North American Dredging Co.*, which established that:

> The contractor and all persons who, as employees or in any other capacity, may be engaged in the execution of the work under this contract either directly or indirectly [...] shall not claim, nor shall they have, with regard to the interests and the business connected with this contract, any other rights or means to enforce the same than those granted by the laws of the Republic [of Mexico] to Mexicans, nor shall they enjoy any other rights than those established in favour of Mexicans.[93]

A US official document employing the wording of one the most fought-upon Latin American doctrines on the treatment of aliens surely represents a turning point in this area of international law. The reasons behind this radical change of mind in US authorities are found in the report of the Senate Finance Committee on the bill from which the Trade Promotion Act's provisions derived. As this document explained:

> one concern expressed about investment agreements currently in force is that the concept of what constitutes an expropriation may be interpreted more broadly than the concept of what constitutes a 'taking' under U.S. law. U.S. takings law has evolved through more than two centuries of decisions by the Supreme Court and lower courts. While there is no fixed set of criteria, that jurisprudence has given rise to certain guidelines, such as criteria for determining when a government regulation (as opposed to a physical appropriation of land) amounts to a compensable 'taking'. By contrast, certain complaints under NAFTA chapter 11 have urged arbitrators to find expropriations where the applicable tests under U.S. law may not support compensation for a taking. While there is unlikely ever to be a perfect overlap, and U.S. courts themselves differ on these issues, section 2 (b) (3) (D) directs

> negotiators to draw on the guidelines developed in U.S. takings jurisprudence in seeking to refine the concept of expropriation for purposes of international investment agreements. This should help ensure that investment agreements do not confer on foreign investors in the United States a right to compensation for expropriation that differs substantially from the right to compensation for takings that U.S. citizens already enjoy.[94]

After the Trade Promotion Act was enacted, the USA has signed and ratified FTAs and BITs which include a description of indirect expropriation in the form of the three *Penn Central* factors developed in US regulatory-takings doctrine.[95] In this way, international tribunals are generally guided towards a police-powers solution in those expropriation cases where the USA is involved, under any of these treaties.[96] Among the US treaties that include such a statement, as well as other clarifications that spring from the same doctrine,[97] are the Chile and Singapore FTAs;[98] the Australia, Central America and Dominican Republic (CAFTA–DR), and Morocco FTAs;[99] the Oman FTA;[100] and the Korea FTA.[101] Besides the latest Canadian FTAs,[102] most of the EIAs concluded by countries other than the USA have not yet included the qualifications put forward by this state in its treaties.[103] The Panamá–Singapore FTA is still one of the few exceptions to this trend.[104]

In the same period that NAFTA was concluded, a regional and a sectorial treaty came to regulate the expropriation of aliens in Africa and Eurasia. The 1993 Treaty establishing the Common Market for Eastern and Southern Africa (COMESA), describes the right of the host-state to take the property of aliens in its Article 159.4, from a clear effects perspective:

> expropriation shall include any measures attributable to the government of a Member State which have the effect of depriving an investor of his ownership or control of, or a substantial benefit from his investment and shall be interpreted to include all forms of expropriation such as nationalisation and attachment as well as creeping expropriation in the form of imposition of excessive and discriminatory taxes, restrictions in the procurement of raw materials, administrative action or omission where there is a legal obligation to act or measures that frustrate the exercise of the investors rights to dividends, profits and proceeds of the right to dispose of the investment.[105]

The 1994 ECT was concluded as an international effort to integrate the energy sector of former Soviet states with that of Western Europe, and provide legal foundations for energetic security in an open and competitive market. Today, it has more than 50 member-states in Asia and Europe.[106] The investment regime of the ECT was largely based on UK BITs and NAFTA's Chapter 11.[107] As a consequence, the definition of investment is wide, followed by a list of examples that comprise tangibles and intangibles, though limited to a specific sector of the economy: energy.[108] Article 13 repeats the four conditions of a lawful taking, Hull formula included, and mentions measures having an effect equivalent to an expropriation or nationalisation. The wording of this provision reflects neither an effects nor a police-powers solution. Article 26 regulates the settlement of investor-to-state disputes. It gives the claimant the choice of initiating arbitrations proceedings under the Washington Convention, the ICSID Additional Facility Rules, the UNCITRAL Arbitration Rules, or before the Arbitration Institute of the Stockholm Chamber of Commerce (SCC), after consultation. Slowly, the case-law of ECT arbitrations has begun to join that of NAFTA and BITs in furthering the international law of expropriation.

6.2.2 A Good Idea Wrongly Executed

The 2007 COMESA Common Investment Area Agreement and the 2009 Comprehensive Investment Agreement of the Association of Southeast Asian Nations (ASEAN) are plurilateral treaties which exclusively regulate the property of aliens. Of these two, only the ASEAN investment agreement is currently in force.[109] While the COMESA investment agreement includes an implicit police-powers rule which is reminiscent of that of the 1961 Harvard Draft,[110] the ASEAN treaty repeats to a large extent the declaration on indirect takings of last-generation US BITs and FTAs,[111] following an innovation introduced in the 2007 Korea–USA FTA:[112] to combine the character of the government action, the last of three *Penn Central* factors,[113] with the proportionality test, first applied to international law by the European Court of Human Rights and to investment treaty arbitration by *TECMED*'s tribunal.[114]

A decade before the conclusion of the ASEAN Comprehensive Investment Agreement, the last effort to regulate foreign investment in a multilateral treaty of universal reach came to naught. MAI's negotiations took place within the OECD between 1995 and 1998, when the first NAFTA arbitrations were being settled; more precisely, among its then 29 members, mostly developed states,[115] and the European Communities. Eight non-OECD members participated as observers only[116] – other non-OECD members were informed on a regular basis about the status and substance of the negotiations. MAI had been planned as a multilateral treaty open to all OECD members and non-OECD members, based on three pillars: investment liberalisation, investment protection, and dispute settlement.[117] It followed, and improved, the investment protections of NAFTA and ECT.[118] BITs, modelled on the 1967 OECD

Draft Convention on the Protection of Foreign Property, were also an important source for the international minimum standard included in it. MAI had a clear leaning towards foreign investors and was promoted as an effort to transform these protections into multilateral rules, with some additional provisions.[119] The concept of property included in its consolidated text was broad.[120] Chapter II, Article 2, defined investment as every kind of asset owned or controlled, directly or indirectly, by an alien. Some OECD members and NGOs expressed their concerns over the inclusion of investments indirectly owned.[121] An interpretative note was added to this provision, stating that in order to qualify as an investment under MAI, 'an asset must have the characteristics of an investment, such as the commitment of capital or other resources, the expectation of gain or profit, or the assumption of risk'.[122] The definition was followed by an illustrative list, including portfolio investment and FDI. The commentary to the consolidated text explained that this list of assets covered 'all recognised and evolving forms of investment'.[123]

Chapter IV, Article 2, was the expropriation provision. It protected foreign investments against direct and indirect takings, as well as 'any measure or measures having equivalent effect'. The four requirements of a lawful taking, normally found in BITs and EIAs, were mentioned in this provision. The first one was described as 'a purpose which is in the public interest'. According to the commentary, the terms 'public purpose' and 'public interest' have similar meanings, but derive from different legal traditions. The wording chosen was considered to be consistent with them.[124] Chapter IV, Article 2, employed the Hull formula to describe the payment of compensation, and due process was construed as expressly including the judicial review of the expropriatory measure by a competent and independent authority of the host-state.

Concerns over the contours of indirect takings led to an explicative note in the commentary to this provision, stating that the violation of criminal laws resulting in the total or partial loss of an investment would not be deemed an expropriation, 'provided those laws and their application are non-discriminatory and otherwise consistent with the standards of this agreement'.[125] This approach conforms to the police-powers exception acknowledged by the effects doctrine. The 1998 report by the chairman of the negotiating group added that the takings provision was intended to incorporate into MAI existing international norms, and that the reference to expropriation or nationalisation, and measures tantamount to either, reflected the fact that international law requires compensation for a taking without regard to the label applied to it, even if the title to the property is not taken. In other words, as the report said, it did not establish 'a new requirement that Parties pay compensation for losses which an investor or investment may incur through regulation, revenue raising and other normal activity in the public interest undertaken by governments'.[126] A declaration adopted by the OECD Council of Ministers that same year further stated that 'the MAI would establish mutually beneficial international rules which would not inhibit the normal non-discriminatory exercise of regulatory powers by governments and such exercise of regulatory powers would not amount to expropriation'.[127]

The commentary to the consolidated text explained that the phrase 'measure or measures having equivalent effect' meant, in general, creeping expropriation.[128] Regarding the practical consequence of distinguishing between a lawful and an unlawful taking, it said that the former would be subject to the Hull formula, while the latter would give rise to a right of restitution under customary law.[129] Such a view is not found expressly stated in BITs or EIAs, but has been endorsed in doctrine and exceptionally in case-law.[130] To effectively protect the property of aliens, MAI included a dispute settlement device for investor-to-state controversies. Chapter V gave the investor the choice, commonly found in BITs and some EIAs, to submit the respective controversy to the domestic courts or administrative tribunals of the host-state, or to international arbitration under *ad hoc*, ICSID, UNCITRAL, or the ICC rules.

Though the provisions of MAI were not particularly new in international law, it failed mainly for the lack of a representative body of states in the negotiations.[131] One of the main reasons for the adoption of MAI was to liberalise and protect foreign investment in developing countries. These states, however, were not adequately represented in the negotiating process from the beginning. The OECD, unlike the World Bank group or other international organizations, proved not to be the most adequate *forum* for drafting a multilateral treaty aimed at being universal. Additionally, NGOs resented not being invited to participate in the negotiations and criticised the secretiveness of the whole process.[132] The clear inclination of MAI towards foreign investors, derived from BITs and EIAs, became suspicious and a prime target of criticism for developing states and NGOs, which related the treaty with the widespread anti-globalisation campaigning against international economic organisations.[133] The growing opposition even distressed European governments, eager not to upset their electorates.[134] The timing of MAI was also not the best. At the end of the 1990s, claims of indirect takings were lodged against developed countries in the context of NAFTA. *Ethyl* and *Metalclad*, for instance, affected the negotiations.[135] There were other problems too. For example, the right of entry and establishment, borrowed from NAFTA and US BITs, was only accepted with significant general and country-specific exceptions, resulting in what was called a

'Swiss cheese' agreement.[136] Several countries had expressed their concern about the liberalisation of the media sector to foreign investment, fearing an 'Americanisation' of this industry. The cultural exception to the national treatment standard of MAI became a deal breaker for these states, particularly for France.[137] Eventually, it was the Prime Minister of this country, Lionel Jospin, who declared in 1998 that his government would take no further part in the negotiations of MAI. A few days later, the OECD announced that it would not proceed with them.[138]

6.3 THE CASE-LAW OF FTAS AND ECT

NAFTA awards have generally upheld the substantial and permanent deprivation standard, emphasising the economic result of the expropriatory measure on the affected investment.[139] On the threshold question, NAFTA case-law initially followed an effects approach, best described in *Metalclad*.[140] Willingly or not, all parties of this treaty accepted this rule, when capital-exporting countries were equated with developed states, and capital-importing countries with developing states. The potential application of an effects solution to claims that challenge the regulatory powers of the USA and Canada, in sensitive areas like the protection of the environment or public health, and taxation, *inter alia*, changed this.

The interpretation given by NAFTA panels to 'investment' and 'measures', two concepts closely related to the article on expropriation, have expanded the scope of the protection afforded by this provision.[141] This and the potential application of the effects rule explains the unlikely circumstance of Canada and Mexico supporting a police-powers solution to the problem of indirect takings in their written submissions to the tribunal in *Methanex*; a proceeding where the respondent was the USA, advocating the same approach.[142] Recently, the jurisprudence of NAFTA has oscillated between these rules. Some awards have mentioned the proportionality test of the European Court of Human Rights, without elaborating on how to conciliate this notion with the text of NAFTA's takings provision. So far, the case-law of other FTAs and ECT has recognised the substantial and permanent deprivation standard, following an effects approach.

6.3.1 Early NAFTA Awards

Pope & Talbot is an early example of an effects solution to the problem of indirect takings in NAFTA case-law.[143] In this arbitration, the claim filed by the US investor against Canada was rejected, applying the test of substantial deprivation.[144] The respondent had argued that regulations constitute an exercise of police-powers which is beyond the reach of NAFTA rules on expropriation, unless employed in a discriminatory manner. *Pope & Talbot* expressly denied such a contention, declaring that regulations can indeed be exercised in a way that would constitute creeping expropriation.[145] According to the panel, a blanket exception for regulatory measures would create a 'gaping loophole in international protections against expropriation'.[146] The tribunal identified different examples of indirect takings, against which it assessed the claim of Pope & Talbot:

> [...] the Investor remains in control of the Investment, it directs the day-to-day operations of the Investment, and no officers or employees of the Investment have been detained by virtue of the [export control] Regime. Canada does not supervise the work of the officers or employees of the investment, does not take any of the proceeds of company sales (apart from taxation), does not interfere with management or shareholders' activities, does not prevent the Investment from paying dividends to its shareholders, does not interfere with the appointment of directors or management and does not take any other actions ousting the Investor from full ownership and control of the Investment.[147]

These examples resemble those of the case-law of the Iran-US CT.[148] In *Pope & Talbot*, the claimant argued that the phrase 'measure tantamount to nationalization or expropriation' of Article 1110 broadens the ordinary concept of takings in international law, requiring compensation for measures affecting property without regard to the magnitude or severity of their effect. In this respect, the award simply stated: '"Tantamount" means nothing more than equivalent. Something that is equivalent to something else cannot logically encompass more'.[149] This position has been normally followed by subsequent NAFTA arbitrations.[150]

In 2000, a second expropriation claim was settled under NAFTA from an effects standpoint. Metalclad was a US investor that bought a Mexican company to develop and operate a hazardous-waste landfill located in the municipality of Guadalcázar, in the state of San Luis Potosí, Mexico.[151] After obtaining authorisations from the Mexican federal state, the national ecological institute, and the state of San Luis Potosí, the claimant was refused a construction permit by the municipality of Guadalcázar. Its request for reconsideration of the denial of the permit was also rejected by the municipality, which then effectively prevented Metalclad from opening the finished landfill. The claimant unsuccessfully lodged an administrative complaint, as well as a constitutional action. Finally, the governor of the state of San Luis Potosí issued an ecological decree declaring a natural area for the protection of a rare cactus encompassing the landfill.

The panel concluded that Mexico had violated Article 1110. According to it, the exclusive authority regarding a hazardous-waste landfill resided with the Mexican federal state, which permitted or tolerated the conduct of Guadalcázar towards Metalclad, and participated or acquiesced in the denial of its right to operate the landfill, notwithstanding the fact that the project had been fully approved and endorsed by federal authorities. As a result, Mexico's conduct amounted to a measure equivalent to expropriation in breach of NAFTA.[152] Quoting *Biloune*,[153] the tribunal held that the actions of the municipality effectively and unlawfully prevented the claimant's operation of the landfill. These measures, together with the representations of the Mexican federal government, on which Metalclad had relied, 'and the absence of a timely, orderly or substantive basis for the denial by the Municipality of the local construction permit', were equivalent to an indirect taking.[154] The ecological decree of the governor of the state of San Luis Potosí was considered by the tribunal as a further ground for a finding of expropriation.[155] *Metalclad* based its conclusions in one of the most famous statements of the effects doctrine in international case-law:

> expropriation under NAFTA includes not only open, deliberate and acknowledged takings of property, such as outright seizure or formal or obligatory transfer of title in favour of the host State, but also covert or incidental interference with the use of property which has the effect of depriving the owner, in whole or in significant part, of the use or reasonably-to-be-expected economic benefit of property even if not necessarily to the obvious benefit of the host State.[156]

That same year, a third decision of a NAFTA panel implicitly endorsed the effects rule, rejecting an expropriation claim lodged against Canada. In *S.D. Myers*, the tribunal differentiated takings from regulations in their results: the former tends to involve the deprivation of ownership right, while the latter a lesser interference.[157] This award accepted the possibility of partial or temporary takings, and agreed with *Pope & Talbot*'s conclusion that the phrase 'measure tantamount to' means 'equivalent to', because the drafters of NAFTA intended the word 'tantamount' to embrace the concept of creeping expropriation, 'rather than to expand the internationally accepted scope of the term expropriation'.[158]

Another expropriation claim was turned down two years later, applying a rather confusing effects solution to the threshold question. *Feldman* expressly declared in 2002:

> If there is a finding of expropriation, compensation is required *even if* [*sic*] the taking is for a public purpose, non-discriminatory and in accordance with due process of law and Article 1105(1) [on FET, and full protection and security].[159]

This award mentioned some examples of indirect takings, and then recognised a police-powers rule similar to that of the Harvard Draft:

> The Tribunal notes that the ways in which governmental authorities may force a company out of business, or significantly reduce the economic benefits of its business, are many. In the past, confiscatory taxation, denial of access to infrastructure or necessary raw materials, imposition of unreasonable regulatory regimes, among others, have been considered to be expropriatory actions. At the same time, governments must be free to act in the broader public interest through protection of the environment, new or modified tax regimes, the granting or withdrawal of government subsidies, reductions or increases in tariff levels, imposition of zoning restrictions and the like. Reasonable governmental regulation of this type cannot be achieved if any business that is adversely affected may seek compensation, and it is safe to say that customary international law recognizes this.[160]

The panel relied heavily on the Third Restatement of the Foreign Relations of the United States and its comments in this respect. *Feldman* also referred to *Azinian*, when it stated that:

> not all government regulatory activity that makes it difficult or impossible for an investor to carry out a particular business, change in the law or change in the application of existing laws that makes it uneconomical to continue a particular business, is an expropriation under Article 1110. Governments, in their exercise of regulatory power, frequently change their laws and regulations in response to changing economic circumstances or changing political, economic or social considerations. Those changes may well make certain activities less profitable or even uneconomic to continue.[161]

Regarding the interpretation of the phrase 'measure tantamount to nationalization or expropriation', *Feldman* followed *Pope & Talbot* and *S.D. Myers*.[162] The panel quoted *Metalclad* on the problem of the degree of interference, but had its doubts as to whether the lack of transparency alone constitutes a violation of NAFTA or general international law.[163]

In 2004, two other claimants were not successful either. According to the panel in *Waste Management 2*:

> Article 1110 (1) distinguishes between direct or indirect expropriation on the one hand and measures tantamount to an expropriation on the other. An indirect expropriation is still a taking of property. By contrast where a measure tantamount to an expropriation is alleged, there may have been no

> actual transfer, taking or loss of property by any person or entity, but rather an effect on property which makes formal distinctions of ownership irrelevant. […]
>
> Evidently the phrase 'take a measure tantamount to nationalization or expropriation of such an investment' in Article 1110 (1) was intended to add to the meaning of the prohibition, over and above the reference to indirect expropriation.[164]

The tribunal did not regard the conduct of Mexico as an expropriation, 'within the meaning attributed to that term in *Metalclad*'.[165] For this panel, statements 'made by local political figures in the heat of public debate may or may not be wise or appropriate, but they are not tantamount to expropriation unless they are acted on in such a way as to negate the rights concerned without any remedy'.[166] For the tribunal in *Waste Management 2*:

> The mere non-performance of a contractual obligation is not to be equated with a taking of property, nor (unless accompanied by other elements) is it tantamount to expropriation. Any private party can fail to perform its contracts, whereas nationalization and expropriation are inherently governmental acts, as is envisaged by the use of the term 'measure' in Article 1110 (1).[167]

In other words:

> […] it is one thing to expropriate a right under a contract and another to fail to comply with the contract. Non-compliance by a government with contractual obligations is not the same thing as, or equivalent or tantamount to, an expropriation. [I]t is necessary to show an effective repudiation of the right, unredressed by any remedies available to the Claimant, which has the effect of preventing its exercise entirely or to a substantial extent.[168]

No indirect taking, or measures tantamount to an expropriation, were found in this case.[169] Nor in *GAMI*, where the panel cited *Metalclad*, and the non-NAFTA case of *Santa Elena*,[170] to conclude that the property of the US investor was not expropriated by Mexico under Article 1110.[171] *GAMI* supported the proposition that the partial destruction of the value of an investment may amount to a taking.[172] The tribunal quoted *Pope & Talbot* and *S.D. Myers* on the issue, but considered their references to Article 1110 as inconclusive *obiter dicta*.[173]

6.3.2 In a Current State of Flux

The first NAFTA award to embrace a police-powers rule was *Methanex*, in 2005.[174] In this arbitration, a Canadian investor claimed compensation for the losses caused by the state of California's ban on the sale and use of a gasoline additive, to which its main product was a feedstock. Methanex alleged damages to 'a substantial portion of [its] customer base, goodwill, and market for methanol in California' as a result of the ban.[175] The award agreed with *Pope & Talbot*'s broad concept of property.[176] Nevertheless, it concluded that items such as goodwill and market share may figure in the valuation of a comprehensive taking, '[b]ut it is difficult to see how they might stand alone, in a case like the one before the Tribunal'.[177] The panel considered the claim within the limits of the phrase 'measure tantamount to [...] expropriation' of NAFTA's Article 1110, analysing it from a police-powers perspective, worded in these terms:

> as a matter of general international law, a non-discriminatory regulation for a public purpose, which is enacted in accordance with due process and, which affects, inter alios, a foreign investor or investment is not deemed expropriatory and compensable unless specific commitments had been given by the regulating government to the then putative foreign investor contemplating investment that the government would refrain from such regulation.[178]

The tribunal quoted the *Revere Copper* arbitration and *Waste Management 2* on the issue of assurances, representations or undertakings given by host-states to aliens.[179] According to *Methanex*, public purpose, non-discrimination and due process of law are differentiating aspects between non-compensable regulations and expropriations, rather than conditions of a lawful taking. Although the panel started its declaration by saying 'as a matter of general international law', such an interpretation owes more to the US regulatory-takings doctrine than to international norms.[180] The problem with this statement is that it confuses the constitutive elements of a taking with the requirements of a lawful expropriation. By doing this, *Methanex* limited indirect takings to those measures that go against specific commitments made by the host-state to a foreign investor. In fact, the tribunal concluded that because in this case there were no such commitments, and the California ban complied with the conditions of public purpose, non-discrimination and due process, '[f]rom the standpoint of international law [it] was a lawful regulation and not an expropriation'.[181]

After *Methanex*, NAFTA panels have rejected the expropriation claims lodged against the parties to this treaty, either applying an effects or a police-powers rule. In *Fireman's Fund*, the tribunal explicitly followed a traditional approach, separating the constitutive elements of an expropriation from its conditions of lawfulness.[182] The award identified those elements, as recognised in NAFTA case-law, confirming that actions and omissions may constitute a taking.[183] *Fireman's Fund* expressly mentioned the substantial and permanent deprivation standard, the effects rule, and respect for the investor's legitimate expectations.[184] Then it declared:

> To distinguish between a compensable expropriation and a noncompensable regulation by a host State, the following factors (usually in combination) may be taken into account: whether the measure is within the recognized police powers of the host State; the (public) purpose and effect of the measure; whether the measure is discriminatory; the proportionality between the means employed and the aim sought to be realized; and the bona fide nature of the measure.[185]

In support of this asseveration, the panel quoted two BIT arbitrations: *TECMED* and *Saluka*.[186] This statement contradicts the reasoning of the same tribunal that issued it, exposed not only previously, but also subsequently in the award – for instance, when it openly admitted that '[i]t cannot be argued that because there is discrimination, there is expropriation', and that the proportionality test 'is used by the European Court of Human Rights [...] and it may be questioned whether it is a viable source of interpreting Article 1110 of the NAFTA'.[187] *Archer Daniels* adopted an unorthodox effects solution, close to that of *Fireman's Fund*.[188] The award started describing indirect takings as state measures which have equivalent effects to a direct expropriation.[189] On the threshold question, it simply declared:

> The test on which other Tribunals and doctrine have agreed – and on which the Claimants' rely – is the 'effects test'. Judicial practice indicates that the severity of the economic impact is the decisive criterion in deciding whether an indirect expropriation or a measure tantamount to expropriation has taken place. An expropriation occurs if the interference is substantial and deprives the investor of all or most of the benefits of the investment. There is a broad consensus in academic writings that the intensity and duration of the economic deprivation is the crucial factor in identifying an indirect expropriation or equivalent measure.[190]

The tribunal cited different arbitrations in this regard, both NAFTA (*Pope & Talbot*, *Feldman* and *Metalclad*) and non-NAFTA (*Norwegian Shipowners* and *LG&E*).[191] Subsequently, *Archer Daniels* added other factors to the answer for this question, some of which cannot be easily reconciled with an effects approach: the respect of legitimate expectations; the discriminatory nature of the correspondent state measure; its due process; and the proportionality between this measure and the alleged public purpose.[192] *Archer Daniels* gave no explanation as to how to integrate these elements with the effects solution adopted before. It only observed that the discriminatory character of a state measure, standing alone, 'is not a sufficient criterion for an expropriation'.[193] *Glamis Gold* explicitly labelled the threshold question as such, stating that it 'is an inquiry as to the degree of the interference with the property right. This often dispositive inquiry involves two questions: the severity of the economic impact and the duration of that impact'.[194] The tribunal applied an effects rule on the issue, quoting *Pope & Talbot* and *GAMI*,[195] even though it had already agreed with the Third Restatement's view, that '[a] State is not responsible [...] for loss of property or for other economic disadvantage resulting from bona fide ... [*sic*] regulation ... [*sic*] if it is not discriminatory'.[196] *Cargill* analysed the expropriation claim from the same perspective, focusing on the degree of Mexico's interference with the property of the US investor, studying the severity and duration of the economic impact of the challenged measure, with references to *S.D. Myers*, *GAMI* and *Fireman's Fund*.[197]

NAFTA case-law returned to the police-powers rule in 2010, with *Chemtura*. In this case, the panel stated that:

> [...] the practice of NAFTA tribunals has been to follow a three-step approach focusing on (i) whether there is an investment capable of being expropriated, (ii) whether that investment has in fact been expropriated, and (iii) whether the conditions set in Article 1110 (1) (a)–(d) have been satisfied.[198]

The second step of this analysis requires an answer to the threshold question. For this purpose, *Chemtura* followed the substantial deprivation standard, as a 'fact-sensitive exercise to be conducted in the light of the circumstances of each case'.[199] Applying this standard, the panel concluded that the measures adopted by Canada did not amount to such an interference with the US investor's property.[200] Notwithstanding its own previous statement differentiating the constitutive elements of an expropriation from the conditions of a lawful taking, *Chemtura* recognised thereupon a police-powers rule similar to that described in *Methanex*.[201] It declared that 'in any event [...] the measures challenged by the Claimant constituted a valid exercise of the Respondent's police powers' because the Canadian agency had acted within its mandate, in a non-discriminatory manner, motivated by a public purpose.[202] In the tribunal's view, '[a] measure adopted under such circumstances is a valid exercise of the State's police powers and, as a result, does not constitute an expropriation'.[203] The panel quoted a BIT arbitration (*Saluka*) in support of this asseveration.[204] This police-powers solution was not followed in later NAFTA awards, like *Merrill & Ring* or *Grand River*.[205]

The case-law of other plurilateral treaties follows the general trend of BIT and NAFTA arbitrations on the threshold question. *RDC* was the first award issued on the merits in an investment dispute under CAFTA–DR. This tribunal rejected in 2012 the expropriation claim of the US investor, applying the effects rule and the substantial deprivation standard, as developed in NAFTA case-law (*Metalclad* and *Fireman's Fund*) and BIT arbitrations (*CMS* and *Telenor*).[206] Concerning the ECT jurisprudence on indirect takings, *Petrobart*'s declaration of 2005 is worth recalling:

> As to Article 13 (1) of the Treaty, which deals with expropriation, the Arbitral Tribunal notes that this provision gives protection not only in respect of expropriation but also in regard to measures having effect equivalent to expropriation. Such measures are sometimes referred to as 'indirect', 'creeping' or '*de facto*' expropriation and are frequently assimilated to formal expropriation as regards their legal consequences.[207]

In this arbitration, the tribunal turned down the expropriation claim[208] – as in *Nykomb*, *Plama* and *AES*, where the respective panels implicitly or explicitly recognised the effects rule and the substantial and permanent deprivation standard.[209] In the case of *Plama*, the panel applied this rule citing the jurisprudence of the Iran–US CT (*Starrett*),[210] BIT arbitrations (*TECMED*),[211] and NAFTA jurisprudence (*Fireman's Fund*).[212]

6.4 CONCLUSION

The attempts to regulate expropriation in a multilateral treaty span the whole of the 20th century. Various instruments emerged from these efforts. Early ones, like the 1949 ICC Code or the 1959 Abs/Shawcross Draft, implicitly or explicitly recognised the international minimum standard and briefly referred to takings. The first of these instruments to adopt an open police-powers approach was the 1967 OECD Draft Convention, highly influential in the BITs subsequently concluded by Western European states, but not in this aspect. Inspired by the domestic takings doctrine of the USA, the 1961 Harvard Draft and the 1987 Third Restatement of the Foreign Relations Law of the United States also adopted a police-powers solution, only recently included in US BITs and FTAs, as a reaction to the case-law of NAFTA. The 1990 UN Draft Code of Conduct of TNCs and the 1992 World Bank Guidelines on the Treatment of FDI followed the traditional requirements of a lawful expropriation, not referring expressly to the problem of intent.

Plurilateral treaties that mention or regulate expropriation, effectively concluded and in force today, have usually not opted for an effects or a police-powers rule in explicit terms. NAFTA is silent on the issue, unlike its case-law. Arbitral panels established under Chapter 11 have answered the threshold question mostly from an effects standpoint. Examples of this solution can be found in *Pope & Talbot*, *Metalclad*, *S.D. Myers*, *Feldman*, *GAMI*, *Glamis Gold*, *Cargill*, *Merrill & Ring* and *Grand River*. Exceptionally, *Methanex* and *Chemtura* adopted a police-powers rule, while *Fireman's Fund* and *Archer Daniels* identified proportionality as one of the factors that should help decision-makers to distinguish non-compensable regulation from indirect takings. The jurisprudence of other plurilateral treaties, particularly ECT and CAFTA–DR, have hitherto recognised the substantial and permanent deprivation standard and the effects rule, quoting the case-law of the Iran–US CT, BIT arbitrations and NAFTA awards.

The response of the USA to the threat posed by international claims directed against it, within the context of the effects approach endorsed by NAFTA case-law, was made official in the 2002 Trade Promotion Act. After this statute, BITs and FTAs concluded by the USA have incorporated its domestic takings doctrine, expressly mentioning the *Penn Central* factors as a guideline for arbitral panels facing claims of indirect expropriation. This means the actual replacement of the long-advocated international minimum standard, by a national treatment standard limited to that offered by US domestic laws. Such an effort has been well received by Canada and a few other countries. Some NGOs, mainly those concerned with the protection of the environment, have joined the heterogeneous group which favours this approach.

NOTES

1. G Jaenicke, 'Havana Charter', in R Bernhardt (ed.), *EPIL* (1995), Vol. 2, 680. *See* A Lowenfeld, *International Economic Law* (2008), 483.
2. *See* Jaenicke (1995), 680; and M Matsushita, T Schoenbaum and P Mavroidis, *The World Trade Organization: Law, Practice, and Policy* (2006), 1–2.
3. P Muchlinski, *Multinational Enterprises & the Law* (2007), 654. *See* S Picciotto, 'Linkages in International Investment Regulation: The Antinomies of the Draft Multilateral Agreement on Investment', (1998) 19/3 *U. Penn. JIEL* 731, at 742–3; S Montt, *State Liability in Investment Treaty Arbitration: Global Constitutional and*

Administrative Law in the BIT Generation (2009), 52–4; and A Newcombe and L Paradell, *Law and Practice of Investment Treaties: Standards of Treatment* (2009), 15–7.
4. Jaenicke (1995), 679.
5. Available at http://www.worldtradelaw.net/misc/havana.pdf (last visited 30 June 2013).
6. Matsushita, Schoenbaum & Mavroidis (2006), 2. *See* Newcombe and Paradell (2009), 20.
7. Lowenfeld (2008), 483.
8. Lowenfeld (2008), 28. *See* S Schill, *The Multilateralization of International Investment Law* (2009), 34.
9. F Tschofen, 'Multilateral Approaches to the Treatment of Foreign Investment', (1992) 7/2 *ICSID Rev.* 384, at 387.
10. P Muchlinski, 'The Rise and Fall of the Multilateral Agreement on Investment: Where Now?', (2000) 34/3 *IL* 1033, at 1037; and Muchlinski (2007), 655.
11. S Riesenfeld, 'Foreign Investments', in R Bernhardt (ed.), *EPIL* (1995), Vol. 2, 436.
12. L Loppacher and W Kerr, 'Investment Rules. The U.S. Agenda in Bilateral Trade Agreements', (2006) 7/1 *JWIT* 39, at 40.
13. J Salacuse, *The Law of International Investment Treaties* (2010), 87–8.
14. Tschofen (1992), 388. *See* Newcombe and Paradell (2009), 20–1.
15. Tschofen (1992), 388. *See* Newcombe and Paradell (2009), 20.
16. *See* Tschofen (1992), 389 & 407; and Newcombe and Paradell (2009), 21–2.
17. 'Comment on the Draft Convention by Its Authors', (1960) 9/1 *JPL* 119, at 121.
18. Art. III of the Abs/Shawcross Draft, available at http://www.unctad.org/sections/dite/iia/docs/Compendium//en/137%20volume%205.pdf (last visited 30 June 2013). *See* K Vandevelde, *Bilateral Investment Treaties: History, Policy, and Interpretation* (2010), 285.
19. *See* H Abs and H Shawcross, 'Comment on the Draft Convention by Its Authors', (1960) 9/1 *JPL* 119, at 121.
20. S Metzger, 'Multilateral Conventions for the Protection of Private Foreign Investment', (1960) 9/1 *JPL* 133, at 133–4.
21. G Schwarzenberger, 'The Abs-Shawcross Draft Convention on Investments Abroad: A Critical Commentary', (1960) 9/1 *JPL* 147, at 156.
22. Tschofen (1992), 389. *See* Vandevelde (2010), 54.
23. This draft was done with the help of an advisory committee formed by professors of other law schools and practising lawyers in the USA. *See* L Sohn and R Baxter, 'Responsibility of States for Injuries to the Economic Interests of Aliens', (1961) 55/3 *AJIL* 545, at 545–6.
24. *Ibid.*, 547.
25. Art. 10, paras. 1 (a) & 2, of the Harvard Draft.
26. Sohn and Baxter (1961), 556.
27. *Ibid.*, 555–6.
28. Art. 10, paras. 2 & 6, of the Harvard Draft. *See* Sohn and Baxter (1961), 557–8 & 562–3.
29. *Ibid.*, 556–7.
30. Art. 10, para. 4, of the Harvard Draft. *See* Sohn and Baxter (1961), 557 & 559–61.
31. *See* Art. 10, para. 7, of the Harvard Draft.
32. Art. 10, para. 3 (a), of the Harvard Draft.
33. Sohn and Baxter (1961), 559.
34. *See* Chapter 4 above.
35. Art. 10, para. 3 (b) of the Harvard Draft. *See* Sohn and Baxter (1961), 554.
36. *Ibid.*, 559.
37. *See* Chapter 7 below.

38. Art. 10, para. 5, of the Harvard Draft. *See* Sohn and Baxter (1961), 561–2.
39. *Ibid.*, 559.
40. Muchlinski (2000), 1036; and Muchlinski (2007), 655. *See* Schill (2009), 38–9.
41. R Dolzer and M Stevens, *Bilateral Investment Treaties* (1995), 1–2. *See* Schill (2009), 36.
42. 'O.E.C.D. Draft Convention on the Protection of Foreign Property', (1968) 7 *ILM* 117, note 4 (b) at 125–6.
43. *Ibid.*, note 4 (b) at 126.
44. *Ibid.*, note 4 (c) at 126.
45. *Ibid.*, note 4 (a) at 125.
46. *See ibid.*, notes 1 (a) & 3 at 125.
47. *Ibid.*, note 4 (b) at 125.
48. *Ibid.*. *See* Chapter 4 above.
49. OECD Draft Convention (1968), note 5 at 126.
50. *Ibid.*, notes 8 & 9 at 127.
51. *Ibid.*, note 6 at 126.
52. *Ibid.*, note 6 (c) at 126.
53. American Law Institute, *Restatement of the Law Third, the Foreign Relations Law of the United States* (1987), 196–7 & 200.
54. *Ibid.*, 200.
55. *Ibid.*.
56. Third Restatement (1987), 201. *See* Chapter 7 below.
57. Third Restatement (1987), 211.
58. *See* Muchlinski (2007), 660–2.
59. Muchlinski (2000), 1037.
60. Available at http://www.unctad.org/sections/dite/iia/docs/Compendium//en/13%20volume%201.pdf (last visited 30 June 2013).
61. *See* UN Code of Conduct, para. 54.
62. Muchlinski (2007), 661.
63. Muchlinski (2000), 1037.
64. Available at http://ita.law.uvic.ca/documents/WorldBank.pdf (last visited 30 June 2013). *See generally* I Shihata, *Legal Treatment of Foreign Investment: The World Bank Guidelines* (1993).
65. *I.e.*, the International Bank for Reconstruction and Development (IBRD), the International Finance Corporation (IFC), the International Development Association (IDA), ICSID, and MIGA.
66. *See* Muchlinski (2007), 662–3. *See also* Newcombe and Paradell (2009), 49; and Salacuse (2010), 104–5.
67. Preamble, para. 6. In fact, investment treaties take precedence to the Guidelines, in case of conflict between the two. Guideline I, Section 1.
68. *See* C Chinkin, 'The Challenge of Soft Law: Development and Change in International Law', (1989) 38/4 *ICLQ* 850; H Hillgenberg, 'A Fresh Look at Soft Law', (1999) 10/3 *EJIL* 499; C Chinkin, 'Normative Development in the International Legal System', in D Sheldon (ed.), *Commitment and Compliance. The Role of Non-Binding Norms in the International Legal System* (2003); A Boyle and C Chinkin, *The Making of International Law* (2006), 210–29; P Birnie, A Boyle and C Redgwell, *International Law & the Environment* (2009), 34–7; and A Boyle, 'Soft Law in International Law-Making', in M Evans (ed.), *International Law* (2010).
69. The expression 'soft-law' is attributed to Lord Arnold McNair. Although this choice of words is certainly poor, for it reveals a contradiction in terms, the concept has generally been accepted in international doctrine. Not without dissenters, most notably Jan Klabbers and Prosper Weil. *See* P Weil, 'Towards Relative Normativity

in International Law?', (1983) 77/3 *AJIL* 413; and J Klabbers, 'The Redundancy of Soft Law', (1996) 65/2 *Nord. JIL* 167.

70. Guideline II.
71. Guideline IV, Section 1.
72. Guideline IV, Sections 2–9.
73. Guideline IV, Section 10. Regarding the settlement of investment disputes, the Guidelines declared that they should normally be resolved through negotiations. If not possible, through domestic courts or other agreed mechanisms, including binding independent arbitration, agreed upon in writing, in which case the Guidelines encourage states to accept ICSID's jurisdiction. Guideline V.
74. Art. 9.2 of the 1980 Unified Agreement for Arab Capital. *See ibid.*, Arts. 1.5 & 1.6. This treaty entered into force in 1981, and is available at http://www.unctad.org/sections/dite/iia/docs/Compendium//en/36%20volume%202.pdf (last visited 30 June 2013). *See* Salacuse (2010), 97–8.
75. In force since 1988.
76. It also advises developing governments on how to attract foreign investment, shares information by means of online services, and mediates investor-to-state disputes. *See* http://www.miga.org (last visited 30 June 2013). *See also* Schill (2009), 47–9.
77. Art. 11 of the 1985 MIGA Convention. *See ibid.*, Art. 12. This treaty is available at http://www.unctad.org/sections/dite/iia/docs/Compendium//en/16%20volume%201.pdf (last visited 30 June 2013).
78. *See* Newcombe (2005), note 88 at 22.
79. *See* A Aust, *Modern Treaty Law and Practice* (2007), 17.
80. NAFTA entered into force in 1994 and is available at http://www.international.gc.ca/trade-agreements-accords-commerciaux/agr-acc/nafta-alena/gen-nafta.aspx?view=d (last visited 30 June 2013).
81. Instead, the disputes under the Canada–USA FTA had to be brought before an intergovernmental commission, which had the discretionary power to refer them later to arbitration. *See* Arts. 1801–6 of the Canada–US FTA, (1988) 27 *ILM* 281. *See also* V Been and J Beauvais, 'The Global Fifth Amendment: NAFTA's Investment Protection and the Misguided Quest for an International "Regulatory Takings" Doctrine', (2003) 78/1 *NYU LR* 30, at 51–2.
82. These rules authorise the ICSID Secretariat to administer conciliation and arbitration proceedings between host-states and foreign investors for disputes which fall outside the scope of the Washington Convention. The 2006 ICSID Additional Facility Rules are available at https://icsid.worldbank.org/ICSID/StaticFiles/facility/AFR_English-final.pdf (last visited 30 June 2013).
83. The 2010 UNCITRAL Arbitration Rules are available at http://www.uncitral.org/pdf/english/texts/arbitration/arb-rules-revised/arb-rules-revised-2010-e.pdf (last visited 30 June 2013).
84. Been and Beauvais (2003), 40.
85. *See* Art. 1139 of NAFTA.
86. Daniel Price, quoted in Been and Beauvais (2003), 55. *See also* Z AlQurashi, 'Indirect Expropriation in the Field of Petroleum', (2004) 5/6 *JWIT* 897, at 901, note 45 at 904.
87. *See* Art. 1114, para. 1, of NAFTA. On general exception clauses, *see* S Spears, 'The Quest for Policy Space in a New Generation of International Investment Agreements', (2010) 13/4 *JIEL* 1037, at 1059–64; and S Nikièma, *L'expropriation indirecte en droit international des investissements* (2012), 77–9.
88. And EIAs or BITs of other countries too. *See* Chapter 5 above.
89. The 2002 Trade Promotion Act is available at http://www.bilaterals.org/IMG/pdf/TPAA_2002.pdf (last visited 30 June 2013).

90. F Francioni, 'Compensation for Nationalisation of Foreign Property: The Borderline between Law and Equity', (1975) 24/2 *ICLQ* 255, at 269. *See* Chapter 2 above.
91. J Paulsson, *Denial of Justice in International Law* (2005), 21. *Cf.* Vandevelde (2010), 73.
92. *See* Garcia-Amador (1992), 521.
93. D Shea, *The Calvo Clause: A Problem of Inter-American and International Law and Diplomacy* (1955), 200. *See North American Dredging Company of Texas* (USA v. Mexico), US–Mexican General Claims Commission, Decision. (1926) 4 *RIAA* 26. On the US Trade Promotion Act and the Calvo doctrine, *see* S Subedi, *International Investment Law: Reconciling Policy and Principle* (2012), 141–3.
94. Cited in G Sampliner, 'Arbitration of Expropriation Cases under U.S. Investment Treaties – a Threat to Democracy or the Dog That Didn't Bark?', (2003) 18/1 *ICSID Rev.* 1, at 37. *See also* M Porterfield, 'State Practice and the (Purported) Obligation under Customary International Law to Provide Compensation for Regulatory Expropriations', (2011) 37/1 *NC JILCR* 159, at 187–8.
95. *See Penn Central Transportation Co. v. New York City*, (1978) 438 US 104. *See* Chapter 5 above.
96. *See* Y Fortier and S Drymer, 'Indirect Expropriation in the Law of International Investment: I Know It When I See It, or *Caveat Investor*', (2004) 19/2 *ICSID Rev.* 293, at 317–19; G Gagné and J-T Morin, 'The Evolving American Policy on Investment Protection: Evidence from Recent FTAs and the 2004 Model BIT', (2006) 9/2 *JIEL* 357, at 359 & 381–2; and UNCTAD, *Investment Provisions in Economic Integration Agreements* (2006), 107–8.
97. *E.g.*, these treaties also exclude judicial or administrative actions from the open-ended definition of investment.
98. *See* Chapter 10 & Annexes 10-A & 10-D of the 2003 Chile–USA FTA, and Chapter 15 & Exchange Letter on Expropriation of the 2003 Singapore–USA FTA.
99. *See* Chapter 11 & Annexes 11-A & 11-B of the 2004 Australia–USA FTA; Chapter 10 & Annexes 10-B & 10-C of the 2004 CAFTA–DR; and Chapter 10 & Annexes 10-A & 10-B of the 2004 Morocco–USA FTA.
100. *See* Chapter 10 & Annexes 10-A & 10-B of the 2006 Oman–USA FTA.
101. *See* Chapter 11 & Annexes 11-A & 11-B of the 2007 Korea–USA FTA.
102. *See e.g.* Art. 811 & Annex 811 of the 2008 Canada–Colombia FTA,; and Art. 9.11 & Annex 9.11 of the 2010 Canada–Panamá FTA.
103. *See e.g.* Chapter XIII of the 2003 Mexico–Uruguay FTA; Chapter 10 of the 2004 Chile–South Korea FTA; and Chapter X of the 2004 FTA between the Caribbean Community (CARICOM) and Costa Rica. All these treaties are available at http://www.sice.oas.org (last visited 30 June 2013). *See also* 2005 Economic Partnership Agreement between Japan and Malaysia, Chapter 7, available at http://www.mofa.go.jp/region/asia-paci/malaysia/epa/content.pdf (last visited 30 June 2013).
104. *See* Chapter 9 of the 2006 Panamá–Singapore FTA, available at http://www.sice.oas.org (last visited 30 June 2013). *See also* Spears (2010), 1051.
105. The COMESA treaty entered into force in 1994. *See also* Art. 159.3 of this treaty. In conformity with this international agreement, investment comprises tangibles and intangibles. *See* Art. 159.2. COMESA is an international organisation aimed at the establishment of a customs union in the East of Africa among its 20 member states. COMESA treaties are available at http://www.comesa.int (last visited 30 June 2013).
106. ECT is in force since 1998, and is available at http://www.encharter.org/fileadmin/user_upload/document/EN.pdf (last visited 30 June 2013). *See generally* E Gaillard and M McNeill, 'The Energy Charter Treaty', in K Yannaca-Small (ed.), *Arbitration under International Investment Agreements: A Guide to the Key Issues* (2010).

107. T Waelde, 'Energy Charter Treaty-based Investment Arbitration. Controversial Issues', (2004) 5/3 *JWIT* 373, at 376. *See* Salacuse (2010), 102–3; and R Dolzer and C Schreuer, *Principles of International Investment Law* (2012), 15–17.
108. Art. 1 (6) of ECT.
109. Since 2012. This treaty terminated the 1987 ASEAN Agreement for the Promotion and Protection of Investments, as amended by its 1996 Protocol. ASEAN is an international organisation aimed at the economic, social and cultural development of its ten member states, all located in Southeast Asia. ASEAN treaties are available at http://www.asean.org (last visited 30 June 2013).
110. Worded as follows:

> Consistent with the right of states to regulate and the customary international law principles on police powers, bona fide regulatory measures taken by a Member State that are designed and applied to protect or enhance legitimate public welfare objectives, such as public health, safety and the environment, shall not constitute an indirect expropriation under this Article. (Art. 20.8 of the 2007 COMESA Common Investment Area Agreement.)

111. *See* Art. 14 & Annex 2 of the 2009 ASEAN Comprehensive Investment Agreement. This treaty protects foreign tangibles and intangibles against expropriation. *See* Art. 1.
112. *See* Annex 11-B of the 2007 Korea–USA FTA. *See also* Art. 6 of the 2009 Colombia–India BIT; and Annex A of the 2010 Canada–Slovakia BIT.
113. *See* Chapter 7 below.
114. *See* Chapters 4 & 5 above. *See also* Chapter 11 & Annex on Expropriation and Compensation of the 2009 ASEAN–Australia–New Zealand FTA.
115. Australia, Austria, Belgium, Canada, Czech Republic, Denmark, Finland, France, Germany, Greece, Hungary, Iceland, Ireland, Italy, Japan, Korea, Luxembourg, Mexico, Netherlands, New Zealand, Norway, Poland, Portugal, Spain, Sweden, Switzerland, Turkey, UK, and the USA.
116. Argentina, Brazil, Chile, Estonia, Hong Kong, China, Latvia, Lithuania, and the Slovak Republic. Neither Chile nor the Slovak Republic were then members of OECD.
117. G Sacerdoti, 'Bilateral Treaties and Multilateral Instruments on Investment Protection', (1997) 269 *RCADI* 251, at 293–4.
118. T Waelde and A Kolo, 'Environmental Regulation, Investment Protection and "Regulatory Taking" in International Law', (2001) 50/4 *ICLQ* 811, at 816. *See* Schill (2009), 53–4; and Salacuse (2010), 105.
119. Muchlinski (2000), 1036 & 1038.
120. MAI, Draft Consolidated Text, DAFFE/MAI(98)7/REV1, 22 April 1998, available at http://www1.oecd.org/daf/mai/pdf/ng/ng987r1e.pdf (last visited 30 June 2013).
121. Picciotto (1998), 755–6, M Vallianatos, 'De-Fanging the MAI', (1998) 31/3 *Corn. ILJ* 713, at 714–5, and Muchlinski (2000), 1041.
122. MAI, Draft Consolidated Text, note 2 at 11.
123. MAI, Commentary to the Consolidated Text, DAFFE/MAI(98)8/REV1, 22 April 1998, available at http://www1.oecd.org/daf/mai/pdf/ng/ng988r1e.pdf (last visited 30 June 2013).
124. *Ibid.*, para. 1, at 30.
125. *Ibid.*, para. 2, at 30.
126. MAI, Report by the Chairman of the Negotiating Group, DAFFE/MAI(98)17, 4 May 1998, note 2 at 13, available at http://www1.oecd.org/daf/mai/pdf/ng/ng9817e.pdf (last visited 30 June 2013). *See* E Graham, 'Regulatory Takings, Supernational Treatment, and the Multilateral Agreement on Investment: Issues Raised by Nongovernmental Organizations', (1998) 31/3 *Corn. ILJ* 599, at 611.

127. OECD (2004), 9.
128. MAI Commentary, para. 5, at 30.
129. *Ibid.*, para. 6, at 30.
130. *See* Chapters 1, 4 & 5 above.
131. *See* P Juillard, 'MAI: A European View', (1998) 31/3 *Corn. ILJ* 477, at 478–9, Picciotto (1998), 741–2, Muchlinski (2000), 1039, R Geiger, 'Regulatory Expropriations in International Law: Lessons from the Multilateral Agreement on Investment', (2003) 11/1 *NYU ELJ* 94, at 98; Muchlinski (2007), 667; Salacuse (2010), 107; and Dolzer and Schreuer (2012), 10.
132. *E.g.*, the consolidated negotiating text was a restricted internal document of the OECD, only published on the internet in 1997, after it was leaked out.
133. Waelde and Kolo (2001), 816; Muchlinski (2007), 667–8; Schill (2009), 55–7; Salacuse (2010), 106; Sornarajah (2010), 3–4; and Vandevelde (2010), 69.
134. Salacuse (2010), 106; Sornarajah (2010), 258; and Vandevelde (2010), 69.
135. *See* Been and Beauvais (2003), 35–6; Geiger (2003), 96–7; UNCTAD, *International Investment Agreements: Key Issues* (2004), Vol. 1, at 241–2; G Akpan, 'The Investment Provisions of the United States–Singapore Free Trade Agreement and the NAFTA. Old Wine in a New Skin or Something Else?', (2005) 6/6 *JWIT* 873, at 874; A Newcombe, 'The Boundaries of Regulatory Expropriation in International Law', (2005) 20/1 *ICSID Rev.* 1, at 1–3; Newcombe and Paradell (2009), 55; S Robert-Cuendet, *Droits de l'investisseur étranger et protection de l'environnement: contribution à l'analyse de l'expropriation indirect* (2010), 34–6; and Sornarajah (2010), 258.

   See also Ethyl Corporation v. The Government of Canada, NAFTA, UNCITRAL arbitration, Award on Jurisdiction, 24 June 1998; and *Metalclad Corporation v. United Mexican States*, NAFTA, ICSID case No. ARB(AF)/97/1, Award, 30 August 2000.
136. Picciotto (1998), 760; and Muchlinski (2000), 1042.
137. *See* Vallianatos (1998), 718–9; Schill (2009), 54; Muchlinski (2000), 1948; and Dolzer and Schreuer (2012), 10.
138. *See* Muchlinski (2000), 1048–9; and Geiger (2003), 95–6.
139. *See e.g. Pope & Talbot. Inc. v. The Government of Canada*, NAFTA, UNCITRAL arbitration, Interim Award, 26 June 2000, paras. 101–2; *Metalclad*, Award, 30 August 2000, para. 103; *S.D. Myers, Inc. v. The Government of Canada*, NAFTA, UNCITRAL arbitration, Partial Award, 13 November, 2000, para. 283; *Marvin Feldman v. Mexico*, NAFTA, ICSID case No. ARB(AF)/99/1, Award, 16 December 2002, para. 103; *GAMI Investments, Inc. v. The Government of the United Mexican States*, NAFTA, UNCITRAL arbitration, Award, 15 November 2004, paras. 123, 125, 128, 131 & 133; *Fireman's Fund Insurance Company v. United Mexican States*, NAFTA, ICSID case No. ARB(AF)/02/1, Award, 17 July 2006, para. 176; *Archer Daniels Midland Company and Tate & Lyle Ingredients Americas, Inc. v. United Mexican States*, NAFTA, ICSID case No. ARB(AF)/04/05, Award, 21 November 2007, paras. 238, 240–2 & 249; *Glamis Gold, Ltd. v. United States of America*, NAFTA, UNCITRAL arbitration, Award, 8 June 2009, paras. 355–8 & 366; *Cargill, Incorporated v. United Mexican States*, NAFTA, ICSID case No. ARB(AF)/05/2, Award, 18 September 2009, paras. 359–61; and *Grand River Enterprises et al v. United States of America*, NAFTA, UNCITRAL arbitration, Award, 12 January 2011, paras. 147–51 & 154.
140. *Metalclad*, Award, 30 August 2000, para. 103.
141. Even a company's market share is regarded as part of the concept of investment. Akpan (2005), 877. Legislative and administrative action, as well as judicial decisions, are considered within the notion of measures. Been and Beauvais (2003), 41. *See* Madalena (2003), 73.

142. *Methanex Corporation v. United States of America*, NAFTA, UNCITRAL arbitration, Final Award, 3 August 2005, Part II, Chapter C, paras. 31–2.
143. *See Pope & Talbot*, Interim Award, 26 June 2000.
144. The tribunal cited both the Harvard Draft and the Third Restatement for this purpose. *See Pope & Talbot*, Interim Award, 26 June 2000, paras. 96, 102 & 105.
145. *Pope & Talbot*, Interim Award, 26 June 2000, para. 99. *See ibid.*, para. 96.
146. *Ibid.*, para. 99.
The tribunal added:

> This is not to say that every regulatory restraint can be likened to expropriation. The *Restatement* [*sic*] recognizes that the distinction between taking and regulation is not always clear but may rest on the degree of interference with the property interest.

Pope & Talbot, Interim Award, 26 June 2000, note 73 at para. 99.
147. *Ibid.*, para. 100.
148. *See* Chapter 4 above.
149. *Pope & Talbot*, Interim Award, 26 June 2000, para. 104. *See ibid.*, para. 96.
150. *See e.g. S.D. Myers*, Partial Award, 13 June,2000, paras. 285–6; *Feldman*, Award, 16 December 2002, para. 100; *Fireman's Fund*, Award, 17 July 2006, note 159 at para. 176; and *Glamis Gold*, Award, 8 June 2009, para. 355. *Cf. Waste Management, Inc. v. United Mexican States*, NAFTA, ICSID case No. ARB(AF)/00/3, Award, 30 April 2004 ('Waste Management 2'), paras. 143–4.
As Jeswald Salacuse notes (Salacuse (2010), 300):

> In practice, the distinction between indirect expropriations and measures equivalent to expropriations does not appear to be a meaningful one. No case has yet identified a measure that was tantamount to an indirect expropriation but not itself an indirect expropriation.

151. *See Metalclad*, Award, 30 August 2000.
152. *Ibid.*, paras. 104–5.
153. *See Biloune and Marine Drive Complex Ltd v. Ghana Investments Centre and the Government of Ghana*, UNCITRAL arbitration, Award on Jurisdiction and Liability, 27 October 1989, (1994) 95 *ILR* 183. *See* Chapter 5 above.
154. *Metalclad*, Award, 30 August 2000, paras. 106–8 & 112.
155. *Ibid.*, paras. 106–9 & 111.
156. *Ibid.*, para. 103.
157. *See S.D. Myers*, Partial Award, 13 November, 2000, paras. 282, 284 & 288.
158. *S.D. Myers*, Partial Award, 13 June, 2000, paras. 283 & 285–6. *See* Been and Beauvais (2003), 52–3; Sampliner (2003), 6; E Shenkman, 'Could Principles of Fifth Amendment Takings Jurisprudence Be Helpful in Analyzing Regulatory Expropriation Claims under International Law?', (2003) 11/1 *NYU ELJ* 174, at 177–8; and Newcombe (2005), 22–3.
159. *Feldman*, Award, 16 December 2002, para. 98.
160. *Ibid.*, para. 103.
161. *Feldman*, Award, 16 December, 2002 para. 112. *See Robert Azinian, Kenneth Davitian, & Ellen Baca v. The United Mexican States*, NAFTA, ICSID case No. ARB (AF)/97/2, Award, 1 November 1999.
162. *Feldman*, Award, 16 December, 2002 para. 100. *See* Fortier & Drymer (2004), note 10 at 297, and B Kunoy, 'Developments in Indirect Expropriation Case Law in ICSID Transnational Arbitration', (2005) 6/3 *JWIT* 467, at 475–6.
163. *Feldman*, Award, 16 December 2002, paras. 133 & 145.
164. *Waste Management 2*, Award, 30 April 2004, paras. 143–4.
165. *Ibid.*, para. 159.

166. *Ibid.*, para. 161.
167. *Ibid.*, para. 174.
168. *Waste Management 2*, Award, 30 April 2004, para. 175. *See* Chapter 7 below.
169. *See Waste Management 2*, Award, 30 April 2004, paras. 177–8.
170. *See Compañía del Desarrollo de Santa Elena S.A. v. Republic of Costa Rica*, ICSID case No. ARB/96/1, Award, 17 February 2000. *See* Chapter 5 above.
171. *GAMI*, Award, 15 November 2004, paras. 131–3. The tribunal also referred to the case-law of the Iran–US CT (*Starrett Housing*). *Ibid.*, para. 123. *See Starrett Housing Corporation, Starrett Systems, Inc., Starrett Housing International, Inc., v. The Government of the Islamic Republic of Iran et al*, Iran-US CT, Interlocutory Award No. ITL 32-24-1, 19 December 1983, (1985) 4 *Iran-US CTR* 122. *See* Chapter 4 above.
172. *GAMI*, Award, 15 November 2004, para. 131.
173. *Ibid.*, paras. 124–30.
174. *See Methanex*, Final Award, 3 August 2005.
175. *Ibid.*, Part IV, Chapter A, para. 2.
176. According to this case, access to a market is a property interest subject to protection under Article 1110 of NAFTA. *See Pope & Talbot*, Interim Award, 26 June 2000, para. 96.
177. *Methanex*, Final Award, 3 August 2005, Part IV, Chapter D, para. 17.
178. *Ibid.*, Part IV, Chapter D, para. 7.
179. *Methanex*, Final Award, 3 August 2005, Part IV, Chapter D, para. 8. *See Revere Copper and Brass, Incorporated v. Overseas Private Investment Corporation* (OPIC), Haight, Wetzel and Bergan, arbitrators, Award, 24 August 1978. (1978) 17/6 *ILM* 1321.
180. *See* Chapter 7 below. *Cf.* Vandevelde (2010), 301–2.
181. *Methanex*, Final Award, 3 August 2005, Part IV, Chapter D, paras. 9 & 15.
182. *Fireman's Fund*, Award, 17 July 2006, para. 174.
183. *Fireman's Fund*, Award, 17 July 2006, para. 176.
184. *Ibid.*
185. *Ibid.*
186. *See Técnicas Medioambientales TECMED S.A. v. The United Mexican States*, ICSID case No. ARB (AF)/00/2, Award, 29 May 2003; and *Saluka Investments BV v. The Czech Republic*, UNCITRAL arbitration, Partial Award, 17 March 2006. *See* Chapter 5 above. Surprisingly, the tribunal did not refer to *Methanex*.
187. *Fireman's Fund*, Award, 17 July 2006, para. 205 & note 161 at para. 176.
188. *See Archer Daniels*, Award, 21 November 2007.
189. *Ibid.*, para. 238.
190. *Ibid.*, para. 240. *See ibid.*, para. 251.
191. *See Archer Daniels*, Award, 21 November 2007, paras. 241–9. *See Norwegian Shipowners* (Norway v. USA), Anderson, Vogt and Valloton, arbitrators, Award, 13 October 1922. (1922) 1 RIAA 307; and *LG&E Energy Corp., LG&E Capital Corp., LG&E International Inc. v. Argentine Republic*, ICSID case No. ARB/02/1, Decision on Liability, 3 October 2006.
192. *Archer Daniels*, Award, 21 November 2007, para. 250.
193. *Ibid.*, para. 251.
194. *Glamis Gold*, Award, 8 June 2009, para. 356.
195. *See ibid.*, paras. 357–66.
196. *Ibid.*, para. 354,
197. *See Cargill*, Award, 18 September 2009, paras. 359–78.
198. *Chemtura Corporation v. Government of Canada*, NAFTA, UNCITRAL arbitration, Award, 2 August 2010, para. 242. *See ibid.*, para. 257.
199. *Ibid.*, para. 249. *See ibid.*, paras. 244–8, 259 & 263–4.

200. *Ibid.*, para. 265.
201. However, the tribunal made no explicit reference to *Methanex*, in this respect.
202. *Chemtura*, Award, 2 August 2010, para. 266.
203. *Ibid.*
204. *See* Chapter 5 above.
205. *See Merrill & Ring Forestry L.P. v. Canada*, NAFTA, UNCITRAL arbitration, Award, 31 March 2010, paras. 143–53; and *Grand River*, Award, 12 January 2011, paras. 146–55.
206. *Railroad Development Corporation* (RDC) *v. Republic of Guatemala*, CAFTA–DR, ICSID case No. ARB/07/23, Award, 29 June 2012, para. 151. *See CMS Gas Transmission Company v. Republic of Argentina*, ICSID case No. ARB/01/8, Award, 12 May 2005; and *Telenor Mobile Communications A.S. v. The Republic of Hungary*, ICSID case No. ARB/04/15, Award, 13 September 2006. *See* Chapter 5 above.
207. *Petrobart Limited v. The Kyrgyz Republic*, ECT, SCC case No. 126/2003, Award, 29 March 2005, at 77.
208. *Ibid.*
209. *Nykomb Synergetics Technology Holding AB v. The Republic of Latvia*, ECT, SCC arbitration, Award, 16 December 2003, at 33; *Plama Consortium Limited v. Republic of Bulgaria*, ECT, ICSID case No. ARB/03/24, Award, 27 August 2008, paras. 191–3; and *AES Summit Generation Ltd. v. The Republic of Hungary*, ECT, ICSID case No. ARB/01/04, Award, 23 September 2010, para. 14.3.1.
210. *See* Chapter 4 above.
211. *See* Chapter 5 above.
212. *See Plama*, Award, 27 August 2008, paras. 191–3.

7. The applicable standard

International case-law has traditionally answered the threshold question of indirect takings applying an effects rule, supplemented by the substantial and permanent deprivation standard. This rule recognises a restricted police-powers exception, and the principle of respect for legitimate expectations. International tribunals have generally avoided assessing the intentions of the host-states adopting the challenged measures. As a consequence, the police-powers doctrine has rarely been followed by judges and arbitrators at the moment of identifying the boundaries between non-compensable state measures and compensable indirect expropriations. Capital-exporting states in North America and Europe upheld the effects rule when its application was restricted to Latin American, Asian and African countries. Now that any host-state can see its regulatory policy challenged by an expropriation claim, this rule has fallen into disfavour.

National treatment, as an absolute maximum standard, is currently suggested to decision-makers settling investment disputes arising out of last-generation US and Canadian BITs and EIAs. Supported by its main historical adversary, the Calvo doctrine threatens again the international minimum standard of treatment on which the protection against expropriation is based. In this new version of the old doctrine, the national treatment conventionally promoted as a maximum standard is not that of just any country. The expropriation clause of these BITs and EIAs is linked to a particular domestic case-law: the US regulatory takings doctrine. Under the interpretative declarations of these treaties, arbitrators can easily conclude that the expropriation clause allows for the application of a police-powers rule, or even a proportionality test. GAL theory has given the necessary theoretical support to both of these approaches, still exceptional in investment treaty arbitrations. But it is not only the international case-law which has reacted slowly to this new scenario – so has state practice. Apart from US and Canadian BITs and EIAs, not many countries have included interpretative declarations in their treaties. Most investment treaties in force have expropriation clauses with a wording that essentially does not depart from that of the first BIT concluded in 1959.

The present chapter outlines the re-emergence of the national treatment standard in international law, the standpoint of the GAL theory, and the possible application of the proportionality principle of European human rights law in international investment law. The following pages explain the traditional approach to the threshold problem of indirect takings, recognising the state's wide margin of appreciation in expropriation claims and focusing on the substantial and permanent deprivation standard, while acknowledging a limited police-powers exception and the principle of respect for the investor's legitimate expectations. This chapter finally discusses the relationship between the protection of aliens in international law, the minimum standard of treatment, good governance and the rule of law.

7.1 A RESTLESS JURISPRUDENCE

Christoph Schreuer recalls that '[e]ven before the introduction of pertinent treaty provisions, international courts and tribunals have treated indirect takings and equivalent measures in the same way as direct expropriations'.[1] This case-law, however, rarely addressed the threshold question before the 1980s. For years, the only clear references to the international law of expropriation were found in the *Norwegian Shipowners* arbitration and the *Oscar Chinn* case of the PCIJ, regarding indirect takings, and the same court's *Chorzow Factory* case, concerning restitution and compensation.[2] It was not until the 1970s that international arbitral tribunals dealt again with this area of law. The Libyan oil concession cases and *AMINOIL* illustrated the uncertainties that surrounded the question of nationalisation and its compensation.[3] Nonetheless, they did not refer to indirect takings. In the same period, *Revere Copper* explicitly recognised an essential aspect of the international law of expropriation: the protection of legitimate expectations, derived from those commitments made by host-states towards foreign investors.[4]

The problem of takings came before the ICJ in *Anglo-Iranian Oil Co.*, *Certain Norwegian Loans* and *Barcelona Traction*, but the substantive issue remained undecided due to lack of jurisdiction.[5] It reappeared in the *ELSI* case, where a claim of disguised expropriation was rejected. Once again, the ICJ avoided providing any insight on this point, concluding that the alleged deprivation could not be attributed to the state authorities.[6] In the recent *Diallo* case, the ICJ simply dismissed a claim of indirect taking, without much explanation.[7] The first institutions to develop a comprehensive case-law on the international law of expropriation, within the boundaries of their respective jurisdictions, were the

European Court of Human Rights and the Iran–US CT. Their judgments and awards not only construed the concepts of property, expropriation and compensation, but also attempted to answer the threshold question. Arbitral panels established under the dispute settlement provisions of investment codes, investment agreements, BITs and EIAs have enlarged this case-law in the last decades. Unfortunately, the sum of these judgments and awards merely offers contradictory guidelines to decision-makers identifying the boundaries that separate non-compensable state measures from compensable indirect takings.

At present, the effects rule is still dominant in international law. However, the police-powers approach followed by some investment treaty arbitrations and recommended by the BITs and FTAs of certain countries, along with the jurisprudential and doctrinal attempts to apply the proportionality test of the European Court of Human Rights in international investment law, provide too many possible answers to the same question.

7.1.1 Replacing the Minimum for a Maximum

Judges and arbitrators facing claims of indirect takings apply the sources of international law described in Article 38 of the Statute of the ICJ. For this purpose, they resort to the judicial decisions of other international tribunals, as a subsidiary means for determining the rules of law. In the case of the international law of expropriation, judgments of the European Court of Human Rights and the Iran–US CT have necessarily influenced the awards of ICSID, UNCITRAL, SCC and *ad hoc* arbitrations, which in turn influence each other. This process has been named cross-fertilisation.[8] In investment treaty arbitration, it derives from the fact that many of the members of tribunals settling controversies have already sat in the Iran–US CT or other arbitral panels dealing with investment disputes, and are familiar with the case-law of the European Court of Human Rights due to their academic and professional backgrounds. This trend has been strengthened by the publication and ready availability of judicial decisions, the growing *esprit de corps* among arbitrators, and a body of law predisposed to jurisprudential development.[9]

No *jurisprudence constant*, however, arises out of these intertwined decisions. It is not only jurisdictional issues, or the *ad hoc* nature of most tribunals dealing with expropriation claims, which prevent judges and arbitrators from giving a structured response to the problem of indirect takings – it is also the system of *res judicata* in international law.[10] This principle is a feature of the ICJ, as well as of the European Court of Human Rights, the Iran–US CT, and ICSID, UNCITRAL, SCC and *ad hoc* arbitration.[11] While Article 59 of the ICJ Statute provides that the decisions of the Court have no binding force except between the parties and in respect of that particular case, Article 53 (1) of the Washington Convention declares that the award of ICSID panels is only binding on the parties to the investment dispute. The principle of *res judicata* is also established, with different wording, in Article 44 and 46 (1) of the European Convention on Human Rights; Article IV of the 1981 Claims Settlement Declaration, establishing the Iran–US CT; Article 34 (2) of the UNCITRAL Arbitration Rules; Article 40 of the SCC Arbitration Rules;[12] and Article 34 (6) of the ICC Rules of Arbitration.[13]

In spite of these provisions, international tribunals normally consider the judicial decisions of other tribunals as authoritative statements, giving them great weight in practice.[14] Judges and arbitrators refer and quote regularly the judgments and awards of other international tribunals, to a degree unseen in domestic jurisdictions where the principle of *res judicata* is also applied. The steady reliance on case-law by arbitrators in international investment disputes has derived from what has been labelled *de facto* or soft precedent jurisprudence.[15] Regarding indirect takings, this case-law has resorted largely to an effects solution, based on the impact of the challenged measure and the duration of the respective interference, not only in the Iran–US CT, *ad hoc* and ICSID arbitral panels, but also in NAFTA, CAFTA–DR and ECT arbitrations. Not a few of these awards emphasise the importance of respect for legitimate expectations, created by commitments made explicitly or implicitly by the host-state, in the case-by-case identification of a taking. The police-powers rule adopted in some NAFTA awards (*Methanex* and *Chemtura*)[16] and BIT arbitrations (*Saluka* and *El Paso*)[17] casts a shadow of doubt over such a trend. The purported application of the proportionality test to investment treaty arbitration in BIT case-law (*TECMED*, *Azurix*, *LG&E*, *Continental Casualty* and *Tza*)[18] and NAFTA jurisprudence (*Fireman's Fund* and *Archer Daniels*)[19] also undermines the basic legal certainty that the international law of expropriation is required to provide for both foreign investors and host-states.

How does the police-powers rule, traditionally exceptional in the protection of aliens in international law, become a threat to the generally accepted effects approach to indirect takings? The answer to this question lies in NAFTA case-law.[20] The main concern of the Canadian and US governments at the moment of signing this treaty in 1992 was the taking of foreigners' property by Mexican authorities.[21] Nevertheless, most expropriation claims lodged under NAFTA to date have been directed against Canada and the USA, rather than Mexico.[22] As Philippe Sands notes, '[t]he rules which were intended to constrain others became constraining of their creators'.[23] Because amending treaties is more difficult than modifying domestic legislation, this situation has gained some permanence, particularly in countries outside of North America.[24] In this region, the USA and Canada have discarded the position on the treatment of aliens that their own authorities had previously defended for more than a century in the international *fora*. This is a likely turning point in the history of the international law of expropriation. Muthucumaraswamy Sornarajah recognises three moments in the post-colonial protection of aliens in international law:

> In [the first] period, there was an effort to construct theories [...] which sought to remove the foreign investment process from the scope of the host state's control. [...] The second phase was the reaction of the host states to these attempts through the efforts to relocalise the process. In this period, the host states articulated norms like permanent sovereignty over natural resources and the competing standard of appropriate compensation for nationalisation [and the NIEO] [...] The third phase is one of accommodation of these principles through efforts to make bilateral investment treaties which set out the rules of investment protection as between the parties to these treaties.[25]

These periods cover the establishment of the international minimum standard, its challenge by the national treatment standard, and the interaction of the two principles in treaties that enshrine, in practice, the supremacy of the former over the latter. But, as the same author admits, '[i]n international life, nothing seems final. It would be brash to say that one regime has had a final triumph over another'.[26] So there is now a fourth period, heralded by the attempts of the USA and other countries to transform the international minimum standard into a national one. An essential part of this endeavour is the support of the police-powers approach over the effects rule.

The USA now advocates a specific national treatment standard: that of its takings doctrine, the most influential source of state practice in the international law of expropriation.[27] What does this local standard imply? The Fifth Amendment of the US Constitution, passed in 1791, declares that no person shall be deprived of property without due process of law, nor shall it be taken for public use, without just compensation. This provision is commonly known as the takings clause.[28] The inherent power of federal and state authorities to expropriate privately owned property under these conditions is called eminent domain.[29] Until the 20th century, the takings clause was applied by the US Supreme Court exclusively to the direct appropriation of property.[30] After *Lochner*, this tribunal combined the Fifth Amendment with the Fourteenth Amendment, adopted in 1868, which insists on the prohibition of deprivations without due process of law, to construe virtually any change in the law or its application that altered property as a taking.[31] The concept of regulatory taking emerged in *Pennsylvania Coal*, where the US Supreme Court recognised that regulation could amount to an expropriation depending on the extent of the diminution of the property's value.[32] In conformity with *Loretto*, any permanent physical occupation must be compensated, irrespective of its economic impact.[33] The US Supreme Court held later in *Lucas* that a measure which eliminates all or substantially all the value of a property will normally be considered a taking.[34] *Concrete Pipe* added that the mere diminution, however serious, is insufficient to establish an expropriation.[35]

The two *per se* rules in the US takings doctrine establish that the permanent physical occupation of property, or a 100 per cent destruction of its value as a result of a regulatory measure, will require compensation.[36] Outside these situations, an *ad hoc* inquiry is needed for determining whether a regulation constitutes a taking. The three factors that aid this inquiry were first articulated in *Penn Central*: *i.e.*, the economic impact of the regulation on the claimant, the extent to which it has interfered with distinct investment-backed expectations, and the character of the governmental action.[37] Nonetheless, as Vicki Been and Joel Beauvais explain:

> it is extremely difficult to prove a regulatory taking under U.S. takings jurisprudence: U.S. Courts almost never find that a regulation has destroyed one hundred percent of the value of the property, and they seldom find that a regulation effects a taking under the *Penn Central* analysis.[38]

Recent US BITs and FTAs include an international protection against expropriation strongly rooted in this domestic regime.[39] Timidly introduced in international instruments during the second half of the 20th century, it was only after the regulatory powers of developed states began to be challenged in investor-to-state disputes that the US openly adopted the *Penn Central* factors in its treaties.[40] Supporters of this new policy claim that '[it] has sought to conciliate strong protection for foreign investors with the normal non-discriminatory exercise of government regulatory power'.[41] The truth is that it deliberately confuses the threshold question with the requirements of a lawful expropriation, prescribing a police-powers rule for expropriation claims. Canadian BITs and FTAs have included a similar declaration to that of the USA, but few other countries have incorporated it up to now in their treaties.[42] One of the international agreements that does include the *Penn Central* factors is the

2007 Korea–USA FTA, which exceptionally relates 'the character of the government action' to its objective and context, expressly stating that '[r]elevant considerations could include whether the government action imposes a special sacrifice that exceeds what a particular investor or investment should be expected to endure for the public interest'.[43] This balancing test resembles the proportionality principle, first applied in international law by the European Court of Human Rights, and currently advocated by certain authors inspired by those awards in investment-treaty arbitration that have associated this principle with the expropriation provisions of BITs and EIAs.[44]

7.1.2 GAL Theory and the Proportionality Test

Although the police-powers doctrine dates back to the *Oscar Chinn* case, it was not until NAFTA arbitrations challenged regulatory measures in the USA that it became a serious contender to its established counterpart, the effects rule. The undefined terms of indirect expropriation and measures tantamount to it, once promoted by US negotiators and drafters, opened the door to a mass of regulatory-taking claims.[45] According to Sands:

> The US is belatedly recognizing that foreign investment is a two-way street, and that the US too is vulnerable to challenge. This is forcing a rethink as to the real purpose of the international rules on expropriation.[46]

The US reaction must be seen within the broader context of its relations with the once-called law of nations, for this deflection from well-accepted and frequently observed norms currently involves other areas of international law too. Particularly, diplomatic protection; trade law; the protection of the environment; international criminal law; the use of force; and international humanitarian law.[47] Other developed countries have joined the USA in its attempt to replace the effects approach for a police-powers rule. These states, like the USA, had accepted the application of the international minimum standard and the effects rule in the past, when investment disputes referred to the implementation of treaty provisions in favour of their nationals investing in developing countries. Not anymore.

The uncertainty produced by this new scenario is worsened by the implicit, and sometimes explicit, endorsement given by some NGOs and developing states to such a position, derived from what has been called the legitimacy crisis of international investment law.[48] These NGOs have formed an unexpected alliance with mainly capital-exporting, pro-globalisation governments. Each party, nevertheless, approaches the issue from different angles. While NGOs are concerned about sustainable development and protection of the environment, among other things, developed states now fear what developing countries have fought against for decades, and not always with success: the encroachment of their sovereignty. Developing states, normally weak and very sensitive to any threat to their already limited political and economic powers, have long cared about protecting their ability to regulate the commercial, industrial and services activity within their borders – more so, when it involves a potential confrontation with affluent TNCs. These countries used to resort to the Calvo doctrine for this purpose. Currently, the doctrine is promoted by its main historical contender, with an important caveat: national treatment, yes, but mine.[49]

The factual association between states other than the USA and certain NGOs gives more weight to the attempt to replace the international standard by one of national treatment, for it adds a much-needed touch of legitimacy to the original claim. This new national maximum standard of treatment, as opposed to the old international minimum standard, has received the support of the GAL theory, a position which sees governance as a regulatory system based on principles of administrative law like transparency, participation, review and accountability.[50] According to some of the authors who support this theory, there is currently an increasing body of law to which the strict distinction between domestic and international is no longer applicable, originating from institutions not hierarchically organised, issuing binding and non-binding but highly effective regulations.[51] There are several approaches to this theory: as many as there are authors developing it.[52] Stephan Schill gives a convincing description of the main aspects of its application to international investment law:

> [...] rather than only being concerned with backing up private ordering between foreign investors and host states, international investment law has a broader function in providing a legal framework for a public international economic order within which investment relations take place by establishing principles of investment protection under international law that endorse rule of law standards for the treatment of foreign investors. Investment treaty arbitration, in turn, is viewed as a mechanism not only to resolve individual investor-state disputes but also to implement, in reviewing the legality of state conduct, these principles of international investment law. Investment treaty arbitration, therefore, is viewed more akin to administrative or constitutional judicial review than to commercial arbitration, even though investment law makes use of the arbitral process to settle disputes.[53]

GAL theory not only supports a police-powers approach, akin to the US takings doctrine. Depending on the author, it advocates the application of the proportionality principle, as developed in German constitutional law and the jurisprudence of the European Court of Human Rights, or a mixture of both, by linking the character of the state measure of *Penn Central* with the balancing test of the European Court. With or without other states and NGOs, or GAL theory, there is an unavoidable issue pending. Been and Beauvais rightly point out that:

> even if it were possible to tie international compensation requirements to U.S. takings jurisprudence, this would not be a desirable solution from an international standpoint. [a]ny effort simply to equate NAFTA's Chapter 11 with the Fifth Amendment would ignore differences between domestic and international contexts that render the reasons for affording regulatory takings protections within any given country inapplicable in the context of international investment agreements.[54]

The same problem which affects the application of domestic solutions to international problems is also pertinent regarding the indiscriminate use of concepts advanced in other *fora*.[55] International courts and arbitral panels are born and exist within a certain context: that provided by their respective constituent treaty. From this perspective, not only the attempt to bring the factors of the US doctrine to international investment law must be critically assessed, but also the intention to transfer the fair balance test of international human rights law to this area of international law.

Proportionality restrains state powers and protects individual autonomy.[56] As Jasper Kommendijk and John Morijn explain, '[t]he principle is used to determine whether a measure has gone too far. It helps to construe the border between legitimate governmental regulation and excessive interference with rights and obligations [...]'.[57] In comparative law, this principle requires state measures to comply with three sub-principles: be appropriate to their objectives (suitability); the least burdensome possible on the affected persons (necessity); and respect a fair or reasonable balance between the community and individual interests involved (proportionality *stricto sensu*).[58] Proportionality was already an established principle of German constitutional law when the European Court of Human Rights applied it for the first time in the *Belgian Linguistics* case of 1968.[59] Since then, the Court has relied extensively and sometimes merely rhetorically on this principle to construe the three-rule system of Article 1 of the First Optional Protocol, focusing mostly in proportionality *stricto sensu*, without expressly identifying any of its sub-principles.[60] In the Americas, the application of proportionality began in 2002, with the *Cantos* case.[61] Probably because the wording of Article 21 of the American Convention on Human Rights slightly resembles that of Article 1 of the First Protocol, the Inter-American Court of Human Rights has started to use this principle to interpret the protection of property offered by the Pact of San José de Costa Rica.[62]

Inspired by European human rights law, Ursula Kriebaum has suggested an alternative to what she calls the 'all or nothing' paradigm in the international law of foreign investment, which requires full compensation for an indirect expropriation, leaving the tribunal 'no discretion to apportion the economic burden resulting from the measure between the investor and the State'.[63] In her opinion, the application of the proportionality principle would allow arbitral panels in investment disputes to give property-owners less compensation than the fair market value, if there is a special interest of the host-state to interfere and this causes no excessive burden for the individual.[64] According to Kriebaum, the difference between *TECMED*'s solution and her approach is that, while the former applied the balance test at the moment of establishing whether an expropriation had occurred, the latter applies it at the moment of establishing the amount of compensation due for a lawful taking.[65] The problem with this theory is that most BITs and EIAs currently in force provide for a prompt, adequate and effective compensation, or similar formulas. Adjusting the large network of these treaties, to allow the application of the proportionality principle by decision-makers in investment disputes, would involve across-the-board negotiations throughout the international society – not a particularly easy task.[66]

Besides Ursula Kriebaum, other authors have proposed the application of the proportionality principle in international investment law. To Anne Hoffman, for instance, 'the proportionality requirement recently introduced into investment treaty arbitration appears to be a convincing and methodologically clear approach when attempting to balance the interests of both the State and the investor fairly'.[67] Jeswald Salacuse also favours the use of this principle to appraise 'whether the means employed are proportionate to the ends pursued, and whether there are less restrictive alternatives available'.[68] Other scholars have apparently changed their views in this respect. Andrew Newcombe declared in 2005 that:

> the role of international expropriation law is to provide a minimum standard of protection to foreign investors against expropriatory measures. It need not, and should not, attempt to find the optimal balance between state interests and property protection.[69]

Four years later, in his work with Lluís Paradell, the proportionality test was described as '[a] significant consideration in assessing police power regulations, absent a breach of specific commitments which arguably (if clear and unambiguous) may give rise to a duty to compensate'.[70] Benedict Kingsbury and Stephan Schill advocate the application of the proportionality analysis in investor-state arbitration as a general principle of law.[71] They even see an incorporation of this test in those treaties stating that, except in rare circumstances, non-discriminatory regulatory actions by a party aimed at protecting legitimate public objectives, do not constitute indirect expropriation.[72] Andreas Kulick also supports the application of proportionality as a general principle of law.[73] For Caroline Henckels:

> the use of an appropriately deferential approach to proportionality analysis in the consideration of indirect expropriation claims, tailored to a case's factual matrix and applicable to each stage of proportionality analysis' discrete stages of review, would provide greater policy space for host states to take measures in the public interest, yet would provide sufficient scrutiny to control misuse of public power.[74]

For any of these proposals to succeed, the takings provisions of most BITs and EIAs must first be modified. One alternative is to add the US declaration, associating the last factor of *Penn Central* with the proportionality principle. At present, few treaties have explicitly made this connection. Another possibility is to introduce the distinction between deprivations of property, controls on its use, and other interferences of European human rights law in investment treaties. Norway released in 2007 a new draft BIT model, which stated in its Article 6:

1. A Party shall not expropriate or nationalise an investment of an investor of the other Party except in the public interest and subject to the conditions provided for by law and by the general principles of international law.
2. The preceding provision shall not, however, in any way impair the right of a Party to enforce such laws as it deems necessary to control the use of property in accordance with the general interest or to secure the payment of taxes or other contributions or penalties.[75]

The comments on the draft treaty openly recognised that '[t]he expropriation provision in the model agreement is primarily derived from protocol 1, article 1 of the European Convention for the Protection of Human Rights and Fundamental Freedoms'.[76] This new BIT model was ultimately aimed at balancing the investment protections with the exercise of state regulatory-powers.[77] The opposition of both pro-investor and pro-state groups, however, prevented the Norwegian government from pursuing the negotiations of this treaty, which was finally abandoned in 2009.[78]

7.2 EXPLAINING AN APPROACH

Can property be limited by the state? This is a question that can only be duly answered on philosophical grounds.[79] International law has traditionally approached the issue pragmatically, from the perspective of the affected owner. This should come as no surprise. The international law of expropriation has its origin in the protection of aliens offered by the law of nations, particularly those of capital-exporting countries. The aim of these rules and principles was the limitation of state interferences with the rights of individuals, because it was then assumed that the state would benefit from their undertakings and enterprises. International investment law derives from these rules and principles on the treatment of aliens, and the protection of property in international human rights law can also trace its origins back to this area of the law of nations. This explains the close link between the international law of expropriation and the notion of rule of law.

In this regard, Rudolf Dolzer's answer to the question of the future of European BITs is worth mentioning. It is a persuasive statement, applicable not only to these treaties, but to the international minimum standard in general:

> We have every reason to believe that the product and brand which was successful in the past will continue to adapt, grow and succeed.
>
> Is it true that the European BIT has not yet stood the real test of time? Has Europe's BIT not yet lost its innocence inasmuch as the BIT in practice has been translated only into a legal instrument that is used by European companies against non-European host states and not the other way around?
>
> Will the picture change in the future when European States or the European Union find themselves in the uncomfortable position of being the respondent before international tribunals, as the United States has been in the NAFTA context during the past decades?
>
> We do not know. It is true that in such a setting, the new role as the defendant may prompt two very different responses. One would be an attempt to change the substantive rules and to lower the standards so that the likelihood of an award against 'my own country' would be reduced. The alternative response

would be fundamentally different. This second approach would accept that BIT rules continue to serve as useful external disciplines for all states and would facilitate housekeeping for the legal order. In more modern terms, this approach would assume that BITs promote good governance, multilateral administrative rulemaking and the rule of law in general.

It is my view that Europe should not and will not go down the first route of lowering standards for the sake of defending itself as a respondent against unjustified or justified claims. Under such circumstances, the legal culture of Europe which has grown and prospered since 1945 is not likely to prompt a political reflex that holds up the banner of sovereignty and weakens international dispute settlement for the sake of protecting that sovereignty.

The practice within Europe in the implementation of the European Convention on Human Rights shows that, even in sensitive legal areas, European States are today inclined to accept that the rule of law as expressed on the international level is not fundamentally different from the domestic rule of law, and that the price to be paid for it will, in the long run, turn out to be a benefit.[80]

7.2.1 On Public Purpose

The concept of sovereignty still lies at the heart of international law.[81] In the often-quoted passage of the *Isle of Palmas* case, Judge Max Huber equated it with independence, defining sovereignty as the right to exercise the functions of a state within a portion of the globe, to the exclusion of any other state.[82] Based on this notion, international tribunals will normally not question the public purpose requirement claimed by a host-state, except in the most evident cases of abuse.[83] According to the Third Restatement of the Foreign Relations Law of the United States, '[p]resumably, a seizure by a dictator or oligarchy for private use could be challenged under [the public purpose] rule'.[84] *LETCO* offers a good example of an evident case of abuse. This arbitration referred to the successive reduction of the territorial scope of a concession by Liberia, which the tribunal concluded to have 'the effect of greatly reducing the concession area and of effectively rendering the investment by LETCO useless'.[85] No public purpose was found in the measures adopted by the host-state. On the contrary, 'evidence was given to the Tribunal that areas of the concession taken from LETCO were granted to other foreign owned companies [run] by people who were "good friends" of the Liberian authorities'.[86] Most expropriation cases, however, do not present such an open disregard for this requirement.[87]

There is no internationally agreed-upon definition of public purpose, policy or interest. What in fact constitutes it will rest, to a large extent, with the respective host-state.[88] To question the existence of public purpose in a specific situation would entail evaluating the motivation of a sovereign state-policy. For this reason, international tribunals generally abstain from such an assessment. Otherwise, courts and arbitral panels with even less structural independence and democratic legitimacy than domestic judges would be second-guessing decisions of the executive or the legislative, without the necessary protections and institutional credibility to review them.[89] In any case, the fact that international tribunals normally provide host-states a wide margin of appreciation in this regard does not mean that the requirement of public purpose is a legal concept devoid of meaning.[90] The European Court of Human Rights has supported this view. It has refrained from challenging the host-state's motives not only in *James* and other judgments on deprivations of property, but also on those decisions related to controls of its use and other interferences.[91] In this respect, Yutaka Arai-Takahashi notes that '[i]t is possible to consider the application of the proportionality principle as the other side of the margin of appreciation. The more intense the standard of proportionality becomes, the narrower the margin allowed to national authorities'.[92] The Iran–US CT also granted an extensive discretion to the host-state in *Amoco* and other judgments.[93] Arbitral panels in investment disputes have consistently followed this trend too.[94] At least until recently, for the police-powers rule or the proportionality test to apply to claims of indirect expropriation presupposes the assessment of the public purpose involved in the challenged state measure. As Kulick explains:

> It is an achievement of liberal democracy and the rule of law that while judges usually assume the position and competency to control State conduct by independent legal review, they acknowledge their role as judicial bodies and hence their limited competences and legitimacy as political decision-makers. Whether we call it standards of review or *Kontrolldichte* (German Federal Constitutional Court), margin of appreciation (ECtHR) or levels of scrutiny (US Supreme Court), all those instruments aim at adequate allocation of competencies in a separation of power and thus a functional context. Whether such separation is horizontal – between the three branches of government within a State – or vertical – between the State and an international Tribunal [*sic*] – is of no relevance in this regard. The underlying rationale of either of these standards of review is that the judge has to exercise judicial self-restraint in cases where political, cultural and moral core questions are at stake that the State or a particular branch of government is much more competent to evaluate. On the other hand, review grows stricter the more intense and the more suspicious the intrusion on the individual is.[95]

Public interest or utility is an old principle of international law. It was identified by Grotius as one of the two conditions for the exercise of the right of eminent domain. The other was the payment of compensation.[96] Today, non-discrimination and due process complete the conditions of a lawful expropriation. There is no distinction between direct and indirect taking, to this effect. The basic structure of modern takings provisions can be found in 19th-century FCNs. Kenneth Vandevelde describes it as 'a prospective prohibition on any expropriation of foreign property unless full compensation is paid'.[97] Ursula Kriebaum sees a major departure from the traditional approach of international law towards expropriation, in the position of those that consider public purpose as an element of the existence of an indirect taking, rather than an element of its lawfulness.[98] In her view:

> If the approach of the *Methanex* and *Saluka* tribunals were to be followed, this would lead to a considerable gap in international investment protection: any non discriminatory measure, taken in the public interest that interferes with property rights will no longer be an expropriation regardless of its consequences.[99]

This conclusion is similar to that of Judge Dionisio Anzilotti, expressed in his individual opinion to the *Oscar Chinn* case: 'It is clear that international law would be merely an empty phrase if it sufficed for a State to invoke the public interest in order to evade the fulfilment of its engagements'.[100] This is a statement that still resonates in the international *fora*. For instance, *Aguas del Aconquija* affirmed: 'If public purpose automatically immunises the measure from being found to be expropriatory, then there would never be a compensable taking for a public purpose'.[101] As Kriebaum adds, the concept of indirect taking would lose its current meaning.[102] Arbitral panels in both NAFTA and BIT arbitrations have explicitly recognised that the requirements of a lawful taking should not be confused with the constitutive elements of expropriation itself.[103] Compensation is an essential part of the minimum standard of protection granted by international law to those investing abroad. Already in 1933, the US–Panama Claims Commission declared in the *de Sabla* case: 'It is axiomatic that acts of a government in depriving an alien of his property without compensation impose international responsibility'.[104] In international law, the deprivation of an alien's property should generally be compensated by the host-state, even if there is a legitimate general interest involved in the adoption of the expropriatory measure. Christoph Schreuer points out:

> the fact that a measure is in the public interest and non-discriminatory cannot be the answer to the question whether an expropriation has occurred. An

expropriation may take place under perfectly legitimate circumstances. Arbitrariness, bad faith, lack of proportionality and other improprieties are not constitutive elements of expropriation. Their absence does not mean that an expropriation could not have taken place.[105]

Rosalyn Higgins supports this view; so does Yoram Dinstein, among others.[106] Kingsbury and Schill do not, but they accurately outline this traditional approach:

> Proportionality analysis [...] is open to the criticisms that it confers power on arbitrators to take policy-driven decisions about the proper balance between conflicting rights and interests, and that it encourages a focus on principles above rules. This criticism may be less problematic in the domestic context as the legislature there has power to reverse court decisions on administrative and legislative standards, at least with regard to future cases. Yet, in the investment treaty context, the revision of BITs is a slow process requiring the consent of both contracting state parties. Furthermore, most investment treaties do not provide for an institutional procedure that can be triggered in order to adapt the interpretation of investment treaties in response to interpretations by investment tribunals, for example along the lines of the NAFTA Free Trade Commission, an organ through which NAFTA parties can jointly issue authoritative interpretations of the rules and standards applicable to investor-state disputes. While the application of proportionality analysis to constitutional rights has some parallels with its application in the context of interpreting investor rights under investment treaties, national constitutional courts and standing international courts, such as ECJ and the ECtHR, may well be in better institutional position to bear this weight than are ad hoc and evanescent investment treaty tribunals.[107]

Currently, the greatest challenge to this view comes from those investment treaties that include declarations and explanations aimed at guiding decision-makers in future claims of indirect expropriation, which implicitly encourage them to review the public purpose involved in the respective state measure through the application of a police-powers rule or the proportionality principle. In practice, this means replacing an objective approach to the threshold question, based on the effects rule, for a subjective one, centred in the judicial analysis of the motives behind the adoption of the challenged measure.[108] Vandevelde tracks down the emergence of BIT models, identifying three eras or periods in the history of investment treaties.[109] The first era spans the end of the 1950s to the end of the 1980s. In this period, developed states prepared model treaties that were simply presented to developing countries. Few treaties were concluded in these years because of the developing states' suspicion with regard to foreign investment. The second era spans the end of the 1980s to the end of the 20th century. Here, developing countries abandoned their scepticism and concluded several treaties, not only with developed states, but also with other developing countries. They even prepared their own models, which did not differ greatly from those of developed states, and used them as drafts and counterdrafts in treaty negotiations. The third era began in the 21st century. This period was triggered by the growing worldwide resistance to globalisation and the first awards issued by NAFTA arbitral panels, particularly in those of cases dealing with US and Canadian environmental regulations. Here new model treaties were issued, 'intended to preserve host state regulatory discretion by clarifying or diminishing host state obligations or by limiting the scope of investor–state arbitral review'.[110]

Is this conventional challenge to the traditional approach justified? Do investment treaties really undermine the regulatory powers of the host-states party to them? Vandevelde offers a plausible answer to these questions, summarising some of the arguments put forward by part of the international doctrine. In his opinion, investment treaties 'can contribute greatly to institutional quality in host countries', because these treaties rest in six principles: access, security, non-discrimination, reasonableness, transparency and due process, all elements of the rule of law.[111] From this standpoint, investment treaties are nothing more than 'mutual commitments to principles of good governance. Their success should be measured not by the amount of foreign investment that they attract, but by the quality of the legal environment they create'.[112] As Vandevelde remarks:

> The arbitral jurisprudence to date, taken as a whole, suggests that the BITs have meant little more as a practical matter than an insistence that host countries abide by these basic rule of law principles. For the most part, host states that honor their commitments, that refrain from the complete destruction of the value of the investment, that act on the basis of legitimate policy concerns rather than animus against foreign investors, and that deal candidly with investors have had little to fear from arbitral awards.[113]

7.2.2 Substantial and Permanent Deprivation

Legal notions are often threshold concepts, which apply in 'an all-or-nothing fashion' when certain conditions are satisfied or have reached a certain level of intensity.[114] The main issue regarding indirect takings is a threshold question. The answer to it does not lie in the intention of the host-state that adopted the challenged measure; it lies in the result of the respective interference in the property of the affected individual or legal entity. For this reason, the threshold problem was aptly described by Santiago Montt as:

> not an ontological enterprise, but a more pragmatic one: it is simply the ex-post effects of regulation on one or more investors, that causes it to be expropriatory; and it is not expropriatory per se, but only with respect to that investor or those investors.[115]

To be considered a taking, a state measure must substantially and permanently deprive a foreign investor of his/her/its property. This is the applicable standard in international investment law.[116] The European Court of Human Rights and the Iran–US CT require a similar result in their case-laws.[117] Some authors see a more flexible approach in the judgments of the Iran–US CT than in those of the European Court.[118] Both standards, nonetheless, involve at least a substantial and permanent interference; the same threshold usually required by *ad hoc*, ICSID, UNCITRAL or ICC arbitral panels in their awards.[119] Concluding that a deprivation complies with these requirements is a matter of degree, where no numerical formulas apply.[120] But a finding of indirect taking also depends on what has been taken.[121] Treaties do not include an autonomous definition of property, so a *renvoi* to municipal law is needed not only to supplement the conventional notion, which is open and general, but also to establish the existence of the corresponding right under the applicable domestic norms.[122] Even though contracts are property under the international law of expropriation, not just any contractual breach necessarily leads to a taking. *Waste Management 2* summarised the general approach in international case-law towards violations of contracts and expropriations: the respective host-state must have acted in an official capacity, in the exercise of its public authority.[123] A breach of contract is a commercial risk not protected by international investment law. If not accompanied by another governmental measure repudiating the contract, like a decree or a law nullifying its rights, it does not amount to a taking. In this case, the alien will have to exercise the corresponding remedies in the contractually agreed *forum*.[124]

The problem of defining the protected property, the *renvoi* to municipal law and the relationship between breaches of contracts and expropriations are only some of the challenges decision-makers face in claims of indirect takings. The question of whether it is possible to divide the property into identifiable, distinct rights is one of the most difficult tasks that a tribunal will face when settling an indirect expropriation case.[125] Newcombe and Paradell highlight that:

> a fundamental issue in the expropriation analysis is the characterization of the affected property. This, in turn, requires an analysis of the extent to which the affected property can be severed or segregated into distinct parts from the rest of the investment. This analysis will necessarily be context specific. Relevant

> facts will include whether the applicable law recognizes the right or interest in question as a distinct property right, how the investment is legally structured and operated, the extent to which elements of the investment are treated as distinct in the applicable law (e.g., for purposes of regulation and taxation) and [...] the purpose of the measure and the investor's legitimate investment-backed expectations. The tendency has been for tribunals to consider that the investment must be viewed as a whole. In contrast, if there has been a taking of a specific asset, such as a ship in *Middle East*, or a specific contractual right, such as in *Eureko*, that qualified as investment in its own right, tribunals have found that there was an expropriation of the specific investment in question.[126]

Conceptual severance of the expropriated property is generally not accepted in international and comparative law. This favours the host-state, for it diminishes the possibilities of a finding of substantial and permanent deprivation in an indirect takings case.[127]

Related to the problem of degree is that of partial expropriations.[128] Measures that affect an investment by merely reducing its value or profitability are normally not considered expropriatory in case-law and doctrine. This approach would rule out the possibility of partial takings. International judicial decisions, however, are divided on the issue. BIT, NAFTA and ECT arbitrations have denied partial expropriations (*Feldman*, *Nykomb*, *Occidental*, *CMS*, *Telenor* and *Grand River*) or accepted them (*S.D. Myers*, *Middle East Cement*, *Waste Management 2*, *GAMI*, *Eureko* and *EnCana*), either implicitly or explicitly.[129] Kriebaum argues that an answer to this question depends on the notion of substantial deprivation, which she describes in these words:

> What it obviously does not mean is a total taking that leaves the investor without any residual rights. In a wider sense, almost all cases of indirect expropriation are only partial. Typically, there is no transfer of title and the physical property is not taken but the investor is deprived of the substance of the investment. The decisive point for an expropriation is the destruction of the capability to make use of the investment in an economic sense. The investor need not be deprived of its physical property, but it has to be deprived of the economic benefit of its investment.[130]

The author concludes that a partial expropriation should be accepted if three requirements are fulfilled. First, the overall investment project must be able to be separated into a number of discrete rights. Second, the host-state must have deprived the foreign investor of a right which is covered by one of the items in the definition of investment in the applicable treaty. And third, this right must be capable of economic exploitation independently of the remainder of the investment.[131]

Focusing on the effects of the measures adopted, to establish whether a regulation amounts to a taking does not exclude the intent of the domestic authorities from playing a role in this determination. Nonetheless, this role is quite a different one from that attributed to it by the supporters of the police-powers doctrine. Michael Reisman and Robert Sloane explain that:

> Even though a state's responsibility to pay compensation for expropriation does not, in any event, 'depend on proof that the expropriation was intentional', the manifestation of that intent at some level of the state's government generally furnishes a tribunal with a useful demarcation.[132]

Newcombe agrees with them. According to him, the intent will be relevant in the determination of whether a government measure is expropriatory or not, for a tribunal is more likely to find a taking where there is clear evidence of intent to expropriate. As he notes, '[t]hat intent is not a necessary element of expropriation simply means that a government cannot use lack of intent as a defence to a claim of expropriation'.[133] In any case, Rudolf Dolzer and Christoph Schreuer add: '[w]hat is uncontroversial is that the mere post-facto explanation by the host state of its intention will in itself carry no decisive weight'.[134]

To sum up, decision-makers should follow a three-step assessment when settling indirect expropriation claims. The first one corresponds to the application of the substantial and permanent deprivation standard, already mentioned. The second stage consists of the identification of possible police-powers exceptions to the payment of compensation, which are necessarily limited under international law.[135] How can decision-makers identify these exceptions? According to Dolzer and Schreuer, one way of doing this is 'to clarify whether the measure in question was taken in the exercise of functions that are generally considered part of a government's powers to regulate the general welfare. This approach calls for a comparison of domestic legal orders'.[136] The third step requires the decision-makers to assess the fulfilment of the obligation of respecting legitimate expectations, arguably a general principle of law.[137] Regulations breaching distinct prior commitments of the host-state deprive foreign investors of the respective rights created by such commitments, as long as they are covered by the respective treaty.[138]

7.3 INVESTMENT TREATIES AND THE RULE OF LAW

Property is currently protected against expropriation in investment treaties and regional human rights conventions. Both areas of international law provide a minimum standard of treatment, comprising several guaranteed rights which duly respected by the state are the embodiment of the rule of law. In the case of investment treaties, their provisions generally offer stability, predictability, consistency, transparency and coherency in the conduct of host-states towards foreign entrepreneurs, thus reducing political risk.[139] These treaties compensate for gaps in domestic law and customary international norms, therefore encouraging good governance in host-states.[140] For Dolzer:

> BITs are intended to create a level playing field between host states and investors. The host's sovereignty implies that the government can unilaterally set, in principle, those standards which will protect its national policies and will also create an investment-friendly climate. The investor must accept these standards at the time of the investment; his main concern is that these standards are not subsequently altered or modified in a manner which upsets his legitimate expectations.[141]

Vandevelde's sporting explanation of what he considers the core principles of investment treaties offers a vivid description of the protection given to aliens by host-states through these international agreements:

> The decision of a foreign investor to enter a foreign market might be analogized to the decision of an athlete to compete in a game held in unfamiliar territory. Such an athlete would want certain assurances.
>
> First, before preparing to compete, the athlete would want an assurance that he or she would be deemed eligible to participate. This is the principle of access.
>
> Second, the athlete would want an assurance that the competition would be governed by rules, that is, the result of the game would not be determined by arbitrary factors, but by reference to principles. This is the principle of reasonableness.
>
> Third, the athlete would want an assurance that the rules would not be changed after the game began. This is the principle of security.
>
> Fourth, the athlete would want an assurance that the rules would not favor one participant over another or, to use a colloquial expression, that the playing field would be level. This is the principle of nondiscrimination.
>
> Fifth, the athlete would want an assurance that he or she would be informed of the rules that would govern the competition before the game began. This is the principle of transparency.
>
> Finally, the athlete would want an assurance that the game would be supervised by an impartial referee. This is the principle of due process.[142]

Principles like these not only protect foreign investors, but also promote the rule of law in host-states.

7.3.1 Aliens under International Law

Why should the treatment of aliens in international law require a higher standard of protection than that established by the major domestic legal orders?[143] The relevance of this question is not limited to the problem of indirect expropriation, for in its answer lies the *raison d'être* of international investment law as a whole. Sornarajah contends that the dominance of this regime, originally designed by the USA to protect its investors abroad, can only be explained in terms of power, and not in terms of logic or reasoning:

> The positivist notions of sovereignty which were the dominant notion in public international law during this period should have supported the claims of the Latin American states for the regime they argued [was] more consistent with state sovereignty than the intrusive regime which the [US government] argued for on the basis of values which were not universal but were constructed to achieve investment protection.[144]

If power played a role in the establishment of the minimum standard protecting aliens abroad, so did sovereignty and its synonym in international law: independence.[145] The sovereign state is not subject within its territory to the jurisdiction of any state other than itself, or bound by any law other than its own and international law.[146] As a sovereign, the state can choose to bind itself to international law, whether customary or conventional, hence limiting its own independence. In the words of Steven Lee:

> A state, by agreeing to provisions of international law, chooses to create constraints on its own behavior in order to get other states to constrain their behavior, thereby achieving some control over the actions of outside interference to which it is subject, on the calculation that the chosen constraints are less onerous than the unrestrained actions of outside interference. But these constraints are legal constraints, and thus seem to undermine the state's legal independence. The existence of international law seems to entail the loss of the state's legal sovereignty.[147]

The consent of the state to a customary norm may be express or implied. It requires state practice and *opinion juris* – or, in the words of Article 38 (1) (b) of the ICJ's Statute: a general practice accepted as law. The consent of the state may even be presumed in case of acquiescence; that is to say, the silence or passivity of the state towards the conduct of other states that would otherwise deserve a protest. The consent in treaties will generally be explicit.[148] Once given, the state will have to keep its agreement under the principle of *pacta sunt servanda*.[149] This principle does not only apply to treaties, but to any international obligation assumed by the state.[150] But there is more to sovereignty and the protection of aliens. It can be fairly claimed that the international minimum standard is the forerunner of the international system of human rights that governs the treatment of nationals and foreigners alike. Currently, an international minimum standard is enshrined in BITs and EIAs, as well as in the UN Covenants, the European Convention, the American Convention, and the African Charter on human rights.[151] Arguing that the norms on the treatment of aliens go against the state's sovereignty is equivalent to arguing that the norms on human rights go against it. Like international human rights law, investment treaties are aimed at supplementing the treatment given by domestic norms.[152]

Sornarajah has dubbed the international law on foreign investment a law of greed.[153] His answer to Dolzer's question can only be formulated in negative terms:

> there is no reason why a foreigner investor who voluntarily assumes a risk by entering a host state should be insulated from the risks inherent in the host state and should not bear the costs of his own adventure.[154]

However, there are reasons for protecting aliens – and good ones. Relying on the law of the host-state alone has never been an attractive option for foreign investors. Salacuse points out some of the risks to which an alien is subject abroad. It is not only that domestic law can be easily changed after the investment has been made by the host-state, or that the government officials of the latter may act impartially towards him. It is also that, in the past, host-states have treated foreign investors in an arbitrary and discriminatory manner in the past, imposing onerous conditions on the operation of foreign investment.[155] Once an investment is made, it is difficult for the respective foreigner to withdraw to another state.[156] Vandevelde sums up this situation as follows:

> BITs are drafted to address a specific circumstance: that of an investor of one state (the home state) locating assets in the territory of another state (the host state). History demonstrated the vulnerability of the foreign investor in that circumstance and thus BITs are remedial documents, drafted to ameliorate the condition of these investors and their investments. The remedy provided by BITs is that they ensure that the treatment of foreign investment is subject to the rule of law.

> The success of a BIT program depends upon the willingness of host states to accept the legal obligations imposed by the treaties. The inducement offered to host states is that BITs promote economic development by establishing a more liberal international investment regime. More specifically, BITs purport to create conditions under which foreign investors are more likely to enter the host state market.[157]

The same line of reasoning is applicable to other investment treaties, like EIAs. The US–Mexican General Claims Commission had already observed in the 1926 *Hopkins* case that:

> The citizens of a nation may enjoy many rights which are withheld from aliens, and, conversely, under international law aliens may enjoy rights and remedies which the nation does not accord to its own citizens.[158]

Frederick Dunn developed this idea two years later:

> From a practical point of view, the foreigner, although he may be accorded full civil rights on the same basis as citizens, is often at a disadvantage in any dispute which he may have with the agents of the state of his sojourn merely by reason of the fact that he is a foreigner. Furthermore, being deprived of political rights outside of his own country, he is not at liberty to participate in the determination of the social and economic order and has not the political means for the protection of his interests that are at the disposal of the citizen. Perhaps for these reasons as much as any other, it has been found necessary, in a world of diverse cultures and heterogeneous peoples, of strong governments and weak governments, of orderly countries and disorderly countries, to work out a common code of treatment of aliens in order that there might be some basis of security and predictability upon which to build the present complex structure of international intercourse.
>
> This common code of treatment is technically called the 'minimum standard of justice'.[159]

Aliens constitute a minority that requires special protection. Michael Ignatieff illustrates this fact by reference to the problem of balancing liberty and security in the fight against terrorism. He says:

> Democratic citizens do not actually have to balance their liberty against their security, but their security against the liberty of others, usually non-citizens. Decisions to abridge civil liberties for non-nationals have aroused little public resistance since September 11, while measures aimed at citizens, like national identity cards or more intrusive security screenings at airports, have been stymied.[160]

Ignatieff concludes that '[o]bserving international law is the best way to correct the partiality that states feel towards their own citizens and mitigate the discrimination that it meets out towards non-citizens'.[161] The same conclusion is applicable to the international law of expropriation. In the *James* case, the European Court of Human Rights recognised aliens as a minority that should receive special protection.[162] So did the arbitral panel in *TECMED.*[163] Thomas Waelde elaborated on this point, in his separate opinion to the award in *International Thunderbird*:

> Investment arbitration [...] governs the situation of a foreign investor exposed to the sovereignty, the regulatory, administrative and other governmental powers of a state. The investor is frequently if not mostly in a position of structural weakness, exacerbated often by inexperience (in particular in the case of smaller, entrepreneurial investors). Investment arbitration therefore does not set up a system of resolving disputes between presumed equals as in commercial arbitration, but a system of protection of foreign investors that are by exposure to political risk, lack of familiarity with and integration into, an alien political, social, cultural, commercial, institutional and legal system, at a disadvantage.[164]

7.3.2 Expectations and Governance

Human rights treaties are essentially oriented towards the victims of their violation.[165] In the case of investment treaties, the potential victims are aliens. The protection expected by foreign investors from host-states comprises the payment of compensation, in case of takings, and of damages, in case of breaches of the applicable investment treaty. This protection is, nevertheless, not unlimited: it does not cover aliens from any risk faced while investing abroad. The tribunal in *Maffezini*, for example, emphasised that BITs are not insurance policies against bad business judgements.[166] In other words, ordinary commercial risks are excluded from investment treaty protection.[167] This approach goes back to *Oscar Chinn.*[168]

Whether a taking is total or partial, the host-state's obligation to pay an amount of money to a foreign investor may be based either on the law of expropriation or on the law of state responsibility. In practice, both the requirement of a lawful taking and the obligation derived from an internationally wrongful act are normally referred to as compensation.[169] Irmgard Marboe argues that a lawful taking would require a prompt, adequate and effective compensation, while an unlawful one would require full compensation.[170] International case-law generally does not differentiate between the two types of expropriation, at the moment of awarding the respective amount of money to the foreign investor.

International tribunals will require the payment of compensation in conformity to the fair market value, *i.e.* the Hull formula, whether the expropriation was lawful or unlawful.[171] But there is more to compensation than takings in international investment law. The expropriation clause is not the only treaty protection that will engage the international responsibility of the host-state if breached. Others include national and MFN treatment; the obligation of full protection and security; non-discrimination; and, most notably, FET.

The following observation of the arbitral panel in *PSEG* illustrates a common situation these days:

> As it is by now customary in investment arbitration, the aggrieved party invokes the breach of every BIT clause dealing with the standards of the investor's protection, while the Respondent vehemently denies any breach.[172]

From these protections, that against takings is one of the two most relied-upon by claimants in investor-to-state disputes – the other is FET.[173] In fact, findings of indirect takings are relatively rare, unlike favourable decisions on state liability for other substantive treaty standards.[174] In the case-law of the Iran–US CT, every time the judges wanted to award compensation for measures that did not amount to a taking, the tribunal applied the concept of other measures affecting property rights.[175] FET has sometimes been seen as a somewhat equivalent notion.[176] In several arbitrations where no expropriation was found, the tribunal concluded that the FET clause was breached. These cases include BIT arbitrations (*Maffezini*, *MTD*, *Occidental*, *Saluka*, *PSEG* and *Enron*) and NAFTA disputes (*S.D. Myers*, *Pope & Talbot* and *Cargill*).[177]

At first sight, it would appear that an interference that amounts to a substantial and permanent deprivation of the alien's property will constitute an indirect taking, while a lesser interference will amount to a breach of the FET clause. However, an indirect expropriation can overlap with an unfair and inequitable treatment. In a number of cases where a taking was found, the tribunal concluded that the FET clause was also breached by the host-state. These include BIT arbitrations (*CME*, *Middle East Cement*, *TECMED*, *ADC*, *Siemens* and *Alpha Projektholding*) and a NAFTA dispute (*Metalclad*).[178] These cases show that FET and the protection against indirect expropriation are related but distinct standards. They do share some of their constitutive elements. Within those identified by arbitral panels in the FET obligation are due process, non-discrimination, due diligence, respect for legitimate expectations, transparency and good faith.[179] Out of these elements, due process and the respect of legitimate expectations are common to the protection against expropriation and FET. Nevertheless, the legal nature of these obligations is different. While the FET clause establishes an *obligation de moyens*, the protection against expropriation combines the latter with an *obligation de résultat* – the payment of compensation.

The respect for legitimate expectations, based on prior distinct commitments, is an obligation which generally requires stability, predictability and consistency in the conduct of host-states towards foreign investors.[180] Far from being opposed to the effects rule, this obligation supplements the traditional approach on indirect takings. Although the threshold question is answered by the application of the substantial and permanent deprivation test, other elements will help the decision-maker to confirm the expropriatory nature of the respective measure. The intention of the host-state is one of them; the respect of the alien's legitimate expectations is another. This duty derives from those promises or undertakings made explicitly or implicitly by the governmental authorities.[181] These commitments can have a legal nature, either national or international, or a non-legal nature: they can be found in a treaty, a law, a license or a permit, or even an investment brochure.[182] The host-state's legal and administrative framework is an important source of expectations for foreign investors.[183] To be legitimate, these expectations must be reasonable. For instance, expecting the host-state not to change any of its legal or administrative norms, which are applicable to a foreign investor, would not be within reason.[184] Yves Fortier and Stephen Drymer point out that the level of interference allowed with the foreign investor's legitimate expectations is a matter of degree. Because it is largely a question of transparent and coherent conduct by the host-state, the essence of this duty is a requirement of procedural propriety, of fairness in its treatment towards aliens.[185] It is not strange, then, that this concept reappears as one of the elements of the FET standard, and hence as a separate cause of action for claiming damages.

Human rights and investment treaties are mutual commitments to rule of law principles.[186] Their aim is to provide a minimum standard of treatment. In the case of the protection of property, the purpose of both areas of law is to reduce political risk or the possibility that the state might interfere with the corresponding right of the owner. This is achieved by the establishment of a basic legal and administrative framework that would ensure the compliance of the respective international obligation assumed by the state in question. Such a basic framework constitutes a requirement of good governance from the state, which would allow it to become an *état de droit* or *rechstaat*: a law-governed state.[187] The rule of law is, therefore, the main objective of international investment law and international human rights law, and this objective has a content – at least, a minimum one.[188] Jeremy Waldron notes: 'The Rule of Law is commonly seen as a way of limiting the power of the state, keeping the power of the state under control'.[189] This concept, coined in 1885 by Albert Dicey, can be traced back to Aristotle's writings.[190] According to Tom Bingham, the minimum content of the rule of law is 'that all persons and authorities within the state, whether public or private, should be bound by and entitled to the benefit of laws publicly made, taking effect (generally) in the future and publicly administered in the courts'.[191] This core principle implies a number of sub-principles: accessible law (*i.e.*, intelligible, clear and predictable), equally applicable to all (except when objective differences justify differentiation); establishing public powers reasonably exercised by state organs (for the purposes for which they were conferred, without exceeding their limits); affording adequate protecting of human rights (including property); providing means for resolving disputes (without undue delay or costs), through fair adjudicative procedures (provided by the state).[192] Needless to say, the rule of law requires the state to comply with its international obligations.[193]

7.4 CONCLUSION

It is difficult to say in which direction the international law of expropriation is heading. The effects approach is still the dominant trend in international treaty arbitration. However, a growing number of treaties have incorporated an interpretative declaration guiding decision-makers towards the application of the *Penn Central* factors in claims of indirect takings. This goes against the wide margin of appreciation, normally accorded the state by judges and arbitrators in these cases. *Methanex*, *Saluka*, *Chemtura* and *El Paso* unduly followed a police-powers approach without the aid of interpretative declarations. With them, decision-makers can easily construe the third factor of *Penn Central* (*i.e.*, the character of the governmental action) as an invitation to assess the public interest pursued by the host-state with the challenged measure, applying a police-powers rule allegedly supported by the text of the corresponding treaty. Some of these new treaties link the third factor of *Penn Central* with a balancing test which resembles that of the European Court of Human Rights. *TECMED*, *Azurix*, *Fireman's Fund*, *LG&E*, *Archer Daniels*, *Continental Casualty* and *Tza* have already applied the proportionality principle in expropriation claims without any interpretative declaration. With them, arbitrators can continue to misconstrue this principle, applying a proportionality test to answer the threshold question.

The doctrinal turmoil produced by what has been called the legitimacy crisis of international investment law has reinstated old queries. One of these challenges the international minimum standard of treatment, of which the protection against expropriation is an essential part. Why do aliens need to be protected beyond the treatment offered by states to their nationals? This question can only be answered by explaining, once again, the often-misunderstood relationship between sovereignty and international law. Today, investment treaties protect aliens via the promotion of a basic legal and administrative framework, equivalent to the fundamental requirements of the rule of law. In the case of protection against takings, this means complying with the requirements of a lawful expropriation, one of which is payment of compensation. The principles of substantial and permanent deprivation and of respect for legitimate expectations offer useful guidance to decision-makers in claims of indirect takings. Even though the threshold question will always have to be answered on a case-by-case basis, these principles provide foreign investors and host-states a basic sense of legal certainty.

NOTES

1. C Schreuer, 'The Concept of Expropriation under the ECT and Other Investment Protection Treaties', in C Ribeiro (ed.), *Investment Arbitration and the Energy Charter Treaty* (2006), 115.
2. *See Norwegian Shipowners* (Norway v. USA), Anderson, Vogt and Valloton, arbitrators, Award, 13 October 1922, (1922) 1 *RIAA* 307; *Oscar Chinn* (UK v. Belgium), PCIJ, Judgment, 12 December 1934, (1934) *PCIJ Rep.* Series A/B No 63; *Factory at Chorzow* (Germany v. Poland), PCIJ, Judgment, 13 September 1928, (1928) *PCIJ Rep.* Series A No 17.
3. *See British Petroleum Exploration Co. v. Libyan Arab Republic*, Lagergren, sole arbitrator, Award, 10 October 1973, (1973) 53 *ILR* 297; *Texas Overseas Petroleum Co. & California Asiatic Oil Co.* (TOPCO/CALASIATIC) *v. Libyan Arab Republic*, Dupuy, sole arbitrator, Award, 19 January 1977, (1978) 17/1 *ILM* 1; *Libyan American Oil Co.* (LIAMCO) *v. Libyan Arab Republic*, Mahmassani, sole arbitrator, Award, 12 April 1977, (1981) 20/1 *ILM* 1; and *American Independent Oil Co.* (AMINOIL) *v. Kuwait*, Reuter, Sultan and Fitzmaurice, arbitrators, Award, 24 March 1982, (1982) 21/4 *ILM* 976.

   See also R von Mehren and P Kourides, 'International Arbitration between States and Foreign Private Parties: The Libyan Nationalization Cases', (1981) 75/3 *AJIL* 476; and P Norton, 'A Law of the Future or a Law of the Past? Modern Tribunals and the International Law of Expropriation', (1991) 85/3 *AJIL* 474, at 479–82.

4. *See Revere Copper and Brass, Incorporated v. Overseas Private Investment Corporation* (OPIC), Haight, Wetzel and Bergan, arbitrators, Award, 24 August 1978, (1978) 17/6 *ILM* 1321.
5. *See Anglo-Iranian Oil Co.* (UK v. Iran), ICJ, Judgment on Jurisdiction, 22 July 1952, (1952) *ICJ Rep.* 93; *Certain Norwegian Loans* (France v. Norway), (1957) *ICJ Rep.* 9; and *Barcelona Traction* (Belgium v. Spain), ICJ, Judgment, 5 February 1970, (1970) 9/2 *ILM* 227.
6. *See Elettronica Sicula S.p.A.* (ELSI) (USA v. Italy), ICJ, Judgment, 20 July 1989, (1989) 28/5 *ILM* 1111, para 119.
7. *See Ahmadou Sadio Diallo* (Guinea v. Congo), ICJ, Judgment, 30 November 2010, (2011) 50/1 *ILM* 40, paras. 157 & 159.
8. *See* M Sornarajah, *The International Law on Foreign Investment* (2010), 333; and S Subedi, *International Investment Law: Reconciling Policy and Principle* (2012), 153–5. *See also* O Fauchald, 'The Legal Reasoning of ICSID Tribunals – an Empirical Analysis', (2008) 19/2 *EJIL* 301, at 333–43; K Yannaca-Small, 'Indirect Expropriation and the Right to Regulate: How to Draw the Line?', in K Yannaca-Small (ed.), *Arbitration under International Investment Agreements: A Guide to the Key Issues* (2010), 455–6; and J Weeramantry, 'The Future Role of Past Awards in Investment Arbitration', (2010) 25/2 *ICSID Rev.* 111.
9. *See* J Commission, 'Precedent in Investment Treaty Arbitration. A Citation Analysis of a Developing Jurisprudence', (2007) 24/2 *JIA* 129, at 135–42. *See generally* A Rigo Sureda, 'Precedent in Investment Treaty Arbitration', in C Binder et al (eds.), *International Investment Law for the 21st Century: Essays in Honour of Christoph Schreuer* (2009); J Paulsson, 'The Role of Precedent in Investment Arbitration', in K Yannaca-Small (ed.), *Arbitration under International Investment Agreements: A Guide to the Key Issues* (2010), and A Rigo Sureda, *Investment Treaty Arbitration: Judging under Uncertainty* (2012), 109–31.
10. *See* M Pellonpää and M Fitzmaurice 'Taking of Property in the Practice of the Iran–United States Claims Tribunal' (1988), 56; C Gibson and C Drahozal, 'Iran–United States Tribunal Precedent in Investor–State Arbitration', (2006) 23/6 *JIA* 521; B Kunoy, 'The Notion of Time in ICSID's Case Law on Indirect Expropriation', (2006) 23/4 *JIA* 337, at 337; S Schill, *The Multilateralization of International Investment Law* (2009), 281–93; and Sornarajah (2010), note 6 at 333 & 368–9.
11. *Res judicata*, unlike a system of *stare decisis*, does not abide by precedents. *See* J Trayner, *Latin Maxims and Phrases* (1986), 585.
12. The 2010 SCC Arbitration Rules are available at http://www.sccinstitute.com/filearchive/3/35894/K4_Skiljedomsregler%20eng%20ARB%20TRYCK_1_100927.pdf (last visited 30 June 2013).
13. The 2012 ICC Rules of Arbitration are available at http://www.iccwbo.org/WorkArea/DownloadAsset.aspx?id=2147489109 (last visited 30 June 2013).
14. *See* A Boyle and C Chinkin, *The Making of International Law* (2006), 293–300. Judge Philadelpho Azevedo had already recognised the 'quasi-legislative value' of international case-law back in 1950. *Asylum* or *Víctor Raúl Haya de la Torre* (Colombia v. Perú), ICJ, Judgment, 20 November 1950, Dissenting Opinion of Judge Azevedo, (1950) *ICJ Rep.* 266, para. 1.
15. *See* Commission (2007), 142; S Montt, *State Liability in Investment Treaty Arbitration: Global Constitutional and Administrative Law in the BIT Generation* (2009), 20, 107 & 113; L Reed, 'The De Facto Precedent Regime in Investment Arbitration: A Case for Proactive Case Management', (2010) 25/1 *ICSID Rev.* 95, at 95–100; and S Robert-Cuendet, *Droits de l'investisseur étranger et protection de l'environnement: contribution à l'analyse de l'expropriation indirect* (2010), 5–6.

See also T Cheng, 'Precedent and Control in Investment Treaty Arbitration', (2007) 30/4 *Fordh. ILJ* 1014; C Schreuer and M Weiniger, 'A Doctrine of Precedent?', in P Muchlinski, F Ortino and C Schreuer (eds.), *The Oxford Handbook of International Investment Law* (2008), 1189–98; A Newcombe and L Paradell, *Law and Practice of Investment Treaties: Standards of Treatment* (2009), 59–61 & 102–7; Schill (2009), 321–39; and J Gill, 'Is There a Special Role for Precedent in Investment Arbitration?', (2010) 25/1 *ICSID Rev.* 87.

See e.g. Bayindir Insaat Turizm Ticaret Ve Sanayi A.S. v. Islamic Republic of Pakistan, ICSID case No. ARB/03/29, Decision on Jurisdiction, 14 November 2005, para. 76; *Fireman's Fund Insurance Company v. United Mexican States*, NAFTA, ICSID case No. ARB(AF)/02/1, Award, 17 July 2006, para. 172; *Noble Energy, Inc. and Machalapower Cia. Ltda. v. The Republic of Ecuador and Consejo Nacional de Electricidad*, ICSID case No. ARB/05/12, Decision on Jurisdiction, 5 March 2008, para. 50; *Saipem S.p.A. v. People's Republic of Bangladesh*, ICSID case No. ARB/05/7, Award, 30 June 2009, para. 90; and *Railroad Development Corporation* (RDC) *v. Republic of Guatemala*, CAFTA–DR, ICSID case No. ARB/07/23, Award, 29 June 2012, para. 217. *Cf.* Z Douglas, 'Can a Doctrine of Precedent Be Justified in Investment Treaty Arbitration?', (2010) 25/1 *ICSID Rev.* 104.

16. *See Methanex Corporation v. United States of America*, NAFTA, UNCITRAL arbitration, Final Award, 3 August 2005; and *Chemtura Corporation v. Government of Canada*, NAFTA, UNCITRAL arbitration, Award, 2 August 2010. *See* Chapter 6 above.
17. *See Saluka Investments BV v. The Czech Republic*, UNCITRAL arbitration, Partial Award, 17 March 2006; and *El Paso Energy International Company v. Argentine Republic*, ICSID case No. ARB/03/15, Award, 31 October 2011. *See* Chapter 5 above.
18. *See Técnicas Medioambientales TECMED S.A. v. The United Mexican States*, ICSID case No. ARB (AF)/00/2, Award, 29 May 2003; *Azurix Corp. v. The Argentine Republic*, ICSID case No. ARB/01/12, Award, 14 July 2006; *LG&E Energy Corp., LG&E Capital Corp., LG&E International Inc. v. Argentine Republic*, ICSID case No. ARB/02/1, Decision on Liability, 3 October 2006; *Continental Casualty Company v. Argentine Republic*, ICSID case No. ARB/03/9, Award, 5 September 2008; and *Tza Yap Shum c. La República de Perú*, ICSID case No. ARB/07/6, Award, 7 July 2011. *See* Chapter 5 above.
19. *See Fireman's Fund*, Award, 17 July 2006; and *Archer Daniels Midland Company and Tate & Lyle Ingredients Americas, Inc. v. United Mexican States*, NAFTA, ICSID case No. ARB(AF)/04/05, Award, 21 November 2007. *See* Chapter 6 above.
20. *See* Chapters 5 & 6 above.
21. R Jones, 'NAFTA Chapter 11 Investor-to-State Dispute Resolution: A Shield to Be Embraced or a Sword to Be Feared?', (2002) 2 *BYU LR* 527, at 541; G Gagné and J-T Morin, 'The Evolving American Policy on Investment Protection: Evidence from Recent FTAs and the 2004 Model BIT', (2006) 9/2 *JIEL* 357, at 360; Loppacher and Kerr (2006), 46; and G Gagné, 'The U.S. Policy on the Protection of Foreign Investment: From the NAFTA to the U.S.–Korea FTA', (2011) 12/5 *JWIT* 807, at 810.
22. Gagné (2011), 811. By Canadian and US investors, not Mexicans. G Aguilar and W Park, 'The New Face of Investment Arbitration: NAFTA Chapter 11', (2003) 28/2 *Yale JIL* 365, at 370.
23. P Sands, *Lawless World. America and the Making and Breaking of Global Rules* (2005), xi. *See* Aguilar and Park (2003), 366–71 & 398; G Sampliner, 'Arbitration of Expropriation Cases under U.S. Investment Treaties – a Threat to Democracy or the Dog That Didn't Bark?', (2003) 18/1 *ICSID Rev.* 1, at 23; Gagné and Morin (2006), 363; A Falsafi, 'The International Minimum Standard of Treatment of

Foreign Investor's Property: A Contingent Standard', (2007) 30/1 *Suff. TLR* 317, at 332–5; M Sornarajah, 'A Coming Crisis: Expansionary Trends in Investment Treaty Arbitration', in K Sauvant (ed.), *Appeals Mechanism in International Investment Disputes* (2008), 39–41; M Clodfelter, 'The Adaptation of States to the Changing World of Investment Protection through Model BITs', (2009) 24/1 *ICSID Rev.* 165, at 168–9; S Spears, 'The Quest for Policy Space in a New Generation of International Investment Agreements', (2010) 13/4 *JIEL* 1037, at 1042; K Vandevelde, *Bilateral Investment Treaties: History, Policy, and Interpretation* (2010), 72–3; K Vandevelde, 'Model Bilateral Investment Treaties: The Way Forward', (2011) 18/1 *Sw JIL* 307, 308; and Subedi (2012), 141.

24. *See* V Been and J Beauvais, 'The Global Fifth Amendment: NAFTA's Investment Protection and the Misguided Quest for an International "Regulatory Takings" Doctrine', (2003) 78/1 *NYU LR* 30, at 138–9.
25. M Sornarajah, 'Power and Justice in International Law', (1997) 1/1 *SJICL* 28, at 62.
26. *Ibid.*, 52.
27. *See* M Porterfield, 'State Practice and the (Purported) Obligation under Customary International Law to Provide Compensation for Regulatory Expropriations', (2011) 37/1 *NC JILCR* 159, at 174. For differences between this doctrine and the current international minimum standard, *see ibid.*, 174–8.
28. B Garner (ed.), *Black's Law Dictionary* (2009), 1592.
29. Garner (2009), 601. In the UK it is called compulsory acquisition of property. F Mann, 'Outlines of a History of Expropriation', (1959) 75/2 *LQR* 188, at 188.
30. E Graham, 'Regulatory Takings, Supernational Treatment, and the Multilateral Agreement on Investment: Issues Raised by Nongovernmental Organizations', (1998) 31/3 *Corn. ILJ* 599, at 604; R Stumberg, 'Sovereignty by Subtraction: The Multilateral Agreement on Investment', (1998) 31/3 *Corn. ILJ* 491, at 557; and J Stanley, 'Keeping Big Brother out of Our Backyard: Regulatory Takings as Defined in International Law and Compared to American Fifth Amendment Jurisprudence', (2001) 15/1 *Emory ILR* 349, at 366.
31. *See Lochner v. People of the State of New York*, (1905) 198 *US* 45. *See also* Graham (1998), 604–5.
32. *See Pennsylvania Coal Co. v. Mahon*, (1922) 260 *US* 393. *See also* Graham (1998), 605–6; Stumberg (1998), 557; E Shenkman, 'Could Principles of Fifth Amendment Takings Jurisprudence be Helpful in Analyzing Regulatory Expropriation Claims under International Law?', (2003) 11/1 *NYU ELJ* 174, at 174; Porterfield (2011), 176; and Stanley (2001), 367.
33. *See Loretto v. Teleprompter Manhattan CATV Corp.*, (1982) 458 *US* 419. *See also* Montt (2009), 187.
34. *See Lucas v. South Carolina Coastal Council*, (1992) 505 *US* 1003. *See also* Stumberg (1998), 557–8; and Stanley (2001), 370.
35. *See Concrete Pipe and Products of California, Inc. v. Construction Laborers Pension Trust for Southern California*, (1993) 508 *US* 602. *See also* Stumberg (1998), 558.
36. *See* Been and Beauvais (2003), 61–2; and M Perkams, 'The Concept of Indirect Expropriation in Comparative Public Law – Searching for Light in the Dark', in S Schill (ed.), *International Investment Law and Comparative Public Law* (2010), 126–9.
37. *See Penn Central Transportation Co. v. New York City*, (1978) 438 *US* 104. *See also* Stanley (2001), 367–8; and F González de Cossío, *Arbitraje de inversión* (2009), 214–5.
38. Been and Beauvais (2003), 61–2. *See* G Alexander, *The Global Debate over Constitutional Property: Lessons from American Takings Jurisprudence* (2006), 206; and Montt (2009), 219.

39. For more on this and other domestic regimes *see generally* A van der Walt, *Constitutional Property Clauses: A Comparative Analysis* (1999); T Allen, *The Right to Property in Commonwealth Constitutions* (2000); Alexander (2006); and R Alterman (ed.), *Takings International: A Comparative Perspective on Land Use Regulation and Compensation Rights* (2012). *See also* Montt (2009), 168–77.
40. *See* Chapters 5 & 6 above.
41. Gagné (2011), 825.
42. *See* Chapters 5 & 6 above.
43. Annex 11-B, para. 3 (a) (iii) of the 2007 Korea–USA FTA. *See ibid.*, para. 3 (b). *See* J Kommendijk and J Morijn, 'Proportional by What Measure(s)? Balancing Investor Interests and Human Rights by Way of Applying the Proportionality Principle in Investor–State Arbitration', in P Dupuy, F Francioni and E Petersmann (eds.), *Human Rights in International Investment Law and Arbitration* (2009), 442; and Gagné (2011), 817. *See also* Annex 2 of the 2009 ASEAN Comprehensive Agreement; Art. 6 of the 2009 Colombia–India BIT; and Annex A of the 2010 Canada–Slovakia BIT.
44. *See* Chapters 3, 5 & 6 above. On the relation between the *Penn Central* factors and the proportionality test, *see* Montt (2009), 217–9. *See also* T Allen, 'Compensation for Property under the European Convention of Human Rights', (2007) 28/2 *Mich. JIL* 287, at 302–4; Montt (2009), 194–7; and Kulick (2012), 195–7.
45. *See* Been and Beauvais (2003), 120 & 128.
46. Sands (2005), 141. *See* Sornarajah (2010), 24–5; and Gagné (2011), 809.
47. *See generally* Sands (2005). *See also* J Dugard, 'The Future of International Law: A Human Rights Perspective – with Some Comments on the Leiden School of International Law', (2007), 20/4 *LJIL* 729, at 732.
48. *See* Sornarajah (2008), 41–5; C Brower and S Schill, 'Is Arbitration a Threat or a Boon to the Legitimacy of International Investment Law?', (2009) 9/2 *Chic. JIL* 471, at 473; Montt (2009), 127 & 133–41; B Kingsbury and S Schill, 'Public Law Concepts to Balance Investors' Rights with State Regulatory Actions in the Public Interest – the Concept of Proportionality', in S Schill (ed.), *International Investment Law and Comparative Public Law* (2010), 75–6; S Schill, 'International Investment Law and Comparative Public Law', in S Schill (ed.), *International Investment Law and Comparative Public Law* (2010), 6–7; Spears (2010), 1039–40; and S Schill, 'Enhancing International Investment Law's Legitimacy: Conceptual and Methodological Foundations of a New Public Law Approach', (2011) 52/1 *Virg. JIL* 57, at 63–7.

    See generally C Brower, 'Structure, Legitimacy, and NAFTA's Investment Chapter', (2003) 36/1 *Vand. JTL* 37; A Afilalo, 'Towards a Common Law of International Investment: How NAFTA Chapter 11 Panels Should Solve Their Legitimacy Crisis', (2004) 17/1 *Geo. IELR* 51; A Afilalo, 'Meaning, Ambiguity and Legitimacy: Judicial (Re-)Construction of NAFTA Chapter 11', (2005) 25/2 *Nw JILB* 279; S Franck, 'The Legitimacy Crisis in Investment Treaty Arbitration: Privatizing Public International Law through Inconsistent Decisions', (2005) 73/5 *Fordh. LR* 1521; O Chung, 'The Lopsided International Investment Law Regime and Its Effect on the Future of Investor–State Arbitration', (2007) 47/4 *Virg. JIL* 953; and Sornarajah (2008).
49. *See* Chapters 5 & 6 above.
50. *See generally* the GAL Project at New York University School of Law.
51. *See* working definition of GAL at NYU Project.
52. *See e.g.* S Cassese, 'Global Standards for National Administrative Procedure', (2005) 68/3–4 *LCP* 109; B Chimni, 'Co-option and Resistance: Two Faces of Global Administrative Law', (2005) 37/4 *NYU JILP* 799; B Kingsbury, N Krisch and R Stewart, 'The Emergence of Global Administrative Law', (2005) 68/3–4 *LCP*

15; S Cassese, 'The Globalization of Law', (2006) 37/4 *NYU JILP* 973; D Esty, 'Good Governance at the Supranational Scale: Globalizing Administrative Law', (2006) 115/7 *Yale LJ* 1490; C Harlow, 'Global Administrative Law: The Quest for Principles and Values', (2006) 17/1 *EJIL* 187; N Krisch, 'The Pluralism of Global Administrative Law', (2006) 17/1 *EJIL* 247; N Krisch and B Kingsbury, 'Global Governance and Global Administrative Law in the International Legal Order', (2006) 17/1 *EJIL*1; S Marks, 'Naming Global Administrative Law', (2006) 37/4 *NYU JILP* 995; G Van Harten and M Loughlin, 'Investment Treaty Arbitration as a Species of Global Administrative Law', (2006) 17/1 *EJIL* 121; D Dyzenhaus, 'Accountability and the Concept of (Global) Administrative Law', in *IILJ Working Paper* (2008), Nr. 7; N Krisch, 'Global Administrative Law and the Constitutional Ambition', in *LSEWP* (2009), Nr. 10; A Mitchell and J Farnik, 'Global Administrative Law: Can It Bring Global Governance to Account?', (2009) 37/2 *Fed. LR* 237; and Kingsbury and Schill (2010).

See also S Cassese, *Oltre lo stato* (2006); G Van Harten, *Investment Treaty Arbitration and Public Law* (2007); B Kingsbury, 'The Concept of "Law" in Global Administrative Law', (2009) 20/1 *EJIL* 23; Montt (2009); J-B Auby, *La globalisation, le droit et l'état* (2010); M Kuo, 'The Concept of "Law" in Global Administrative Law: A Reply to Benedict Kingsbury', (2010) 20/4 *EJIL* 997; A Somek, 'The Concept of "Law" in Global Administrative Law: A Reply to Benedict Kingsbury', (2010) 20/4 *EJIL* 985, and A Kulick, *Global Public Interest in International Investment Law* (2012).

53. Schill (2010), 3–4. *See generally ibid.*; Schill (2011); and the project of the Max Planck Institute for Comparative Public Law and International Law, titled 'Transnational Private–Public Arbitration as Global Regulatory Governance: Charting and Codifying the Lex Mercatoria Publica', under the charge of Stephan Schill.
54. Been and Beauvais (2003), 141. *See* Shenkman (2003), 180–2, & 196–7.
55. *See* J Paulsson and Z Douglas, 'Indirect Expropriation in Investment Treaty Arbitrations', in N Horn (ed.), *Arbitrating Foreign Investment Disputes. Procedural and Substantive Legal Aspects* (2004), 147–8.
56. *See* Y Arai-Takahashi, *The Margin of Appreciation Doctrine and the Principle of Proportionality in the Jurisprudence of the ECHR* (2002), 2. *See also* A Legg, *The Margin of Appreciation in International Human Rights Law: Deference and Proportionality* (2012), 178.
57. Kommendijk and Morijn (2009), 438. *See ibid.*, 442. *See also* Kingsbury and Schill (2010), 79–80; and C Henckels, 'Indirect Expropriation and the Right to Regulate: Revisiting Proportionality Analysis and the Standard of Review in Investor–State Arbitration', (2012) 15/1 *JIEL* 223, at 226.
58. *See* Arai-Takahashi (2002), 14–15 & 156–7; A Sweet and J Mathews, 'Proportionality Balancing and Global Constitutionalism', (2008) 47/1 *Colum. JTL* 72, at 75–6; Kommendijk and Morijn (2009), 438; Kingsbury and Schill (2010), 85–8; Henckels (2012), 227–8; and Kulick (2012), 186–8.
59. *See Certain Aspects of the Laws on the Use of Languages in Education in Belgium*, Eur. Court HR, Series A No. 6, Judgment, 23 July 1968. *See also* Sweet and Mathews (2008), 97–111 & 145–52; Kingsbury and Schill (2010), 80–81 & 84–5; Henckels (2012), 226; Kulick (2012), 174–8, 182–3 & 189–92; and Legg (2012), 178. On the German expropriation law and the proportionality principle, *see* Alexander (2006), 97–147. *See also* Montt (2009), 196–7; and Perkams (2010), 130–7.
60. *See* Arai-Takahashi (2002), 15–6 & 193; and Henckels (2012), 243 & 245–54. *See also* Chapter 3 above.
61. *See José María Cantos c. Argentina*, I/A Court HR, Series C No. 97, Judgment, 28 November 2002. *See also* Legg (2012), 178–9.

62. *See* Chapter 3 above.
63. U Kriebaum, 'Regulatory Takings: Balancing the Interests of the Investor and the State', (2007) 8/5 *JWIT* 717, at 720. *See* U Kriebaum, 'Is the European Court of Human Rights an Alternative to Investor–State Arbitration?', in P Dupuy et al (2009), 239 & 245.
64. Kriebaum, (2007) 8/5 *JWIT* 717, at 730.
65. Kriebaum, (2007) 8/5 *JWIT* 717, at 727–44. *See* Kriebaum (2009), 240–2. *See also* Henckels (2012), note 103 at 242.
66. *See* Clodfelter (2009), 175.
67. A Hoffmann, 'Indirect Expropriation', in A Reinisch (ed.), *Standards of Investment Protection* (2008), 168. *See ibid.*, 167–70. *See also* Kommendijk and Morijn (2009), 448–46.
68. Salacuse (2010), 317. *See ibid.*, 313–5 & 317–8.
69. A Newcombe, 'The Boundaries of Regulatory Expropriation in International Law', (2005) 20/1 *ICSID Rev*. 1, at 7. *See* Montt (2009), note 34 at 240.
70. Newcombe and Paradell (2009), 363. *See ibid*. 363–6.
71. *See* Kingsbury and Schill (2010), 88–96. *See also* Henckels (2012), 226.
72. Kingsbury and Schill (2010), 95–6. *E.g.* Letter on Expropriation, para. 4 (b), of the 2003 Singapore–USA FTA.
73. *See* Kulick (2012), 168–206 & 209–17.
74. Henckels (2012), 224–5. *See also ibid*. 228–9, 238–41 & 245–54.
75. Available at http://italaw.com/investment-treaties (last visited 30 June 2013).
76. Comments on the draft model treaty issued in 2007 by the Norwegian government, available at http://italaw.com/sites/default/files/archive/ita1029.pdf (last visited 30 June 2013).
77. Cover letter of the draft model treaty sent in 2008 by the state of Norway to several governmental departments, NGOs, companies and universities, available at http://italaw.com/sites/default/files/archive/ita1030.pdf (last visited 30 June 2013).
78. D Vis-Dunbar, 'Norway Shelves Its Draft Model Bilateral Investment Treaty', *Investment Treaty News*, June 2009, at 7, available at http://www.iisd.org/itn/wp-content/uploads/2009/06/ITN-June-2009.pdf (last visited 30 June 2013). *See also* Clodfelter (2009), 174; and Spears (2010), note 27 at 1043–4.
79. *See e.g.* J Waldron, *The Rule of Law and the Measure of Property* (2012). On property theories, *see generally* G Alexander and E Peñalver, *An Introduction to Property Theory* (2012).
80. R Dolzer, 'The European Approach to BITs', (2009) 24/2 *ICSID Rev*. 368, at 375–6.
81. *See generally* S Lee, 'A Puzzle of Sovereignty', (1997) 27/2 *Cal. West. ILJ* 241; B Kingsbury, 'Sovereignty and Inequality', (1998) 9/4 *EJIL* 599; N Schrijver, 'The Changing Nature of State Sovereignty', (1999) 70 *BYIL* 65; and J Jackson, 'Sovereignty-Modern: A New Approach to an Outdated Concept', (2003) 97/4 *AJIL* 782.
82. *Isle of Palmas* (Netherlands v. USA), Huber, sole arbitrator, Award, 4 April 1928, (1928) 2 *RIAA* 829, at 838.
83. *See* G White, *Nationalisation of Foreign Property* (1961), 146; Pellonpää and Fitzmaurice (1988), 63; R Dolzer and M Stevens *Bilateral Investment Treaties* (1995), 104; G Sacerdoti, 'Bilateral Treaties and Multilateral Instruments on Investment Protection', (1997) 269 *RCADI* 251, at 387; and Kriebaum (2007) 8/5 *JWIT* 717, at 727.

    See also Montt (2009), 182, 184, 188 & 206–7; and J Waincymer, 'Balancing Property Rights and Human Rights in Expropriation', in P Dupuy et al (2009), 306–8.
84. American Law Institute (1987), 200.

85. *Liberian Eastern Timber Corporation* (LETCO) *v. The Government of the Republic of Liberia*, ICSID case No. ARB/83/2, Award, 31 March 1986, (1987) 26/3 *ILM* 647, at 662.
86. *LETCO*, Award, 31 March 1986, at 665.
87. *Cf. ADC Affiliate Limited and ADC & ADMC Management Limited v. The Republic of Hungary*, ICSID case No. ARB/03/16, Award, 2 October 2006, paras. 429–33; *Siemens A.G. v. The Argentine Republic*, ICSID case No. ARB/02/8, Award, 6 February 2007, para. 273; and *Waguih Elie George Siag and Clorinda Vecchi v. Arab Republic of Egypt*, ICSID case No. ARB/05/15, Award, 1 June 2009, paras. 429–33.
88. American Law Institute, *Restatement of the Law Third. The Foreign Relations Law of the United States* (1987), 200. *See* Newcombe and Paradell (2009), 371.
89. *See* Been and Beauvais (2003), 105–6 & 108; and W Burke-White and A von Staden, 'Private Litigation in a Public Sphere: The Standard of Review in Investor–State Arbitrations', (2010) 35/2 *Yale JIL* 283, at 329–33.

    See also Afilalo (2004), 52–3; Afilalo (2005), 282; Sands (2005), xvii & 122–3; B Choudhury, 'Recapturing Public Power: Is Investment Arbitration's Engagement of the Public Interest Contributing to the Democratic Deficit', (2008) 41/3 *Vand. JTL* 775, at 782–9; A Reinisch, 'Legality of Expropriations', in A Reinisch (ed.), *Standards of Investment Protection* (2008), 179 & 183; Montt (2009), 133–5 & 228–9; Waincymer (2009), 306; and Henckels (2012), 243–5.
90. Newcombe and Paradell (2009), 371–3.
91. *See James and Others v. United Kingdom*, Eur. Court HR, Series A No. 98, Judgment, 21 February 1986. *See* Chapter 3 above.
92. Arai-Takahashi (2002), 14. *See ibid.*, 2, 152–3 & 156–7. *See also* Burke-White and von Staden (2010), 307–8.
93. *See Amoco International Finance Corporation v. The Government of the Islamic Republic of Iran et al.*, *Iran–US CT*, Partial Award No. 310-56-3, 14 July 1987, (1988) 15 *Iran–US CTR* 189. *See* Chapter 4 above.
94. *See* Chapter 5 above.
95. Kulick (2012), 189. *See ibid.*, 190–1. *See also* Sweet and Mathews (2008), 76–8 & 159–64; Montt (2009), 228–9; and W Burke-White and A von Staden (2010), 304–11 & 314–22.
96. White (1961), 145. *See* B Wortley, 'Some Early but Basic Theories of Expropriation', (1977) 20 *GYIL* 236, at 239–43.
97. Vandevelde (2010), 282. *See ibid.*, 284–9.
98. Kriebaum, (2007) 8/5 *JWIT* 717, at 726. *See* Hoffmann (2008), 166.
99. Kriebaum, (2007) 8/5 *JWIT* 717, at 726. *See* Chapter 1 above.
100. *Oscar Chinn* (UK v. Belgium), PCIJ, Judgment, 12 December 1934, Individual Opinion of Judge Anzilotti, (1934) *PCIJ Rep. Series* A/B No 63, para. 6.
101. *Compañía de Aguas del Aconquija S.A. and Vivendi Universal S.A. v. Argentine Republic* (Vivendi II), ICSID case No. ARB/97/3, Award, 20 August 2007, para. 7.5.21.
102. Kriebaum, (2007) 8/5 *JWIT* 717, at 727. *See* Vandevelde (2010), 301–2 & 307–8.
103. *See e.g. Fireman's Fund*, Award, 17 July 2006, para. 174; *Siemens*, Award, 6 February 2007, para. 270; *Aguas del Aconquija*, Award, 20 August 2007, para. 7.5.21; *Chemtura*, Award, 2 August 2010, para. 242; and *Nations Energy Inc., et al. c. La República de Panamá*, ICSID case No. ARB/06/19, Award, 24 November 2010, para. 680.
104. *Marguerite de Joly de Sabla* (USA v. Panama), US–Panama Claims Commission, Decision, 29 June 1933, (1933) 6 *RIAA* 358, at 366.
105. Schreuer (2006), at 110–11.

106. R Higgins, 'The Taking of Property by the State: Recent Developments in International Law', (1982) 176/3 *RCADI* 259, at 331; and Dinstein (2002), 869. *See* Chapter 1 above.
107. Kingsbury and Schill (2010), 102–3. These authors envision possible solutions to all these problems. *See ibid.* 103–4. *See also* Henckels (2012), 237–8; and Kulick (2012), 171–3.
108. *See* Robert-Cuendet (2010), 6–8 & 21–7. This author expressly differentiates her position from the police-powers doctrine and the proportionality approach to indirect takings, even though it is essentially a mixture of both. *See generally ibid.*
109. *See* Vandevelde (2011), 307–10. *See also* Clodfelter (2009), 166–9.
110. Vandevelde (2011), 311.
111. Vandevelde (2011), 313. *See* Vandevelde (2010), 2–4.
112. Vandevelde (2011), 314. *See* Vandevelde (2010), 1–2. *See also* Schill (2009), 4–6.
113. Vandevelde (2011), 313. *See* Vandevelde (2010), 11.
114. Lee (1997), 245.
115. Montt (2009), 234. *See ibid.* 234–5.
116. *See* Chapters 5 & 6 above.
117. *See* Chapters 3 & 4 above.
118. I Madalena, 'Foreign Direct Investment and the Protection of the Environment: The Border between National Environmental Regulation and Expropriation', (2003) 12/3 *Eur. ELR* 70, at 78; and M Gutbrod and S Hindelang, 'Externalization of Effective Legal Protection against Indirect Expropriation. Can the Legal Order of Developing Countries Live Up to the Standards Required by International Investment Agreements? A Disenchanting Comparative Analysis', (2006) 7/1 *JWIT* 59, at 64–5.
119. *See* Kriebaum, (2007) 8/5 *JWIT* 717, at 723; and Salacuse (2010), 307–11. *See also* Chapters 5 & 6 above.
120. *See e.g.* F Orrego Vicuña, 'Carlos Calvo, Honorary NAFTA Citizen', (2002) 11/1 *NYU ELJ* 19, at 27–8; Montt (2009), 241–2; and Newcombe and Paradell (2009), 344–5.
121. Sometimes called the denominator. *See e.g.* Montt (2009), 265–73.
122. *See* Montt (2009), 244–51; Newcombe and Paradell (2009), 351–2; and Alvik (2011), 174–7.
123. *See* Robert-Cuendet (2010), 101–2; Salacuse (2010), 302–4; Vandevelde (2010), 303–6; I Alvik, *Contracting with Sovereignty: State Contracts and International Arbitration* (2011), 161–77; and R Dolzer and C Schreuer, *Principles of International Investment Law* (2012), 126–9.

    See also Consortium RFCC c. Royaume du Maroc, ICSID case No. ARB/00/6, Award, 22 December 2003, paras. 60–2, 65–9 & 85–9; *Waste Management, Inc. v. United Mexican States*, NAFTA, ICSID case No. ARB(AF)/00/3, Award, 30 April 2004 ('Waste Management 2'), paras. 174–5; *Azurix*, Award, 14 July 2006, para. 315; *Siemens*, Award, 6 February 2007, paras. 248 & 253; and *Alpha Projektholding GmbH v. Ukraine*, ICSID case No. ARB/07/16, Award, 8 November 2010, para. 412.
124. *See* Newcombe and Paradell (2009), 352–6; Salacuse (2010), 60–2; Vandevelde (2010), 303 & 305–6; J Crawford, *Brownlie's Principles of Public International Law* (2012), 627–9; and S Nikièma, *L'expropriation indirecte en droit international des investissements* (2012), 113–6. *See also EnCana Corporation v. Republic of Ecuador*, UNCITRAL arbitration, LCIA Case No. UN3481, Award, 3 February 2006, para. 194; *Aguas del Aconquija*, Award, 20 August 2007, para. 7.5.4; and *Parkerings-Compagniet AS v. Republic of Lithuania*, ICSID case No. ARB/05/8, Award, 11 September 2007, paras. 440–54.
125. *See* Newcombe and Paradell (2009), 348–50. *See also* Montt (2009), 265–73.
126. Newcombe and Paradell (2009), 349–50.

127. *See* Montt (2009), 189–90. *See also* Vandevelde (2010), 280–2.
128. *See* J Herz, 'Expropriation of Foreign Property', (1941) 35/2 *AJIL* 243, at 251.
129. U Kriebaum, 'Partial Expropriation', (2007) 8/1 *JWIT* 69, at 69, & 73–82; Montt (2009), 265–73; Newcombe and Paradell (2009), 348–50; and Dolzer and Schreuer (2012), 119.
See Marvin Feldman v. Mexico, NAFTA, ICSID case No. ARB(AF)/99/1, Award, 16 December 2002, paras. 111, 142 & 152; *Nykomb Synergetics Technology Holding AB v. The Republic of Latvia*, ECT, SCC arbitration, Award, 16 December 2003, para. 4.3.1; *Occidental Exploration and Production Co.* (OEPC) *v. The Republic of Ecuador*, UNCITRAL arbitration, Award, 1 July 2004, para. 89; *CMS Gas Transmission Company v. Republic of Argentina*, ICSID case No. ARB/01/8, Award, 12 May 2005, paras. 262–4; *Telenor Mobile Communications A.S. v. The Republic of Hungary*, ICSID case No. ARB/04/15, Award, 13 September 2006, para. 67; and *Grand River Enterprises et al. v. United States of America*, NAFTA, UNCITRAL arbitration, Award, 12 January 2011, para. 146.
See also S.D. Myers, Inc. v. The Government of Canada, NAFTA, UNCITRAL arbitration, Partial Award, 13 November 2000, para. 283; *Middle East Cement Shipping and Handling Co. v. Arab Republic of Egypt*, ICSID case No. ARB/99/6, Award, 12 April 2002, paras. 101, 105, 107, 127, 138, 144, 152–6 & 163–5; *Waste Management 2*, Award, 30 April 2004, paras. 141, 155, 159 & 162–75; *GAMI Investments, Inc. v. The Government of the United Mexican States*, NAFTA, UNCITRAL arbitration, Award, 15 November 2004, paras. 126–7, 131 & 133; *Eureko B.V. v. Republic of Poland*, Ad hoc arbitration, Partial Award, 19 August 2005, paras. 239–41; and *EnCana*, Award, 3 February 2006, paras. 182–3.
130. Kriebaum, (2007) 8/1 *JWIT* 69, at 71. *See* Y Fortier and S Drymer, 'Indirect Expropriation in the Law of International Investment: I Know It When I See It, or Caveat Investor', (2004) 19/2 *ICSID Rev*. 293, at 308.
131. *See* Kriebaum, (2007) 8/1 *JWIT* 69, at 83. *See also* Montt (2009), 270–2.
132. Reisman and Sloane (2003), 131–2. *See* Vandevelde (2010), 291–2.
133. Newcombe (2005), 25. *See* Newcombe and Paradell (2009), 342–3.
134. Dolzer and Schreuer (2012), 115.
135. *See e.g.* G Christie, 'What Constitutes a Taking of Property under International Law?', (1962) *BYIL* 307, at 338; G Aldrich, 'What Constitutes a Compensable Taking: The Decisions of the Iran–United States Claims Tribunal', (1994) 88/4 *AJIL* 585, at 609; M Ruffert, 'The Protection of Foreign Direct Investment by the European Convention on Human Rights', (2000) 43 *GYIL* 116, at 132–3; R Dolzer, 'Indirect Expropriations: New Developments?', (2003) 11/1 *NYU ELJ* 64, at 80; Sampliner (2003), 9–10; Fortier and Drymer (2004), 308 & note 66 at 320; Montt (2009), 274–7; Newcombe and Paradell (2009), 344, 358–62 & 366; Salacuse (2010), 298–9; Crawford (2012), 621 & 624; and Dolzer and Schreuer (2012), 120–3.
The power of the sovereign state to intervene with private property to preserve public security, order, health, etc. is normally referred to as police-powers. Garner (2009), 1276. *See* Vandevelde (2010), 271. *See also* B Wortley, *Expropriation in Public International Law* (1959), 38–57 & 105–14; and Wortley (1977), 240–3.
136. Dolzer and Schreuer (2012), 120. *See ibid.*, 104. *See also* Newcombe and Paradell (2009), 360–1.
137. *See e.g.* C McLachlan, L Shore and M Weiniger, *International Investment Arbitration: Substantive Principles* (2008), 289 & 302–4; Newcombe and Paradell (2009), 350–1; Salacuse (2010), 311–13; Yannaca-Small (2010), 474–6; and Dolzer and Schreuer (2012), 115–17.

138. *See* Waelde and Kolo (2001), 844; Paulsson and Douglas (2004), 154 & 157; Newcombe and Paradell (2009), 351; Alvik (2011), 169; and Crawford (2012), 624. *See also* Alvik (2011), 167–9. *Cf.* Robert-Cuendet (2010), 94–6 & 166–75.
139. *See* Schill (2009), 4–6; J Zhan, 'The Spread of BITs and Their Changing Face', (2009) 24/2 *ICSID Rev.* 339, at 339; Vandevelde (2010), 2–4; and Vandevelde (2011), 313–4.
140. *See* J Steffens, 'Expectations of Governments and Investors vs. Practice: The Government View on BITs', (2009) 24/2 *ICSID Rev.* 347, at 348.
141. Dolzer (2009), 369.
142. Vandevelde (2010), 2. *See ibid.*, 1–4.
143. *See* Dolzer (2003), at 91. *See also* Gutbrod and Hindelang (2006), note 23 at 64.
144. Sornarajah (1997), 55.
145. For an historical survey of sovereignty, *see generally* R Jackson, *Sovereignty: The Evolution of an Idea* (2007).
146. *See* Lee (1997), 247, 252–3 & 260–1; Schrijver (1999), 70–2; and H Steinberger, 'Sovereignty', in R Bernhardt (ed.), *EPIL* (2000), Vol. 4, at 511–12. *See also* J Shen, 'National Sovereignty and Human Rights in a Positive Law Context', (2000) 26/2 *Brook. JIL* 417, at 419–28.
147. Lee (1997), 256. *See ibid.*, 256–7. In the case of investment treaties, *see* Salacuse (2010), 109–11; and Dolzer and Schreuer (2012), 20–1.
148. Regarding treaties providing rights for third states, Art. 36 of the 1969 Vienna Convention on the Law of Treaties – in force since 1980 – declares that the consent of the third state is presumed 'so long as the contrary is not indicated' and 'unless the treaty otherwise provides'. Available at http://untreaty.un.org/ilc/texts/instruments/english/conventions/1_1_1969.pdf (last visited 30 June 2013).
149. *See* Lee (1999), 258–9.
150. *See generally* I Lukashuk, 'The Principle Pacta Sunt Servanda and the Nature of Obligation under International Law', (1989) 83/3 *AJIL* 513; R Hyland, 'Pacta Sunt Servanda: A Meditation', (1994) 34/2 *Virg. JIL* 405; and M Lachs, 'Pacta Sunt Servanda', in R Bernhardt (ed.), *EPIL* (1997), Vol. 3. *See also* T Treves, 'Customary International Law', in R Wolfrum (ed.), *EPIL* online edition, available at http://www.mpepil.com/sample_article?id=/epil/entries/law-9780199231690-e1393& (last visited 30 June 2013).
151. *See* J Paulsson, *Denial of Justice in International Law* (2005), 35. *See also* Arai-Takahashi (2002), 3 & 152–3; and Robert-Cuendet (2010), 217–18.
152. *See* Shen (2000), 434–41. *See also* T Bingham, *The Rule of Law* (2010), 110–19. *Cf. e.g.* Choudhury (2008), 777–9; Sornarajah (2008), 48–9; and Montt (2009), 141–5.
153. A Newcombe, 'Sustainable Development and Investment Treaty Law', (2007) 3/8 *JWIT* 357, at 359.
154. Sornarajah (1997), 55. *Cf.* Sornarajah (2008), 50–1 & 79.
155. J Salacuse, 'BIT by BIT: The Growth of Bilateral Investment Treaties and Their Impact on Foreign Investment in Developing Countries', (1990) 24/3 *IL* 655, at 659.
156. *See* Been and Beauvais (2003), 107 & 118. *See also* Newcombe (2005), 46–8.
157. Vandevelde (2010), 1–2.
158. *George W. Hopkins* (USA v. Mexico), US–Mexican General Claims Commission, Decision, 31 March 1926, (1926) 4 *RIAA* 41, para. 16. This case was quoted in *S.D. Myers*, Partial Award, 13 November 2000, para. 260.
159. F Dunn, 'International Law and Private Property Rights', (1928) 28/2 *Colum. LR* 166, at 174. *See* E Root, 'The Basis of Protection to Citizens Residing Abroad', (1910) 4/3 *AJIL* 517, at 521–2.
160. M Ignatieff, *The Lesser Evil. Political Ethics in an Age of Terror* (2005), xvi.
161. *Ibid.*

162. *James and Others v. United Kingdom*, European Court, Series A No. 98, Judgment, 21 February 1986, para. 63. *See Lithgow and Others v. United Kingdom*, European Court, Series A No. 102, Judgment, 8 July 1986, paras. 111–19. *See also* Montt (2009), 213–16.
163. *TECMED*, Award, 29 May 2003, para. 122. *See* Newcombe (2005), 46–8.
164. *International Thunderbird Gaming Corporation v. The United Mexican States*, UNCITRAL arbitration, Award, 26 January 2006, Separate Opinion of Thomas Waelde, para. 12.
165. A Cançado Trindade, *El ejercicio de la función judicial internacional* (2011), 64.
166. *Emilio Agustin Maffezini v. The Kingdom of Spain*, ICSID case No. ARB/97/7, Award, 13 November 2000, para. 64. *See also Robert Azinian, Kenneth Davitian, & Ellen Baca v. The United Mexican States*, NAFTA, ICSID case No. ARB (AF)/97/2, Award, 1 November 1999, paras. 83, 87 & 90–1; *Middle East Cement*, Award, 12 April 2002, para. 153; *Generation Ukraine, Inc. v. Ukraine*, ICSID case No. ARB/00/9, Award, 16 September 2003, para 20.30; *Waste Management 2*, Award, 30 April 2004, para. 160; and *MTD Equity Sdn. Bhd. and MTD Chile S.A. v. Republic of Chile*, ICSID case No. ARB/01/7, Award, 25 May 2004, para. 178.
167. *See e.g.* B Kunoy, 'Developments in Indirect Expropriation Case Law in ICSID Transnational Arbitration', (2005) 6/3 *JWIT* 467, at 477–8; Gutbrod and Hindelang (2006), 63; Kunoy (2006), 342; Newcombe and Paradell (2009), 350; Salacuse (2010), 4, 8–9, 26–9 & 285–7; Alvik (2011), 239; and Dolzer and Schreuer (2012), 21–2.
168. *See Oscar Chinn*, Judgment, 12 December 1934, at 88. It can also be found in the case-law of the Iran–US CT. *See e.g. Starrett Housing Corporation, Starrett Systems, Inc., Starrett Housing International, Inc., v. The Government of the Islamic Republic of Iran et al.*, Interlocutory Award No. ITL 32-24-1, 19 December 1983, reprinted in (1985) 4 *Iran–US CTR* 122, at 149.
169. I Marboe, 'Compensation and Damages in International Law. The Limits of the "Fair Market Value"', (2006) 7/5 *JWIT* 723, at 725–6. *See* Chapter 1 above.
170. *See* Marboe (2006), 729–34.
171. *See ibid.*, 731 & 755–8.
172. *PSEG Global Inc. and Konya Ilgin Elektrik Üretim ve Ticaret Limited Şirketi v. Republic of Turkey*, ICSID case No. ARB/02/5, Award, 19 January 2007, para. 220.
173. R Dolzer, 'Fair and Equitable Treatment: A Key Standard in Investment Treaties', (2005) 39/1 *International Lawyer* 87. *See also* C Schreuer, 'Fair and Equitable Treatment in Arbitral Practice', (2005) 6/3 *JWIT* 357, at 357; and M Kantor, 'Fair and Equitable Treatment: Echoes of FDR's Court-Packing Plan in the International Law Approach towards Regulatory Expropriation', (2006) 5/2 *LPICT* 231, at 238.
174. *See* Hoffmann (2008), 167; and Vandevelde (2010), 291.
175. *See* Chapter 4 above.
176. *See e.g.* V Heiskanen, 'The Doctrine of Indirect Expropriation in Light of the Practice of the Iran–United States Claims Tribunal', (2007) 8/2 *JWIT* 215, at 218–9; and Montt (2009), 149 & 234.
177. *See Maffezini*, Award, 13 November 2000; *MTD*, Award, 25 May 2004; *Occidental*, Award, 1 July 2004; *Saluka*, Partial Award, 17 March 2006; *PSEG*, Award, 19 January 2007; and *Enron Corporation Ponderosa Assets, L.P. v. Argentine Republic*, ICSID case No. ARB/01/3, Award, 22 May 2007. *See also S.D. Myers*, Partial Award, 13 November 2000; *Pope & Talbot. Inc. v. The Government of Canada*, NAFTA, UNCITRAL arbitration, Award, 10 April 2001; and *Cargill, Incorporated v. United Mexican States*, NAFTA, ICSID case No. ARB(AF)/05/2, Award, 18 September 2009.
178. *CME Czech Republic B.V. v. The Czech Republic*, UNCITRAL arbitration, Partial Award, 13 September 2001; *Middle East Cement*, Award, 12 April 2002; *TECMED*,

Award, 29 May 2003; *ADC*, Award, 2 October 2006; *Siemens*, Award, 6 February 2007; and *Alpha Projektholding*, Award, 8 November 2010. *See also Metalclad Corporation v. United Mexican States*, NAFTA, ICSID case No. ARB(AF)/97/1, Award, 30 August 2000.

179. On FET, *see generally* I Tudor, *The Fair and Equitable Treatment Standard in the International Law of Foreign Investment* (2008); and R Kläger, *'Fair and Equitable Treatment' in International Investment Law* (2011).
180. *See* Hoffmann (2008), 162; and Montt (2009), 174 & 222.
181. *See* Paulsson and Douglas (2004), 158; Kunoy (2005), 478–82; Salacuse (2010), 311; and Dolzer and Schreuer (2012), 115.
182. *See* Waelde and Kolo (2001), 843–5; Madalena (2003) 77; Kunoy (2005), 482; Newcombe (2005) 45; and Gutbrod and Hindelang (2006), note 33 at 65–6.
183. Dolzer and Schreuer (2012), 115.
184. *See* Kunoy (2005), 479; and Gutbrod and Hindelang (2006), 73–4. *See also* Salacuse (2010), 313; and Dolzer and Schreuer (2012), 115–6.
185. *See* Fortier and Drymer (2004), 306; and Montt (2009), 222.
186. *See e.g.* Vandevelde (2010), 2–4, 8–9 & 113–14.
187. Bingham (2010), 7. *See* Salacuse (2010), 6–9, 109–11 & 114; and Dolzer and Schreuer (2012), 24–5. *See also* S Moyn, *The Last Utopia: Human Rights in History* (2012), 1 & 223–4. *Cf. e.g.* Montt (2009), 146–55.
188. On the rule of law, *see generally* B Tamanaha, *On the Rule of Law: History, Politics, Theory* (2004).
189. Waldron (2012), 88.
190. Bingham (2010), 3. *See* Tamanaha (2004), 8–9.
191. Bingham (2010), 8 & 37.
192. *See* Bingham (2010), 37–109. *See also* Waldron (2012), 6–7, 15–16 & 52–8.
193. *See* Bingham (2010), 110–29.

8. Conclusion

Trying to establish when a state measure is compensable as an indirect expropriation feels like walking towards the horizon: one is apparently closer, but actually never there. At the end, you can only point others in what you think is the right direction, and walk with them towards this elusive destination. This is a common problem in international and comparative public law. Some rules are nothing more than principles, *i.e.*, standards which acquire a specific content in their application to a concrete situation. This is the case with notions like arbitrariness, reasonableness, margin of appreciation or discretion. Several of these concepts can be found in the international law of expropriation. Not only public purpose, non-discrimination, prompt, adequate and effective compensation, and due process, but also deprivation, police-powers, legitimate expectations and proportionality: all of them are open standards which merely orientate interpreters in a direction. The main principle guiding the answer to the threshold question is part of a minimum treatment currently required by investment treaties and regional human rights conventions. This international minimum standard of treatment protects property against takings, by recognising the right of states to expropriate under certain conditions. One of these requirements is the payment of compensation for substantial and permanent deprivations, unless the circumstances allow for the application of a limited police-powers exception.

Property is protected against expropriation in the three regional systems of human rights. The case-law of the European Court of Human Rights on Article 1 of the First Optional Protocol is prominent among these conventional guarantees. Its jurisprudence identifies deprivations of properties, controls on its use and other interferences as distinct rules, to which certain principles are commonly applicable. One of these principles is proportionality, normally described as a requirement of fair balance between the public and private interests in the adoption of the challenged measure by the state. Another one is the margin of appreciation, widely recognised by the European Court to the state adopting this measure. The three rules of Article 1 of the First Optional Protocol are not present in BITs and EIAs. By distinguishing among deprivations of property, controls on the use and other interferences, and applying the principles of proportionality and margin of appreciation, the European Court of Human Rights has been able to avoid choosing between an effects or a police-powers rule in property cases. While the fair balance test is a common feature in the jurisprudence of the European Court of Human Rights, arbitral tribunals in investment disputes have exceptionally resorted to it, applying the proportionality principle to answer the threshold question, rather than to allocate the compensation due, only required in the European human rights law for deprivations of property, in an amount best labelled as appropriate. Otherwise, the approach of the European Court on expropriations is not far from that of international investment law. Public purpose, deprivation, lawfulness and legitimate expectations are construed by this tribunal, as in investment disputes.

According to the European Court of Human Rights, Article 1 includes negative and positive obligations. Not only should the state refrain from interfering with the right of property, but it also must act appropriately; that is to say, in a clear, consistent and coherent manner, avoiding legal uncertainty and ambiguity for those within its jurisdiction. Good governance is part of the protection guaranteed in Article 1 – a provision that can only be understood from the perspective of the rule of law. This is a rather recent language in the case-law of the European Court of Human Rights, which is reminiscent of that in investment treaty arbitrations, and can also be found in the modest jurisprudence of the Inter-American Court of Human Rights on Article 21 of its constitutive treaty. Such a language implies that the protection of property under these human rights conventions offers an international minimum standard of treatment not essentially different from that of BITs and EIAs, aimed at reducing political risk through the promotion of good governance and the rule of law.

The jurisdiction of the Iran–US CT included expropriations and other measures affecting property rights. This tribunal settled cases dealing with traditional forms of interference with property by host-states, recognising the three conditions of a lawful taking, giving the host-state a wide margin of appreciation on its assessment of the required public purpose of the challenged measure, and generally following an effects approach to answer the threshold question of indirect expropriations. For the Iran–US CT, compensation was part of the minimum standard of treatment offered by the protection against takings of the Iran–USA FCN and customary international law. In conformity with its case-law, an interference amounted to an expropriation when it was non-ephemeral and unreasonable, irreversibly depriving the owner of the effective use and control of his/her/its property. The Iran–US CT required full compensation for both lawful and unlawful takings. This standard, however, was not extended to other measures affecting property rights, which were only partially compensated. To construe this phrase in the Claims Settlement Declaration, the Iran–US CT relied on the residual category of other interferences with the peaceful enjoyment of possessions, as developed in European human rights law. This interpretation offered the Iran–US CT an alternative to the effects rule and the full compensation standard for those few cases where an interference with property was found, not amounting to an indirect taking.

Investment treaty arbitrations generally rely on the case-law of the Iran–US CT and, to a lesser extent, on that of the European Court of Human Rights. The awards of these arbitral panels recognise the right of the state to expropriate the property of aliens, following the conditions of customary international law, which BITs and EIAs repeat with similar wording, adding due process as a fourth requirement. In this regard, arbitrators in investment disputes normally give host-states a wide margin of appreciation, like that of the Iran–US CT and the European Court of Human Rights. Claims of indirect takings are generally settled in international investment law applying an effects rule, supplemented by the principles of substantial and permanent deprivation and respect for legitimate expectations. Lawful and unlawful expropriations receive prompt, adequate and effective compensation in investment treaty arbitrations. This general trend was rather uncontroversial, until the first expropriation claims against the USA and Canada were filed under Chapter 11 of NAFTA. A new interpretative declaration was then added to the expropriation provisions of the investment treaties of these countries, which expressly mentions the three *Penn Central* factors of the US regulatory takings doctrine, instructing decision-makers to go beyond the effects rule in cases of indirect takings. Before this, only the Harvard Draft Convention on the International Responsibility of States for Injuries to Aliens, the OECD Draft Convention on the Protection of Foreign Property and the Third Restatement of the Foreign Relations Law of the United States had timidly incorporated a police-powers solution to the question of intent – none of them a treaty. It was more than a coincidence that, while this interpretative declaration was being attached to the latest US and Canadian models, the NAFTA and BIT-based cases of *Methanex* and *Saluka* applied a police-powers rule in 2005 and 2006, respectively. Such a solution had not been adopted in international case-law since *Sea-Land*, the 1984 judgment of the Iran–US CT.

The international minimum standard is currently challenged by the national treatment conventionally proposed by the USA, Canada and a few other countries. By adding the *Penn Central* factors, these states are trying to limit the discretion of decision-makers, when in fact they are doing quite the opposite. The third factor, *i.e.*, the character of the governmental action, opens the door to judicial assessment of the requirement of public purpose, allowing the application of a police-powers rule or a proportionality test to claims of indirect takings. This intrusive approach goes against the wide margin of appreciation normally accorded to national authorities, raising legitimacy issues for international tribunals now encouraged to appraise the adoption of measures of public policy by sovereign states. Wealthy countries can hire expensive teams to defend the adoption of these measures by their national authorities. No defence team, however, no matter how expensive, can ensure that an arbitral panel will favourably assess the public purpose asserted by the respective state. The abandonment of the principle of margin of appreciation, to enable the application of a police-powers rule or a proportionality test to expropriation cases, opens a Pandora's box which offers even less legal certainty than the effects rule. This leaves the international law of expropriation in disarray, again.

Anyone investing wants a stable, predictable, consistent, transparent and coherent legal and administrative framework in the respective state, and expects that its governmental authorities will fulfil their international obligations. In the case of the law of takings, these include respect for prior distinct commitments and the exercise of the right of expropriation in conformity with certain conditions. Governmental authorities simply aspire to promote foreign investment, and for that they have to undertake obligations of an international nature aimed at reducing political risk, which as a whole constitute a pledge with good governance and the rule of law. The protection against expropriation is one of these international obligations – currently not just a part of investment treaties, but of regional human rights conventions as well. The minimum standard of treatment offered by the international law of expropriation should be necessarily understood from this standpoint. After all, law-abiding countries have nothing to fear from international obligations assumed in the exercise of their sovereignty, fundamentally designed to complement the national protection of the right of property.

Bibliography

BOOKS

Aldrich, G, *The Jurisprudence of the Iran-United States Claims Tribunal* (1996).
Alexander, G, *The Global Debate over Constitutional Property: Lessons from American Takings Jurisprudence* (2006).
Alexander, G, and Peñalver, E, *An Introduction to Property Theory* (2012).
Allen, T, *Property and The Human Rights Act 1998* (2005).
Allen, T, *The Right to Property in Commonwealth Constitutions* (2000).
Alvik, I, *Contracting with Sovereignty: State Contracts and International Arbitration* (2011).
Amerasinghe, C, *Diplomatic Protection* (2008).
Arai-Takahashi, Y, *The Margin of Appreciation Doctrine and the Principle of Proportionality in the Jurisprudence of the ECHR* (2002).
Auby, J-B, *La globalisation, le droit et l'état* (2010).
Aust, A, *Modern Treaty Law and Practice* (2007).
Avanessian, A, *Iran–United States Claims Tribunal in Action* (1993).
Bello, A, *Principios de derecho de jentes* (1833).
Beveridge, F, *The Treatment and Taxation of Foreign Investment under International Law* (2000).
Bingham, T, *The Rule of Law* (2010).
Birnie, P, Boyle, A, and Redgwell, C, *International Law & the Environment* (2009).
Bishop, R, Crawford, J, and Reisman, M, *Foreign Investment Disputes. Cases, Materials and Commentary* (2005).
Blackaby et al, N, *Redfern & Hunter on International Arbitration* (2009).
Boyle, A, and Chinkin, C, *The Making of International Law* (2006)
Brower, C, and Brueschke, J, *The Iran–United States Claims Tribunal* (1998).
Brownlie, I, *Principles of Public International Law* (2008).
Calvo, C, *Le droit international théorique et pratique* (1896).
Cassese, A, *International Law* (2005).
Cassese, A, *International Law in a Divided World* (1994).
Cassese, S, *Oltre lo stato* (2006).
Clayton, R, and Tomlinson, H, *The Law of Human Rights* (2000).

Comeaux, P, and Kinsella, N, *Protecting Foreign Direct Investment under International Law. Legal Aspects of Political Risk* (1996).
Crawford, J, *Brownlie's Principles of Public International Law* (2012).
Crawford, J, *The International Law Commission's Articles on State Responsibility. Introduction, Text and Commentaries* (2005).
Davidson, S, *The Inter-American Human Rights System* (1997).
Dolzer, R, and Schreuer, C, *Principles of International Investment Law* (2012).
Dolzer, R, and Stevens, M, *Bilateral Investment Treaties* (1995).
Dugard, J, *International Law. A South African Perspective* (2000).
Fletcher, G, and Sheppard, S, *American Law in a Global Context: The Basics* (2005).
García Roca, J, *El margen de apreciación nacional en la interpretación del Convenio Europeo de Derechos Humanos: soberanía e integración* (2010).
González de Cossío, F, *Arbitraje de inversión* (2009).
Guzmán Brito, A, *Vida y obra de Andrés Bello especialmente considerado como jurista* (2008).
Harris, D, O'Boyle, M, Warbrick, C, and Bates, E, *Law of the European Convention on Human Rights* (2009).
Higgins, R, *Problems & Process. International Law and How We Use It* (1994).
Ignatieff, M, *The Lesser Evil. Political Ethics in an Age of Terror* (2005).
Jackson, R, *Sovereignty: The Evolution of an Idea* (2007).
Jennings, R, and Watts, A, *Oppenheim's International Law* (1996).
Katzarov, K, *The Theory of Nationalisation* (1964).
Kläger, R, *'Fair and Equitable Treatment' in International Investment Law* (2011).
Kulick, A, *Global Public Interest in International Investment Law* (2012).
Legg, A, *The Margin of Appreciation in International Human Rights Law: Deference and Proportionality* (2012).
Lowenfeld, A, *International Economic Law* (2008).
Malanczuk, P, *Akehurst's Modern Introduction to International Law* (1997).
Marboe, I, *Calculation of Compensation and Damages in International Investment Law* (2009).
Matsushita, M, Schoenbaum, T, and Mavroidis, P, *The World Trade Organization: Law, Practice, and Policy* (2006).
McLachlan, C, Shore, L, and Weiniger, M, *International Investment Arbitration: Substantive Principles* (2008).
Merrills, J, and Robertson, A, *Human Rights in Europe. A Study of the European Convention on Human Rights* (2001).

Montt, S, *State Liability in Investment Treaty Arbitration: Global Constitutional and Administrative Law in the BIT Generation* (2009).
Mouri, A, *The International Law of Expropriation as Reflected in the Work of the Iran–U.S. Claims Tribunal* (1994).
Mowbray, M, *Cases and Materials on the European Convention on Human Rights* (2007).
Moyn, S, *The Last Utopia: Human Rights in History* (2012).
Muchlinski, P, *Multinational Enterprises & the Law* (2007).
Newcombe, A, and Paradell, L, *Law and Practice of Investment Treaties: Standards of Treatment* (2009).
Nikièma, S, *L'expropriation indirecte en droit international des investissements* (2012).
Pastor Ridruejo, J-A, *Curso de derecho internacional y organizaciones internacionales* (2009).
Paulsson, J, *Denial of Justice in International Law* (2005).
Reynolds, S, *Before Eminent Domain: Toward a History of Expropriation of Land for the Common Good* (2010).
Rigo Sureda, A, *Investment Treaty Arbitration: Judging under Uncertainty* (2012).
Ripinski, S, and Williams, K, *Damages in International Investment Law* (2008).
Robert-Cuendet, S, *Droits de l'investisseur étranger et protection de l'environnement: contribution à l'analyse de l'expropriation indirect* (2010).
Robertson, A, and Merrills, J, *Human Rights in the World: An Introduction to the Study of the International Protection of Human Rights* (1996).
Sabahi, B, *Compensation and Restitution in Investor–State Arbitration: Principles and Practice* (2011).
Salacuse, J, *The Law of International Investment Treaties* (2010).
Sands, P, *Lawless World. America and the Making and Breaking of Global Rules* (2005).
Schill, S, *The Multilateralization of International Investment Law* (2009).
Schrijver, N, *Sovereignty over Natural Resources. Balancing Rights and Duties* (1997).
Seidl-Hohenveldern, I, *International Economic Law* (1992).
Shea, D, *The Calvo Clause: A Problem of Inter-American and International Law and Diplomacy* (1955).
Shihata, I, *Legal Treatment of Foreign Investment: The World Bank Guidelines* (1993).
Sornarajah, M, *The International Law on Foreign Investment* (2010).
Subedi, S, *International Investment Law: Reconciling Policy and Principle* (2012).

Tamanaha, B, *On the Rule of Law: History, Politics, Theory* (2004).
Trayner, J, *Latin Maxims and Phrases* (1986).
Trindade, A Cançado, *El ejercicio de la función judicial internacional* (2011).
Tudor, I, *The Fair and Equitable Treatment Standard in the International Law of Foreign Investment* (2008).
van der Walt, A, *Constitutional Property Clauses: A Comparative Analysis* (1999).
Vandevelde, K, *Bilateral Investment Treaties: History, Policy, and Interpretation* (2010).
Van Harten, G, *Investment Treaty Arbitration and Public Law* (2007).
Vattel, E, *Les droits des gens ou principes de la loi naturelle* (1758).
Waldron, J, *The Rule of Law and the Measure of Property* (2012).
White, G, *Nationalisation of Foreign Property* (1961).
White, R, and Ovey, C, *Jacobs, White and Ovey: The European Convention on Human Rights* (2010).
Wortley, B, *Expropriation in Public International Law* (1959).
Yourow, H, *The Margin of Appreciation Doctrine in the Dynamics of European Human Rights Jurisprudence* (1995).
Zweigert, K, and Kötz, H, *Introduction to Comparative Law* (1998).

ARTICLES

Afilalo, A, 'Meaning, Ambiguity and Legitimacy: Judicial (Re-) Construction of NAFTA Chapter 11' (2005) 25/2 *Northwestern Journal of International Law & Business* 279.
Afilalo, A, 'Towards a Common Law of International Investment: How NAFTA Chapter 11 Panels Should Solve Their Legitimacy Crisis' (2004) 17/1 *Georgetown International Environmental Law Review* 51.
Aguilar, G, and Park, W, 'The New Face of Investment Arbitration: NAFTA Chapter 11' (2003) 28/2 *Yale Journal of International Law* 365.
Akpan, G, 'The Investment Provisions of the United States–Singapore Free Trade Agreement and the NAFTA. Old Wine in a New Skin or Something Else?' (2005) 6/6 *Journal of World Investment & Trade* 873.
Aldrich, G, 'What Constitutes a Compensable Taking: The Decisions of the Iran–United States Claims Tribunal' (1994) 88/4 *American Journal of International Law* 585.
Allen, T, 'Compensation for Property under the European Convention of Human Rights' (2007) 28/2 *Michigan Journal of International Law* 287.

AlQurashi, Z, 'Indirect Expropriation in the Field of Petroleum' (2004) 5/6 *Journal of World Investment & Trade* 897.

Anaya, J, and Williams, R, 'The Protection of Indigenous Peoples' Rights over Lands and Natural Resources under the Inter-American Human Rights System' (2001) 14 *Harvard Human Rights Journal* 33.

Anderson, D, 'Compensation for Interference with Property' (1999) 4/6 *European Human Rights Law Review* 543.

Appleton, B, 'Regulatory Takings: The International Law Perspective' (2003) 11/1 *New York University Environmental Law Journal* 35.

Been, V, and Beauvais, J, 'The Global Fifth Amendment: NAFTA's Investment Protection and the Misguided Quest for an International "Regulatory Takings" Doctrine' (2003) 78/1 *New York University Law Review* 30.

Bernardini, P, 'Investment Protection under Bilateral Investment Treaties and Investment Contracts' (2001) 2/2 *Journal of World Investment & Trade* 235.

Bowett, D, 'State Contracts with Aliens: Contemporary Developments on Compensation for Termination or Breach' (1988) 59 *British Year Book of International Law* 49.

Brower, C, 'Current Developments in the Law of Expropriation and Compensation: A Preliminary Survey of Awards of the Iran–United States Claims Tribunal' (1987) 21/3 *International Lawyer* 639.

Brower, C, 'Structure, Legitimacy, and NAFTA's Investment Chapter' (2003) 36/1 *Vanderbilt Journal of Transnational Law* 37.

Brower, C, and Schill, S, 'Is Arbitration a Threat or a Boon to the Legitimacy of International Investment Law?' (2009) 9/2 *Chicago Journal of International Law* 471.

Brunetti, M, 'Indirect Expropriation in International Law' (2003) 5/3 *International Law FORUM du Droit International* 150.

Brunetti, M, 'The Iran–United States Claims Tribunal, NAFTA Chapter 11, and the Doctrine of Indirect Expropriation' (2001) 2/1 *Chicago Journal of International Law* 203.

Burke-White, W, and von Staden, A, 'Private Litigation in a Public Sphere: The Standard of Review in Investor–State Arbitrations' (2010) 35/2 *Yale Journal of International Law* 283.

Cassese, S, 'Global Standards for National Administrative Procedure' (2005) 68/3–4 *Law and Contemporary Problems* 109.

Cassese, S, 'The Globalization of Law' (2006) 37/4 *New York University Journal of International Law and Politics* 973.

Cheng, T, 'Precedent and Control in Investment Treaty Arbitration' (2007) 30/4 *Fordham International Law Journal* 1014.

Chimni, B, 'Co-option and Resistance: Two Faces of Global Administrative Law' (2005) 37/4 *New York University Journal of International Law and Politics* 799.

Chinkin, C, 'The Challenge of Soft Law: Development and Change in International Law' (1989) 38/4 *International & Comparative Law Quarterly* 850.

Choudhury, B, 'Recapturing Public Power: Is Investment Arbitration's Engagement of the Public Interest Contributing to the Democratic Deficit' (2008) 41/3 *Vanderbilt Journal of Transnational Law* 775.

Christie, G, 'What Constitutes a Taking of Property under International Law?' (1962) *British Year Book of International Law* 307.

Chung, O, 'The Lopsided International Investment Law Regime and Its Effect on the Future of Investor–State Arbitration' (2007) 47/4 *Virginia Journal of International Law* 953.

Clodfelter, M, 'The Adaptation of States to the Changing World of Investment Protection through Model BITs' (2009) 24/1 *ICSID Review – Foreign Investment Law Journal* 165.

Commission, J, 'Precedent in Investment Treaty Arbitration. A Citation Analysis of a Developing Jurisprudence' (2007) 24/2 *Journal of International Arbitration* 129.

Dalrymple, C, 'Politics and Foreign Direct Investment: The Multilateral Investment Guarantee Agency and the Calvo Clause' (1996) 29/1 *Cornell International Law Journal* 161.

del Toro, M, 'El derecho de propiedad colectiva de los miembros de comunidades y pueblos indígenas en la jurisprudencia de la Corte Interamericana de Derechos Humanos' (2010) 10 *Anuario Mexicano de Derecho Internacional* 49.

Dolzer, R, 'Fair and Equitable Treatment: A Key Standard in Investment Treaties' (2005) 39/1 *International Lawyer* 87.

Dolzer, R, 'Indirect Expropriations: New Developments?' (2003) 11/1 *New York University Environmental Law Journal* 64.

Dolzer, R, 'Indirect Expropriation of Alien Property' (1986) 1/1 *ICSID Review – Foreign Investment Law Journal* 41.

Dolzer, R, 'New Foundations of the Law of Expropriation of Alien Property' (1981) 75/3 *American Journal of International Law* 553.

Dolzer, R, 'The European Approach to BITs' (2009) 24/2 *ICSID Review – Foreign Investment Law Journal* 368.

Dolzer, R, 'The Impact of International Investment Treaties on Domestic Administrative Law' (2006) 37/4 *New York University Journal of International Law and Politics* 953.

Dolzer, R, and Bloch, F, 'Indirect Expropriation: Conceptual Realignments?' (2003) 5/3 *International Law FORUM du Droit International* 155.

Douglas, Z, 'Can a Doctrine of Precedent Be Justified in Investment Treaty Arbitration?' (2010) 25/1 *ICSID Review – Foreign Investment Law Journal* 104.

Dugard, J, 'The Future of International Law: A Human Rights Perspective – with Some Comments on the Leiden School of International Law' (2007), 20/4 *Leiden Journal of International Law* 729.

Dunn, F, 'International Law and Private Property Rights' (1928) 28/2 *Columbia Law Review* 166.

Elkins, Z, Guzman, A, and Simmons, B, 'Competing for Capital: The Diffusion of Bilateral Investment Treaties, 1960–2000' (2008) 1 *University of Illinois Law Review* 265.

Escobar, A, 'Introductory Note on Bilateral Investment Treaties Recently Concluded by Latin American States' (1996) 11/1 *ICSID Review – Foreign Investment Law Journal* 86.

Esty, D, 'Good Governance at the Supranational Scale: Globalizing Administrative Law' (2006) 115/7 *Yale Law Journal* 1490.

Falsafi, A, 'The International Minimum Standard of Treatment of Foreign Investor's Property: A Contingent Standard' (2007) 30/1 *Suffolk Transnational Law Review* 317.

Fauchald, O, 'The Legal Reasoning of ICSID Tribunals – an Empirical Analysis' (2008) 19/2 *European Journal of International Law* 301.

Forero, F, 'Conectividad: alcances del derecho a la propiedad aborigen y tribal en la jurisprudencia de la Corte Interamericana de Derechos Humanos' (2010) 16 *International Law – Revista Colombiana de Derecho Internacional* 177.

Fortier, Y, and Drymer, S, 'Indirect Expropriation in the Law of International Investment: I Know It When I See It, or Caveat Investor' (2004) 19/2 *ICSID Review – Foreign Investment Law Journal* 293.

Francioni, F, 'Compensation for Nationalisation of Foreign Property: The Borderline between Law and Equity' (1975) 24/2 *International & Comparative Law Quarterly* 255.

Franck, S, 'The Legitimacy Crisis in Investment Treaty Arbitration: Privatizing Public International Law through Inconsistent Decisions' (2005) 73/5 *Fordham Law Review* 1521.

French, D, 'From Seoul with Love – the Continuing Relevance of the 1986 Seoul ILA Declaration on Progressive Development of Principles of Public International Law Relating to a New International Economic Order' (2008) 55/1 *Netherlands International Law Review* 3.

Gagné, G, 'The U.S. Policy on the Protection of Foreign Investment: From the NAFTA to the U.S.–Korea FTA' (2011) 12/5 *Journal of World Investment & Trade* 807.

Gagné, G, and Morin, J-F, 'The Evolving American Policy on Investment Protection: Evidence from Recent FTAs and the 2004 Model BIT' (2006) 9/2 *Journal of International Economic Law* 357.

Garcia-Bolívar, O, 'Sovereignty vs. Investment Protection: Back to Calvo?' (2009) 24/2 *ICSID Review – Foreign Investment Law Journal* 464.

Garcia-Mora, M, 'The Calvo Clause in Latin American Constitutions and International Law' (1950) 33/4 *Marquette Law Review* 205.

Geiger, R, 'Regulatory Expropriations in International Law: Lessons from the Multilateral Agreement on Investment' (2003) 11/1 *New York University Environmental Law Journal* 94.

Gibson, C, and Drahozal, C, 'Iran–United States Tribunal Precedent in Investor–State Arbitration' (2006) 23/6 *Journal of International Arbitration* 521.

Gill, J, 'Is There a Special Role for Precedent in Investment Arbitration?' (2010) 25/1 *ICSID Review – Foreign Investment Law Journal* 87.

Graham, E, 'Regulatory Takings, Supernational Treatment, and the Multilateral Agreement on Investment: Issues Raised by Nongovernmental Organizations' (1998) 31/3 *Cornell International Law Journal* 599.

Graham, F, 'The Calvo Clause: Its Current Status as a Contractual Renunciation of Diplomatic Protection' (1970) 6/2 *Texas International Law Forum* 289.

Gutbrod, M, and Hindelang, S, 'Externalization of Effective Legal Protection against Indirect Expropriation. Can the Legal Order of Developing Countries Live up to the Standards Required by International Investment Agreements? A Disenchanting Comparative Analysis' (2006) 7/1 *Journal of World Investment & Trade* 59.

Guzman, A, 'Why LDCs Sign Treaties That Hurt Them: Explaining the Popularity of Bilateral Investment Treaties' (1998) 38/4 *Virginia Journal of International Law* 639.

Hallward-Driemeier, M, 'Do Bilateral Investment Treaties Attract Foreign Direct Investment? Only a Bit … and They Could Bite' (2003) 3121 *World Bank Policy Research Working Paper*.

Harlow, C, 'Global Administrative Law: The Quest for Principles and Values' (2006) 17/1 *European Journal of International Law* 187.

Heiskanen, V, 'The Contribution of the Iran–United States Claims Tribunal to the Development of the Doctrine of Indirect Expropriation' (2003) 5/3 *International Law FORUM du Droit International* 176.

Heiskanen, H, 'The Doctrine of Indirect Expropriation in Light of the Practice of the Iran–United States Claims Tribunal' (2007) 8/2 *Journal of World Investment & Trade* 215.

Henckels, C, 'Indirect Expropriation and the Right to Regulate: Revisiting Proportionality Analysis and the Standard of Review in Investor–State Arbitration' (2012) 15/1 *Journal of International Economic Law* 223.

Herz, J, 'Expropriation of Foreign Property' (1941) 35/2 *American Journal of International Law* 243.

Higgins, R, 'The Taking of Property by the State: Recent Developments in International Law' (1982) 176/3 *Recueil des Cours* 259.

Hillgenberg, H, 'A Fresh Look at Soft Law' (1999) 10/3 *European Journal of International Law* 499.

Hindelang, S, 'Bilateral Investment Treaties, Custom and a Healthy Investment Climate – the Question of Whether BITs Influence Customary International Law Revisited' (2004) 5/5 *Journal of World Investment & Trade* 769.

Hyland, R, 'Pacta Sunt Servanda: A Meditation' (1994) 34/2 *Virginia Journal of International Law* 405.

Jackson, J, 'Sovereignty-Modern: A New Approach to an Outdated Concept',(2003) 97/4 *American Journal of International Law* 782.

Jones, R, 'NAFTA Chapter 11 Investor-to-State Dispute Resolution: A Shield to Be Embraced or a Sword to Be Feared?' (2002) 2 *Brigham Young University Law Review* 527.

Juillard, P, 'MAI: A European View' (1998) 31/3 *Cornell International Law Journal* 477.

Kantor, M, 'Fair and Equitable Treatment: Echoes of FDR's Court-Packing Plan in the International Law Approach towards Regulatory Expropriation' (2006) 5/2 *Law and Practice of International Courts and Tribunals* 231.

Kantor, M, 'Little Has Changed in the New US Model Bilateral Investment Treaty' (2012) 27/2 *ICSID Review – Foreign Investment Law Journal* 335.

Kaushal, A, 'Revisiting History: How the Past Matters for the Present Backlash against the Foreign Investment Regime' (2009) 50/2 *Harvard International Law Journal* 491.

Kingsbury, B, 'The Concept of "Law" in Global Administrative Law' (2009) 20/1 *European Journal of International Law* 23.

Kingsbury, B, 'Sovereignty and Inequality' (1998) 9/4 *European Journal of International Law* 599.

Kingsbury, B, Krisch, N, and Stewart, R, 'The Emergence of Global Administrative Law' (2005) 68/3–4 *Law and Contemporary Problems* 15.

Kishaiyian, B, 'The Utility of Bilateral Investment Treaties in the Formulation of Customary International Law' (1994) 14/2 *Northwestern Journal of International Law and Business* 327.

Klabbers, J, 'The Redundancy of Soft Law' (1996) 65/2 *Nordic Journal of International Law* 167.

Kriebaum, U, 'Human Rights of the Population of the Host State in International Investment Arbitration' (2009) 10/5 *Journal of World Investment & Trade* 653.

Kriebaum, U, 'Partial Expropriation' (2007) 8/1 *Journal of World Investment & Trade* 69.

Kriebaum, U, 'Regulatory Takings: Balancing the Interests of the Investor and the State' (2007) 8/5 *Journal of World Investment & Trade* 717.

Krisch, N, 'The Pluralism of Global Administrative Law' (2006) 17/1 *European Journal of International Law* 247.

Krisch, N, and Kingsbury, B, 'Global Governance and Global Administrative Law in the International Legal Order' (2006) 17/1 *European Journal of International Law* 1.

Kunoy, B, 'Developments in Indirect Expropriation Case Law in ICSID Transnational Arbitration' (2005) 6/3 *Journal of World Investment & Trade* 467.

Kunoy, B, 'The Notion of Time in ICSID's Case Law on Indirect Expropriation' (2006) 23/4 *Journal of International Arbitration* 337.

Kuo, M, 'The Concept of "Law" in Global Administrative Law: A Reply to Benedict Kingsbury' (2010) 20/4 *European Journal of International Law* 997.

Lee, S, 'A Puzzle of Sovereignty' (1997) 27/2 *California Western International Law Journal* 241.

Lipstein, K, 'The Place of the Calvo Clause in International Law' (1945) 22 *British Year Book of International Law* 130.

Loppacher, L, and Kerr, K, 'Investment Rules. The U.S. Agenda in Bilateral Trade Agreements' (2006) 7/1 *Journal of World Investment & Trade* 39.

Lowenfeld, A, 'Investment Agreements and International Law' (2003) 42/1 *Columbia Journal of Transnational Law* 123.

Lukashuk, I, 'The Principle Pacta Sunt Servanda and the Nature of Obligation under International Law' (1989) 83/3 *American Journal of International Law* 513.

Madalena, I, 'Foreign Direct Investment and the Protection of the Environment: The Border between National Environmental Regulation and Expropriation' (2003) 12/3 *European Environmental Law Review* 70.

Maniruzzaman, A, 'Expropriation of Alien Property and the Principle of Non-Discrimination in International Law of Foreign Investment: An Overview' (1998) 8/1 *Journal of Transnational Law & Policy* 57.

Mann, F, 'British Treaties for the Promotion and Protection of Investments' (1981) 52 *British Year Book of International Law* 241.
Mann, F, 'Outlines of a History of Expropriation' (1959) 75/2 *Law Quarterly Review* 188.
Marboe, I, 'Compensation and Damages in International Law. The Limits of the "Fair Market Value"' (2006) 7/5 *Journal of World Investment & Trade* 723.
Marks, S, 'Naming Global Administrative Law' (2005) 37/4 *New York University Journal of International Law and Politics* 995.
Metzger, S, 'Multilateral Conventions for the Protection of Private Foreign Investment' (1960) 9/1 *Journal of Public Law* 133.
Mitchell, A, and Farnik, J, 'Global Administrative Law: Can It Bring Global Governance to Account?' (2009) 37/2 *Federal Law Review* 237.
Mountfield, H, 'Regulatory Expropriations in Europe: The Approach of the European Court of Human Rights' (2003) 11/1 *New York University Environmental Law Journal* 136.
Muchlinski, P, 'The Rise and Fall of the Multilateral Agreement on Investment: Where Now?' (2000) 34/3 *International Lawyer* 1033.
Neumayer, E, and Spess, L, 'Do Bilateral Investment Treaties Increase Foreign Direct Investment to Developing Countries?' (2005) *London School of Economics and Political Science Research Online*.
Newcombe, A, 'The Boundaries of Regulatory Expropriation in International Law' (2005) 20/1 *ICSID Review – Foreign Investment Law Journal* 1.
Newcombe, A, 'Sustainable Development and Investment Treaty Law' (2007) 3/8 *Journal of World Investment & Trade* 357.
Norton, P, 'A Law of the Future or a Law of the Past? Modern Tribunals and the International Law of Expropriation' (1991) 85/3 *American Journal of International Law* 474.
Orrego Vicuña, F, 'Carlos Calvo, Honorary NAFTA Citizen' (2002) 11/1 *New York University Environmental Law Journal* 19.
Orrego Vicuña, F, 'Regulatory Authority and Legitimate Expectations: Balancing the Rights of the State and the Individual under International Law in a Global Society' (2003) 5/3 *International Law FORUM du Droit International* 188.
Parra, A, 'Principles Governing Foreign Investment, as Reflected in National Investment Codes' (1992) 7/2 *ICSID Review – Foreign Investment Law Journal* 428.
Paulsson, J, 'Arbitration without Privity" (1995) 10/2 *ICSID Review – Foreign Investment Law Journal* 232.
Paulsson, J, and Petrochilos, G, '*Neer*-ly Misled?' (2007) 22/2 *ICSID Review – Foreign Investment Law Journal* 242.

Pellonpää, M, and Fitzmaurice, M, 'Taking of Property in the Practice of the Iran–United States Claims Tribunal' (1988) 19 *Netherlands Yearbook of International Law* 53.

Picciotto, S, 'Linkages in International Investment Regulation: The Antinomies of the Draft Multilateral Agreement on Investment' (1998) 19/3 *University of Pennsylvania Journal of International Economic Law* 731.

Porterfield, M, 'State Practice and the (Purported) Obligation under Customary International Law to Provide Compensation for Regulatory Expropriations' (2011) 37/1 *North Carolina Journal of International Law and Commercial Regulation* 159.

Puig, S, and Kinnear, M, 'NAFTA Chapter Eleven at Fifteen: Contributions to a Systemic Approach in Investment Arbitration' (2010) 25/2 *ICSID Review – Foreign Investment Law Journal* 225.

Reed, L, 'The De Facto Precedent Regime in Investment Arbitration: A Case for Proactive Case Management' (2010) 25/1 *ICSID Review – Foreign Investment Law Journal* 95.

Reisman, M, and Sloane, R, 'Indirect Expropriation and Its Valuation in the BIT Generation' (2003) 74 *British Year Book of International Law* 115.

Root, E, 'The Basis of Protection to Citizens Residing Abroad' (1910) 4/3 *American Journal of International Law* 517.

Ruffert, M, 'The Protection of Foreign Direct Investment by the European Convention on Human Rights' (2000) 43 *German Yearbook of International Law* 116.

Ruiz Fabri, H, 'The Approach Taken by the European Court of Human Rights to the Assessment of Compensation for "Regulatory Expropriations" of the Property of Foreign Investors' (2003) 11/1 *New York University Environmental Law Journal* 148.

Sacerdoti, G, 'Bilateral Treaties and Multilateral Instruments on Investment Protection' (1997) 269 *Recueil des Cours* 251.

Sacerdoti, G, 'The Admission and Treatment of Foreign Investment under Recent Bilateral and Regional Treaties' (2000) 1/1 *Journal of World Investment & Trade* 105.

Salacuse, J, 'BIT by BIT: The Growth of Bilateral Investment Treaties and Their Impact on Foreign Investment in Developing Countries' (1990) 24/3 *International Lawyer* 655.

Salacuse, J, and Sullivan, N, 'Do BITs Really Work: An Evaluation of Bilateral Investment Treaties and Their Grand Bargain' (2005) 46/1 *Harvard International Law Journal* 67.

Sampliner, G, 'Arbitration of Expropriation Cases under U.S. Investment Treaties – a Threat to Democracy or the Dog That Didn't Bark?' (2003) 18/1 *ICSID Review – Foreign Investment Law Journal* 1.

Schill, S, 'Enhancing International Investment Law's Legitimacy: Conceptual and Methodological Foundations of a New Public Law Approach' (2011) 52/1 *Virginia Journal of International Law* 57.

Schreuer, C, 'Fair and Equitable Treatment in Arbitral Practice' (2005) 6/3 *Journal of World Investment & Trade* 357.

Schrijver, N, 'The Changing Nature of State Sovereignty' (1999) 70 *British Year Book of International Law* 65.

Schwarzenberger, G, 'The Abs-Shawcross Draft Convention on Investments Abroad: A Critical Commentary' (1960) 9/1 *Journal of Public Law* 147.

Schwebel, S, 'A BIT about ICSID' (2008) 23/1 *ICSID Review – Foreign Investment Law Journal* 1.

Schwebel, S, 'The Influence of Bilateral Investment Treaties on Customary International Law (2004) 98 *American Society of International Law Proceedings* 27.

Schwelb, E, 'The Protection of the Right of Property of Nationals under the First Protocol to the European Convention on Human Rights' (1964) 13/4 *American Journal of Comparative Law* 518.

Sedigh, H, 'What Level of Host State Interference Amounts to a Taking under Contemporary International Law' (2001) 2/2 *Journal of World Investment & Trade* 631.

Shen, J, 'National Sovereignty and Human Rights in a Positive Law Context' (2000) 26/2 *Brooklyn Journal of International Law* 417.

Shenkman, E, 'Could Principles of Fifth Amendment Takings Jurisprudence Be Helpful in Analyzing Regulatory Expropriation Claims under International Law?' (2003) 11/1 *New York University Environmental Law Journal* 174.

Sohn, L, and Baxter, R, 'Responsibility of States for Injuries to the Economic Interests of Aliens' (1961) 55/3 *American Journal of International Law* 545.

Somek, A, 'The Concept of "Law" in Global Administrative Law: A Reply to Benedict Kingsbury' (2010) 20/4 *European Journal of International Law* 985.

Sornarajah, M, 'Power and Justice in International Law' (1997) 1/1 *Singapore Journal of International & Comparative Law* 28.

Spears, S, 'The Quest for Policy Space in a New Generation of International Investment Agreements' (2010) 13/4 *Journal of International Economic Law* 1037.

Stanley, J, 'Keeping Big Brother out of Our Backyard: Regulatory Takings as Defined in International Law and Compared to American Fifth Amendment Jurisprudence' (2001) 15/1 *Emory International Law Review* 349.

Steffens, J, 'Expectations of Governments and Investors vs. Practice: The Government View on BITs' (2009) 24/2 *ICSID Review – Foreign Investment Law Journal* 347.

Stewart, R, 'The Global Regulatory Challenge to U.S. Administrative Law' (2006) 37/4 *New York University Journal of International Law and Politics* 695.

Stumberg, R, 'Sovereignty by Subtraction: The Multilateral Agreement on Investment' (1998) 31/3 *Cornell International Law Journal* 491.

Sweet, A, and Mathews, J, 'Proportionality Balancing and Global Constitutionalism' (2008) 47/1 *Columbia Journal of Transnational Law* 72.

Swenson, D, 'Why Do Developing Countries Sign BITs?' (2006) 12/1 *University of California–Davis Journal of International Law and Policy* 131.

Tobin, J, and Rose-Ackerman, S, 'Foreign Direct Investment and the Business Environment in Developing Countries: the Impact of Bilateral Investment Treaties' (2004) 293 *Yale Law and Economics Research Paper*.

Tobin, J, and Rose-Ackerman, S, 'When BITs Have Some Bite' (2006) *Yale Law School Draft Working Paper*.

Tschofen, F, 'Multilateral Approaches to the Treatment of Foreign Investment' (1992) 7/2 *ICSID Review – Foreign Investment Law Journal* 384.

Vallianatos, M, 'De-Fanging the MAI' (1998) 31/3 *Cornell International Law Journal* 713.

Van Harten, G, and Loughlin, M, 'Investment Treaty Arbitration as a Species of Global Administrative Law' (2006) 17/1 *European Journal of International Law* 121.

Vandevelde, K, 'A Brief History of International Investment Agreements' (2006) 12/1 *University of California-Davis Journal of International Law and Policy* 157.

Vandevelde, K, 'Investment Liberalization and Economic Development: The Role of Bilateral Investment Treaties' (1998) 36/3 *Columbia Journal of Transnational Law* 501.

Vandevelde, K, 'Model Bilateral Investment Treaties: The Way Forward' (2011) 18/1 *Southwestern Journal of International Law* 307.

Vandevelde, K, 'Sustainable Liberalism and the International Investment Regime' (1998) 19/2 *Michigan Journal of International Law* 373.

Vandevelde, K, 'The Bilateral Investment Treaty Program of the United States' (1988) 21/2 *Cornell International Law Journal* 201.

Vandevelde, K, 'The Political Economy of a Bilateral Investment Treaty' (1998) 92/4 *American Journal of International Law* 621.

Vandevelde, K, 'U.S. Bilateral Investment Treaties: the Second Wave' (1993) 14/4 *Michigan Journal of International Law* 621.

von Mehren, R, and Kourides, P, 'International Arbitration between States and Foreign Private Parties: The Libyan Nationalization Cases' (1981) 75/3 *American Journal of International Law* 476.

Waelde, T, 'Energy Charter Treaty-based Investment Arbitration. Controversial Issues' (2004) 5/3 *Journal of World Investment & Trade* 373.

Waelde, T, and Kolo, A, 'Environmental Regulation, Investment Protection and "Regulatory Taking" in International Law' (2001) 50/4 *International & Comparative Law Quarterly* 811.

Weeramantry, J, 'The Future Role of Past Awards in Investment Arbitration' (2010) 25/2 *ICSID Review – Foreign Investment Law Journal* 111.

Weil, P, 'Towards Relative Normativity in International Law?' (1983) 77/3 *American Journal of International Law* 413.

Weiner, A, 'Indirect Expropriations: The Need for a Taxonomy of "Legitimate" Regulatory Purposes' (2003) 5/3 *International Law FORUM du Droit International* 166.

Westberg, J, 'Applicable Law, Expropriatory Takings and Compensations in Cases of Expropriation: ICSID and Iran–United States Claims Tribunal Case Law Compared' (1993) 8/1 *ICSID Review – Foreign Investment Law Journal* 1.

Westberg, J, 'Compensation in Cases of Expropriation and Nationalization: Awards of the Iran–United States Claims Tribunal' (1990) 5/2 *ICSID Review – Foreign Investment Law Journal* 256.

Weston, B, '"Constructive Takings" under International Law: A Modest Foray into the Problem of "Creeping Expropriation"' (1975) 16/1 *Virginia Journal of International Law* 103.

Wortley, B, 'Protection of Property Situated Abroad' (1960) 35/4 *Tulane Law Review* 739.

Wortley, B, 'Some Early but Basic Theories of Expropriation' (1977) 20 *German Yearbook of International Law* 236.

Zhan, J, 'The Spread of BITs and Their Changing Face' (2009) 24/2 *ICSID Review – Foreign Investment Law Journal* 339.

CONTRIBUTIONS TO COMPILATIONS & EDITED VOLUMES

Alterman, R (ed.), *Takings International: A Comparative Perspective on Land Use Regulation and Compensation Rights* (2012).

American Law Institute, *Restatement of the Law Third, the Foreign Relations Law of the United States* (1987).

Benedek, W, 'Drago-Porter Convention (1907)', in Bernhardt, R (ed.), *Encyclopedia of Public International Law* (1992), Vol. 1.

Blackaby, N, and Paradell, L, 'Investment Treaty Arbitration', in Tackaberry, J, and Marriott, A (eds.), *Bernstein's Handbook of Arbitration and Dispute Resolution Practice* (2003), Vol. 1.

Blumemwitz, D, 'Treaties of Friendship, Commerce and Navigation', in Bernhardt, R (ed.), *Encyclopedia of Public International Law* (2000), Vol. 4.

Boyle, A, 'Soft Law in International Law-Making', in Evans, M (ed.), *International Law* (2010).

Brower, B, 'Natural Resources, Sovereignty over', in Bernhardt, R (ed.), *Encyclopedia of Public International Law* (1997), Vol. 3.

Buxbaum, R, and Riesenfeld, S, 'Investment Codes', in Bernhardt, R (ed.), *Encyclopedia of Public International Law* (1995), Vol. 2.

Chinkin, C, 'Normative Development in the International Legal System', in Sheldon, D (ed.), *Commitment and Compliance. The Role of Non-Binding Norms in the International Legal System* (2003).

Condorelli, L, 'Premier Protocole Additionnel. Article 1', in Pettiti, L-E, Decaux, E, and Imbert, P-H (eds.), *La Convention Europeénne des Droits de l'Homme* (1999).

D'Amato, A, 'Good Faith', in Bernhardt, R (ed.), *Encyclopedia of Public International Law* (1995), Vol. 2.

Davidson, S, 'The Civil and Political Rights Protected in the Inter-American Human Rights System', in Harris, D, and Livingstone, S (eds.), *The Inter-American System of Human Rights* (1998).

De Sena, P, 'Economic and Non-Economic Values in the Case Law of the European Court of Human Rights', in Dupuy, P, Francioni, F, and Petersmann, E (eds.), *Human Rights in International Investment Law and Arbitration* (2009).

De Witte, B, 'Balancing of Economic Law and Human Rights by the European Court of Human Rights', in Dupuy, P, Francioni, F, and Petersmann, E (eds.), *Human Rights in International Investment Law and Arbitration* (2009).

Dinstein, Y, 'Deprivation of Property of Foreigners under International Law', in Ando, N, et al (eds.), *Liber Amicorum Judge Shigeru Oda* (2002).

Dolzer, R, 'Expropriation and Nationalization', in Bernhardt, R (ed.), *Encyclopedia of Public International Law* (1995), Vol. 2.

Dolzer, R, 'Requisitions', in Bernhardt, R (ed.), *Encyclopedia of Public International Law* (2000), Vol. 4.

Dolzer, R, 'Sequestration', in Bernhardt, R (ed.), *Encyclopedia of Public International Law* (2000), Vol. 4.

Dyzenhaus, D, 'Accountability and the Concept of (Global) Administrative Law', in *International Law and Justice Working Paper* (2008), Nr. 7.

Evans, M, and Murray, R (eds.), *The African Charter on Human and Peoples' Rights: The System in Practice, 1986–2000* (2002).
Gaillard, E, and McNeill, M, 'The Energy Charter Treaty', in Yannaca-Small, K (ed.), *Arbitration under International Investment Agreements: A Guide to the Key Issues* (2010).
Garcia-Amador, F, 'Calvo Doctrine, Calvo Clause', in Bernhardt, R (ed.), *Encyclopedia of Public International Law* (1992), Vol. 1.
Garner, B (ed.), *Black's Law Dictionary* (2009).
Gretton, G, 'The Protection of Property Rights', in Boyle, A, et al (eds.), *Human Rights and Scots Law* (2002).
Hartwig, M, 'Colonies and Colonial Régime', in Bernhardt, R (ed.), *Encyclopedia of Public International Law* (1992), Vol. 1.
Heyns, C, 'Civil and Political Rights in the African Charter', in Evans, M, and Murray, R (eds.), *The African Charter on Human and Peoples' Rights: The System in Practice, 1986–2000* (2002).
Hoffmann, A, 'Indirect Expropriation', in Reinisch, A (ed.), *Standards of Investment Protection* (2008).
Houde, M-F, and Yannaca-Small, K, 'Relationships between International Investment Agreements', in *OECD Working Papers on International Investment* (2004), Nr. 1.
Jaenicke, G, 'Havana Charter', in Bernhardt, R (ed.), *Encyclopedia of Public International Law* (1995), Vol. 2.
Janis, M, 'Equity in International Law', in Bernhardt, R (ed), *Encyclopedia of Public International Law* (1995), Vol. 2.
Kingsbury, B, and Schill, S, 'Public Law Concepts to Balance Investors' Rights with State Regulatory Actions in the Public Interest – the Concept of Proportionality', in Schill, S (ed.), *International Investment Law and Comparative Public Law* (2010).
Kinnear, M, 'Damages in Investment Treaty Arbitration', in Yannaca-Small, K (ed.), *Arbitration under International Investment Agreements: A Guide to the Key Issues* (2010).
Kommendijk, J, and Morijn, J, 'Proportional by What Measure(s)? Balancing Investor Interests and Human Rights by Way of Applying the Proportionality Principle in Investor–State Arbitration', in Dupuy, P, Francioni, F, and Petersmann, E (eds.), *Human Rights in International Investment Law and Arbitration* (2009).
Kriebaum, U, 'Is the European Court of Human Rights an Alternative to Investor–State Arbitration?', in Dupuy, P, Francioni, F, and Petersmann, E (eds.), *Human Rights in International Investment Law and Arbitration* (2009).
Krisch, N, 'Global Administrative Law and the Constitutional Ambition', in *London School of Economics and Political Science (LSE) Law Society and Economy Working Papers* (2009), Nr. 10.

Lachs, M, 'Pacta Sunt Servanda', in Bernhardt, R (ed.), *Encyclopedia of Public International Law* (1997), Vol. 3.

Lillich, R, 'Lump Sum Agreements', in Bernhardt, R (ed.), *Encyclopedia of Public International Law* (1997), Vol. 3.

Muir Watt, H, 'Globalization and Comparative Law', in Reimann, M, and Zimmermann, R (eds.), *The Oxford Handbook of Comparative Law* (2006).

Müller, D, 'Other Specific Regimes of Responsibility: The Iran–US Claims Tribunal', in Crawford, J, Pellet, A, and Olleson, S (eds.), *The Law of International Responsibility* (2010).

Nikken, P, 'Balancing of Human Rights and Investment Law in the Inter-American System of Human Rights', in Dupuy, P, Francioni, F, and Petersmann, E (eds.), *Human Rights in International Investment Law and Arbitration* (2009).

Olaniyan, K, 'Civil and Political Rights in the African Charter: Articles 8–14', in Evans, M, and Murray, R (eds.), *The African Charter on Human and Peoples' Rights: The System in Practice, 1986–2006* (2010).

Paulsson, J, 'The Role of Precedent in Investment Arbitration', in Yannaca-Small, K (ed.), *Arbitration under International Investment Agreements: A Guide to the Key Issues* (2010).

Paulsson, J, and Douglas, Z, 'Indirect Expropriation in Investment Treaty Arbitrations', in Horn, N (ed.), *Arbitrating Foreign Investment Disputes. Procedural and Substantive Legal Aspects* (2004).

Perkams, M, 'The Concept of Indirect Expropriation in Comparative Public Law – Searching for Light in the Dark', in Schill, S (ed.), *International Investment Law and Comparative Public Law* (2010).

Petersmann, E-U, 'Charter of Economic Rights and Duties of States', in Bernhardt, R (ed.), *Encyclopedia of Public International Law* (1992), Vol. 1.

Reinisch, A, 'Expropriation', in Muchlinski, P, Ortino, F, and Schreuer, C (eds.), *The Oxford Handbook of International Investment Law* (2008).

Reinisch, A, 'Legality of Expropriations', in Reinisch, A (ed.), *Standards of Investment Protection* (2008).

Riesenfeld, S, 'Foreign Investments', in Bernhardt, R (ed.), *Encyclopedia of Public International Law* (1995), Vol. 2.

Riesenfeld, S, and Caron, D, 'United States–Iran Agreement of January 19, 1981 (Hostages and Financial Agreements)', in Bernhardt, R (ed.), *Encyclopedia of Public International Law* (2000), Vol. 4.

Rigo Sureda, A, 'Precedent in Investment Treaty Arbitration', in Binder, C, et al (eds.), *International Investment Law for the 21st Century: Essays in Honour of Christoph Schreuer* (2009).

Rubins, N, 'The Notion of "Investment" in International Investment Arbitration', in Horn, N (ed.), *Arbitrating Foreign Investment Disputes. Procedural and Substantive Legal Aspects* (2004).
Schill, S, 'International Investment Law and Comparative Public Law', in Schill, S (ed.), *International Investment Law and Comparative Public Law* (2010).
Schlemmer, E, 'Investment, Investor, Nationality, and Shareholders', in Muchlinski, P, Ortino, F, and Schreuer, C (eds.), *The Oxford Handbook of International Investment Law* (2008).
Schreuer, C, 'Denunciation of the ICSID Convention and Consent to Arbitration', in Waibel, M, et al, *The Backlash against Investment Arbitration: Perceptions and Reality* (2010).
Schreuer, C, 'The Concept of Expropriation under the ECT and other Investment Protection Treaties', in Ribeiro, C (ed.), *Investment Arbitration and the Energy Charter Treaty* (2006).
Schreuer, C, 'The Future of Investment Arbitration', in Arsanjani, M, et al (eds.), *Looking at the Future: Essays on International Law in Honor of W. Michael Reisman* (2011).
Schreuer, C, and Weiniger, M, 'A Doctrine of Precedent?', in Muchlinski, P, Ortino, F, and Schreuer, C (eds.), *The Oxford Handbook of International Investment Law* (2008).
Seidl-Hohenveldern, I, 'Aliens, Property', in Bernhardt, R (ed.), *Encyclopedia of Public International Law* (1992), Vol. 1.
Silagi, M, 'Preferential Claims against Venezuela Arbitration', in Bernhardt, R (ed.), *Encyclopedia of Public International Law* (1997), Vol. 3.
Sornarajah, M, 'A Coming Crisis: Expansionary Trends in Investment Treaty Arbitration', in Sauvant, K (ed.), *Appeals Mechanism in International Investment Disputes* (2008).
Steinberger, H, 'Sovereignty', in Bernhardt, R (ed.), *Encyclopedia of Public International Law* (2000), Vol. 4.
Tomuschat, C, 'New International Economic Order', in Bernhardt, R (ed.), *Encyclopedia of Public International Law* (1997), Vol. 3.
Tomuschat, C, 'The European Court of Human Rights and Investment Protection', in Binder, C, et al (eds), *International Investment Law for the 21st Century: Essays in Honour of Christoph Schreuer* (2009).
UNCTAD, *Denunciation of the ICSID Convention and BITs: Impact on Investor–State Claims* (2010).
UNCTAD, *International Investment Agreements: Key Issues* (2004), Vol. 1.
UNCTAD, *Investment Provisions in Economic Integration Agreements* (2006).

UNCTAD, *Recent Developments in International Investment Agreements* (2005).
UNCTAD, *Recent Developments in Investor–State Dispute Settlement* (2013).
UNCTAD, *Recent Developments in International Investment Agreements 2008–June 2009* (2009).
UNCTAD, *The Entry into Force of Bilateral Investment Treaties* (2006).
UNCTAD, *World Investment Report* (2011).
UNCTAD, *World Investment Report* (2012).
UNCTAD, *World Investment Report* (2013).
Vagts, D, 'Minimum Standard', in Bernhardt, R (ed.), *Encyclopedia of Public International Law* (1997), Vol. 3.
van Dijk, P, van Hoof, F, van Rijn, A, and Zwaak, L (eds.), *Theory and Practice of the European Convention on Human Rights* (2006).
Waelde, T, 'Requiem for New International Economic Order', in Hafner, G, et al (eds.), *Liber Amicorum I. Seidl-Hohenveldern* (1998).
Waelde, T, and Sabahi, B, 'Compensation, Damages, and Valuation', in Muchlinski, P, Ortino, F, and Schreuer, C (eds.), *The Oxford Handbook of International Investment Law* (2008).
Waincymer, J, 'Balancing Property Rights and Human Rights in Expropriation', in Dupuy, P, Francioni, F, and Petersmann, E (eds.), *Human Rights in International Investment Law and Arbitration* (2009).
Wallace, D, 'Case Study under NAFTA: Lessons for the Wise?', in Horn, N (ed.), *Arbitrating Foreign Investment Disputes. Procedural and Substantive Legal Aspects* (2004).
Wildhaber, L, and Wildhaber, I, 'Recent Case Law on the Protection of Property in the European Convention on Human Rights', in Binder, C, et al (eds.), *International Investment Law for the 21st Century: Essays in Honour of Christoph Schreuer* (2009).
Yannaca-Small, K, 'Definition of "Investment": An Open-ended Search for a Balanced Approach', in Yannaca-Small, K (ed.), *Arbitration under International Investment Agreements: A Guide to the Key Issues* (2010).
Yannaca-Small, K, 'Indirect Expropriation and the Right to Regulate: How to Draw the Line?', in Yannaca-Small, K (ed.), *Arbitration under International Investment Agreements: A Guide to the Key Issues* (2010).

Index